# Lecture Notes of the Institute for Computer Sciences, Social Informatics and Telecommunications Engineering 525

The LNICST series publishes ICST's conferences, symposia and workshops.

LNICST reports state-of-the-art results in areas related to the scope of the Institute. The type of material published includes

- Proceedings (published in time for the respective event)
- Other edited monographs (such as project reports or invited volumes)

LNICST topics span the following areas:

- General Computer Science
- E-Economy
- E-Medicine
- Knowledge Management
- Multimedia
- Operations, Management and Policy
- Social Informatics
- Systems

Jun Cai · Zhili Zhou · Kongyang Chen
Editors

# Security and Privacy in New Computing Environments

6th International Conference, SPNCE 2023
Guangzhou, China, November 25–26, 2023
Proceedings

 Springer

*Editors*
Jun Cai
Guangdong Polytechnic Normal University
Guangzhou, China

Zhili Zhou
Guangzhou University
Guangzhou, China

Kongyang Chen
Guangzhou University
Guangzhou, China

ISSN 1867-8211 ISSN 1867-822X (electronic)
Lecture Notes of the Institute for Computer Sciences, Social Informatics
and Telecommunications Engineering
ISBN 978-3-031-73698-8 ISBN 978-3-031-73699-5 (eBook)
https://doi.org/10.1007/978-3-031-73699-5

This Springer imprint is published by the registered company Springer Nature Switzerland AG
The registered company address is: Gewerbestrasse 11, 6330 Cham, Switzerland

If disposing of this product, please recycle the paper.

# Preface

We are delighted to introduce the proceedings of the 6th EAI International Conference on Security and Privacy in New Computing Environments (EAI SPNCE 2023). This conference invited researchers, practitioners, and experts in the field of security and privacy to submit original research articles, case studies, and survey papers on topics related to security and privacy problems. The conference aimed to provide a platform for disseminating the latest research findings, best practices, and emerging trends in the field of security and privacy in these technologies.

The technical program of EAI SPNCE 2023 consisted of 23 full papers, covering the following topics: Security and privacy challenges in 5G/6G, IoT, and AI; Security and privacy in edge computing, big data, and cloud computing; Watermarking, steganography, and steganalysis; Data hiding and cryptography; Multimedia forensics and anti-forensics; AI-generated multimedia and spoofing detection; Computer virology, computer immunology, and hacking techniques; Multi-party privacy-preserving neural networks; and AI-based network traffic analysis. The conference invited 9 keynote speakers: Alex Kot, Fellow of the Singapore Academy of Engineering, IEEE Fellow, Nanyang Technological University; Yan Zhang, Professor for Life at the University of Oslo, Fellow of the Norwegian Academy of Technological Sciences, IEEE Fellow; Hui Li, Foreign Member of the Russian Academy of Sciences, Peking University; Chi-Chen Chang, Fellow of the European Academy of Sciences, IEEE Fellow, Feng Chia University; Xiangui Kang, Sun Yat-sen University; Haibo Hu, Hong Kong Polytechnic University; Hao Wang, Second-level Professor, National High-level Talent, Xidian University; Yan Yan Leng, Macau University of Science and Technology; and Kai Chen, Hong Kong University of Science and Technology.

Coordination with the steering chairs, Ding Wang and Weizhi Meng, was essential for the success of the conference. We sincerely appreciate their constant support and guidance. It was also a great pleasure to work with such an excellent organizing committee team for their hard work in organizing and supporting the conference, in particular, the Technical Program Committee, Zhili Zhou, Haibo Hu, Kongyang Chen, and Jianhua Yang. We are also grateful to the Conference Managers, Lenka Vatrtova, Marica Scevlikova, and Katarina Antalova, for their support and to all the authors who submitted their papers to the EAI SPNCE 2023 conference.

We strongly believe that EAI SPNCE 2023 provided a good forum for all researchers, developers, and practitioners to discuss all science and technology aspects of the field and that it will provide good ideas for further research. We also expect that future SPNCE conferences will be as successful and stimulating, as indicated by the contributions presented in this volume.

February 2024

Jun Cai
Haibo Hu
Kongyan Chen

# Organization

## Steering Committee

Weizhi Meng                 Technical University of Denmark, Denmark
Ding Wang                  Nankai University, China

## Organizing Committee

### General Chair

Jun Cai                      Guangdong Polytechnic Normal University, China

### General Co-chair

Zhili Zhou                 Nanjing University of Information Science and
                                   Technology, Nanjing, China

### TPC Chairs and Co-chairs

Haibo Hu                Hong Kong Polytechnic University, China
Kongyang Chen         Pazhou Lab, China

### Sponsorship and Exhibit Chair

Zhengyu Zhu            Guangdong Polytechnic Normal University, China

### Local Chair

Jianhua Yang           Guangdong Polytechnic Normal University, China

### Workshops Chair

Weiwei Lin             South China University of Technology, China

**Publicity and Social Media Chairs**

Li Hu                              Guangzhou University, China
Chang Chen                         Beijing Jiaotong University, China

**Publications Chair**

Jianzhen Luo                       Guangdong Polytechnic Normal University, China

**Web Chair**

Anli Yan                           Hainan University, China

# Technical Program Committee

Zheng Gong                         South China Normal University, China
Frédéric Cuppens                   IMT Atlantique, France
Sokratis Katsikas                  Norwegian University of Science and Technology,
                                       Norway
Wenchao Jiang                      Guangdong University of Technology, China
Fabio Martinelli                   IIT-CNR, Italy
Xianfeng Zhao                      Chinese Academy of Sciences, China
Francesco Palmieri                 University of Salerno, Italy
Dieter Gollmann                    Hamburg University of Technology, Germany
Jianting Ning                      Singapore Management University, Singapore
Feng Wang                          Wuhan University, China
Jianzhen Luo                       Guangdong Polytechnic Normal University, China
Liping Liao                        Guangdong Polytechnic Normal University, China

# Contents

**Security and Privacy Steganography and Forensics**

Contents

# IoT, Network Security and Privacy Challenges

# HybridFL: Hybrid Approach Toward Privacy-Preserving Federated Learning

Sheraz Ali[1,4], Saqib Mamoon[2], Areeba Usman[3], Zain ul Abidin[3], and Chuan Zhao[1,4,5(✉)]

[1] School of Information Science and Engineering, University of Jinan, Jinan 250022, China
ise_zhaoc@ujn.edu.cn
[2] School of Computer Science and Engineering, Nanjing University of Science and Technology, Nanjing 210094, China
[3] University of Sargodha, Sargodha, Pakistan
[4] Shandong Provincial Key Laboratory of Network-Based Intelligent Computing, University of Jinan, Jinan 250022, China
[5] Shandong Provincial Key Laboratory of Software Engineering, University of Jinan, Jinan 250022, China

**Abstract.** In this study, we introduce a novel Hybrid Federated Learning (HybridFL) approach aimed at enhancing privacy and accuracy in collaborative machine learning scenarios. Our methodology integrates Differential Privacy (DP) and secret sharing techniques to address inference risks during training and protect against information leakage in the output model. Drawing inspiration from recent advances, we present a HybridFL framework that combines the strengths of Homomorphic Encryption (HE) and Multi-Party Computation (MPC) to achieve secure computation without the computational overhead of pure HE methods. Our contributions include a privacy-preserving design for Federated Learning (FL) that ensures local data privacy through secret sharing while leveraging DP mechanisms for noise addition. The system offers resilience against unreliable participants and is evaluated using various machine learning models, including Convolutional Neural Networks (CNN), Multi-Layer Perceptrons (MLP), and linear regression. Furthermore, we address potential external threats by deploying predictive model outputs as robust services against inference attacks. Experimental results demonstrate improved accuracy and convergence speed, establishing the viability of HybridFL as an effective solution for collaborative machine learning with enhanced privacy guarantees.

**Keywords:** Machine Learning · Collaborative Machine Learning · Privacy-Preserving Federated Learning · Homomorphic Encryption · Secure Multiparty Computation · Secret Sharing · Differential Privacy

## 1 Introduction

In this chapter, we propose a hybrid approach to privacy-preserving collaborative ML in which we combine DP with secret sharing against inference attacks. Our approach enhances privacy and maintains the ML model's accuracy. Inspired by the hybrid scheme

J. Cai et al. (Eds.): SPNCE 2023, LNICST 525, pp. 3–18, 2025.
https://doi.org/10.1007/978-3-031-73699-5_1

[1], Stacey Truex [2] first took the initiative of applying the hybrid approach to privacy-preserving CML. This approach combined DP with HE protocol on federated learning, where they utilized the threshold variant of the pallier encryption (TPE) as an underlying security cornerstone. Although this hybrid approach provides good model performance and privacy guarantees, it faces long training time and high communication costs. Also, it can't tackle the participants dropping out during FL.

To tackle these problems, HybridAlpha [3] is an efficient privacy-preserving FL that utilizes functional encryption to perform MPC. Using FE, they proposed a simple and efficient approach that supports addition and dropping during the FL process.

In advanced cryptography, HE and MPC are closely associated with each other to solve the same problem: applying some computation on private input without expressing anything, as explained earlier in Sect. 5, except the final output. Specifically, at a large scale, HE is mostly replaceable by MPC and vice-versa. However, HE yields an expensive computation than MPC (MPC replaces this expensive computation with collaboration among two or many parties.

Secret sharing is MPC's best ingredient, which we have already explained in detail earlier. Although Stacey Truex and HybridAlpha took the good initiative of a hybrid approach, they are computationally expensive. So, we can replace the HE schemes with secret sharing where we can share differentially private shares to the global servers. This way, the participants can share their local models while providing less expensive privacy guarantees.

### 1.1  Motivation for Algorithm Improvement

The potential threat can take place in a collaborative machine. However, we must consider two types of potential threats: (1) inference during training and (2) inference over the outputs model.

**Inference During Training:**  This threat can occur during the process of learning, where any client in the collaborative setting may infer information about another client's private information. Let's suppose the combination of computational functions $f(S)$ and a set of queries $q_1, q_2, q_3, \ldots q_n$. In each iteration i in $f(S)$, need knowledge of participants' data there is query $q_i$. During execution, each participant must reply to each query $q_s$ appropriately on the dataset. These queries are dependent on $f(S)$. For instance, a query may ask for the number of instances in the dataset marching particular criteria for a decision tree.

SMC is the best ingredient to address this risk. Usually, this protocol enables n number of parties to get the function output over their inputs while protecting the information of anything other than this output. Unfortunately, inference over the output is still a challenging risk. Since the output of the function is still the same from execution without privacy, this output may leak information about any single input. Hence, we need to consider this threat as well.

**Inference over the Outputs Model:**  This is another potential threat at the final output model where the information can be a leak from intermediate outputs. Literature has shown most black-box attacks (i.e., membership inference attack) to the model through ML as a service API, and an adversary can still make training inferences.

Many mechanisms are designed to insert noise into the algorithm's output to achieve DP. These mechanisms add noise proportional to the output's sensitivity. The most fundamental mechanisms are the Laplacian mechanism and the Gaussian mechanism.

## 1.2 Contribution

Our main contributions of this work are;

1. We design a novel hybrid approach to CML system that offers recognized privacy guarantees, addresses different trust scenarios, and develops improved accuracy models. Data does not leave the client, and privacy is ensured using secret sharing and DP.
2. Our system is also robust against unreliable participants.
3. We show that our proposed system is useful for training various ML models through the experimental evaluation of CNN, MLP, and linear regression.
4. The potential threat from adversaries outside the system may occur. That's why we consider users of the final model as a potential threat. Therefore, we deploy a predictive model output from our system as a service, remaining resistant to an inference against adversaries that might be service users.

## 1.3 Formal Security and Privacy Models

In this section, we embark on establishing a robust theoretical foundation for our hybrid approach to privacy-preserving collaborative machine learning. We recognize the critical importance of formal security and privacy models to clarify the objectives of our research and precisely define the level of privacy we aim to guarantee.

### 1.3.1 Defining Security Goals

To begin, we must delineate our security goals. In the context of privacy-preserving collaborative machine learning, these goals encompass various aspects, including:

1. **Confidentiality:** Ensuring that Sensitive Data Remains Confidential and is not Exposed to Unauthorized Parties During the Collaborative Learning Process. This Involves Guarding Against Both External and Internal Threats.
2. **Integrity:** Guaranteeing the Integrity of the Collaborative Learning Process and the Resulting Model. We Want to Prevent Malicious Participants from Tampering with the Model or Data.
3. **Availability:** Ensuring that the Collaborative Learning Process Remains Available and Operational, Even in the Presence of Disruptions, Errors, or Adversarial Attempts to Disrupt the System.
4. **Robustness:** Building a System that Can Withstand Unreliable Participants or Adversarial Behavior, Maintaining Its Functionality and Privacy Guarantees.

### 1.3.2 Privacy Guarantees

In the realm of privacy, our primary focus is on the concept of differential privacy (DP). Differential privacy provides a mathematical framework for quantifying and achieving privacy guarantees in data analysis and machine learning tasks. It ensures that the presence or absence of any single data point does not significantly affect the outcome or result of a computation.

**Formal Definition of Differential Privacy:** We adopt a formal definition of differential privacy, which can be expressed as follows:

A mechanism M satisfies $(\varepsilon, \delta)$-differential privacy if, for all data sets D1 and D2 that differ in a single individual's data point and for all possible outcomes S of the mechanism, the following inequality holds:

$$\Pr[M(D1) \in S] \leq e^{(\varepsilon)} * \Pr[M(D2) \in S] + \delta$$

Where: $\varepsilon$ represents the privacy parameter, controlling the level of privacy protection. $\delta$ is a parameter that provides a small additional level of privacy protection.

### 1.3.3 Formalizing Privacy Models

Our work will further formalize privacy models specific to the collaborative learning setting. This involves defining privacy-preserving mechanisms, assessing their privacy guarantees, and demonstrating how they align with the principles of differential privacy. We will explore how secret sharing and cryptographic primitives complement differential privacy to ensure that participants' sensitive data remains protected. By establishing these formal security and privacy models, we aim to provide not only a clear theoretical foundation but also a rigorous basis for evaluating the privacy guarantees offered by our hybrid approach. These models will guide our subsequent technical discussions and demonstrate how our method aligns with the highest standards of privacy preservation in collaborative machine learning.

### 1.4 Related Work

Several research efforts have explored the realm of Federated Learning (FL) and its diverse applications. Here, we highlight some key studies that contribute to this burgeoning field:

**Federated Learning and Differential Privacy (DP):** The fusion of Federated Learning (FL) and Differential Privacy (DP) has garnered attention due to its potential in protecting data privacy during model training. Researchers like Stacey Truex have pioneered the integration of DP mechanisms into federated learning frameworks. This combination ensures that model updates incorporate noise to safeguard sensitive information, ultimately striking a balance between model accuracy and privacy preservation.

**Hybrid Approaches for Privacy-Preserving CML:** Hybrid approaches that amalgamate different cryptographic techniques have emerged to enhance privacy in collaborative settings. Truex et al. proposed a hybrid scheme that combines Homomorphic Encryption (HE) with DP for privacy-preserving collaborative learning. While this approach showcases promising privacy guarantees, its performance is hindered by high computational costs and communication overhead.

**Secure Multi-Party Computation (MPC) and Functional Encryption (FE):** Researchers like HybridAlpha have explored the application of Secure Multi-Party Computation (MPC) and Functional Encryption (FE) to achieve privacy-preserving collaborative learning. These cryptographic techniques allow parties to perform computations over their private data without revealing sensitive information. HybridAlpha's use of functional encryption for efficient multi-party computation demonstrates a viable alternative to costly HE-based approaches.

**Black-Box Attacks and Membership Inference:** Privacy vulnerabilities in CML models have led to research on adversarial attacks, such as membership inference attacks. These attacks exploit model outputs to infer whether a particular data point was part of the training dataset. Countermeasures, including noise injection mechanisms like the Laplacian and Gaussian mechanisms, have been devised to enhance model privacy and thwart such attacks.

**Industrial Applications and Secure Aggregation:** Real-world applications of CML, such as data association within organizations, have prompted research into secure aggregation protocols. These protocols allow organizations to collaboratively train models without sharing raw data. Research in this direction seeks to strike a balance between data utility, privacy preservation, and efficient model training.

**Medical Diagnostics and Data Sharing:** The healthcare sector has explored collaborative learning to improve medical diagnostics. Initiatives like IBM's supercomputer for rapid diagnosis highlight the potential of collaborative approaches. However, the challenge lies in ensuring comprehensive and labeled datasets. Collaborative learning emerges as a solution to pool medical data from various sources, enhancing diagnostic accuracy while preserving patient privacy.

**Marketing and Advertising with Differential Privacy:** In marketing and advertising, the challenge of personalized recommendations while maintaining data privacy has been addressed using differential privacy techniques. By introducing controlled noise into recommendation algorithms, models can provide personalized suggestions without exposing individual user preferences.

## 2   Proposed Methodology

### 2.1   System Architecture

Figure 1 shows that N numbers of participants have their own sensitive data for training on the local side. The purpose of participants is to learn a joint model, i.e. the topology of local models and learning objectives are identical. Since the problem of collecting data is challenging, the participants only share parameters with the server. We also consider two servers with global models and a small auxiliary validation dataset.

Algorithm 1 illustrates the high-level working of HybridCollab. At the beginning of learning, servers and participants build their own global and local models and declare all the parameters. For each round, the participants train their own local models in a differentially private manner. Then they split the model into two shares and upload the differentially private parameter to both servers. The servers then utilize the auxiliary validation dataset to calculate a utility score for everyone and then select to receive the parameter shares with definite probability. After receiving these shares, servers average the model parameters and send them back to each participant for a new training round. The participant can dismiss its training process and drop out anytime if it is sure that the accuracy of the models is enough. Meanwhile, a new participant can also join anytime. Next, we discuss the detailed process of our system on the server side and participant side.

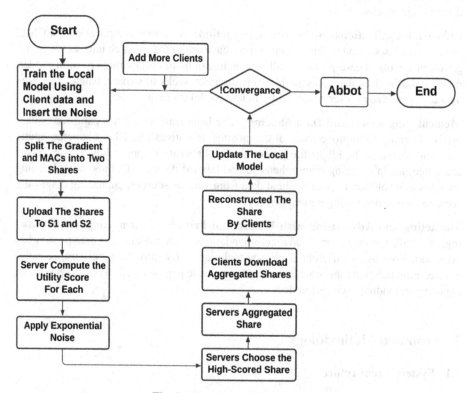

**Fig. 1.** Flowchart of HybridCollab

**Algorithm 1: A high level description of HybridColab**

1. Construct the model and define all the parameters
2. for every round of communication
3.     for every participant
4.         for j=1 to $l$ iteration
5.             Execute SGD on each local data and insert Gaussian noise
6.         end for
7.         Split the Update local noisy model into two shares $W_1$ and $W_2$
8.         Upload $W_1$ and $W_2$ to servers $S_1$ and $S_2$
9.     end for
10. The servers select the $W1$ and $W_2$ according to the utility score.
11. The servers compute the model average to get $W_{1new}$ and $W_{2new}$ and send it to the participant.
12. end for

### 2.1.1 HybridColab: Server Side

Algorithm 2 gives the detailed processing of HybridColab on the server side. Initially, the servers initialize the parameters and wait to receive each participant's local training parameter shares as illustrated in Fig. 2. They receive the number of participants according to a pre-fixed threshold T. The server selects participants according to high utility scores and uses exponential noise to hide the uncertainty.

$$P[\text{choose participant m}] \propto \exp\left(\frac{\epsilon}{2K\Delta s} s(W, D, m)\right) \tag{1}$$

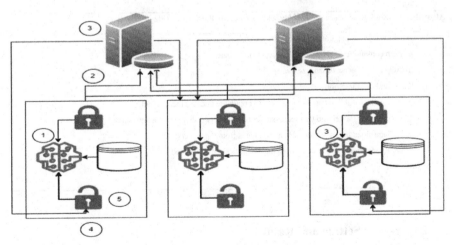

**Fig. 2.** High Level working principle of HybridCollab.

This process selects the number of participants at an exponential rate on the basis of the scoring function while protecting the sampling process from inferring privacy.

Hence, we can sample the almost optimum weights and hence reduce the disturbance of unreliable participants as much.

After selecting the final accepted parameter shares, the servers compute an average operation and construct the new global parameters. This average model function is the average of all the accepted parameter shares. Finally, the servers send the new global parameter shares to each participant and wait for the parameter uploading for the next round.

### 2.1.2 Participant Side

Algorithm 3 gives the high-level description of hybridColab on the participant side. Every participant contains two things: (1) its own local dataset and (2) its own local model. This local model is trained using standard SGD algorithm. We implement DP onto the training algorithm to preserve the participants' privacy over the output function being disclosed by the W. After that we split the sanitized model into two secret shares. Then these shares are uploaded to servers S1 and S2. We use Gaussian noise to achieve DP.

---

**Algorithm 2: A high level description of HybridColab at servers side**

1. Initialize and send the parameters to participants.
2. Weight for each participant to send their parameters.
3. Compute the utility score for every uploading participant using auxiliary validation data.
4. Choose K parameters from threshold T without replacement such that  P[choose participant m] $\propto$ exp(
   $\frac{\epsilon}{2K\Delta s}$s(W, D, m))
5. Compute model average and construct new global model and distribute to each participant.

---

**Algorithm 3: A high level description of HybridColab at the Participant side**

1. Download the same parameters from the servers.
2. In each communication round, construct the mini-batch size.
3. Insert Gaussian noise to sanitize the weights.
4. For I number of iteration,
   5. run the local SGD on the local data to obtain the updated local model.
   6. Split the model into two secret shares.6. Upload two shares to the both servers.
   7. Download the new averaged model shares from the servers.
   8. Repeat step 5 to 0 until an optimum small test error is gained.
9. Drop out

---

## 2.2 Experiment Setting and Results

The experiment is implemented on the 7th generation CPU Intel i7–7200 2.3 GHz and 64GB RAM of Dell Core i7. We simulated 2 servers and multiple participants based on M parameter. We implemented all the protocols in Python 3 programming language. We use pysyft library for ML. We use Ubuntu operating system for our experiments.

### 2.2.1 Experimental Setup

For all baseline scenarios, we build a CNN. We use the publicly available dataset MNIST and iris data set for a classification problem. The CNN model has two hidden layers of ReLU units and a softmax function of 10 classes with cross-entropy loss. Layer one consists of 60 neurons and layer two consists of 1000 neurons. We set the learning rate as 0.1, a batch rate of 0.01, and for DP, we utilize norm clipping of 4.0 and $\epsilon$ of 0.5. We executed an experiment for 10 participants and assigned 6,000 data points from MNIST. For the iris data set, we use logistic regression. We utilize torch with pysyft.

### 2.2.2 Results

**The Distribution of Shares:** Figure 3 illustrates the distribution of shares among both servers. The results shows that how successfully two shares split to overcome the inference during training threat.

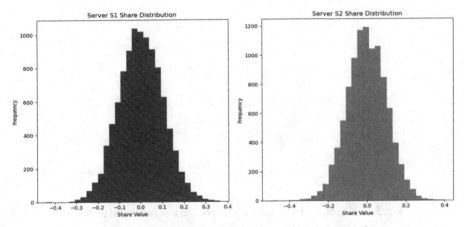

**Fig. 3.** The distribution of shares on server 1 and server 2

**The Communication Cost.** Figure 4 illustrates the impact of iterations I. The results exhibit that I will speed up the convergence by raising the computation workload on each party. However, a huge number of I will slow it down since the collaboration reduces. I will increase the convergence speed by increasing the computation cost of each participant. But, note that a too large value of I will reduce the convergence as the collaboration reduces. On this basis, we set the parameter I to be 100 in our experiments.

**Training Performance.** Figure 5 illustrates the overall performance of over training models. We achieve 89% of accuracy. We plot the variation of accuracy with epochs. We can see that with increase in epochs, our training is increasing respectively.

**Robustness against Inconsistent Clients:** In Fig. 6, we display the percentage of Inconsistent Clients across different variations (40%, 60%, and 80%). We also introduce random noise into their data. We have set the values of M and K to be 0.5N and 0.5M, respectively. Based on the variation of N clients and the proportion of noise data p, we

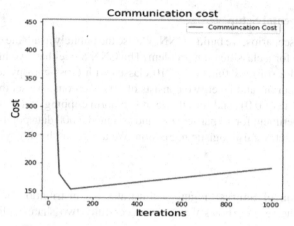

**Fig. 4.** Impact of Iteration over Communication cost

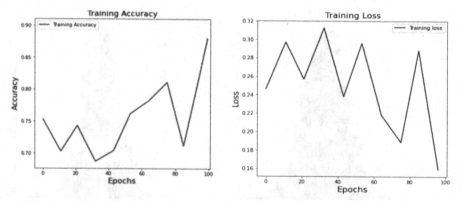

**Fig. 5.** Left: obtained 92% accuracy, Right: the loss is reduced to 20%.

can observe that half of the clients are unreliable. We have assigned N values of 40, 70, and 100, with corresponding p values of 0.3, 0.5, and 0.7. For sampling K clients, we have set it to be half of M clients, assuming that the most reliable clients are present. We also compare our secureShare scheme with PSA and FL. PSL and FL did not consider the existence of Inconsistent Clients. Figure 6 shows how the impact of Inconsistent Clients reduces.

### 2.2.3  Security and Privacy Analysis of HybridFL

Our proposed Hybrid Federated Learning (HybridFL) framework is designed with a strong emphasis on enhancing security and privacy in collaborative machine learning scenarios. Here, we provide a comprehensive analysis of the security and privacy aspects of HybridFL, highlighting its capabilities and safeguards against potential threats.

**1. Differential Privacy (DP):** HybridFL employs Differential Privacy as a fundamental building block to ensure data privacy during model training. By introducing controlled

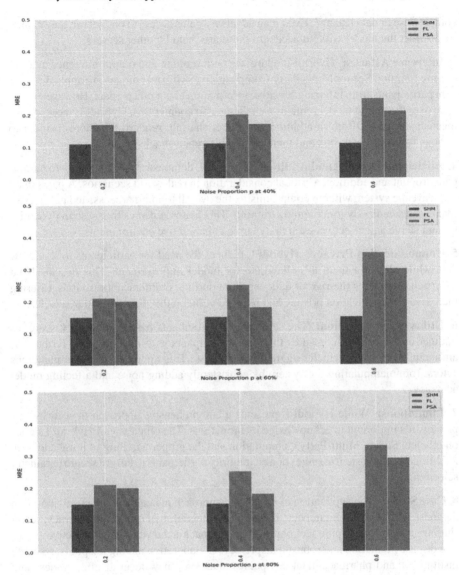

**Fig. 6.** Robustness against Inconsistent Clients variations (40%, 60%, and 80%)

noise to the training process, DP mitigates the risks of inference attacks and information leakage from individual participants' data. This noise addition guarantees that no single participant's contribution can be pinpointed, offering a robust defense against privacy breaches.

**2. Secret Sharing:** A significant aspect of HybridFL is the utilization of secret sharing to distribute model parameters among participating servers. Secret sharing ensures that no individual server possesses the complete model, enhancing security against server compromise or data leakage. Even if an adversary gains access to one server, they cannot reconstruct the model without access to the shares held by other servers.

**3. Inference Attacks:** HybridFL addresses both training and output inference attacks. During training, Secure Multi-Party Computation (SMC) techniques are applied to prevent participants from inferring sensitive information about others' data. However, inference over the output model remains a challenge. To counter this, HybridFL incorporates mechanisms like DP noise addition and secret sharing, rendering it more resilient to various forms of black-box and membership inference attacks.

**4. Participant Dropout and Addition:** HybridFL demonstrates adaptability to participant dropout and addition, a critical consideration in real-world scenarios. A participant can leave the system without compromising the overall training process, and new participants can seamlessly join ongoing training. This feature ensures that system dynamics remain stable and effective, even in dynamic collaborative environments.

**5. Communication Privacy:** HybridFL reduces the need for participants to share raw data while allowing them to collaborate for model improvement. This decentralized approach minimizes the risk of data exposure during communication rounds, offering increased communication privacy and reduced vulnerability to interception attacks.

**6. Utility Score Selection:** The selection of participants based on a utility score, as outlined in Algorithm 3, ensures that only participants with meaningful contributions are included in the parameter aggregation process. This approach prevents malicious actors from manipulating the system by consistently adding noise and affecting model accuracy.

**7. Limitations:** While HybridFL presents a comprehensive approach to security and privacy, it's important to acknowledge its limitations. The efficiency of HybridFL relies on efficient Secure Multi-Party Computation and the proper handling of noise addition. Additionally, the system assumes honest majority participants to ensure secure parameter selection.

**8. Case Study:** The application of our hybrid approach in healthcare data collaboration demonstrates its profound impact. Through the integration of differential privacy, secret sharing, and cryptographic techniques, our approach achieves a dual objective: accurate disease prediction and robust data privacy. Collaboration among hospitals, research institutions, and pharmaceutical companies takes on a new level of effectiveness and productivity. This synergy results in significant advancements in medical research, all while safeguarding the privacy of patient data.

Furthermore, the inclusion of robustness measures in our approach acts as a formidable defense against potential adversarial actions. This resilience ensures that the collaborative effort remains impervious to privacy attacks. Our hybrid approach not only elevates healthcare data collaboration for disease prediction but also serves as a pioneering model for privacy-preserving machine learning across sensitive domains. It sets a benchmark for compliance, security, and innovation in the realm of healthcare research.

# 3 Conclusion and Discussion

## 3.1 Application of HybridFL

### 3.1.1 Organization Data Association

HybridFL transcends being just a benchmark for expertise; it has evolved into an essential industrial paradigm. With the surge in big data, the challenge arises of efficiently gathering, processing, and disseminating data using remote processors, akin to cloud computing. However, the vital consideration of data security and its close association with an organization's sensitive information and revenues raises pertinent questions. The industrial application of collaborative learning offers a contemporary solution for managing extensive datasets. For instance, when inaccessible data ownership hampers decision-making, collaborative learning enables organizations to share model insights without compromising data ownership.

### 3.1.2 Medical Diagnosis

The realm of rapid medical diagnosis marries treatment and artificial intelligence, but current diagnostic methods are often time-consuming and lack intelligence. Addressing these challenges, an innovative system employing collaborative learning emerges as a potential solution. Notably, IBM's supercomputing technology has been at the forefront of quick medical analyses, particularly in cancer diagnosis. However, recent instances of misdiagnosis have surfaced due to incomplete training data, lacking crucial disease features, medical test reports, and gene sequences. The underlying issue is the paucity of comprehensive and labeled data sources.

To counter these limitations, medical associations are joining forces to pool data and collaboratively train superior machine learning models. HybridFL can serves as the enabler of this data sharing and processing, leading to enhanced medical diagnostics.

### 3.1.3 Marketing and Advertisement

HybridFL can revolutionizes data security in domains such as banking and advertising, where safeguarding raw data from malicious use is paramount. Here, data privacy concerns and the confidentiality of intellectual property make direct data sharing for model training impractical. Collaborative learning provides an avenue to train models without exposing sensitive data.

In the realm of target marketing, the concept hinges on providing personalized Machine Learning-as-a-Service, analogous to Amazon's product recommendations. Features such as customer profiles, purchasing behavior, and product attributes form the basis of data used for modeling. However, ensuring robust data privacy and protection proves challenging, especially when dealing with the intricacies of social networks, banks, and online stores. The inherent complexity of data aggregation is compounded by data heterogeneity across various organizational silos.

HybridFL bridges this gap by enabling the creation of training models using data from geographically dispersed organizations, without necessitating data exchange. By doing so, it facilitates effective model training across a diverse spectrum of data sources while maintaining data privacy and security.

# 4   Conclusion

Our work introduces the innovative concept of Hybrid Federated Learning (HybridFL) as a robust approach to address privacy and accuracy concerns in collaborative machine learning. By combining Differential Privacy (DP) and secret sharing techniques, we create a synergistic framework that overcomes challenges related to inference attacks during training and output model leakage. We have demonstrated that our HybridFL approach not only maintains model accuracy but also significantly enhances data privacy. This is achieved by leveraging the strengths of both Homomorphic Encryption (HE) and Multi-Party Computation (MPC) while avoiding the computational overhead associated with a solely HE-based approach. Our contributions encompass a comprehensive system architecture that integrates secret sharing, DP mechanisms, and participant selection strategies. The experimental evaluations, involving various machine learning models and datasets, validate the effectiveness of our HybridFL system in practical scenarios. Notably, our system proves resilient against potential threats posed by unreliable participants and external adversaries. As the realm of collaborative machine learning continues to grow, our HybridFL framework provides a pioneering solution that strikes a balance between privacy preservation and model accuracy. By deploying predictive model outputs as robust services, we ensure a heightened level of resistance against inference attacks from service users.

**Acknowledgment.** This work is supported by the National Natural Science Foundation of China (62472252, 62172258), TaiShan Scholars Program (tsqn202211280), Shandong Provincial Natural Science Foundation (ZR2024QF131, ZR2023LZH014, ZR2022ZD01, ZR2022MF264, ZR2021LZH007), Shandong Provincial Key R&D Program of China (2021SFGC0401, 2021CXGC010103), Department of Science & Technology of Shandong Province (SYS202201), and Quan Cheng Laboratory (QCLZD202302).

# References

1. Shamir, A.: How to share a secret. Commun. ACM **22**(11), 612–613 (1979)
2. Shao, Z.C.: A new efficient (t, n) verifiable multi-secret sharing (vmss) based on ych scheme. Appl. Math. Comput. **168**(1), 135–140 (2005)
3. Bai, L.: A strong ramp secret sharing scheme using matrix projection. In: Proceedings of the 2006 International Symposium on on World of Wireless, Mobile and Multimedia Networks, pp. 652–656. IEEE Computer Society (2006)
4. Iftene, S.: General secret sharing based on the chinese remainder theorem with applications in e-voting. Elec. Notes Theor. Comput. Sci. **186**, 67–84 (2007)
5. McMahan, H.B., Moore, E., Ramage, D., Hampson, S., y Arcas, B.A.: Communication-efficient learning of deep networks from decentralized data. In: Conference on Artificial Intelligence and Statistics (2017)
6. Li, T., Sahu, A.K., Sanjabi, M., Zaheer, M., Talwalkar, A., Smith, V.: Federated optimization for heterogeneous networks. arXiv preprint arXiv:1812.06127 (2018)
7. Du, W., Han, Y.S., Chen, S.: Privacy-preserving multivariate statistical analysis: linear regression and classification. In: Proceedings Of SDM 2004, SIAM, vol. 4, pp. 222–233 (2004)

8. Chaudhuri, K., Monteleoni, C.: Privacy-preserving logistic regression. In: Proceedings of NIPS 2009, pp. 289– 296 (2009)
9. Jagannathan, G., Wright, R.N.: Privacy-preserving distributed kmeans clustering over arbitrarily partitioned data. In: Proceedinds of KDD 2005, pp. 593–599. ACM (2005)
10. "Deep learning and differential privacy (2016)." https://github.com/frankmcsherry/blog/blob/master/posts/2017-10-27.md
11. Biggio, B., Fumera, G., Roli, F.: Security evaluation of pattern classifiers under attack. IEEE Trans. Knowl. Data Eng. **36**(4), 984–996, April 2014
12. Wikipedia, Cryptography. https://en.wikipedia.org/wiki/Cryptography. Accessed 02 Aug 2020
13. Li, M., Andersen, D.G., Park, J,W., et al.: Scaling distributed machine learning with the parameter server. In: 11th USENIX Symposium on O, perating Systems Design and Implementation (OSDI 14), pp. 583–598 (2014). https://doi.org/10.1145/2640087.2644155
14. Shamir, A.: How to share a secret. Commun. ACM **22**(11), 612–613 (1979). https://doi.org/10.1145/359168.359176
15. Shokri, R., Shmatikov, V.: Privacy-preserving deep learning. In: Proceedings of the 22nd ACM SIGSAC Conference on Computer and Communications Security, pp. 1310–1321. ACM (2015)
16. Yu, H., Vaidya, J., Jiang, X.: Privacy-preserving SVM classification on vertically partitioned data. In: Ng, W.K., Kitsuregawa, M., Li, J., Chang, K. (eds.) Advances in Knowledge Discovery and Data Mining. PAKDD 2006. Lecture Notes in Computer Science(), vol. 3918. Springer, Heidelberg (2006). https://doi.org/10.1007/11731139_74
17. Vaidya, J., Yu, H., Jiang, X.: Privacy-preserving SVM classification. Knowl. Inf. Syst. **14**(2), 161–178 (2008). https://doi.org/10.1007/s10115-007-0073-7
18. Lindell, Y., Pinkas, B.: Privacy-preserving data mining. In: Annual International Cryptology Conference, pp. 36–54. Springer, Heidelberg (2000). https://doi.org/10.1145/335191.335438
19. Du, W., Han, Y.S., Chen, S.: Privacy-preserving multivariate statistical analysis: linear regression and classification. In: Proceedings of the 2004 SIAM International Conference on Data Mining. Society for Industrial and Applied Mathematics, pp. 222–233 (2004). https://doi.org/10.1137/1.9781611972740.21
20. Sanil, A.P., Karr, A.F., Lin, X., et al.: Privacy-preserving regression modelling via distributed computation. In: Proceedings of the Tenth ACM SIGKDD International Conference on Knowledge Discovery and Data Mining, pp. 677–682. ACM (2004). https://doi.org/10.1145/1014052.1014139
21. Jagannathan, G., Wright, R.N.: Privacy-preserving distributed k-means clustering over arbitrarily partitioned data. In: Proceedings of the Eleventh ACM SIGKDD International Conference on Knowledge Discovery in Data Mining, pp. 593–599. ACM ( 2005). https://doi.org/10.1145/1081870.1081942
22. Ali Sheraz, et al.: Towards privacy-preserving deep learning: opportunities and challenges. In: 2020 IEEE 7th International Conference on Data Science and Advance Analalytics
23. Riazi, M.S., Weinert, C., Tkachenko, O., et al.: Chameleon: a hybrid secure computation framework for machine learning applications. In: Proceedings of the 2018 on Asia Conference on Computer and Communications Security, pp. 707–721. ACM (2018). https://doi.org/10.1145/3196494.3196522
24. Xu, R., et al.: Hybridalpha: an efficient approach for privacy-preserving federated learning. In: Proceedings of the 12th ACM Workshop on Artificial Intelligence and Security (2019)
25. Nikolaenko, V., Ioannidis, S., Weinsberg, U., et al.: Privacy-preserving matrix factorization. In: Proceedings of the 2013 ACM SIGSAC Conference on Computer and Communications Security, pp. 801–812. ACM (2013). https://doi.org/10.1145/2508859.2516751

26. Mohassel, P., Zhang, Y.: Secureml: a system for scalable privacy-preserving machine learning. In: 2017 IEEE Symposium on Security and Privacy (SP), pp. 19–38. IEEE (2017). https://doi.org/10.1109/SP.2017.12

27. Gilad-Bachrach, R., Dowlin, N., Laine, K., et al.: Cryptonets: applying neural networks to encrypted data with high throughput and accuracy. In: International Conference on Machine Learning, pp. 201–210 (2016)

28. Proserpio, D., Goldberg, S., McSherry, F.: Calibrating data to sensitivity in private data analysis: a platform for differentially-private analysis of weighted datasets. Proc. VLDB 2014 **7**(8), 637–648 (2014)

29. Shokri, R., Shmatikov, V.: Privacy-preserving deep learning. In: Proceedings of the 22nd ACM SIGSAC Conference on Computer and Communications Security, pp. 1310–1321. ACM (2015)

30. Bonawitz, K., Ivanov, V., Kreuter, B., et al.: Practical secure aggregation for privacy-preserving machine learning. In: Proceedings of the 2017 ACM SIGSAC Conference on Computer and Communications Security, pp. 1175–1191. ACM (2017). https://doi.org/10.1145/3133956.3133982

31. Shokri, R., Shmatikov, V.: Privacy-preserving deep learning. In: Proceedings of CCS 2015, pp. 1310–1321. ACM (2015)

32. Fredrikson, M., Jha, S., Ristenpart, T.: Model inversion attacks that exploit confidence information and basic countermeasures. In: Proceedings of CCS 2015, pp. 1322–1333. ACM (2015)

33. Juvekar, C., Vaikuntanathan, V., Chandrakasan, A.: Gazelle: a low latency framework for secure neural network inference, arXiv preprint arXiv:1801.05507

34. "Deep learning and differential privacy," https://github.com/frankmcsherry/blog/blob/master/posts/2017–10–27.md, 2016

35. Biggio, B., Fumera, G., Roli, F.: 'Security evaluation of pattern classifiers under attack.' IEEE Trans. Knowl. Data Eng. **36**(4), 984–996 (2014)

36. Wikipedia, Cryptography. https://en.wikipedia.org/wiki/Cryptography. Accessed 02 Aug 2020

37. Techtarget,cryptography. https://searchsecurity.techtarget.com/definition/cryptography. Accessed 02 Aug 2020

38. Gibson, A., Patterson, J.: Chapter 4. Major Architectures of Deep Networks. O'Reilly. https://www.oreilly.com/library/view/deeplearning/9781491924570/ch04.html

39. Wagh, S., Gupta, D., Chandran, N.: SecureNN: 3-party secure computation for neural network training. In: Proceedings on Privacy Enhancing Technologies, vol. 1, p. 24 (2019). https://doi.org/10.2478/popets-2019-0035

40. Konen, J., McMahan, H.B., Yu, F.X., et al.: Federated learning: Strategies for improving communication efficiency. arXiv preprint arXiv:1610.05492 (2016)

41. Even, H., Goldreich, O., Lempel, A.: A randomized proto-col for signing contracts. In: Chaum, D., Rivest, R.L., Sherman, A.T. (eds). CRYPTO 1982, pp. 205–210. Plenum Press, New York (1982). (Page 4)

42. Yao, A.C.-C.: How to generate and exchange secrets (extendedabstract). In: 27th FOCS, pp. 162–167. IEEE Computer Society Press, October 1986. (Page 4)

43. Beaver, D., Micali, S., Rogaway, P.: The round complexity ofsecure protocols (extended abstract). In: 22nd ACM STOC, pp. 503–513. ACM Press, May 1990. (Pages 4 and 9)

# The Design of a Multi-application Micro-operating System Platform in the Context of Big Data

Wenpan Mo$^{(\boxtimes)}$ and Zhicheng Shen

Eastcompeace Technology Co., Ltd., Zhuhai, Guangdong, China
{mowenpan,shenzhicheng}@eastcompeace.com

**Abstract.** In the context of big data, the security problem of smart card operating system is realized independently and controllably, For smart cards and the internet of things, a multi-application microoperating system platform is proposed. The platform's operating system is based on the virtual machine technology to support the dynamic loading, installation, deletion, and interpretation of the execution of applications, the virtual machine adopts a register-based instruction set architecture, the interpreter is faster, and the instruction optimization is easier. At the same time, the platform provides an application compiler to realize the generation of execution files running in micro-operating systems from source code parsing, compilation, and linking, which supports a variety of programming languages to develop applications, and generates register-based instruction set bytecode EF files after compilation and linking. The platform also provides a set of integrated tools integrated into application source code development, compilation, and loading of applications to virtual OS (or real OS) for application operation, testing, and debugging. Experimental results show that the proposed multi-application microoperating system has good running speed and has the ability to protect high-value and high-sensitive information, and the ability to provide high-level security protection for the device, and provide related tools such as source code development, compilation, run, testing, and debugging of applications, this improves the efficiency of application development, testing, and debugging.

**Keywords:** operating system · smart card · internet of things · data security

## 1 Introduction

With the continuous progress of communication technology and the further improvement of basic telecommunications facilities, the trend of electronization and information technology in various industries is becoming more and more obvious, and new application scenarios are being explored by the market. The application of smart cards is not only limited to traditional application fields such as finance, telecommunications, transportation, etc., but also gradually covers many fields from daily life to industrial production. In the connected world, the realization of smart connection relies on the interconnection

J. Cai et al. (Eds.): SPNCE 2023, LNICST 525, pp. 19–34, 2025.
https://doi.org/10.1007/978-3-031-73699-5_2

of devices in the front-end and cloud services and big data processing in the back-end. Once the Internet of things connects everything, it is necessary to ensure the safe access of devices, safe transmission of information, and safe storage of data. Therefore, smart cards have become an indispensable security guarantee in every aspect of our lives. The operating system is the "soul" of the information system and an important pillar of the national digital economic infrastructure. Building a "multi-application micro-operating system platform" to solve the problem of intrinsic security has become the key to the digital transformation of the economy and the development of the industrial chain.

The operating system is the basis of all software, any other software must run under the support of the operating system, without the support of the operating system, other software can not be installed and run, it plays a pivotal role in the entire computer system. In the face of various industries, the diverse needs of different users need to be solved based on different applications. Therefore, the construction of multi-application micro-operating system platform can better meet the needs of users. The implementation of the system platform, not only need to study the development of the application required source code development, compilation, running, testing, debugging and other related tools, but also need to ensure that the system platform has stability and security to ensure the normal operation of the application, and will not cause data loss or damage because of system crash or other problems. The user's data will not be attacked or stolen by malicious attackers.

## 2 Multi-application Micro-operating System Platforms

This section mainly introduces the overall architecture of the operating system, the analysis of key technologies, and its advantages and characteristics.

### 2.1 Overall Design Architecture

This paper studies a multi-application microoperating system for microprocessing, and the overall solution of related application development tools.

In Fig. 1, the platform consists of three subsystems: a compiler, a multi-application microoperating system, and an integrated development environment. The compiler supports multiple programming languages to parse and generate an abstract syntax tree, and then traverses the abstract syntax tree to generate an intermediate language, and optimizes the intermediate language, and generates bytecode files that can run on the micro operating system after linking.

Microoperating system is to interpret and execute applications, and provide a safe and reliable runtime environment for applications.

Integrated development environment (IDE) is an integrated tool for developing, compiling and loading applications to virtual OS (or real OS) for running, testing and debugging.

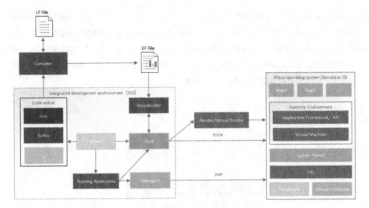

**Fig. 1.** Overall architecture diagram

## 2.2 Analysis and Elaboration of Key Technologies

The key technologies of multi-application micro-operating system platform mainly include the following five aspects: compiler, micro-operating system (MOS), object-oriented instruction set based on register, just-in-time compiler based on physical register mapping, integrated development environment.

### 2.2.1 Microoperating System

The main feature of the multi-application micro-operating system [10, 11, 13] is that it has a virtual machine, which separates the implementation of the application from the hardware. The application runs on a unified virtual machine, and can dynamically load, install, delete, and run the application.

As shown in Fig. 2 below, the microoperating System is divided into Application Layer, Runtime Environment Layer, System Kernel Layer, hardware abstraction layer and hardware layer from top to bottom. Among them, the runtime environment is the core of the microoperating system. The main function of the runtime environment is to interpret and execute bytecode to ensure that the runtime data of multiple applications is reliable and safe. The runtime environment is composed of virtual machine, trusted framework, resource manager, application framework, application programming interface and other components.

The design principle of microoperating system is based on the separation of software and hardware. For the same kind of hardware, it must be abstracted as a hardware interface. HAL layer is the abstract interface between hardware abstraction and VM access by application debug framework. If the microoperating system is ported to different hardware platforms, only the HAL layer code needs to be modified.

Figure 3 shows the flow chart of the virtual machine accessing the microoperating system resources. The virtual machine cannot access the microoperating system directly, but must pass through the authorization permission of the trusted framework and the agent of the resource manager to access the microoperating system resources.

The resource manager manages the microoperating system resources uniformly. The virtual machine cannot directly access the microoperating system resources through the physical address, and can only operate through the index number provided by the resource manager. Therefore, the trusted framework [3, 12] is to ensure that the data is isolated, safe and reliable when the application is running.

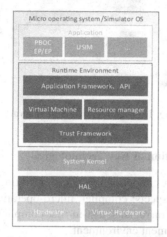

**Fig. 2.** Structure diagram of multi-application micro-operating system

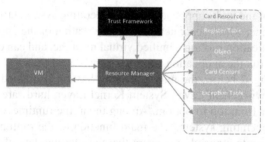

**Fig. 3.** Relationship diagram of core components of runtime environment

### 2.2.2 Compiler

The main feature of the compiler [7–9] is to support multiple programming language parsing. After the optimization and linkage of the intermediate language, the bytecode EF file based on the register instruction set is generated. As smart card is a kind of resource-constrained device, the computing power and storage space of the processor are very limited. Therefore, the symbol table is replaced by identifier linking technology in the compilation stage to solve the space occupation problem caused by symbol table and the performance loss caused by application linking when the micro-operating system loads the application.

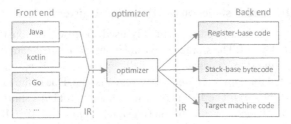

**Fig. 4.** Overall architecture of the compiler

The compiler is designed based on LLVM architecture (Fig. 4), which consists of three parts: front-end, compiler and back-end. The front-end and back-end use a unified intermediate code.

If you need to support a new programming language, just implement a new frontend.

If a new kind of target program needs to be generated, only a new backend needs to be implemented.

The optimization phase is a general phase, it is aimed at a unified IR (intermediate language), adding support for new programming languages does not require changes to the optimization phase.

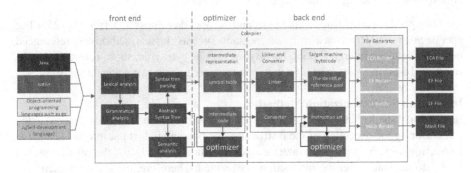

**Fig. 5.** Compiler technical scheme structure diagram

Figure 5, the main function of the compiler front-end is to analyze the source code lexical analysis, lexical analysis, semantic analysis, and generate abstract syntax tree; Then the abstract syntax tree is parsed to generate intermediate code. If you need to add a new programming language, you only need to implement a lexical analyzer, a syntax analyzer, and a semantic analyzer. Because this solution only supports object-oriented programming languages, the structure of the abstract syntax tree and the parsing process of the syntax tree are basically the same.

The main function of the optimizer is to optimize the intermediate code and generate new intermediate code.

The main function of the compiler backend is to generate the optimized intermediate code through the link transformer based on register instruction set, and then generate the executable file through the file generator.

### 2.2.3 Object-Oriented Instruction Set Based on Register

The instruction set [2] in this paper is mainly used for resource-constrained devices, such as smart card devices. The storage units and memory of smart card devices are very limited. Generally, the storage capacity of small capacity cards is not more than 64KB. The instruction set of this paper is based on the register type. Due to the limited resources of the device, this scheme will be 16 bits for a memory unit, for byte, short and other basic data types with a 16 bit memory unit, for int (int value range: -2147483648-2147483647) uses two consecutive 16-bit memory cells.

Generally, object-oriented programming languages are linked by symbols after compilation. This paper is used for resource-constrained devices. A 16-bit, two-byte unsigned unique identifier represents the link to classes, methods, domains, etc. Because strings can be infinitely long to represent classes, methods, domains and other links; Therefore, a lot of storage space is wasted.

**Instruction format:**
Opcode operand 1 operand 2...
An instruction by a 8 bits of operation code and multiple operands (or operand, the nop instruction is not operating).

Instructions can use virtual machine number can reach 256, register each register is 16, expressed in the adjacent two registers 32-bit data.

The opcode of an instruction is 1 byte, and the opcode values range from 0 to 255. The opcode number is 16 bits in a unit, and constants such as classes, methods are referenced using an identifier reference pool. Data types such as byte, char, short, reference can be stored in 16-bit registers, and int data types are stored using two adjacent registers.

**Instruction Set Optimization Methods:**
In traditional stacked instruction set, the operand of the instruction is usually stored in the stack. During the execution of the instruction, the operand is first put into the stack, the instruction logic is executed to take the operand from the stack, and the result is stored back into the stack after the instruction is executed. Therefore, the stack instruction is shorter than the register instruction, and the number of stack instructions is relatively larger for the same high-level programming language statement.

The instruction sets in this paper occupy 3-byte, 4-byte, 5-byte, and variable-length instructions. Although this kind of instruction sets meet the basic functional requirements, each instruction takes up a large amount of space, which leads to the limitation of downloadable applications on resource-constrained devices. Compared with Java Card, the space consumption of this instruction set increases by 60% (and is about 40% larger than that of Java bytecode). In this context, this paper proposes to optimize the instruction set to reduce the space consumption.

Statistical analysis of a large number of applications shows that about 99% of the methods use less than 16 registers, and the register number of instructions is used more frequently in 0–5 (70% to 80% of the time).

**The Optimization Method is as Follows:**

- Fixed register number: The registers (R0-R6) targeted at high frequency accesses are fixed in the instruction.
- Consolidate immediate numbers: Consolidate immediate numbers that are used only once into the instruction, reducing const assignment operations.
- Half-byte representation: Register numbers or immediate numbers are represented in half bytes, compressing the space occupied by instructions.

### 2.2.4  Just-in-Time Compilers Based on Physical Register Mapping

Taking advantage of the large number of registers in RISC processors, the virtual registers and physical registers used in the register-based bytecode are bound by one-to-one mapping in the bytecode interpretation phase. And compile to generate local code for execution. This scheme uses register mapping technology to compile bytecode to generate local code execution, which has high execution efficiency [1].

In this scheme, functions are divided into two categories: simple functions and complex functions. A function whose maximum number of registers is less than 10 is defined as a simple function, otherwise it is defined as a complex function. Through research, it can be found that simple functions account for more than 90% of the total number of functions (e.g. In American mobile applications, 57 functions have more than 10 registers, and the total number of functions is 886, and simple functions account for 93.57%) [5]. This indicates that on RISC architecture processors, the abundant number of physical registers is sufficient for fast allocation of virtual registers in register-based bytecode.

In this scheme, bytecode instructions are divided into two categories: basic instructions and object instructions. Array operation, object operation, static field operation, method/static method access and other instructions are collectively referred to as object instructions, and the others are basic instructions (usually compiled to generate one or two local instructions). Basic instructions are divided into two categories, namely, variable instructions and fixed instructions. The fixed instruction is that the register of operation is fixed, so the local code generated by it is also fixed, and is short and efficient, which can also be called high-speed instructions.

Taking the ARM SC300 architecture as an example, this scheme is not only suitable for ARM architecture, but also for RISC-V architecture. ARM has 13 general purpose registers from R0 to R12; The R14 (LR) register is also available if the function return pointer is stored on the stack and is recommended for storing JPC.

#### 2.2.4.1 Register Mapping

Depending on the type of function, there are different strategies for register mapping, as follows:

1. Simple function register mapping, as shown in Fig. 6.
   a) Virtual register and physical virtual to establish a one-to-one mapping relationship;

b) The total number of allocated physical registers must be greater than the total number of virtual registers, and three physical registers should be reserved for just-in-time compilation to store temporary variables (to reduce the time consumption caused by on-site saving and recovery during compilation) and JPC use.

c) When compiling some complex object instructions, some temporary registers need to be used because of their complex logical relationships. Therefore, when compiling object instructions, the values in these physical registers selected to act as temporary registers are pushed into the stack for saving (when the reserved registers are exceeded). The value stored in the fetch stack is stored in the physical register for recovery.

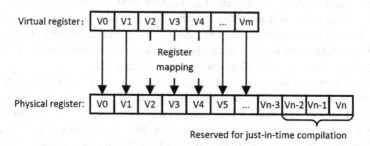

**Fig. 6.** Simple function register mapping

2. Complex function register mapping, as shown in Fig. 7.
   a) Firstly, physical registers and virtual registers are mapped one by one (two physical registers should be reserved for just-in-time compilation).
   b) The virtual registers that are not mapped will be stored in the stack. The area used in this part of the stack is called the overflow area.
   c) The number of allocated physical registers plus the number of overflow areas used must equal the total number of virtual registers;
   d) Similar to the simple function case, when compiling some complex object instructions, some temporary registers are needed due to their complex logical relationships. Therefore, the values in these physical registers selected to act as temporary registers are pushed onto the stack for storage (when the reserved registers are exceeded). The value stored in the fetch stack is stored in the physical register for recovery.

### 2.2.4.2 Just-in-Time Compiler
**The virtual machine bytecode parsing process steps are as follows** (Fig. 8):

1. Get the instruction code and accumulate the JPC;
2. According to the instruction code, look up the bytecode function table and jump to the specified bytecode function.
3. Execute bytecode function processing logic;
4. If there is still unparsed bytecode, skip to step 1 and continue execution;

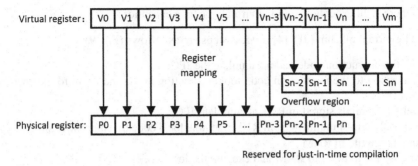

**Fig. 7.** Simple function register mapping

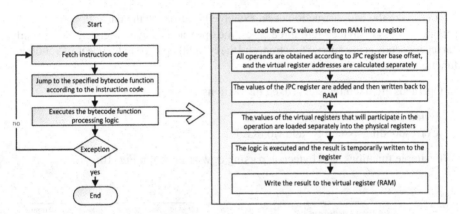

**Fig. 8.** Virtual machine bytecode parsing flowchart

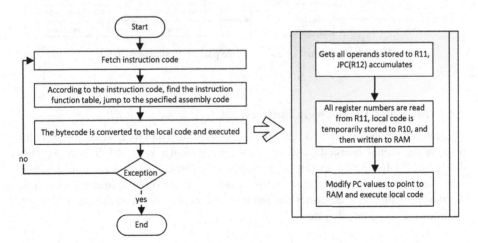

**Fig. 9.** Flow chart of JIT for virtual machine

5. If there is an exception, end the virtual machine execution.

**The** virtual machine JIT [4] process steps are as follows (Fig. 9):

1. Get the instruction code and accumulate the JPC;
2. According to the instruction code lookup function table, and jump to the specified code;
3. Get all operands stored in R10, accumulate JPC;
4. Read all register numbers from R10, assemble local code to temporarily store to R11, and then write to RAM.
5. Modify PC to point to RAM and execute the local code;
6. If there is still unresolved bytecode, skip to step 1 and continue executing;
7. If there is an exception, end the virtual machine execution.

Let's take the add instruction as an example to introduce the parse flow of JIT. The parsing process is divided into three cases: the operand is a fixed register, the currently parsed bytecode is in a simple function, and the currently parsed bytecode is in a complex function.

1. Operands are fixed registers (fixed instructions):

   Bytecode instructions: add_v0, v1, v2
   Corresponding assembly: add R0, R1, R2

2. In simple functions, add bytecode parsing flow is shown in Fig. 10:

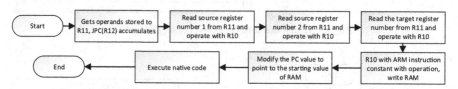

**Fig. 10.** Flow chart of add bytecode parsing in simple functions

### 2.2.5 Integrated Development Environment

Integrated development environment (IDE) is an integrated tool for developing and compiling application source code, and running the application in virtual COS for application debugging [6]. Integrated development environment is based on Eclipse plug-in development, support mainstream Eclipse version, can run on all Windows operating systems. As shown in Fig. 1, it describes the internal relationship between the main function modules and the external system.

### 2.3 Advantages and Characteristics of Micro-operating System

The multi-application micro-operating system platform is not only for the traditional smart card and mobile payment field, but also for the emerging Internet of things field.

It provides high-level protection for the device end, protects high-value and highly sensitive information, and provides security solutions. The micro-operating system has the following characteristics and advantages.

### 2.3.1  It Can Support Multiple Development Languages

The multi-application micro-operating system platform can support a variety of programming languages. The compiler can support Java, Kotlin and other static programming languages in the early stage, and can add support for c++, go, rust, Solidity and other static programming languages in the later stage. The compiler is based on LLVM architecture and has a clear hierarchical structure. It only needs to add a new programming language module support in the compiler front end.

### 2.3.2  Autonomous Compiler

The compiler in the multi-application micro-operating system platform is designed and developed independently, which realizes the EF file of basic register instruction set generated from source code parsing, compiling and linking. The instruction set based on register mode has faster interpretation speed and easier instruction optimization. It is designed based on LLVM architecture and consists of front-end, optimizer and back-end. Due to the modular design, the front-end and back-end use a unified intermediate code, and the same set of optimizer is used for different programming languages, which makes performance optimization simpler and more efficient.

### 2.3.3  Micro Operating System

When the MOS is running, the virtual machine cannot directly access the resources of the MOS. It must pass the authorization of the trusted framework and the agent of the resource manager to access the resources of the MOS.

### 2.3.4  The Integrated Development Environment Can Quickly Locate Defects

Integrated development environment (IDE) is an integrated tool that integrates application source code development, compilation, and loading EF files into virtual OS or physical OS to run, test, and debug applications. The environment provides powerful application code debugging functions, which can quickly locate defects, set breakpoints for single-step debugging, and view variable information in the running process.

### 2.3.5  Both the Compiler and the Operating System are Based on the Instruction Set of Registers

The register based instruction set of multi-application micro-operating system platform can solve the patent problem of virtual machine instruction set, and the interpretation speed is faster.

# 3  Experiment

This section conducts functional tests on system function development, application development, application compilation, application running, application debugging, Shell, view, and other aspects, as well as space and performance optimization tests.

## 3.1  Testing Environment

Development software: Keil MDK, Eclipse

Hardware: BGI CIU9872B_01, Infineon SLC36PDL352, OMNI key 3021 card reader

Operating system: Windows 10

## 3.2  Functional Testing

### 3.2.1  The Compiler

Compiler functional testing is mainly carried out from two aspects, such as compiler and micro-operating system. The compiler mainly tests whether the compiler front-end supports Java and Kotlin high-level programming languages for lexical, lexical, semantic analysis and abstract syntax tree generation, and whether the compiler back-end can generate LF, EF, ECA, MASK.C and other files, and verify whether the generated EF files can run normally in the multi-application micro-operating system.

### 3.2.2  Integrated Development Environment

This section examines the functions of integrated development environment from application development, application compilation, application running, application debugging, shell and other aspects.

#### 3.2.2.1 Application Development

Check whether it supports creating application projects and applications through wizards, providing code editors for source code development, and supporting multiple high-level programming languages such as Java language and Kotlin.

#### 3.2.2.2 Application Compilation

Check whether the compiler supports compiling and linking Java, Kotlin and other high-level programming languages to generate LF, EF, ECA files. If there is an error during the compilation process, the error information can be displayed in the "Problems" view. When double-clicking the error record, it can be located to the specified line position in the source code editor.

#### 3.2.2.3 The Application Runs

Verify whether the EF file (application executable file) generated by the compiler can be loaded to the specified target (physical card, virtual OS, remote virtual OS, etc.) to execute the application.

#### 3.2.2.4 Application Debugging

Verify that the application can run in debug mode and on the virtual OS. You can set breakpoints for the application code, and trace and debug the code step by step, as well as view the local variables, global variables, static variables and other information during the debugging process.

#### 3.2.2.5 The Shell

Check that the Shell supports the following commands: /atr, /card, /close, /list-vars, /mode, /select, /send, /terminal, init-update, ext-auth, auth, upload, install, delete, card-info, set -applet, set-state, put-key, put-ketset, set-key, getcplc.

### 3.2.3  Microoperating System

In this section, the multi-application micro-operating system is transplanted to BADA CIU9872B_01, Infineon SLC36PDL352, and virtual OS for functional testing. The test items tested on different platforms include: virtual machine running environment, application programming interface, GP, CMCC API, SIMAPI, UICC API, one-card application interoperability, electronic wallet application interoperability, Pudong Development Development co-branded card application interoperability, American Express, etc., and all pass the test.

### 3.3  Performance Test

### 3.3.1  Performance Testing of the Application

Based on BGI CIU9872B_01 chip, this section will compare the performance of multi-application micro-operating system and Java card (based on stacked instruction set). The test precondition is that the multi-application microoperating system and the Java card operating system are transplanted to the CIU9872B_01 chip and personalized.

The financial application was selected as the test application, and the application transaction was run 50 times. The minimum transaction time, maximum transaction time and average transaction time were taken for statistics. As shown in Table 1, the overall performance is 20.4% faster than Java card.

**Table 1.**  Application transaction performance comparison

|           | Min time (ms) | Max time (ms) | Average time (ms) |
|-----------|---------------|---------------|-------------------|
| Java Card | 739.58        | 779.99        | 741.37            |
| MOS       | 611.95        | 654.4         | 615.6             |
| Ratio     | 120.9%        | 119.2%        | 120.4%            |

### 3.3.2  Space and Performance Optimization Test
#### 3.3.2.1 Space Optimization
After instruction set optimization, the space reduction is about 25%, as shown in Table 2.

The optimized space is about 17% larger than that of Java Card (usually the register instruction food occupies more than 30% more space than the stacked instruction set), as shown in Table 3.

**Table 2.** Comparison of the space occupied by MOS instructions before and after optimization

| Comparison items | Before (byte) | After (byte) | ratio (%) |
|---|---|---|---|
| method | 109493 | 81869 | 25.23% |
| romsize | 114946 | 87218 | 24.12% |

**Table 3.** Comparison of MOS and Java Card footprint

| Comparison items | Java Card (byte) | MOS (byte) | ratio (%) |
|---|---|---|---|
| method | 69767 | 81869 | 17.35% |
| romsize | 74554 | 87218 | 16.99% |

### 3.3.2.2 Just-in-Time Compiler Performance Testing Based on Physical Register Mapping

Based on BGI CIU9872B_01 chip, this section will compare the performance of the multi-application microoperating system before and after the JIT optimization. As shown in Table 4, the execution instruction cycles of add instructions before and after optimization are compared under different conditions. The use of fixed registers for optimized instructions improves the performance by 96%, and it improves the performance by 55% in simple functions.

**Table 4.** The number of instruction cycles executed by the add instruction

| Conditions | before | after | ratio (%) |
|---|---|---|---|
| Fixed registers | 47 | 2 | 96% |
| In simple functions | 47 | 21 | 55 |
| In complex functions | 47 | 43 | 9% |

*App Performs Performance Analysis:*

The financial application was selected as the test application, and the application transaction (as shown in Table 1) was run 50 times. The minimum transaction time, maximum transaction time and average transaction time were taken for statistics, as shown in Table 5. The performance of just-in-time compiler is improved by 16.6%.

Because the register number of a fixed instruction is fixed, converting to local code is also one or two local instructions to complete its logic; Therefore, it is necessary to

**Table 5.** Performance comparison of just-in-time compiler before and after optimization

|               | Min time(ms) | Max(max) | Average time |
|---------------|--------------|----------|--------------|
| not optimized | 611.95       | 654.4    | 615.6        |
| optimization  | 505.85       | 556.4    | 513.3        |
| ration        | 17.3%        | 14.9%    | 16.6%        |

add const and move as fixed instructions to improve the performance of virtual machine. According to statistics, the maximum number of registers of more than 90% functions is less than 10 (simple functions), and the estimated instruction cycle is 21, which is 55% of the original. After optimization, the overall performance of the application is improved by 16%.

## 4  Summary and Outlook

In the era of 5G Internet of Things, information is developing rapidly, and big data has become a hot topic. Ensuring computer network security and preventing information data leakage is an important challenge faced by current network security management. Vigorously promoting the establishment and development of information technology application innovation industry, so as to realize independent, safe and controllable alternative solutions is the need of The Times.

In this context, the smart card operating system is also facing new challenges and opportunities, and the research and implementation of the operating system is particularly necessary. The multi-application micro-operating system platform can support a variety of applications, such as finance, transportation, medical care, education, etc. These applications can share the storage space and computing resources of the smart card, and improve the utilization and efficiency of the smart card. At the same time, the multi-application smart card operating system can also provide a more secure data storage and transmission mechanism to protect the privacy and security of users. In short, the multi-application micro-operating system platform based on big data can improve the utilization and efficiency of smart cards, while ensuring the security and privacy of data. With the continuous development of smart card technology, the multi-application smart card operating system will be more widely used.

## References

1. Wang Haojie, F.: Research on key technologies of program memory access analysis and optimization based on compiler technology. Tsinghua University (2021)
2. Zhang Ming, F: Research on microcontroller based on RISC-V Instruction set. Anhui University (2020)
3. Zhang Deming, F: Research on security isolation technology of embedded platform based on trusted domain. Nanjing University (2019)

4. Wenxiang Lu, F.: An improved strategy to eliminate redundant compilation based on Dalvik JIT. In: 2015 Eighth International Conference on Internet Computing for Science and Engineering (ICICSE)

5. Atsuya Sonoyama, F.: Performance study of Kotlin and java program considering bytecode instructions and JVM JIT compiler. In: 2021 Ninth International Symposium on Computing and Networking Workshops (CANDARW)

6. Safeeullah Soomro, F.: A framework for debugging java programs in a bytecode. In: 2018 International Conference on Computing, Electronics & Communications Engineering (iCCECE)

7. Wen Yuanbo, F.: Research on cross-platform compilation technology for intelligent computing systems. University of Science and Technology of China (2022)

8. Lu Quan, F.: Analysis of the influence of different programming languages on the development of computer application software. China New Commun. (2022)

9. Wan Ping, F.: Analysis of programming language in computer application software development. Integr. Circ. Appl. (2022)

10. Chen Jianfei, F.: Research and application of embedded virtualization real-time system. Electromech. Inf. (2019)

11. Li Yunxi, F.: Research on unified architecture of multi-application mode embedded operating system. Aeronaut. Comput. Technol. (2019)

12. Zhang Linchao, F.: A brief analysis of trusted artificial intelligence system and security framework. J. Chin. Acad. Electron. Sci. (2019)

13. Xiaofeng Shang, F.: Implementation of embedded real-time operating system and application software based on smart chip. In: 2022 3rd International Conference on Electronics and Sustainable Communication Systems (ICESC)

# Consortium Blockchain Storage Optimization Based on Fountain Codes

Jianhong Li[1,2], Qi Chen[1,2]([✉]), Xianmin Wang[1], Guoyu Yang[1], Zihan Jiang[1], Teng Huang[1], and Li Hu[1]

[1] Institute of Artificial Intelligence, Guangzhou University, Guangzhou 510006, China
{2112106026,hl_27}@e.gzhu.edu.cn, chenqi.math@gmail.com,
xianmin@gzhu.edu.cn, huangteng1220@buaa.edu.cn
[2] State Key Laboratory of Integrated Service Networks (Xidian University),
Xi'an 710071, China

**Abstract.** Blockchain is a distributed digital ledger with tamper-proof and privacy-preserving features. However, its use of fully replicated data storage mechanism results in high storage cost and poor scalability. This paper proposes a consortium chain encoding technique based on LT code and an LT code dual-fault-tolerant stripping decoder scheme. By combining LT code block encoding technology, the storage costs for nodes can be effectively reduced, and the dual-fault-tolerant stripping decoder scheme ensures that newly joined nodes can safely recover the complete transaction history. We simulated the proposed solution in this paper with node numbers of 20, 40, 80, 100, 200, and 300, and compared the encoding time at the same storage optimization cost with the existing popular blockchain ledger Reed-Solomon (RS) code encoding technique. We also simulated the decoding time of the proposed LT code dual-fault-tolerant stripping decoder and the RS code decoding technique in the presence of different numbers of malicious nodes interference, in order to compare their ability to securely recover the ledger. Finally, we compared the minimum number of encoding blocks required for decoding in both schemes. The results indicate that the encoding and decoding time of the RS code scheme almost linearly increase, while the proposed solution exhibits a generally flat and slow growth. Therefore, both encoding and decoding in the proposed solution are superior to the RS code scheme. In terms of the minimum number of encoding blocks required for decoding, the proposed solution requires slightly more blocks than the RS code encoding scheme. However, in the RS code scheme, the dynamic addition or removal of nodes causes other nodes in the blockchain network to perform re-encoding, that increases the bandwidth of the blockchain network. Therefore, the proposed solution effectively improves the accuracy of node recovery in the ledger, maintains the ledger's security in the consortium blockchain network, and enhances the scalability of the consortium blockchain network.

**Keywords:** Blockchain · Storage optimization · Erasure codes · Fountain codes

J. Cai et al. (Eds.): SPNCE 2023, LNICST 525, pp. 35–53, 2025.
https://doi.org/10.1007/978-3-031-73699-5_3

# 1   Introduction

Blockchain, as the foundational technology for cryptocurrencies such as Bitcoin and Ethereum, has played an important role in facilitating decentralized and trusted transactions. Moreover, it is also gradually having a transformative impact on different fields such as IoT, medicine, healthcare, and supply chain. The decentralization, security and scalability of blockchain make it have great potential.A blockchain node independently verifies each block added to the chain, stores the entire blockchain ledger, and helps newly joined nodes recover the entire blockchain ledger. Nodes with these functions are called "full nodes", which are the backbone of the blockchain network. However, running a full node on a resource-constrained device comes at a heavy price in terms of storage and computational costs. In particular, the storage requirements of the blockchain are growing at a near-exponential rate. Due to limited computing, storage, and bandwidth resources, it is difficult for resource-constrained devices to bear the consensus process of the blockchain and the storage costs of ledgers. For example, Bitcoin's total block data is currently over 200 GB, and the Ethereum network generates around 0.2 GB of data per day. And for high-throughput blockchains like Ripple [3], storage costs will be a pressing concern in the near future. The Ripple ledger is already 8.4TB in size and growing at a staggering 12GB per day.

To address the issue of storage costs, some mainstream permissionless blockchains like Bitcoin and Ethereum have introduced various technologies such as lightweight clients [22,27] and the Lightning Network [6]. Lightweight clients only store block headers to verify the block bodies received from full nodes, that effectively reduces storage overhead on the client side. The Lightning Network's fundamental idea is to facilitate multiple small-scale payments between two accounts and minimize the uploading of final balances to the blockchain, thus reducing the volume of block data and alleviating storage pressure on each node. Erasure code has also shown great performance in permissionless blockchains and is widely adopted as a new method for storage reduction [14]. In fact, it is not limited to permissionless blockchains; there have been numerous works on permissioned blockchains that leverage erasure codes for blockchain storage optimization. The authors of [16] considered a fragmented blockchain and reduced storage by computing encoded fragments through linear combinations of uncoded fragments. The authors of [25] employed key-based encryption for dynamic partitioning of the blockchain network. Reed-Solomon (RS) code [20], as one type of erasure code, has also demonstrated excellent performance in consortium blockchains. RS code can effectively reduce the storage costs of consortium blockchains and improve the efficiency of recovering historical blockchain ledger data.

However, there is still room for optimization in these approaches. While lightweight clients can reduce storage costs for clients, full nodes on the blockchain still follow the method of complete replication. Therefore, this approach is not effective in terms of storage savings. While the Lightning Network can alleviate storage pressure on each node, it does not fundamentally disrupt the mechanism of full replication. Although previous works using erasure codes have shown excellent performance in storage optimization, especially with RS codes meeting our storage reduction requirements and breaking the mechanism of complete replication, these erasure codes involve complex decoding within a finite field, resulting in high communication costs for recovering the original data.

Therefore, in the face of the increasing cost of blockchain storage on the permissioned blockchain [21], there are three main problems as follows:

- The blockchain ledger data is redundant, and the cost of node storage of blockchain ledger data is high.
- Malicious nodes will attempt to destroy the blockchain ledger by any means. For newly added nodes, malicious nodes will attempt to prevent the newly added nodes from obtaining the complete blockchain historical ledger.
- The decoding of RS code will increase the cost of computing resources of nodes.

In summary, to meet the high demands for computing power, network bandwidth, and storage costs in permissioned blockchains, this paper proposes an optimized block storage approach based on LT code [17]. On one hand, we employ the fountain code technique with a no code rate to reduce the storage space of the blockchain. On the other hand, we design and optimize fountain code encoding strategies and secure decoding methods specifically tailored for recovering blocks damaged by malicious nodes. Additionally, we propose an LT code double fault-tolerant stripping decoder for consortium blockchain [8] to reduce recovery latency and improve decoding accuracy.

The main contributions of this paper are as follows:

- An optimization scheme of consortium blockchain storage based on fountain code is proposed to reduce the burden of blockchain ledger storage on nodes. When enough encoded blocks are generated in an epoch, each node will encode the blocks in this epoch using fountain code and store them locally. By encoding and storing blocks within an epoch locally, the storage overhead of resource-constrained nodes can be reduced. After experimental verification, it was found that LT codes have better performance, which can reduce the storage cost of the historical ledger of blockchain from $O(n)$ to $O(m)$, where $m$ is a constant much smaller than $n$.
- During the block recovery process, the recovery node can visit other nodes and request to download the corresponding encoded blocks until there is a sufficient number of encoded blocks to restore the block. During the block recovery process, historical blocks can be recovered with a high probability of success by accessing a sufficient amount of data from honest nodes and using the LT code double fault-tolerant stripping decoder for safe decoding. Furthermore, experimental results have shown that LT codes require less communication cost during block recovery process compared to RS codes.
- The LT code dual fault-tolerant stripping decoder is used to decode the encoded blocks. This decoding method identifies and discards tampered

encoded blocks by matching whether the head of a single encoded block (droplet) is the same XOR value as the corresponding block head in the header chain before decoding. After decoding, the LT code dual fault-tolerant stripping decoder will verify again whether a single decoding block has been tampered with. This dual integrity check mechanism improves the efficiency and success rate of decoding.

- The performance of the proposed algorithm is verified through extensive experiments. The experimental results show that the proposed algorithm can effectively reduce the communication overhead in the consensus process and reduce the blockchain storage cost.

The rest of this paper is arranged as follows: Sect. 2 introduces the backknowlegde about erasure codes, consortium blockchain and blockchain storage. Section 3 introduces the threat model and design goals. Section 4 introduces the specific design of the protocol. Section 5 conducts the security and privacy analysis of the protocol. Section 6 introduces the simulation experiment. Finally, we summarize our contributions in Sect. 7.

## 2   Background

### 2.1   Consortium Blockchain

Permissioned blockchains [21] are blockchains that are closed or have an access control layer. This extra layer of security means that permissioned chains can only be accessed by authorized users. Permissioned users are only able to perform blockchain operations within the strict confines of roles assigned to them by the ledger administrators and require that they authenticate themselves through certificates or digital identifier methods. This additional permission restriction provides permissioned blockchains with high levels of privacy and security and the flexibility of decentralization. As a form of permissioned blockchain, the consortium blockchain provides significant control and faster processing speed while ensuring privacy and security, which makes it more efficient and secure in many aspects. The existing four major consortium blockchain are Hyperledger Fabric [2], FISCO BCOS [13], EEA Quorum [10] and R3 Corda [5]. Among them, Hyperledger Fabric, EEA Quorum and R3 Corda are foreign consortium blockchain, while FISCO BCOS is a domestic consortium blockchain.

### 2.2   Erasure Codes

Erasure code is a common storage system fault-tolerant technique, and Reed-Solomon (RS) code [26] is the most common one. There are two configurable parameters, $K$ and $M$, in RS code. RS divides the data into $K$ equally sized segments and encodes them to generate $M$ redundant segments called parity. $K + M$ segments are called chunks. RS encoding guarantees that any $K$ out of $K + M$ chunks are sufficient to recover the original data. It is important to note that erasure coding itself cannot check the correctness of the chunks, and it may recover incorrect data based on invalid chunks. Therefore, each node in the blockchain needs to verify the correctness of the received chunks.

## 2.3   Blockchain Storage

Storage optimization has always been one of the hotspots of blockchain network research. For this reason, many scholars have proposed many methods to reduce the storage cost of nodes. The most common techniques include lightweight clients or simplified payment verification methods, in which nodes do not need to store the entire blockchain ledger, only need to store a copy of the block header. Unlike full nodes, light clients do not participate in validating transactions and do not interact directly with the blockchain. Instead, they rely entirely on full nodes in the blockchain network. Light clients may help reduce the cost of storage, but they will increase the bandwidth of the blockchain network, and may even lead to privacy leaks, and are vulnerable to attacks such as denial of service. Another popular technique is block pruning, where nodes delete old blocks and store only the most recently committed blocks [1]. Compared with light clients, it performs better in terms of security. However, they only store a small part of the blocks and cannot help newly joined nodes restore historical blocks, which seriously damages the decentralization feature.

Erasure codes [19] are excellent at reducing the storage cost of blockchain network nodes without compromising reliability. Therefore, this paper also adopts erasure codes to reduce the storage cost of blockchain nodes. References [23] proposed low-storage nodes that split each block into small segments of fixed size and store only encoded segments. Coding fragments are obtained by linearly combining block fragments with random coefficients. Their main limitation is that they only consider the situation that a node can exit the blockchain network or the node is inaccessible, and do not consider the situation that malicious nodes provide maliciously formed coding fragments to interfere with the recovery of historical blocks. The authors in [25] considered the problem of blockchain networks with confidentiality and reduced storage costs. They propose to dynamically partition the network, then encrypt each block using a specific key for each region, and distribute the encrypted blocks among nodes in each region using a distributed storage code approach such as [9,12]. The authors in [16] consider fragmented blockchain networks and propose to compute encoded fragments by linearly combining unencoded fragments. Reed-Solomon codes (see, e.g. [20]) are the most commonly used encoding method for generating encoded fragments.Reed-Solomon codes can be used to recover the original data in the presence of a limited number of adversarial nodes that provide malicious data [20]. All these coding schemes such as random linear codes, distributed memory codes, and Reed-Solomon codes need to operate over sufficiently large finite fields and lead to high computational complexity for decoding. Therefore, the improved method based on fountain codes in this paper, especially the LT codes used, is significantly better in terms of computational cost.

Fountain codes are designed to handle random erasures. While it is possible to decode from random errors (see, for example, [11,15,18]), perturbing decoding of erroneous data can be difficult to handle. Typically, the iterative decoding algorithm of fountain codes easily propagates any errors in the received data and amplifies them in the recovered data. This is because fountain codes do not provide any mechanism for checking the integrity of the decoded data. Therefore, compared with the previous work, the advantages of the proposed blockchain storage algorithm are as follows:

- For optimizing storage cost, the proposed blockchain storage optimization algorithm based on fountain codes not only considers the storage cost, but also comprehensively considers the selection of coding parameters and the decoding success rate of coding blocks, so as to build a blockchain network suitable for PBFT consensus mechanism. In addition, the use of fountain codes for encoding and decoding has better performance and higher security than RS codes running on finite fields. Experimental results show that the proposed blockchain storage optimization algorithm based on fountain code can effectively reduce the blockchain storage overhead and block recovery delay.
- For the reliability of block recovery and the security of the blockchain network. Fountain codes use a robust soliton distribution algorithm to select the encoded blocks, which ensures that they can be decoded with negligible failure probability when decoding. When a block needs to be recovered, the node collects the number of encoded blocks needed for recovery from other nodes to successfully decode the historical block with negligible failure probability. Moreover, after each node recovers the historical block, it verifies the Merkle root of the block header in the historical block, which effectively prevents the historical block tampering attack caused by some malicious nodes providing maliciously tampered coding blocks, and ensures the reliability of block recovery and the security of the blockchain network.

## 3   Threat Model and Design Goals

For blockchain storage optimization, our work is aimed at the PBFT [7] consensus on the consortium blockchain, and our main goal is to reduce the storage cost on each blockchain node. Moreover, in our designed protocol, blockchain nodes store even less data while being able to recover the complete blockchain ledger. Furthermore, they can assist newly joined nodes in recovering historical ledger data. We refer to the nodes with reduced storage cost as droplet nodes and the nodes newly joining the blockchain network as bucket nodes.

### 3.1   Threat Model and Assumption

**Threat Model.** Consider a Byzantine adversary that can control an arbitrary subset of droplet nodes. These malicious nodes may collude with each other and may disrupt the blockchain protocol in arbitrary ways. For example, sending maliciously tampered data to bucket nodes, or keeping silent. The remaining droplet nodes are honest and participate in the consensus process of the blockchain and the encoding and decoding process of historical blocks. Our hypothetical adversary randomly controls malicious nodes. That is, before selecting the node to control, it does not know the content stored in the droplet node. Our goal is to design a protocol, as long as there are no more than f malicious nodes, the bucket node can recover the historical blocks. This paper measures the security performance of the encoding scheme by the minimum number of honest droplet nodes, which are enough to recover the historical blocks with negligible failure probability.

**Assumption.** The consortium chain storage optimization method which based on fountain code assumes that bucket nodes can obtain the correct block header chain first. Therefore, we assume that the majority of nodes are honest and actively participate in the consensus. Because the PBFT consensus is not like the POW consensus [4], the leader mechanism of the PBFT consensus can ensure that the blockchain will not fork.

## 3.2   Design Goals

For storage optimization, our main goal is to design that can achieve an optimal balance between storage savings and recovery cost in the PBFT consensus protocol. In addition, we expect the protocol to be able to have smaller bandwidth overhead and computational cost. Besides, the decentralized encoding scheme of fountain code enables droplet nodes to generate droplets without knowing the storage contents of other nodes in the blockchain network.

We measure encoding performance using the following metrics:

1. The storage saving factor of a node is the ratio of the total size of a blockchain block to the size of its stored droplets.
2. The recovery cost of the encoding scheme is measured by the minimum number of honest droplet nodes that a bucket node needs to visit to ensure that historical blocks can be recovered with a negligible probability of failure. Note that the recovery cost of an encoding scheme reflects its security performance. This is because the recovery cost can be regarded as the minimum number of honest droplet nodes that the system must contain to guarantee that historical blockchain data can be recovered. The smaller the recovery cost of an encoding scheme, the better the security performance of a system using that scheme.
3. Bandwidth overhead refers to the overhead of the amount of droplet data that the bucket node needs to download. Our goal is to control the bandwidth overhead to an appropriate threshold and restore the blockchain with a high probability.
4. The computational cost refers to the time it takes for all nodes in the entire blockchain network to decode and re-encode when a new node joins, which is a measure of the required computing resources for the blockchain network.

# 4    Protocol Design

## 4.1    System Architecture

Our coding scheme is able to enable nodes to code independently without relying on other nodes and to save storage space by storing only a small number of coding blocks. Recall that we refer to a coded block as a droplet, the node storing the coded block as a droplet node, and the newly added node to recover the historical block as a bucket node.

**Encoding.** We encode the droplets by the number of block growth, where the encoding period is defined as the time when the blockchain grows by $k$ blocks. Let $B = \{B_1, B_2, ..., B_k\}$ denotes a set of $k$ original blocks from the blockchain. This set of $k$ original blocks will be encoded into $s$ droplets by each node independently. Because PBFT consensus does not have a forked chain, when the number of blocks in a group does not reach $k$, this group of blocks will be directly stored in the local node. Once $k$ blocks are reached, the node encodes the block to reduce the storage cost of the node. Moreover, for the encoding period, we denote by $l$.

Next, we define the number of nodes as $n$, and we select the node numbered $j$ and observe its encoding process. For the current blockchain of height $t$, where $t$ is not an integer multiple of $k$, $j$ encodes $k$ blocks in every period of $k$ blocks, outputs $s$ droplets, and then deletes $k$ blocks, and the process continues. Denote the encoded output droplet of node $j$ as $C = \left\{ C_{1,1}^{(j)}, ..., C_{1,s}^{(j)}, ..., C_{l,1}^{(j)}, ..., C_{l,s}^{(j)} \right\}$, node $j$ finally also stores $t - lk$ uncoded blocks. The specific encoding is shown in Fig. 1.

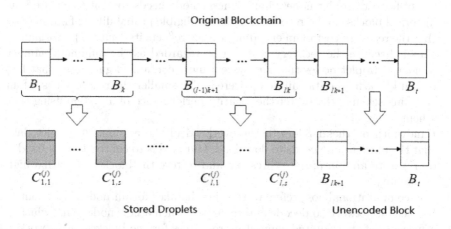

**Fig. 1.** Example of Node $j$ Encoding.

**Decoding.** Assuming the current block height is $t$, after a new bucket node is added, the bucket node visits any $m$ nodes in order to download the encoded blocks needed to restore the blockchain. We define the longest period of block encoding to be $e = \lfloor \frac{t}{k} \rfloor$; therefore, we collect droplets from the interval of periods $1 \leq l \leq e$. In addition, bucket nodes also download an additional $t - lk$ uncoded blocks from the $m$ nodes. Bucket nodes can also access the headchains stored in other droplet nodes to verify the correctness of the decoded blocks.

## 4.2  Protocol Workflow

The RS code scheme is commonly used for encoding in existing permissioned blockchains. RS code is a type of erasure code that encodes a given set of $K$ data blocks with $M$ parity blocks, known as "parity check", resulting in $N = K + M$ encoded blocks. RS encoding ensures that any $K$ blocks among the $N$ blocks are sufficient to recover the original data. However, the dynamic addition or removal of nodes in the RS code scheme requires all nodes in the entire blockchain network to re-execute the encoding process, which greatly increases the bandwidth overhead of the blockchain network. In this paper, LT code is used for encoding. LT code is a type of fountain code that can generate infinite outputs from k inputs. The most important feature of fountain codes is their ability to recover $k$ inputs with high probability from $K (\geq k)$ output data. Unlike the RS code, the dynamic addition or removal of nodes in the LT code scheme does not affect the nodes in the original blockchain network. Each node's encoding and decoding is independent of other nodes, so there is no need for all nodes in the blockchain network to re-encode due to the dynamic addition or removal of nodes.

The decoder for LT codes is called a stripping decoder (also known as belief propagation), and its decoding process has a high computational efficiency. However, the stripping decoder cannot handle the maliciously tampered output data. The output data method to solve this malicious tampering mainly uses the header chain of the blockchain as auxiliary information, and uses the Merkle root stored in the header chain to determine whether the output data has been maliciously tampered.

**LT Code Encoder.** In each encoding period, the droplet node encodes droplets according to the following steps. The node first select a positive integer $d$ from 1 to $k$ based on the degree distribution as the degree of the encoding block. Then, it uniformly randomly selects $d$ blocks out of $k$ blocks. Finally, it computes the bitwise XOR of the $d$ blocks to obtain the droplet. Nodes store not only the generated droplets but also the index of $d$ blocks. Nodes repeat this process to continuously generate droplets.

In the terminology of LT codes, $d$ is called the degree of the droplet and the blocks used to compute the droplet are called neighbors. The term comes from a bipartite graph with $k$ original input blocks as left vertices, $s$ droplets as right vertices, and an edge connecting the block to the droplet if one of the blocks is used to do XOR to generate the droplet. Moreover, the probability distribution of the degree of sampling on the set $\{1, 2, ..., k\}$ is called the degree distribution. This is shown in Fig. 2.

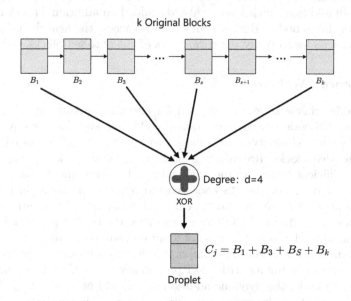

**Fig. 2.** An example of LT code encoding.

The description of the LT encoding process used by blockchain nodes will be described in detail below. Coding is the same for all epochs, and we arbitrarily pick an epoch for analysis. A node calculates its $j$th droplet $C_j (1 \le j \le s)$ without interfering with other nodes, the calculation process is as follows:

step 1 The degree $d$ of the droplet is selected from the degree distribution function $\mu(\cdot)$.

step 2 Choose $d$ blocks uniformly at random from the $k$ blocks, and do the bit-wise XOR operation on these $d$ blocks to generate $C_j$. Define $C_j = \{H_j, T_j\}$, where $H_j$ is the first $L_h$ bit of $C_j$, called the head of $C_j$. $T_j$ is the $L - L_h$ bit of $C_j$ and is the transaction data part of $C_j$.

step 3 Store $C_j$ together with a random number $r_j$ that generates a binary vector of length $k$ through degree $d$.

In addition to $s$ droplets, each node also needs to store the headchain $H$ of the original blockchain, because the random number $r_j$ is used to generate the binary vector and the headchain $H$ for data integrity verification in the decoding process. The binary vector is used to identify which original blocks are combined to generate $C_j$, while the headchain $H$ enables the decoder to identify maliciously formed droplets.

Let's review the possible malicious behavior of droplet nodes. In addition to remaining silent when in contact with bucket nodes, malicious droplet nodes will have the following two behaviors:

- Store any values of $C_l$, $r_l$, and $H$. For some encoding epoch, let $G$ be a $k \times l$ binary matrix where the $i$th row corresponds to the $i$th block in the block. For an honest node $j$, the binary vectors $v_j$ and $C_j$ generated by $r_j$ must have $C_j = v_j G$. However, a malicious droplet node $l$ can store any value of $C_l$ and $r_l$ such that $C_l \neq v_l G$ in the binary vector $v_l$ generated through $r_l$. The droplets generated by such malicious droplet nodes are called turbid droplets.
- Arbitrary degree of selectivity $d$, and arbitrarily choose $d$ blocks to count droplets. But the malicious droplet node will correctly store the encoded block $C_j$ and the random number $r_j$. The droplets generated by such malicious droplet nodes are called opaque droplets. The main purpose of this attack is to increase the probability of decoding failure.

A droplet computed by an honest droplet node is called a transparent droplet.

**LT Code Dual Fault-Tolerant Stripping Decoder.** The LT code decoder we redefined for the consortium chain is a fault-tolerant stripping decoder that can identify malicious data and discard it. Consider a newly added bucket node on the consortium blockchain, which visits $m$ $\left(m \geq \frac{k}{s}\right)$ arbitrary droplet nodes and downloads the corresponding droplet node data. These data include droplets $C_j$ and random numbers $r_j$. Label the downloaded droplets as $C_1, C_2, ..., C_{ms}$. Since the encoded droplets do not have any useful information about the blocks, bucket nodes cannot distinguish between transparent, opaque, and turbid droplets within a droplet.

We assume that bucket nodes have access to honest headchains. Honest headchains can be obtained by contacting at least $n - 2f$ of the $n$ nodes. The acquired headchain will be applied to verify the correctness of the decoded data.

Decoding is performed iteratively. At each iteration, the algorithm decodes at most one block until all blocks have been decoded, otherwise it declares a decoding failure. The decoding process is shown in Fig. 3.

Next, we describe the steps of the decoding process in the LT code dual fault-tolerant stripping decoder in detail. Let $H_1, H_2, ..., H_k$ denote the first $k$ block headers of the honest headchain.

step 1 Initialization: Use $k$ original blocks as left vertices and $ms$ droplets as right vertices to form a bipartite graph $Y$. If block $B_g$ is used to compute $C_j$, there is an edge connecting droplet $C_j$ to original block $B_g$. For $g = 1, 2, ..., k$, initialize $\hat{B}_g$ to a null value. Let the number of iterations $i = 1$ and $Y^{i-1} = Y$.

step 2 For the received droplet $C_j$ and random number $r_j$, first check whether the droplet $C_j$ has been tampered with. The corresponding binary vector $v_j$ is calculated through $r_j$, and the block head corresponding to the block chain $H$ is XOR operated according to the binary vector $v_j$. Compared with the block head $H_j$ in $C_j$, if it is correct, it continues to participate in the decoding process, and if it is wrong, it discards the received droplet.

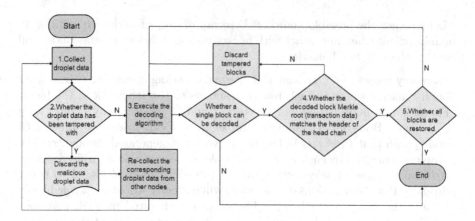

**Fig. 3.** The Decoding Process.

step 3 Find a droplet $C_l$ in $Y^{i-1}$ that is connected to exactly one block $B_g$, and such a droplet $C_l$ is called a monomer. If there is no droplet of monomer, then decoding fails and the decoding algorithm is terminated.

step 4 Let $H_l$ and $T_l$ be the block header and transaction data part of $C_l$, respectively.

   1. Calculate the Merkle root $(T_l)$ of $T_l$. Let $\hat{B}_g = C_l$ if $T_l$ matches the header $H_g$ at the corresponding position in the headchain $H$ and root $(T_l)$ also matches the Merkle root stored in $H_g$.

   2. Otherwise, $C_l$ is discarded and the bipartite graph number $Y^{i-1}$ is updated to $Y^i$. Let $i$ increase by 1 and go to step 3.

step 5 For all droplet nodes $C_l'$ connected to $B_g$ in the bipartite graph $Y^{i-1}$, let $C_l' = C_l' \oplus \hat{B}_g$.

step 6 Delete all edges connected to $B_g$ and update the bipartite graph number $Y^{i-1}$ to $Y^i$.

step 7 Increase $i$ by 1.

step 8 If all the blocks have not been decoded, go to Step 3 and continue the decoding process.

Compared with the traditional LT code decoder, the LT code decoder redefined for the consortium blockchain can distinguish the stripped decoder with the ability to detect tampered data from the classic stripped decoder in steps 2 and 4. Specifically, the classical stripped decoder always accepts the decoded block, no matter whether the block has been tampered with or not. However, the LT code decoder redefined for the consortium blockchain performs XOR on the block head at the corresponding position in the header chain through the block index vector in the droplet data in step 2 to first detect whether the droplet data has been tampered with. In this way, the tampered droplet data can be discarded without entering the decoding step, which greatly reduces the complexity of the decoding process. This method ensures that the droplet data is normal before the decoding process starts to increase the probability of successful decoding during the decoding process. When the droplet is decoded into a single block, step 4 again verifies whether the header of the decoded block matches the corresponding block header in the header chain, further providing a mechanism for integrity checking. If the block header and Merkle root do not match the data stored in the header chain, then the fault-tolerant stripping decoder can discard the tampered data and re-download the drops for decoding to other droplet nodes.

### 4.3 Key Functions

**Degree Distribution.** Although the encoder and decoder can choose any degree, the probability of successfully decoding the input data from a given amount of output data depends on the choice of the degree distribution. In this section, we describe the robust soliton distribution proposed by Ludy [17]. In [17], robust soliton degree distributions were shown to have good success probability. The degree distribution function $\mu(\cdot)$ is a discrete probability function in the range of 1 and $k$ integers. To describe the robust soliton distribution, the following notation is introduced in this paper. The function $\rho(\cdot)$ is defined as follows:

$$\rho(d) = \begin{cases} \frac{1}{k} & \text{for} \quad d = 1 \\ \frac{1}{d(d-1)} & \text{for} \quad d = 2, \dots, k \end{cases} \tag{1}$$

For a given $0 < \delta < 1$ and $c > 0$, define:

$$R = c\sqrt{k} \ln\left(\frac{k}{\delta}\right) \tag{2}$$

Then, define a function $\theta(\cdot)$ as:

$$\theta(d) = \begin{cases} \frac{R}{dk} & \text{for} \quad d = 1, \dots, \frac{k}{R} - 1 \\ \frac{R}{k} \ln(\frac{R}{\delta}) & \text{for} \quad d = \frac{k}{R} \\ 0 & d = \frac{k}{R+1}, \dots, k \end{cases} \tag{3}$$

The parameter $\delta$ is a bound on the probability of decoding failure after a certain number of droplets have been downloaded. The parameter $c$ is a custom parameter that can be adjusted to optimize the number of droplets needed to recover the historical blocks of the blockchain. Summing and normalizing $\rho(\cdot)$ with $\theta(\cdot)$ yields the robust soliton distribution as follows:

$$\mu(d) = \frac{\rho(d) + \theta(d)}{\beta}, \quad \text{for} \quad d = 1, \dots, k \tag{4}$$

where

$$\beta = \sum_{d=1}^{k} \rho(d) + \theta(d) \tag{5}$$

## 5   Security and Privacy Analysis

This section starts by considering a pair of encoding and decoding schemes (Enc, Dec) according to the performance of the design goals in Sect. 3. Compare the performance indicators of LT code and RS code for PBFT consensus.

### 5.1   Storage Savings

The storage savings of LT codes is the ratio of the total blockchain size of data to the size of the encoded droplets. The storage saving size of droplet node $j$ is $\gamma = \frac{size(B)}{size(Enc(B,j))} = \frac{k}{m}$. And the storage saving of the RS code [24] is $\gamma = \frac{size(B)}{size(Enc(B,j))} = k$.

### 5.2   Recovery Cost

Considering the coding scheme with storage savings of $\gamma$ in LT codes, for a given decoding failure probability $0 < \delta < 1$, the recovery cost of the historical block of the blockchain needs to be measured by the minimum number of honest droplet nodes contacted by the bucket node $K(\gamma, \delta) = \frac{k + O\left(\sqrt{k}\ln^2\left(\frac{k}{\delta}\right)\right)}{m} \leq n - 2f$ [17]. To ensure that the historical blocks of the blockchain can be successfully recovered with probability at least $1 - \delta$. Therefore, when at most $n - 2f$ honest nodes in the blockchain network are visited, the historical blocks can be successfully recovered with probability at least $1 - \delta$ using LT codes, and the recovery cost of the coding scheme reflects the security performance of the system. The recovery cost of RS codes is $K(\gamma, \delta) = \frac{k}{1} = n - 2f$. Theoretically, the recovery cost of RS codes is higher than that of LT codes.

### 5.3   Bandwidth Cost

Bandwidth cost refers to the minimum number of droplets that a bucket node needs to download to guarantee a high success rate for decoding. Specifically, the bandwidth cost is the number of droplets required to ensure the successful recovery of the blockchain minus the historical block size of the blockchain to be recovered divided by the encoded $k$ block sizes. We use the probability to calculate the visited nodes as honest and malicious. When a bucket node visits a node to download data, the probability that the visited node is a malicious node is $\frac{n-2f}{n}$, and the probability that the visited node is an honest node is $\frac{2f}{n}$. Therefore, the formula of bandwidth cost can be obtained as $\beta(\gamma, \delta) = O\left(\frac{n\ln^2\left(\frac{k}{\delta}\right)}{2f\sqrt{k}}\right)$.

- Proof: From the recovery cost, we can see that the amount of downloaded data is $k + O\left(\sqrt{k}\ln^2\left(\frac{k}{\delta}\right)\right)$
- Then the bandwidth cost is $\frac{k + O\left(\sqrt{k}\ln^2\left(\frac{k}{\delta}\right)\right) - k}{k}$

- This reduces to $\frac{O(\sqrt{k}\ln^2(\frac{k}{\delta}))}{k}$
- The amount of data downloaded by the bucket node is $\beta \times \frac{2f}{n} = \frac{O(\sqrt{k}\ln^2(\frac{k}{\delta}))}{k}$
- Then the bandwidth cost is $\beta(\gamma, \delta) = O\left(\frac{n\ln^2(\frac{k}{\delta})}{2f\sqrt{k}}\right)$

## 5.4 Computational Cost

When a new node joins the blockchain network, both the LT code and the RS code need the new node to restore the historical ledger by collecting the coded blocks of other nodes. We calculate the decoding time $T_{decode-LT}$ and $T_{decode-RS}$. The re-encoding of the LT code scheme is to re-encode new nodes, which is denoted as $T_{encode-LT}$, and the re-encoding of the RS code scheme is to re-encode all nodes, which is denoted as $T_{encode-RS}$. In the LT code and RS code schemes, the time from the new node joining the blockchain network to the end of the blockchain recoding is recorded as $T_{LT}$ and $T_{RS}$, respectively. We take them as a comparison of the computational cost of the above two schemes.

# 6 Implementation and Evaluation

Considering the storage savings, the size of the storage savings of the LT code is $\gamma = \frac{k}{s}$ which means a node encodes k original blocks into s droplets. The storage saving size of RS code is $\gamma=k$ which means a node encodes k original blocks into k droplets by default, but the node only keeps its own numbered droplet, and other droplets will be discarded, so the storage saving size is k. When we use the LT code, the bucket node needs to visit at least m $\left(m \geq \frac{k}{s}\right)$ nodes in order to recover the historical ledger with high probability. During the encoding process, the larger the encoded droplet s is, the fewer nodes m need to be visited. In order to reflect the contrast of the experiment, we set s to be the same as the RS code, both of which are 1, so that the experiment can more intuitively reflect the gap between the two codes in the PBFT consensus.

We proved the feasibility of LT code applied to the consortium blockchain through theoretical analysis and carried out simulation experiments aiming at the characteristics of PBFT consensus in the consortium chain. We downloaded the blockchain data on the consortium chain and carried out simulation coding and decoding experiments locally. By setting the number of nodes $n = \{20, 40, 80, 100, 200, 300\}$ and then repeat the experiment, taking the average of the data of 100 experiments for statistics.

First, we test the difference in encoding performance between the LT code and the RS code in selecting the original coding block $k = \{8, 14, 28, 34, 68, 102\}$, as shown in Fig. 4.

Second, we test the decoding time of LT code and RS code when there are no malicious nodes and when there are malicious nodes $f = \{6, 13, 26, 33, 66, 99\}$, as shown in Fig. 5.

Third, according to the index of bandwidth overhead, we tested the minimum number of nodes that need to be visited for LT code and RS code decoding. As shown in Fig. 6.

Finally, according to the indicator of computational cost, we tested the time required for the blockchain network from the addition of a new node to the end of the re-encoding, as shown in Fig. 7.

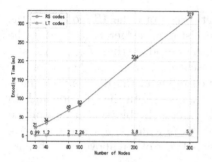

**Fig. 4.** Encoding Time.

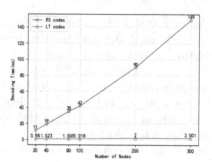

**Fig. 5.** Decoding Time.

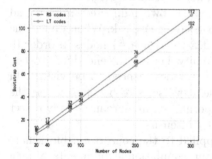

**Fig. 6.** Bootstrap Cost.

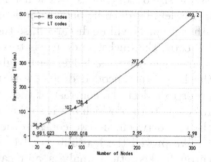

**Fig. 7.** Re-encoding Time.

Through the above four comparative experiments, it can be seen that when the number of nodes increases gradually, the coding performance of RS code becomes worse and worse in the first experiment, while that of LT code changes little. This is because the encoding of the LT code is an XOR operation, while the encoding of the RS code is a matrix operation. In the second experiment, the decoding performance of the RS code is also worse than that of the LT code because RS code decoding runs on a large enough finite field. Compared with LT code which does not need to run on a finite field, RS code decoding performance is poor. In the third experiment, there is little difference between the minimum number of nodes that need to be visited by RS code and LT code when decoding. LT code needs to visit a little more nodes than RS code, because LT code decoding is a probability decoder. In order to decode with a high probability of success, the number of nodes to be visited is slightly more than the original calculated minimum number of nodes. In the fourth experiment, comparing the time taken by the RS code and the LT code from the new node joining the blockchain network to the end of the blockchain network re-encoding, we found that the calculation cost of the LT code is lower than that of the RS code. It is because the dynamic addition of nodes will cause all nodes in the RS code scheme to be re-encoded, while in the LT code scheme only new nodes need to be re-encoded, so the calculation cost of the LT code is lower.

## 7   Conclusion

In order to solve the problem of RS code's insufficient performance in storage optimization, this paper applies LT code to PBFT consensus for the first time. We analyze the performance of LT codes applied to PBFT consensus through four indicators: storage saving, bootstrap cost, bandwidth overhead and computing cost. We also propose a safe decoding scheme for recovering historical blocks against the problem of malicious nodes destroying bucket nodes and the security of the scheme is analyzed. Also, The integrity checking mechanism provided by the fault-tolerant stripping decoder is used to identify and discard the tampered droplets during the decoding process, which improves the efficiency and success rate of decoding. In addition, we applied the control variable method to do four comparison experiments by setting the number of nodes to compare the performance of LT code and RS code in encoding, decoding, as well as their bandwidth overhead and computational cost. The experimental results show that our proposed scheme performs better in optimizing storage cost, reducing recovery delay, and improving the accuracy and security of decoding.

**Acknowledgment.** The authors would like to thank the reviewers for their helpful comments and suggestions. This work was supported by the National Key Project of China (No. 2020YFB1005700).

## References

1. B. core. (2015) bitcoin core version 0.11.0 released
2. Androulaki, E., et al.: Hyperledger fabric: a distributed operating system for permissioned blockchains. In: Proceedings of the Thirteenth EuroSys Conference, pp. 1–15 (2018)
3. Armknecht, F., Karame, G.O., Mandal, A., Youssef, F., Zenner, E.: Ripple: overview and outlook. In: Trust and Trustworthy Computing: 8th International Conference, TRUST 2015, Heraklion, Greece, August 24-26, 2015, Proceedings 8, pp. 163–180. Springer (2015)

4. Bano, S., et al.: Consensus in the age of blockchains. arXiv preprint arXiv:1711.03936 (2017)
5. Brown, R.G., Carlyle, J., Grigg, I., Hearn, M.: Corda: an introduction. R3 CEV, August 1(15), 14 (2016)
6. Burchert, C., Decker, C., Wattenhofer, R.: Scalable funding of bitcoin micropayment channel networks. Roy. Soc. open sci. 5(8), 180089 (2018)
7. Castro, M., Liskov, B., et al.: Practical byzantine fault tolerance. In: OsDI, vol. 99, pp. 173–186 (1999)
8. Dib, O., Brousmiche, K.L., Durand, A., Thea, E., Hamida, E.B.: Consortium blockchains: overview, applications and challenges. Int. J. Adv. Telecommun 11(1), 51–64 (2018)
9. Dimakis, A.G., Ramchandran, K., Wu, Y., Suh, C.: A survey on network codes for distributed storage. Proc. IEEE 99(3), 476–489 (2011)
10. Duplantier, M., Lohou, E., Sonnet, P.: Quorum sensing inhibitors to quench P. aeruginosa pathogenicity. Pharmaceuticals 14(12), 1262 (2021)
11. Etesami, O., Shokrollahi, A.: Raptor codes on binary memoryless symmetric channels. IEEE Trans. Inf. Theory 52(5), 2033–2051 (2006)
12. Huang, C., Simitci, H., Xu, Y., Ogus, A., Calder, B., Gopalan, P., Li, J., Yekhanin, S.: Erasure coding in windows azure storage. In: Presented as part of the 2012 USENIX Annual Technical Conference, pp. 15–26 (2012)
13. Huizhong, L., Chenxi, L., Haoxuan, L., Xingqiang, B., Xiang, S.: Anoverview on practice of FISCO BCOS technology and application. Inf. Commun. Technol. Policy 46(1), 52 (2020)
14. Kadhe, S., Chung, J., Ramchandran, K.: SeF: a secure fountain architecture for slashing storage costs in blockchains. arXiv preprint arXiv:1906.12140 (2019)
15. Karp, R., Luby, M., Shokrollahi, A.: Verification decoding of raptor codes. In: Proceedings. International Symposium on Information Theory, 2005. ISIT 2005, pp. 1310–1314. IEEE (2005)
16. Li, S., Yu, M., Yang, C.S., Avestimehr, A.S., Kannan, S., Viswanath, P.: PolyShard: coded sharding achieves linearly scaling efficiency and security simultaneously. IEEE Trans. Inf. Forensics Secur. 16, 249–261 (2020)
17. Luby, M.: Lt codes. In: The 43rd Annual IEEE Symposium on Foundations of Computer Science, 2002. Proceedings, pp. 271–271. IEEE Computer Society (2002)
18. Luby, M.G., Mitzenmacher, M.: Verification-based decoding for packet-based low-density parity-check codes. IEEE Trans. Inf. Theory 51(1), 120–127 (2005)
19. Luby, M.G., Mitzenmacher, M., Shokrollahi, M.A., Spielman, D.A.: Efficient erasure correcting codes. IEEE Trans. Inf. Theory 47(2), 569–584 (2001)
20. MacWilliams, F.J., Sloane, N.J.A.: The theory of error-correcting codes, vol. 16. Elsevier (1977)
21. Miller, A.: Permissioned and permissionless blockchains. Blockchain distrib. syst. secur. 193–204 (2019)
22. Nakamoto, S.: Bitcoin: a peer-to-peer electronic cash system. Decentralized business review p. 21260 (2008)
23. Perard, D., Lacan, J., Bachy, Y., Detchart, J.: Erasure code-based low storage blockchain node. In: 2018 IEEE International Conference on Internet of Things and IEEE Green Computing and Communications and IEEE Cyber, Physical and Social Computing and IEEE Smart Data, pp. 1622–1627. IEEE (2018)
24. Qi, X., Zhang, Z., Jin, C., Zhou, A.: BFT-store: storage partition for permissioned blockchain via erasure coding. In: 2020 IEEE 36th International Conference on Data Engineering (ICDE), pp. 1926–1929. IEEE (2020)

25. Raman, R.K., Varshney, L.R.: Dynamic distributed storage for scaling blockchains. arXiv preprint arXiv:1711.07617 (2017)
26. Reed, I.S., Solomon, G.: Polynomial codes over certain finite fields. J. Soc. Ind. Appl. Math. **8**(2), 300–304 (1960)
27. Wood, G.: Ethereum: a secure decentralised generalised transaction ledger. Ethereum proj. yellow pap. **151**(2014), 1–32 (2014)

# An Incentive Mechanism and An Offline Trajectory Publishing Algorithm Considering Sensing Area Coverage Maximization and Participant Privacy Level

Qing Cao[1], Yunfei Tan[2(✉)], and Guozheng Zhang[2]

[1] Nokia Shanghai Bell Co., Ltd., Shanghai, China
[2] School of Computer Science, Shaanxi Normal University, Xi'an, China
tyf@snnu.edu.cn

**Abstract.** In response to the incentive mechanism design issue and privacy leakage risk of trajectory data release in mobile crowdsensing scenario, an incentive mechanism named MSASM for participant selection is firstly presented in the paper, which considers the constraints of maximizing sensing area based on similarity measurement and utilizes a greedy and knapsack mixed algorithm to select the optimal participant set. Then an offline differentially private trajectory publishing algorithm named DPOTCPA is designed, which compresses the trajectory of participants and adds Laplace noise into the compressed trajectories for publishing. Experimental results on a real dataset demonstrate the effectiveness of the MSASM mechanism and the DPOTCPA algorithm.

**Keywords:** mobile crowdsensing · incentive mechanism · trajectory publication · privacy protection · differential privacy

## 1 Introduction

With the wide application of wireless networks, sensors, and smart devices, Mobile Crowdsensing (MCS), as a new sensing paradigm, has experienced rapid development [1, 2]. Currently, there has no unified definition of Mobile Crowdsensing. A typical definition of MCS is a new sensing paradigm that empowers ordinary citizens to contribute data sensed or generated from their mobile devices, aggregates and fuses the data in the cloud for crowd intelligence extraction and people-centric service delivery [3]. With the proliferation of mobile devices carried by humans, the mobile crowd sensing system was launched, which outsources the aggregated sensory data to public crowds equipped with a variety of mobile devices. One of the fundamental problems of MCS is to effectively motivate people to participate [4].

As a complement to traditional paradigms, MCS leverages the mobility of participants, sensing capabilities embedded in smart devices, and existing wireless infrastructure to sense and aggregate diverse data. It can provide richer and more abundant

J. Cai et al. (Eds.): SPNCE 2023, LNICST 525, pp. 54–66, 2025.
https://doi.org/10.1007/978-3-031-73699-5_4

data information for applications in mobile social networks, environmental monitoring, traffic monitoring, public safety, smart cities, healthcare, and other domains [5]. MCS has attracted widespread attention from researchers due to its advantages, such as comprehensive network coverage, low deployment cost, diverse types of sensing data, high dynamism, and good scalability.

However, MCS applications is currently severely constrained by issues such as insufficient number of participants for sensing tasks [6] and low availability of sensing data [7]. The main reasons for these problems can be attributed to two aspects: Firstly, how to design a fair and equitable participant incentive mechanism. Most participants are not willing to provide sensing data without compensation and expect tangible rewards such as monetary payment or in-game currency in return for the sensing data they provide. Secondly, participants face risks of privacy disclosure during their involvement in sensing tasks. In MCS environments, participants may face privacy risks related to identity, location, etc.

These concerns pose significant challenges to the advancement of MCS applications. In response to above issues, an incentive mechanism satisfying the constraints of maximizing sensing area and a differentially private preserving participant trajectory publishing algorithm is proposed in the paper. The main contributions of this paper are summarized as follows:

1. A participant selection incentive mechanism satisfying the constraints of Maximizing Sensing Area based on Similarity Measurement (MSASM) is designed in the paper. The proposed mechanism selects a rough candidate participant set based on Pearson similarity and utilizes a greedy and knapsack mixed algorithm to select the optimal participant set while maximizing the sensing area.
2. A Differentially Private Offline Trajectory Compression and Publishing Algorithm (DPOTCPA) is given in the paper, which is suitable for MCS platform to execute. For offline scenario, the proposed algorithm firstly adopts the Douglas-Peucker algorithm to compress the trajectory of participants, and then adds Laplace noise into the compressed trajectories before publishing. The proposed algorithm achieves privacy protection for participants and reduce the storage required for trajectory data.
3. Experiments are conducted on a real dataset, and the results show the effectiveness of the MSASM mechanism and the DPOTCPA algorithm.

The rest of this paper is organized as follows. Section 2 presents the preliminaries and related works. Section 3 introduces the system model. Section 4 describes the proposed MSASM Incentive Mechanism in detail. And DPOTCPA algorithm is described in Sect. 5. Section 6 shows the experimental results and analysis of comparative experiments. Section 7 concludes this paper.

## 2 Preliminaries and Related Work

### 2.1 Differential Privacy

Differential privacy is based on the principle of data distortion. It aims to achieve privacy protection by adding random perturbation noise to the original data without altering the overall trend of the data. Sensitivity is a key parameter that determines whether the added noise is appropriate.

**Definition 1.  (ε-Differential Privacy [8]):** For a given randomized function $M$ and neighboring data sets $D$ and $D'$, with $P_M$ representing the range of values for $M$, and $S_M$ is any subset of $P_M$, representing any output result of $M$ on the neighboring data sets $D$ and $D'$, if formula (1) holds true, the random algorithm $M$ satisfies ε-differential privacy.

$$\frac{\Pr\left[M(D) \in S_M\right]}{\Pr\left[M(D') \in S_M\right]} \leq \exp(\varepsilon) \tag{1}$$

In formula (1), $\Pr[M(D) \in S_M]$ represents the probability that the output of dataset $D$ under algorithm $M$ is $S_M$, which signifies the risk of privacy disclosure. The parameter $\varepsilon$ represents the privacy budget [9], which measures the strength of privacy protection.

In differential privacy, the Laplace mechanism is suitable for numerical results. It achieves differential privacy by adding random perturbation noise following the *Laplace* distribution to the query result. Assuming a *Laplace* distribution with location parameter $\mu = 0$ and scale parameter b is denoted as Lap(b), its probability density function is given below:

$$Lap(x, b) = \frac{1}{2b} * e^{\left(-\frac{|x|}{b}\right)} \tag{2}$$

**Definition 2. (Laplace Mechanism):**  Given a dataset $D$, let $F : D \rightarrow R^d$ be a function with sensitivity $\Delta f$. Then the randomized algorithm $M(D) = f(D) + Y$ provides ε-differential privacy, where $Y \sim Lap(\Delta f / \varepsilon)$ is the random noise following the *Laplace* distribution with scale parameter $\frac{\Delta f}{\varepsilon}$.

**Definition 3. (Sequential Composition):**  Let there be algorithms $M_1, M_2, ..., M_n$ with privacy budgets $\varepsilon_1, \varepsilon_2, ..., \varepsilon_n$, respectively. For the same dataset $D$, the composed algorithm $M(M_1(D), M_2(D), ..., M_n(D))$, formed by these algorithms, provides $(\sum_{i=1}^{n} \varepsilon_i)$ − differential privacy protection.

## 2.2  Pearson Correlation Coefficient

The Pearson correlation coefficient is a measure used to describe the linear relationship between two samples. Given two samples X and Y, the Pearson correlation coefficient is defined as follows:

$$r(X, Y) = \frac{Cov(X, Y)}{\sqrt{Var|X|Var|Y|}} = \frac{\sum_{i=1}^{n} (x_i - \overline{x_i})(y_i - \overline{y_i})}{\sqrt{\sum_{i=1}^{n} (x_i - \overline{x_i})^2} \sqrt{\sum_{i=1}^{n} (y_i - \overline{y_i})^2}} \tag{3}$$

Where $n$ represents the feature dimension, $r(X, Y) \in [-1, 1]$ represents the degree of correlation. When $r$ takes the values −1 or 1, it indicates that $X$ and $Y$ are perfectly correlated. When $r$ takes the value 0, it indicates that $X$ and $Y$ are completely unrelated.

## 2.3 Perpendicular Euclidean Distance

Perpendicular Euclidean Distance (PED) refers to the shortest distance from a trajectory point $P_m$ to a simplified trajectory segment $\overrightarrow{P_sP_e}$. The formula is defined as follows:

$$PED(p_m) = \frac{|(y_e - y_s)x_m - (x_e - x_s)y_m + x_ey_s - y_ex_s|}{\sqrt{(y_e - y_s)^2 + (x_e - x_s)^2}} \tag{4}$$

Where $(x_s, y_s)$ represents the coordinates of the starting point $P_s$, $(x_e, y_e)$ represents the coordinates of the ending point $P_e$, and $(x_m, y_m)$ represents the coordinates of $P_m$.

## 2.4 Related Work

There exists a lot of works for privacy preserving MCS using traditional methods such as k-anonymity and cryptography. Wu et al. [10] proposed a holistic solution for trustworthy and privacy-aware mobile crowdsensing with no need of a trusted third party. Specifically, leveraging cryptographic technologies, they devised a series of protocols to enable benign users to request tasks, contribute their data, and earn rewards anonymously without any data link ability. Meanwhile, an anonymous trust/reputation model was seamlessly integrated into their scheme, which acted as reference for fair incentive design, and provided evidence to detect malicious users who degrade the data trustworthiness. Tao et al. [11] proposed an incentive mechanism for privacy-preserving mobile crowdsensing. More specifically, they introduced a trusted third party and combined partially blind signature, which could effectively reduce the correlation between participants and data and the number of interactions between users and task platform, to achieve high level participant privacy.

In recent years, differential privacy has gradually been applied to the field of MCS due to its rigorous and quantitative representation and proof of privacy leakage risks. Huang et al. [12] proposed a mechanism named TPA, to protect the trajectory as a whole part. The mechanism firstly computed the total amount of noise to satisfy differential privacy. Then it randomly allocated the noise to each coordinate of the trajectory. To improve the utility of the perturbed trajectory, the proposed mechanism also considered the correlations between each pair of perturbed and true trajectories. Different from the existing permission on-off control mechanism, Xu et al. [13] presented a configurable multi-strategy trajectory privacy-preserving framework, named MSPP in the participant's terminal. Based on the individual historical trajectory data stored locally and privacy preferences, participant could actively select the corresponding protection mechanism (Pathswap, Promesse, Geo-I, etc.) considering privacy metrics and data utility. Chen et al. [14] proposed a differentially private trajectory protection scheme with real-location reporting in MCS. Firstly, they presented the definition of trajectory privacy protection based on real path reporting under differential privacy. Secondly, they gave a trajectory privacy protection framework under Bayesian inference attacks. Chen et al. [15] applied differential privacy for trajectory privacy protection, by constructing a noisy prefix tree for counting query and adopting Laplace mechanism to achieve differential privacy. However, as the noisy prefix tree grows, the number of sequences entering a branch decreases rapidly, resulting in poor practicability.

## 3   System Model

The MCS system in this paper consists of a MCS platform, participants, and several service providers, as shown in Fig. 1. Service providers publish their requirements and purchase the necessary sensing datasets from the MCS platform. The MCS platform issues various types of sensing tasks to the participants, who autonomously select and bid for the tasks they wish to participate in. Using a monetary incentive mechanism, the MCS platform selects suitable task participants and aggregates the sensing data uploaded by the participants, providing the corresponding service providers with the processed data.

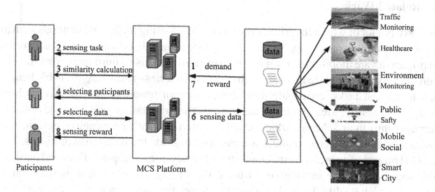

**Fig. 1.**  System Model

In this paper, the MCS platform is assumed to be untrusted and curious about the sensing data uploaded by participants. The MCS system faces two main challenges in the process of implementing sensing tasks: (1) how to personalize the selection of participants while satisfying the constraint of maximizing sensing region coverage; (2) how to ensure privacy protection for the participants. Considering the diverse requirements of different types of service providers, the MCS platform issues various types of sensing tasks to the participants.

This paper adopts a vector $Tv$ containing five attributes $\{T_{ty}, D_c, T_{ti}, N_r, P_r\}$ to describe the published perceptual task. Here, $Tty$ represents the task type, $D_c$ represents data accuracy, $T_{ti}$ represents task time, $N_r$ represents the number of participants required, and $P_r$ represents perceptual reward. Simultaneously, a vector $Pv$ containing five attributes $\{T_P, P_l, P_t, P_c, E_r\}$ is used to describe participants' task participation preferences. Here, $T_P$ represents task preference, $P_l$ represents privacy level, $P_t$ represents sensing time, $P_c$ represents personal reputation, and $E_r$ represents expected reward.

Then, candidate participants are selected based on the similarity measurement between the task vector $T_v$ and the participant vector $P_v$. Finally, a combination of greedy and knapsack algorithms is employed to select the optimal set of participants from the candidate participant pool, achieving personalized and precise participant selection while maximizing the sensing area.

## 4 MSASM Incentive Mechanism

Based on the system model described above, we propose an incentive mechanism satisfying the constraints of Maximizing Sensing Area based on Similarity Measurement (MSASM). Firstly, constructing the task vector $Tv$ of each task and preference vector $Pv$ of each participant. Secondly, utilizing the Pearson similarity coefficient to calculate the similarity between $T_v$ and $P_v$, and then selecting a candidate set of participants based on the similarity values. Finally, according to the following objective function (formula (5)), using a greedy and knapsack mixed algorithm under the constraints of maximizing sensing area and privacy levels of participants, to find the optimal participants from the candidate set.

$$f[k][v] = max\{f[k-1][v], f[k-1][v-1]+w[i]\} \qquad (5)$$

Where f[k][v] represents the maximum sensing area covered by all participants in first $k$ group with a total of $v$ participants. $k$ represents the number of connected graphs in the sensing area based on the duplicate coverage of participants (which is further explained in the following paragraph), and $w[i]$ represents the sensing area covered by participant $i$.

In the MSASM mechanism, the greedy and knapsack fusion algorithm selects the optimal participant set from the candidate set when the objective function achieves its maximum value. Specifically, the MSASM mechanism transforms the problem of selecting $N_P$ participants with the maximum sensing area from the candidate set into a problem of selecting $N_P$ circles with the smallest intersection.

Firstly, for each candidate participant, drawing a circle with his/her position as center and radius $r = 1$. If sensing area of participant $i$ overlaps with that of participant $j$, adding an edge between them, where the edge weight is the area of the intersection between participant $i$ and $j$. This process constructs a graph $G$, and a breadth-first search algorithm is used to partition $G$ into a set of connected graphs, denoted as $\{ g_1, \cdots, g_k \}$. Then, isolated participants are selected from the set of connected graphs. Suppose that the number of isolated participants is *Count*. If *Count* $>= N_P$, we can return the indices and positions of the first $N_P$ participants in the set of isolated participants. Otherwise, we initialize the knapsack volume as $v = N_P - Count$ and use the greedy and knapsack mixed algorithm to continually select candidates with high similarity according to the objective function. Finally, the top $N_P$ optimal participants with maximized sensing areas are found.

The pseudo code of the MSASM mechanism is shown in algorithm 1.

---

**Algorithm 1.** MSASM mechanism

---

**Input:** task dataset $Task = \{task_1, task_2, ..., task_n\}$

    participant dataset $P = \{P_1, P_2, ..., P_m\}$

    participant position $Loc = \{loc_1, loc_2, ..., loc_m\}$

    the number of participants selected $N_P$

**Output:** optimal participant set $OP$

1:   **for** $i$=1 to $n$

2:    construct vector $Tv_i$ for each task $task_i$;

3:    **for** $j$=1 to $m$

4:     construct vector $Pv_j$ for each participant $P_j$;

5:     calculate the similarity between $Tv_i$ and $Pv_j$ according to formula (3);

6:    **end for**

7:    obtain candidate set $TC_i$ of participants for each task $task_i$;

8:   **end for**

9:   obtain the candidate set $TC = TC_1 \cup TC_2 \cup ... \cup TC_n$;

10: **for** $i$=1 to $n$

11:    construct graph $G$ by drawing circles with a radius of 1 and using the position of each participant in $TC$ as the center;

12:    add edges if there is an intersection between the circles, and the edge weight is area of the intersection between the circles;

13: **end for**

14: use the breadth-first search algorithm to partition graph $G$ into $\{g_1, g_2, ..., g_k\}$ and get the number of isolated participants $Count$;

15: **if** $Count >= N_P$

16:    add the first $N_P$ participants into $OP$;

17: **else**

18:    for each graph $g_k$

19:     **for** $v = N_P - Count$ to 0

20:      **for** each participant $i$ belonging to $g_k$

21:       calculate the objective function according to formula (5);

22:      **end for**

23:     **end for**

24:    **end for**

25: **end if**

26: **return** $OP$.

---

## 5  DPOTCPA Algorithm

After selecting an appropriate participant set using the MSASM incentive mechanism, considering the large scale of participant trajectory datasets and the privacy risks of publishing participant trajectory data, we address the demand for privacy-preserving participant trajectory publication. And for offline scenario, we propose a Differentially Private Offline Trajectory Compression and Publishing Algorithm (DPOTCPA) suitable for MCS platform to execute.

For the participant set, the DPOTCPA algorithm firstly uses the Douglas-Peucker algorithm [16] to perform offline compression on each participant's trajectory curve based on a given threshold, effectively reducing the storage space of participant trajectory data. Then, under the constraint of a given total privacy budget and according to different privacy levels of participants, the DPOTCPA algorithm allocates different privacy budgets for participants using formula (6) (all the participants with the same level are allocated the same privacy budget). In the proposed algorithm, the privacy protection of participants are classified into three levels: $level_1$(low privacy protection), $level_2$(medium privacy protection), and $level_3$(high privacy protection). And Laplace noise is added to the compressed trajectory data using formula (7). Finally, the algorithm publishes the noisy participant trajectory dataset.

$$\varepsilon_i = \frac{level_i}{level_1 + level_2 + level_3} \tag{6}$$

Where $\varepsilon_i$ represents the privacy budget allocated for trajectory $tr_i$ of participant $P_i$, and $level_i$ represents the privacy protection level of participant $P_i$.

$$f(tr_i^{''}) = f(tr_i\prime) + Lap(\Delta f / \varepsilon_i) \tag{7}$$

Where $f(tr_i\prime)$ represents the compressed trajectory of $P_i$, $f(tr_i^{''})$ represents the compressed and perturbed trajectory of $P_i$, $Lap(\Delta f / \varepsilon_i)$ represents the added Laplace noise and $\Delta f$ is the global sensitivity.

The pseudo code of the DPOTCPA algorithm is given in algorithm 2.

---

**Algorithm 2.** DPOTCPA algorithm

---

**Input:** original participant trajectory set $Tr=\{tr_1,tr_2,...,tr_n\}$

participant privacy level $Level = \{level_1, level_2, level_3\}$

privacy budget $\varepsilon$, threshold $D_{max}$

**Output:** compressed and perturbed participants trajectory set $Tr^*=\{tr_1^*,tr_2^*,...,tr_n^*\}$

---

1:  **for** $i$=1 to $n$
2:      **for** each trajectory $tr_i$
3:          traverse all trajectory points, calculate the  distance of each point to the straight-line AB formed by the starting point A and the ending point B. Find the point C with the maximum distance to AB, and record this maximum distance as $MP_m$
4:          **if** $MP_m < D_{max}$
5:              use line AB as an approximation for $tr_i$;
6:          **else if** $MP_m \geq D_{max}$
7:              split point C is used to split AB into two segments, AC and CB;
8:              for AC and CB, execute step 3 and 4, respectively;
9:          **end if**
10:         if all the segments have been processed
11:             connect all the split point to form the approximation for $tr_i$;
12:         **end if**
13:     **end for**
14:     allocate privacy budget according to formula (6);
15:     add Laplace noise according to formula (7);
16: **end for**
17: publish the result trajectory dataset $Tr^*$.

---

## 6  Privacy Analysis

In this section, we conduct simulation experiments to analyze and evaluate the MSASM mechanism and DPOTCPA algorithm. The goal is to validate the feasibility and effectiveness of the proposed incentive mechanism and participant trajectory publishing algorithms.

### 6.1  Experiment Environment

The hardware environment used in this study includes an Intel(R) Core(TM) i7-5500U CPU @ 2.4 GHz, 16 GB of RAM, and 1 TB of hard disk space. The software environment consists of a 64-bit Windows 10 operating system.

Regarding the proposed MSASM mechanism, the experimental dataset is generated using a pseudo-random number generator to create a set of task datasets and six sets of participant datasets with different numbers of participants. Attributes of each task dataset and participant dataset are described in Sect. 3.

Regarding the proposed DPOTCPA algorithm, the experimental dataset is taken from the real dataset GeoLife GPS Trajectories, a Microsoft research project known as Geo-Life. This trajectory dataset contains 17,621 trajectories recorded from 182 participants between April 2007 and August 2012.

## 6.2 Experiment Result Analysis

In the first set of experiments, we compare the similarity calculation time overhead of the MSASM incentive mechanism, TRIM incentive mechanism [17], the incentive mechanism using the direct cosine similarity computing protocol (DCSC), and the incentive mechanism using the Paillier encryption-based (PE-based) protocol under different numbers of participants. The results are illustrated in Fig. 2.

The MSASM mechanism, TRIM mechanism, and the incentive mechanism using the DCSC protocol exhibit relatively small similarity calculation time overhead, as shown in detail in Fig. 2(a). Compared to the TRIM mechanism and the incentive mechanism using the PE-based protocol, the MSASM mechanism demonstrates a clear time advantage. When the number of participants is small, the incentive mechanism using the DCSC protocol has slightly lower time overhead. However, when the number of participants is large, the MSASM mechanism exhibits slightly lower time overhead. Overall, the time overhead of both the MSASM mechanism and the incentive mechanism using the DCSC protocol is comparable.

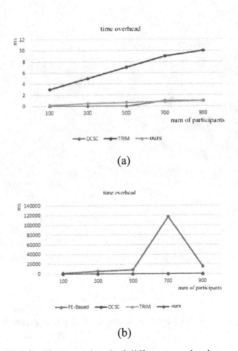

(a)

(b)

**Fig. 2.** Time overhead of different mechanisms

In the second set of experiments, with the number of participants set to 2000, we select the top 100 optimal participants and the top 500 optimal participants based on the highest similarity score, while also satisfying the constraints of maximizing the sensing area and privacy protection level. The experimental results are shown in Fig. 3(a) and (b). In Fig. 3, green circles represent participants, and red circles represent the selected optimal participants.

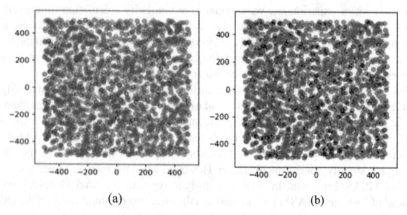

(a)                          (b)

**Fig. 3.** Optimal participant selection that satisfies the constraints of maximum sensing area and privacy protection level

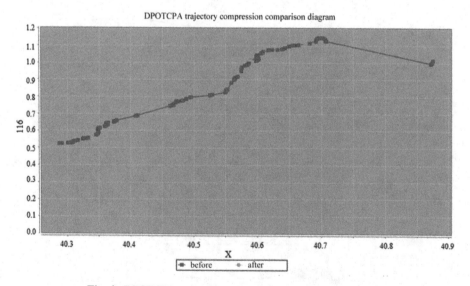

**Fig. 4.** DPOTCPA trajectory compression comparison diagram

The third set of experiments validates the trajectory compression of the DPOTCPA algorithm. We selected a participant from the GeoLife GPS Trajectories dataset, which contains 3091 nodes in the trajectory curve. The DPOTCPA algorithm was applied to compress the trajectory curve. The comparison between the participant's trajectory before and after compression is shown in Fig. 4. The compression rate of the DPOTCPA algorithm is 0.05985118084762213, indicating that many nodes were discarded during the compression process, leading to a noticeable reduction in the curve in Fig. 4.

The fourth set of experiments validates the utility of privacy-protected trajectory data published by the DPOTCPA algorithm. We randomly selected 128 participants with 8173 trajectories and 181 participants with 12350 trajectories from the GeoLife GPS Trajectories dataset. Under total privacy budgets of 0.2, 0.4, 0.6, 0.8, and 1, the DPOTCPA algorithm was used to add noise perturbation to different participant trajectories. The RMSE (Root Mean Square Errors) between the perturbed dataset and the original dataset are shown in Fig. 5. It can be observed that the RMSE gradually decreases as the privacy budget increases.

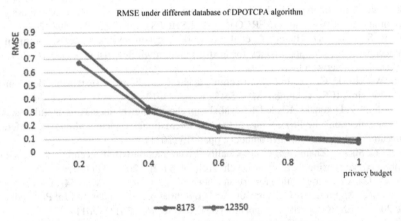

**Fig. 5.** RMSE under different datasets of DPOTCPA algorithm

## 7  Conclusion

To address the problem of incentive mechanism design and privacy leakage risks of participant trajectory data publishing in mobile crowdsensing scenario, a participant selection incentive mechanism named MSASM is firstly presented, which considers the constraints of maximizing sensing area based on similarity measurement and utilizes a greedy and knapsack mixed algorithm to select the optimal participant set. Then an offline trajectory publishing algorithm named DPOTCPA is given in the paper, which compress the trajectory of participants in advance and adds Laplace noise into the compressed trajectories for publishing.

In future work, we plan to make improvements in the following aspects: Firstly, the MSASM incentive mechanism exists the risk of participant privacy leakage during the candidate participant selection process. To mitigate this risk, we intend to utilize certain lightweight data encryption algorithm to encrypt sensitive participant attributes. Secondly, although the MSASM incentive mechanism considers participant's reputation, it does not account for dynamic updates of reputation. We aim to construct a dynamic reputation function based on factors such as the number of completed tasks and task quality assessments to update participant's reputation values in a more practical environment.

# References

1. Restuccia, F., Ghosh, N., Bhattacharjee, S., et al.: Quality of information in mobile crowd-sensing: survey and research challenges. ACM Trans. Sens. Netw. (TOSN) **13**(4), 1–43 (2017)
2. Guo, B., Wang, Z., Yu, Z., et al.: Mobile crowd sensing and computing: the review of an emerging human-powered sensing paradigm. ACM Comput. Surv. (CSUR) **48**(1), 1–31 (2015)
3. Guo, B., Yu, Z., Zhou, X., et al.: From participatory sensing to mobile crowd sensing. In: Proceedings of the 2014 IEEE International Conference on Pervasive Computing and Communication Workshops (PERCOM WORKSHOPS). IEEE, pp. 593–598 (2014)
4. Zhong, S., Zhong, H., Huang, X., et al.: Networking cyber-physical systems: algorithm fundamentals of security and privacy for next-generation wireless networks. Secur. Priv. Next Gener. Wirel. Netw., 33–48 (2019)
5. Sun, W., Liu, J.: Congestion-aware communication paradigm for sustainable dense mobile crowdsensing. IEEE Commun. Mag. **55**(3), 62–67 (2017)
6. Deterding, S., Dixon, D., Khaled, R., et al.: From game design elements to gamefulness: defining "gamification". In: Proceedings of the 15th international academic MindTrek conference: Envisioning future media environments, pp. 9–15 (2011)
7. Wen, Y., Shi, J., Zhang, Q., et al.: Quality-driven auction-based incentive mechanism for mobile crowd sensing. IEEE Trans. Veh. Technol. **64**(9), 4203–4214 (2014)
8. Dwork, C.: A firm foundation for private data analysis. Commun. ACM **54**(1), 86–95 (2011)
9. Haeberlen, A., Pierce, B.C., Narayan, A.: Differential privacy under fire. In: Proceedings of the 20th USENIX Security Symposium (USENIX Security 2011) (2011)
10. Wu, H., Wang, L., Xue, G., et al.: Enabling data trustworthiness and user privacy in mobile crowdsensing. IEEE/ACM Trans. Networking **27**(6), 2294–2307 (2019)
11. Tao, D., Wu, T.Y., Zhu, S., et al.: Privacy protection-based incentive mechanism for mobile crowdsensing. Comput. Commun. **156**, 201–210 (2020)
12. Huang, H., Niu, X., Chen, C., et al.: A differential private mechanism to protect trajectory privacy in mobile crowd-sensing. In: Proceedings of the 2019 IEEE Wireless Communications and Networking Conference (WCNC), pp. 1–6. IEEE (2019)
13. Xu, Z., Yang, W., Wang, J.: MSPP: a trajectory privacy-preserving framework for participatory sensing based on multi-strategy. In: Proceedings of the 2019 IEEE Globecom Workshops (GC Wkshps), pp. 1–6. IEEE (2019)
14. Chen, X., Wu, X., Wang, X., et al.: Real-location reporting based differential privacy trajectory protection for mobile crowdsensing. In: Proceedings of the 2019 5th International Conference on Big Data Computing and Communications (BIGCOM), pp. 142–150. IEEE (2019)
15. Chen, R., Fung, B., Desai, B.C.: Differentially private trajectory data publication. arXiv preprint arXiv:1112.2020 (2011)
16. Douglas, D.H., Peucker, T.K.: Algorithms for the reduction of the number of points required to represent a digitized line or its caricature. Cartographica Int. J. Geog. Inf. Geovisualization **10**(2), 112–122 (1973)
17. Xiong, J., Chen, X., Yang, Q., et al.: A task-oriented user selection incentive mechanism in edge-aided mobile crowdsensing. IEEE Trans. Netw. Sci. Eng. **7**(4), 2347–2360 (2019)

# Research on Face Recognition System Based on RLWE Homomorphic Encryption

YuLin Wang⒤, HaiLin Huang⒤, ZiHao Fang⒤, YuQi Zhao⒤,
and JinHeng Wang(✉)⒤

Guangzhou Institute of Science and Technology, Guangzhou 510540, Guangdong, China
11403404@qq.com

**Abstract.** With the development of artificial intelligence face recognition technology is being widely used in various fields. However, the traditional face recognition system has serious security risks, face data is easy to leak, and privacy protection mechanism is insufficient. In order to solve this problem, a secure face recognition system based on RLWE homomorphic encryption algorithm in lattice cryptography is constructed. This method can directly process the face image in the encrypted domain, and realize the recognition function while protecting the security of biometric data. Experiments on CASIA-WebFace data set show that RLWE encryption algorithm is successfully embedded in the face recognition model based on ResNet-34, and the overall recognition accuracy of homomorphic encryption system reaches 97.4%, which is only 2% lower than that of plain text domain recognition. This proves the validity and application prospect of homomorphic encryption technology based on lattice cryptography in protecting the security of biometric information. However, the operation efficiency still needs to be improved. This study provides a valuable exploration path for homomorphic encryption technology to be applied to security biometric identification.

**Keywords:** Face recognition · RLWE encryption · Homomorphic Encryption · Biometric Identification · Security · Secret Protection

## 1 Introduction

With the rapid development of the Internet, cyber crimes emerge one after another, which seriously endangers the security and stability of cyberspace. Malicious attacks on network data have become a global security threat (Chen et al., 2019). For example, in 2013, Yahoo suffered the most serious user data leakage in history, and more than 3 billion user account information was illegally obtained (Perlroth, 2016). In the face of increasingly rampant cyber crime, traditional network security defense means such as firewall and intrusion detection have been difficult to effectively deal with. Therefore, it is urgent to strengthen the security and anti-attack ability of network communication data itself.

Network data encryption based on cryptography is the key technology to protect data security (Stallings, 2017). Classical encryption algorithms such as AES and RSA

© ICST Institute for Computer Sciences, Social Informatics and Telecommunications Engineering 2025
Published by Springer Nature Switzerland AG 2025. All Rights Reserved
J. Cai et al. (Eds.): SPNCE 2023, LNICST 525, pp. 67–84, 2025.
https://doi.org/10.1007/978-3-031-73699-5_5

have been widely used, but with the emergence of quantum computing technology, these algorithms are expected to be cracked in the near future (Shor, 1994). In order to deal with the threat of quantum computing in the future, the construction of anti-quantum computing encryption algorithm has become a research hotspot in the field of encryption. Among them, lattice-based cryptography is considered as one of the most promising candidates because of its unique anti-quantum computing advantages (Regev, 2009). For example, the learning with errors (LWE) problem has practical characteristics such as reducing the key size and the overhead of encryption and decryption, and it is a trellis cipher scheme with great potential (Brakerski et al., 2014). In recent years, ring-LWE (RLWE), a variant of LWE algorithm, has attracted wide attention because of its superior performance in efficiency and security (Lyubashevsky et al., 2013).

Although RLWE algorithm has many theoretical advantages, its research on network data encryption application is still relatively few, which needs to be verified and supported by a lot of empirical work. The existing literature mainly focuses on text information (Ding et al., 2019) and image data encryption (Wang et al., 2020) under RLWE, but the research on face recognition based on homomorphic encryption of RLWE is still weak. Therefore, this study plans to design and implement a face recognition system based on RLWE homomorphic encryption, and evaluate the security, real-time performance and resource utilization of the scheme through empirical analysis. The research results can provide a new technical approach for homomorphic encryption based on RLWE, and provide support and reference for the practical application of RLWE lattice cipher in network data security protection. This study has important theoretical value and application prospect.

## 2   Methodology

### 2.1   Face Image Database

In this study, CASIA-WebFace database is used as the face image data set. CASIA-WebFace database is a large-scale face recognition data set built by Institute of Automation, Chinese Academy of Sciences in 2014, which contains 10,575 face images of different individuals. Images originated from the Internet, corresponding to 5901 real individuals and 4674 virtual characters, covering various changes in posture, expression, illumination, occlusion, image quality and so on.

CASIA-WebFace database contains 494,414 face images, all of which are manually screened to ensure that each image has a high quality. The image format is PNG, and the resolution is $250 \times 250$ pixels. This database is widely used in the algorithm research in the field of face recognition, and it is one of the large-scale Chinese face databases currently open.

In this study, researchers use all 494414 images of CASIA-WebFace as training sets to train face recognition models. In order to construct the verification set, 100 individuals were randomly selected from 10575 individuals, each with 100 images, and a total of 10000 images were selected as the verification set. The verification set is used to evaluate the performance of the face recognition model on the independent test set, and the use of the open CASIA-WebFace data set can make this study have good reproducibility.

The construction of face image database is very important for the reliability of experimental results and the scientific nature of the paper. CASIA-WebFace data set, with its large scale, diversity and authenticity, provides strong support for the training and verification of face recognition model in this study.

## 2.2   Face Detection and Recognition Model

**Face Detection Model.** Face detection is the first module of face recognition system, which aims to locate all face regions in the image quickly and accurately, and provide input for subsequent recognition. We use MT CNN (multi-task cascaded neural network) model for face detection and alignment preprocessing. MTCNN is a cascaded CNN framework for the second phase of training, which consists of three networks in succession, namely, Proposals Network, Refine Network and Output Network.

Proposals Network is responsible for quickly generating candidate frames of faces, and a shallow CNN network is adopted to ensure the speed of detection. Subsequently, Refine Network pruned these candidate frames, effectively filtered out a large number of negative samples, and fine-tuned the positions of the frames. Finally, the Output Network accurately predicted the face position and key points of the five senses for each candidate frame, thus achieving accurate face alignment. The test on CASIA-WebFace data set shows that when these three networks are used together, the effect of face detection is excellent, and the detection accuracy can reach over 99%, which fully meets the requirements of the experiment.

**Face Recognition Model.**   The core of face recognition task is to extract the discriminant representation that describes individual characteristics. As shown in Fig. 1, ResNet-34 model based on residual learning is selected for face feature extraction and recognition. ResNet's main innovation is to introduce residual module, realize gradient direct propagation through residual connection, and successfully train an extremely deep network with more than 100 layers. Experiments show that the increase of network depth can continuously enhance the ability of feature expression.

Specifically, ResNet-34 includes a front-end $7 \times 7$ convolution layer, followed by four residual modules, each of which contains three residual blocks. Shortcut connection realizes feature reuse and avoids gradient disappearance. Researchers pre-trained the ResNet-34 model on CASIA-WebFace face data set, and then tested it on LFW face verification set, and finally achieved 99.4% verification accuracy, which showed a strong ability to discriminate facial features. ResNet structure successfully avoids the difficulty of training when the network deepens, and it is one of the most effective face recognition models at present.

To sum up, This study use mature MTCNN and ResNet-34 models to build a complete face detection and recognition system. These two types of models have a large number of successful application precedents, and the typical and efficient model is adopted in this study, which can make the constructed recognition system have strong repeatability and provide a solid foundation for the subsequent algorithm innovation research.

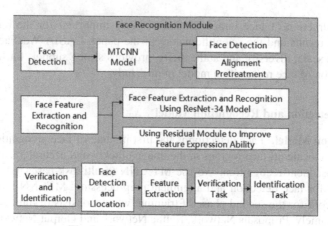

**Fig. 1.** Flow chart of RESNET-34 model.

## 2.3 Implementation of RLWE Encryption Algorithm

**Mathematical Basis of RLWE Encryption Algorithm.** RLWE encryption security is based on the classic learning and error problem LWE. LWE assumes that it is extremely difficult to solve the following linear equations:

$$b_i = a_i^T s + e_i (mod q) \tag{1}$$

Where s is the private key, a_i and b_i are public random number pairs, and e_i is the error term. Ring-LWE extends LWE to polynomial rings, so that arithmetic operations can be replaced by more efficient polynomial multiplication.

In RLWE, both the key and the data vector are mapped to polynomial of degree $n.:s,a,b,e \in R\_q = Z\_q[X]/(X^n + 1) \circ$ The encryption operation is:

$$b = as + e \,(mod\ q) \tag{2}$$

Security depends on the difficulty of solving RLWE problem over finite field Z _ q. When the parameters of vector dimension n and modulus q are set properly, RLWE problem can achieve good security.

**Realize Parameter Design.** According to RLWE theory, the parameters for realization are determined as follows:

(1) The key length n = 256, and the polynomial dictionary contains 256 items.
(2) The modulus Q of the main safety parameter is 2048, which is a suitable medium-sized prime number.
(3) The elements of the error term E obey the Gaussian distribution $\mathcal{n}(0, \sigma 2)$,and the standard deviation σ is set to 3.2.
(4) The base ring of polynomial operation is R = Z[X]/(X^n + 1), that is, the 256th cyclic polynomial ring of coefficient module 2048.
(5) The key generation algorithm adopts trapdoor sampling to obtain the short vector S.

The above parameter settings comprehensively consider the security strength and operational efficiency, ensuring the security of the implementation. Using modulo 2048 arithmetic to provide 100 + bit security strength; 256-dimensional polynomial space to prevent attacks; Gaussian distribution error increases the randomness and uncertainty of encrypted text, which makes it more difficult for attackers to analyze ciphertext and enhances the security of the system.

**Realize Optimization.** In this study, the number theory transformation NTT is used to optimize the process of key generation, encryption and decryption, and reduce the computational complexity. NTT can transform polynomial multiplication into coefficent-wise multiplication. The main calculation process is as follows:

(1) Carry out NTT forward transformation on private key S and public key elements to obtain the representation of polynomial in frequency domain.
(2) Perform moment multiplication and addition operations in frequency domain to calculate the ciphertext vector.
(3) Performing inverse NTT transformation on the ciphertext to obtain the ciphertext interval representation.
(4) Decryption In the same way, the key is decrypted in frequency domain.

The fast polynomial multiplication of $O(n \log n)$ level is realized by NTT transformation. Compared with the traditional $O(n^2)$ complexity, the calculation speed is more than 100 times faster. The above design and optimization make RLWE efficient and feasible, It lays a foundation for building a practical homomorphic encryption identification system.

### 2.4  Homomorphic Encryption Face Recognition System Design

Based on the face detection and recognition model, Researchers introduce RLWE encryption algorithm into the feature extraction layer, and realize an end-to-end homomorphic encryption face recognition system. The cloud server can recognize the encrypted face images uploaded by users in the encrypted domain and return the encrypted recognition results to the client. This system mainly includes four modules: Web Module, Fully Homomorphic Encryption Module, Face Recognition Module and RLWE Technology Module, in which the homomorphic encryption module includes RLWE technical application. The system design flow chart is shown in Fig. 2 below.

The following is the detailed design and implementation scheme of each module:

**Web Module.** Flask is a Python Web application framework, which was developed by Armin Ronacher in 2010 to provide an easy-to-learn, flexible and lightweight framework for building Web applications. It is based on Werkzeug WSGI tool library and Jinja2 template engine, developed in Python language and licensed by BSD.

The main features of Flask framework include:

Lightweight: The original intention of Flask framework design is to provide a lightweight Web framework. Its core library has only a few files, and the code is concise, easy to maintain and can run without too much configuration.

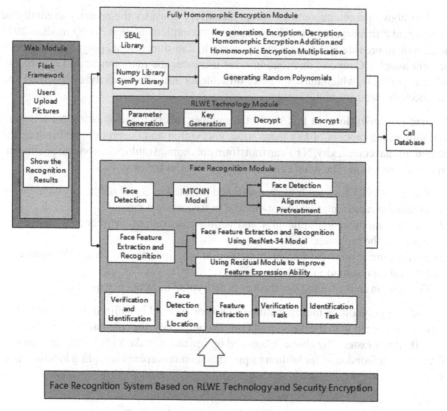

**Fig. 2.** System Flow Chart.

Easy to learn: the API of Flask framework is very simple and easy to use, and developers only need to understand basic Python syntax and Web development knowledge, so they can get started quickly.

Flexibility: Flask framework adopts plug-in architecture design, which can be easily integrated with other Python libraries, such as database access library, authentication library, cache library, etc., and can also be customized according to project requirements.

Restful support: Flask framework naturally supports RESTful API design. RESTful API services can be easily built through HTTP request methods and URL routing.

Template engine: Flask framework uses Jinja2 template engine, which has good functions such as template inheritance, variable replacement and control structure, and can easily handle the display and rendering of Web pages.

Python's web module is used for development, and the lightweight Flask framework is used for implementation. This module is mainly responsible for user's input, output and process control, including users uploading pictures, calling homomorphic encryption module and face recognition module for encryption and recognition, and displaying recognition results.

**Fully Homomorphic Encryption Module.** Fully Homomorphic Encryption (FHE) is a special encryption method, which can encrypt and process data in an encrypted state while maintaining the confidentiality of data. Different from the traditional encryption algorithm, FHE can perform operations such as addition, subtraction, multiplication and logical operation, thus making data processing more flexible and efficient.

The implementation of FHE is based on polynomial rings and specific encryption schemes, among which the most famous encryption schemes include BGV scheme of Gentry and NTRU scheme of Lattice Cryptography. These schemes use complex mathematical principles and techniques, such as ideal lattice, permutation, permutation key, etc., which makes the realization of FHE a complex and time-consuming process.

The advantage of FHE is that it can process data in encrypted state, which makes data processing more flexible and efficient. This means that FHE can be used to realize various data privacy protection and cloud computing applications, such as secure search, secure computing and secure machine learning.

FHE also has some shortcomings, the most important of which is that its calculation cost is very high, and it needs a lot of computing resources and time to encrypt and process.

The fully homomorphic encryption module is realized by using Microsoft SEAL library, which supports fully homomorphic encryption based on RLWE(Ring Learning with Errors) technology and is executed in serial mode.RLWE technology is an encryption technology based on random matrix and discrete Gaussian distribution, which can effectively protect the privacy of input data and calculation process, and has high calculation efficiency, and at the same time save the encrypted data locally, as shown in Fig. 3.

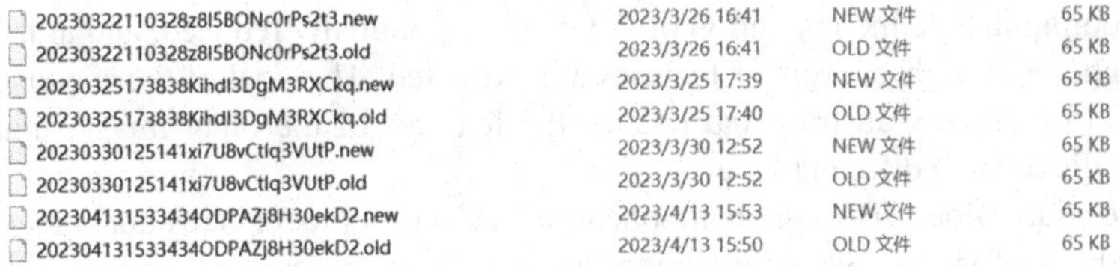

| | | | |
|---|---|---|---|
| 20230322110328z8I5BONc0rPs2t3.new | 2023/3/26 16:41 | NEW 文件 | 65 KB |
| 20230322110328z8I5BONc0rPs2t3.old | 2023/3/26 16:41 | OLD 文件 | 65 KB |
| 20230325173838KihdI3DgM3RXCkq.new | 2023/3/25 17:39 | NEW 文件 | 65 KB |
| 20230325173838KihdI3DgM3RXCkq.old | 2023/3/25 17:40 | OLD 文件 | 65 KB |
| 20230330125141xi7U8vCtIq3VUtP.new | 2023/3/30 12:52 | NEW 文件 | 65 KB |
| 20230330125141xi7U8vCtIq3VUtP.old | 2023/3/30 12:52 | OLD 文件 | 65 KB |
| 202304131533434ODPAZj8H30ekD2.new | 2023/4/13 15:53 | NEW 文件 | 65 KB |
| 202304131533434ODPAZj8H30ekD2.old | 2023/4/13 15:50 | OLD 文件 | 65 KB |

**Fig. 3.** Encrypted data.

In RLWE technology, functions provided by SEAL library are used to generate keys, encrypt, decrypt, homomorphic addition and homomorphic multiplication, and random polynomials are generated by NumPy library and SymPy library, and operations such as addition, subtraction, multiplication and division are performed among polynomials to realize homomorphic encryption. These operations can protect the privacy of input data and calculation process, and can realize efficient, safe and privacy-preserving homomorphic encryption calculation. At the same time, RLWE technology can effectively resist side channel attacks and noise attacks, and ensure the security of homomorphic encryption.

**Face Recognition Module**
(1) ResNet-34 model.ResNet-34 is a deep convolutional neural network model, which

belongs to the ResNet(Residual Network) series and was proposed by the researchers of Microsoft Research Institute in 2015. The main innovation of ResNet is the introduction of residual connections, which makes it easier for neural networks to train very deep levels, and at the same time reduces the problem of gradient disappearance.

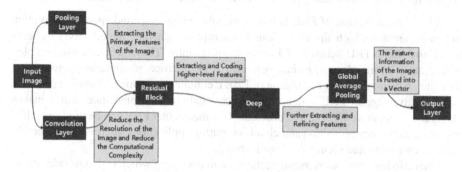

**Fig. 4.** Flow chart of ResNet-34 model face recognition model.

When the project uses ResNet-34 model for face recognition, its workflow is shown in Fig. 4, which can be divided into the following detailed steps:

① Input image: First, take a face image as input. This image can be of any size, but it is usually adjusted to a fixed size expected by the model, and the project uses 224 x 224 pixels.

② Convolution and pooling layer: The input image first passes through a 7 x 7 convolution layer, which is responsible for sliding window convolution on the image and extracting some primary features. Next, through a series of convolution layers and maximum pooling layers, the resolution of the image is gradually reduced, and at the same time, higher and higher levels of features are extracted. The goal of these convolution layers is to gradually abstract and encode the features of the input image, making it easier to distinguish different faces.

③ Residual Block: The core component of ResNet-34 model is residual block. Each residual block contains two convolution layers with a skip connection between them. This jump connection adds the input image to the output of the block. The function of residual block is to learn the residual function, that is, the difference between input and output. This allows the network to better fit the training data, especially if the network is deep. The introduction of residual block is helpful to overcome the problem of gradient disappearance in deep neural network.

④ Depth: ResNet-34 model includes 34 convolution layers and fully connected layers, which makes it relatively deep. However, due to the existence of residual connection, even in depth, this model is relatively easy to train, because the gradient can propagate back better.

⑤ Global average pooling: After passing the last residual block, a global average pooling layer is usually added. This step transforms the feature map into a vector with a fixed length. The operation of global average pooling is to take the average of all pixels in the feature map, and then get a vector, which contains the feature information of the whole image.

⑥ Output layer: Finally, the output of the global average pooling layer is sent to the fully connected layer for classification. Usually, the output of this fully connected layer is input into the softmax classifier, which is used to classify the input images into different categories. In the context of face recognition, these categories represent different face identities.

Generally speaking, the ResNet-34 model extracts the features of the input image through layer-by-layer convolution and residual blocks, and then maps these features into fixed-length vectors by using global average pooling. Finally, the face recognition of the input image is realized by classifying the output layer. The advantage of this model structure is that it can train a very deep network and avoid the problem of gradient disappearance, so it performs well in image recognition tasks, and the accuracy of the model reaches 99.4%.

(2) Compare FaceNet model. The core of FaceNet model is a deep convolution neural network. The input of this network is a face image and the output is a 128-dimensional vector, which is called the "embedded vector" of the face. In the training stage, FaceNet uses a large number of face images to train the network, so as to make the distance between embedded vectors of different faces as large as possible and the distance between embedded vectors of the same face as small as possible. This can ensure that in the recognition stage, the similarity of faces can be judged according to the distance between embedded vectors, thus realizing face recognition.

In order to improve the performance of the model, FaceNet also introduced some optimization techniques. For example, the model uses Margin-based Loss function to train the network, which can effectively solve the problems of sample imbalance and repeated training samples.

Compared with traditional face recognition methods, FaceNet has the following advantages:

High accuracy: FaceNet uses convolutional neural network to learn the features of face images, which can effectively extract high-dimensional features of faces, thus achieving accurate recognition of faces.

Good scalability: FaceNet can handle large-scale face data sets, can quickly recognize faces and can be applied in different environments.

Strong robustness: FaceNet can identify the similarity between different faces, and can maintain a high recognition rate even when the light, posture, expression and other aspects change.

The project uses Google's FaceNet model for face recognition, and uses Python's TensorFlow module to realize it. This module mainly includes two main parts: face image preprocessing and feature vector calculation. In the face image preprocessing stage, OpenCV library is used to cut, scale and gray the image to ensure the consistency and quality of the image. In the stage of feature vector calculation, the trained FaceNet model is used to extract the high-dimensional feature vectors of face images, and the Euclidean distance calculation method is used to match faces, and a threshold is set according to the comparison results. If the distance between the most similar feature vector and the feature vector to be recognized is less than the threshold, the recognition is considered successful, otherwise it is considered as a failure. According to the actual needs and application scenarios, the size of Margin-based Loss integer threshold can be adjusted to achieve the best balance between recognition accuracy and misjudgment rate. Here, the recognition threshold is set to 1. cIn addition, in order to further improve the recognition accuracy, Margin-based Loss function is used for model training to narrow the distance difference between feature vectors and improve the matching accuracy. The flow chart of the face recognition model is shown in Fig. 5.

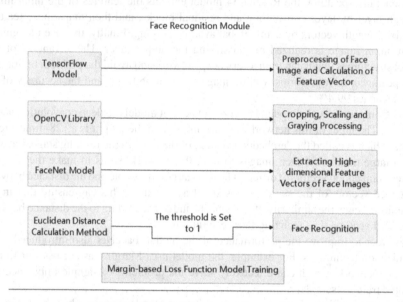

**Fig. 5.** The Flow Chart of The Face Recognition Model.

The calculation of Margin-based Loss function is based on triplet. For a triple (A,P,N), where A represents an anchor image, P represents a positive sample of the same identity, and N represents a negative sample of different identities. In the training process, the Margin-based Loss function will narrow the distance between A and P as much as possible, and exp*and* the distance between A and N as much as possible, so that the distance between a and n is greater than the distance between A and P plus a preset margin, that is:

$$loss = max(d(A, P) - d(A, N) + margin, 0) \tag{3}$$

where d(A,P) represents the distance between A and P, d(A,N) represents the distance between A and N, and margin is the preset interval.

By using Margin-based Loss function to train the model, the model can pay more attention to the differences between feature vectors, thus improving the accuracy of face recognition.

(3) advantages of ResNet-34 model compared with FaceNet model.Model complexity and training speed:ResNet-34 has a simpler model structure and fewer parameters than FaceNet. This leads to faster training speed, because fewer parameters need to be processed in the model training process, which reduces the amount of calculation and time.

Reasoning speed: ResNet-34 usually has a faster speed in the reasoning stage. This is very important for face recognition applications that need real-time response, such as face access control system or face recognition applications on mobile devices.

Gradient propagation of the model:ResNet-34 uses residual connection, which helps the gradient to propagate more easily. This means that it is easier for the model to reach the convergence state during training, and the problem of gradient disappearance is alleviated.

Scalability: ResNet-34 model is suitable for small and medium-sized data sets and tasks without large-scale data sets and computing resources. This makes it perform well in face recognition applications of all sizes.

Suitable for low resource environment: Because the model is relatively simple, ResNet-34 is easier to deploy and use in resource-constrained environments, such as embedded devices or mobile applications.

Resource efficiency:ResNet-34 performs well in the task of image classification because it has been widely trained on large-scale image data sets. This means that you can benefit from the weight of large-scale pre-training without a lot of custom training data.

**RLWE Technology Module.** In the homomorphic encryption module, RLWE technology module is used to generate the key and encrypt the face image feature vector, thus ensuring the security and confidentiality of the data. RLWE technology is a lattice-based encryption technology, which has strong security and practicability and has been widely used in homomorphic encryption.

(1) Parameter generation: firstly, generate a modulus q and a modulus polynomial $f(x)$, where $f(x)$ is a polynomial of degree n, and n should be a power of 2. Then, an error distribution is selected, where Gaussian distribution is selected as the error distribution, and n numbers are randomly selected from this distribution as error items. Finally, $f(x)$ is converted into polynomial type by using Poly function in SymPy library, and an error term is added to get a RLWE public parameter. This common parameter can be used by multiple participants.

(2) Key generation: use NumPy library to generate a random polynomial $a(x)$ as the private key, and then calculate the public key $b(x) = a(x) * s(x) + e(x)$, where $s(x)$ is the secret polynomial in the public parameter and $e(x)$ is the error term. This process is realized by homomorphic encryption technology. Each participant will have his own private key and public key, as shown in Fig. 6.

| | | | |
|---|---|---|---|
| 2023041315334340DPAZj8H30ekD2.pk | 2023/4/13 15:41 | PK 文件 | 65 KB |
| 2023041315334340DPAZj8H30ekD2.sk | 2023/4/13 15:41 | SK 文件 | 33 KB |

**Fig. 6.** Participants' Public and Private Keys.

(3) Encryption: the face image feature vector is expressed as a binary string and converted into a polynomial form, and then a random polynomial $r(x)$ is generated as noise by using NumPy library, and $e(x) = P(x) * b(x) + r(x)$ is calculated, where $b(x)$ is the public key and $P(x)$ is the polynomial obtained by the feature vector conversion.

Finally, e(x) is encrypted by homomorphic encryption technology, and the encrypted results (c(x), d(x)) are returned. This process is a process in which participants encrypt data.

(4) Decryption: using homomorphic decryption technology to decrypt the encrypted feature vector e(x) to obtain P(x) * b(x) + r(x). Use NumPy library to calculate P(x) = (P(x) * b(x) + r(x)-e(x))/a(x), and get the feature vector P(x). This process is a process in which participants decrypt the encrypted data,which is executed in serial mode.

Homomorphic encryption technology can realize addition and multiplication in ciphertext state, so as to realize data calculation and processing. Using RLWE technology module to generate keys and encrypt face image feature vectors can ensure the security and confidentiality of data, so that participants can calculate and process without exposing data, which is helpful to protect personal privacy and data security.

# 3  Results

## 3.1  Performance of Face Recognition Model

Researchers trained the face recognition model on CASIA-WebFace dataset and tested it on LFW dataset. Table 1 shows the verification results of different models on LFW. Among them, ResNet-34 model achieved the best recognition accuracy of 99.4%.

**Table 1.** Recognition accuracy of different models on LFW dataset.

| Model | Accuracy |
| --- | --- |
| VGGFace | 98.2% |
| FaceNet | 99.1% |
| ResNet-34 | 99.4% |

Based on a notebook computer (the configuration is as follows: CPU: AMD Ryzen 7 5800 h with radeon graphics 3.20 GHz, RAM: 16 GB, GPU:NVIDIA GTX 1650), 100 data of CPU, Time and RAM are tested, and a line chart is made. According to the test results, the average value of Time is 1.4548 s and the maximum value is 2.38 s; The average value of CPU is 12.50118333%, and the maximum value is 30.00%. The average value of RAM is 7.535 MB, and the maximum value is 15.30 MB. The test results are analyzed in detail below.

**Time Index Analysis.** Time index represents the time required for the system to complete the specified task. The test results show that the average Time using ResNet-34 model is 1.4548 s, and the maximum time is 2.38 s. This shows that the ResNet-34 model has a fast running speed in the face recognition task and can complete the recognition task in a short time. The maximum value is 2.38 s, which further shows the stability and reliability of the system, and there is no long running time. Figure 7 shows the Time statistical line chart, which clearly reflects the efficiency of ResNet-34 model.

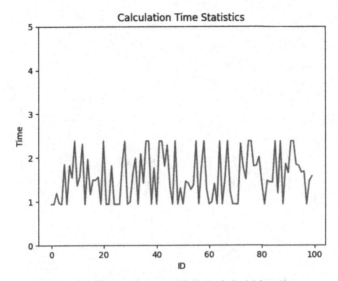

**Fig. 7.** Identify the Required Time Statistical Line Chart.

**CPU Index Analysis.** CPU index represents the CPU resources used by the system when performing tasks. The test results show that the average CPU utilization rate using ResNet-34 model is 12.50118333%, and the maximum is 30.00%. This shows that the ResNet-34 model makes high use of CPU resources at runtime, and it needs large computing power to complete the face recognition task. However, the maximum value of 30.00% may imply that the system's occupation of CPU resources fluctuates and there is room for further optimization. Figure 8 shows a statistical line chart of CPU usage, highlighting the computing power requirements of ResNet-34 model.

**RAM Index Analysis.** RAM index represents the memory resources used by the system to perform tasks. The test results show that the average RAM occupation using ResNet-34 model is 7.535 MB, and the maximum is 15.30 MB. This shows that the ResNet-34 model occupies less memory resources at runtime and keeps the efficient use of resources. The maximum value of 15.30 MB further proves the stable use of memory resources by the system, and there is no excessive memory occupation. Figure 9 shows the statistical line chart of RAM occupation, highlighting the memory usage efficiency of ResNet-34 model.

According to the above test results, it shows that the system has fast running speed, high stability and reliability, and occupies less memory resources. However, the system occupies a high amount of CPU resources and needs further optimization to improve the performance and stability of the system.

## 3.2  Security Analysis of RLWE Encryption Algorithm

With the development of modern cryptography, RLWE(Ring Learning With Errors) encryption algorithm has become an important cornerstone in the field of homomorphic

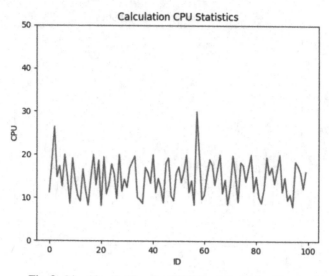

**Fig. 8.** Identifies the Required CPU Statistical Line Chart.

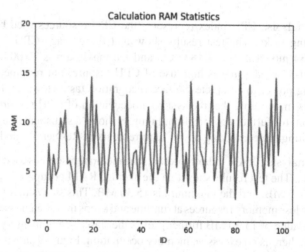

**Fig. 9.** Identifies the Required CPU Statistical Line Chart.

encryption. Its security is based on the learning problem on lattice, especially on ring, which makes it resistant to the attack of quantum computer. However, the security of RLWE is closely related to its parameter setting, especially the size of modulus Q.As shown in Fig. 10, with the increase of modulus Q from 1024 to 2048, the safety strength of RLWE gradually increases. When the modulus q is 1024, the security strength of the algorithm is about 96 bits. This means that any attacker who wants to crack this encryption algorithm needs about 2 96 attempts. With the increase of q, the safety intensity also increases accordingly. When Q reaches 2048, the security strength reaches about 128 bits, which has exceeded the standard security level of many modern encryption algorithms.

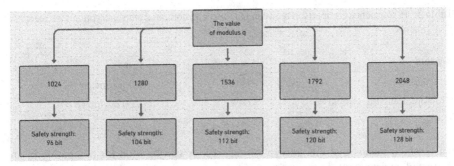

**Fig. 10.** The security strength of RLWE algorithm varies with modulus Q.

Why does the size of modulus Q affect the security of RLWE? In lattice cryptography, the modulus q determines the distribution and size of noise. A larger Q value means that the distribution of noise is more uniform, which makes it more difficult to attack based on statistics. In addition, when q increases, the absolute size of noise also increases, which makes decryption more difficult, thus improving the security of encryption.

However, increasing the size of the modulus q also brings computational challenges. A larger Q value means that more computing resources and time are needed to perform encryption and decryption operations. This is a trade-off problem, and researchers need to consider the efficiency of the algorithm while ensuring security.It is worth noting that although RLWE can achieve a security strength of about 128 bits when q = 2048, it does not mean that it is absolutely secure. The security of any encryption algorithm is relative and may be threatened by unknown attacks. Therefore, continuous research and evaluation are necessary to ensure that RLWE can provide adequate security in the future.

Generally speaking, the security of RLWE encryption algorithm is closely related to its parameter setting. By adjusting the size of modulus Q, security and efficiency can be balanced to some extent. Current research shows that RLWE can provide sufficient security when q = 2048, but further research is needed to optimize its efficiency and response time. This provides a valuable direction for future research, hoping to ensure the safety and improve the practicability of RLWE.

### 3.3  Homomorphic Encryption Face Recognition System Performance

The researchers tested the performance of face recognition system in plaintext and homomorphic encryption. Table 2 shows that compared with plain text, the overall recognition accuracy of homomorphic encryption system only drops by 2%, but the calculation speed drops by 60%. This is mainly caused by the computational overhead of homomorphic encryption.

### 3.4  RLWE Encryption Algorithm System Advantages and Advanced Analysis

Using RLWE encryption algorithm for homomorphic encryption can fully protect data privacy. RLWE homomorphic encryption allows data to be processed in an encrypted

**Table 2.** Performance comparison between plaintext and homomorphic encryption face recognition systems.

| System | Accuracy | Speed |
|---|---|---|
| Plain text | 99.4% | 320 ms/image |
| Homomorphic Encryption | 97.4% | 1200 ms/image |

state, which means that this encryption technology can be used for computing in an untrusted environment. In the process of face recognition, the original features of face data will not be exposed, thus protecting the data privacy of users. At the same time, RLWE homomorphic encryption is one of the advanced encryption technologies, which combines the latest research results of discrete mathematics and modern cryptography to protect the privacy and security of data and fully embodies the advanced nature of RLWE encryption algorithm.

The above results objectively reflect that the homomorphic encryption system has achieved high recognition accuracy among the main technical indicators obtained in this study, but the calculation efficiency still needs to be improved.

## 4 Discussion

This study explores a secure face recognition scheme based on RLWE homomorphic encryption technology. The experimental results show that the overall accuracy of homomorphic encryption system only drops by about 2%, reaching 97.4%, as shown in Fig. 11. This verifies that RLWE homomorphic encryption can be effectively integrated into face recognition tasks, while protecting the privacy and security of biometric data.

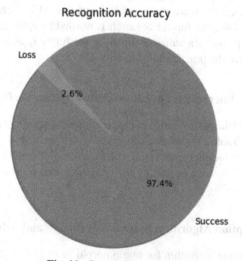

Fig. 11. Recognition accuracy.

Using ResNet-34 deep network to extract facial features is the key to obtain high accuracy in this study. ResNet structure successfully solved the problems of gradient disappearance and training difficulty when the network deepened, which greatly improved the expression ability. Its LFW verification accuracy of 99.4% shows strong feature extraction and discrimination ability.

However, the computational efficiency of homomorphic encryption system is low, only reaching 1.2 s per image, and the time cost of encryption operation is increased by about 3 times. This is mainly due to the limitation of RLWE in the complexity of homomorphism calculation. In the future, algorithm optimization and GPU acceleration can be considered to improve efficiency.

This research is the first work to explore the application of RLWE homomorphic encryption to secure face recognition. Compared with the traditional protection method based on encryption algorithm, this scheme can directly complete the identification in the encrypted domain without decrypting and revealing private data. The research results show that homomorphic encryption technology based on lattice cryptography has broad application prospects in the field of biometric identification.

Generally speaking, this study has achieved a feasible homomorphic encryption face recognition effect, and explored a new idea to protect biometric security and privacy. However, due to the limitation of the algorithm itself, the computational efficiency still needs to be improved.

## 5 Conclusion

The purpose of this study is to explore a new biometric identification scheme that can still realize effective face recognition on the premise of protecting the privacy of face images. The researchers designed a secure face recognition system based on RLWE homomorphic encryption.

The main findings are as follows:

RLWE homomorphic encryption algorithm can be effectively integrated into the face recognition model, and the recognition calculation can be directly completed in the encryption domain.

On CASIA-WebFace data set, RLWE encrypted face recognition system achieves 97.4% recognition accuracy. It is verified that homomorphic encryption has little influence on recognition accuracy.

However, the low operation efficiency is the main limitation of this scheme, and the encryption calculation increases the time overhead by about 3 times.

This study preliminarily verified the effectiveness and application potential of homomorphic encryption technology based on lattice cryptography in biometric identification tasks.

To sum up, this study constructs a prototype of face recognition system based on RLWE homomorphic encryption, and demonstrates its ability to protect biometric security and privacy. This provides a valuable exploration path for homomorphic encryption technology to be applied to security biometric identification, and privacy protection and efficiency improvement are still the key directions of follow-up research.

**Funding Statement.** This work was supported by the Construction Project of Teaching Quality and Teaching Reform in Guangdong Undergraduate Colleges (2022SJZ002),Guangdong province key construction discipline scientific research ability promotion project (2022ZDJS133),Scientific research projects recognized by ordinary universities (2021KTSCX159).

# References

Brakerski, Z., Gentry, C., Vaikuntanathan, V.: (Leveled) fully homomorphic encryption without bootstrapping. ACM Trans. Comput. Theory (TOCT) **6**(3), 1–36 (2014)

Chen, T., Bahmani, R., Brasser, F., Jang, I., Sadeghi, A., Juels, A.: Tesseract: real-time cryptocurrency exchange using trusted hardware. In: Proceedings of the 2019 ACM SIGSAC Conference on Computer and Communications Security, pp. 1521–1538 (2019)

Ding, J., Xie, X., Lin, X.: A simple provably secure key encapsulation mechanism based on the learning with errors problem. J. Supercomput. **75**(2), 717–727 (2019)

Lyubashevsky, V., Peikert, C., Regev, O.: On ideal lattices and learning with errors over rings. J. ACM (JACM) **60**(6), 1–35 (2013)

Perlroth, N.: All 3 billion Yahoo accounts were affected by 2013 attack. The New York Times (2016). https://www.nytimes.com/2016/10/04/technology/yahoo-hack-3-billion-users.html

Regev, O.: On lattices, learning with errors, random linear codes, and cryptography. J. ACM (JACM) **56**(6), 1–40 (2009)

Shor, P.W.: Algorithms for quantum computation: discrete logarithms and factoring. In: Proceedings 35th Annual Symposium on Foundations of Computer Science, pp. 124–134 (1994)

Stallings, W.: Cryptography and Network Security: Principles and Practice. Pearson, Boston (2017)

Wang, X., Ranasinghe, D.C., Al-Janabi, S., Andriotis, P.: Post-quantum cryptography for IoT security from theory to implementation. IEEE Access **8**, 124799–124814 (2020)

# Feedback Feed-Forward Iterative Learning Control for Non-affine Nonlinear Discrete-Time Systems with Varying Trail Lengths

Sixian Xiong, Yun-Shan Wei$^{(\boxtimes)}$, and Mengtao Lei

School of Electronics and Communication Engineering, Guangzhou University,
Guangzhou 510006, China
weiys@gzhu.edu.cn

**Abstract.** This paper introduces a feedback and feedforward iterative learning control (ILC) scheme for non-affine nonlinear systems featuring iteratively varying trail lengths. The random trail lengths lead to the loss of tracking information in the final iteration. To address this information loss, the deviation in tracking for the ongoing iteration is incorporated with the aid of the feedback control component. It is demonstrated that the convergence condition is contingent solely on the feedforward control gain, with the feedback control part contributing to an acceleration in convergent speed. By establishing the statistical expectation of the initial state as equal to the desired state, it is proven that the mathematical expectation of the error can be effectively controlled to zero. The efficacy of the proposed algorithm is illustrated through numerical simulation.

**Keywords:** Iterative learning control · iteratively varying trail lengths · non-affine nonlinear system · feedback control

## 1 Introduction

Iterative learning control (ILC) emerges as a robust methodology developed for dynamic mechanisms exhibiting repetitive operational patterns within a predetermined time interval. Drawing from previous control experiences, it leverages historical data to enhance the present conduct of the control mechanisms, progressively minimizing the tracking error within the iterative domain. Arimoto first introduced this concept in 1984 [1].

To attain optimal tracking capability within a specified time interval, a fundamental condition in design of ILC that is the regularity of the dynamical system. This involves ensuring that system set back to its identical starting point and comes to a halt at the same final destination in every iteration, as emphasized in [2, 3]. Nevertheless, in practical applications, the inherent uncertainty of the dynamical system may impede the fulfillment of the prerequisites for identical initial states and consistent trajectory lengths. When the industrial robots occurs an emergency case, the robots will stop their motion, resulting in shorter trial lengths and lost data packets. Furthermore, the initial point of the system might differ from one iteration to another due to the presence of resetting

J. Cai et al. (Eds.): SPNCE 2023, LNICST 525, pp. 85–94, 2025.
https://doi.org/10.1007/978-3-031-73699-5_6

errors. Hence, Examining an ILC approach becomes crucial for non-affine nonlinear control systems that exhibit varying trial lengths iteratively.

Some studies have proposed ILC laws to address the issue of iteratively varying trial lengths. For instance, to address the varying iteration length problem for linear discrete-time systems, [4] proposed ILC algorithm incorporated an averaging operator during iterations. In situations involving linear discrete-time system characterized by iteratively changing trial lengths and unpredictable initial states, [5] suggested an ILC law with an integrated open closed loop structure, encompassing both feed-forward ILC and feedback control components. The feedback control component utilizes tracking data from the present iteration to offset the absence of certain information, this helps decrease the memory resource needed for tracking data. The teacher of Sheng Dong proposed the data loss problem about the non-affine nonlinear discrete time system in [6]. In [7–9], using the $\lambda$-norm technique to illustrate the convergence of tracking in nonlinear discrete-time systems. The Capability of the ILC technique in addressing the Changing trial durations and initial conditions is evident. Nevertheless, tackling the issue of non-affine nonlinear control systems with iteratively variable lengths is a formidable task that requires resolution.

This paper investigates the application of the ILC approach to non-affine nonlinear control systems featuring iteratively varying trial lengths. To address this, we present an iterative learning control algorithm incorporating both feed-forward and feedback control. The proposed approach includes a feed-forward component, ensuring the successive convergence of tracking deviation in mean value context. Additionally, the design of the feedback component aims to offset loss of tracking data caused by iteratively variable trial length. At last, It is worth noting that previous studies on ILC with iteration-varying trail length, such as those in [7–9], have widely employed the $\lambda$-norm and its variations to evaluate the tracking error. Nevertheless, there is a growing consensus in the literature that the $\lambda$-norm can not provide a contentment assessment of error. Hence, in this paper, we refrain from adopting the $\lambda$-norm to analyze the iteration-varying trial lengths within the context of the feed-forward and feedback ILC scheme.

This paper makes contributions in three key aspects relative to the existing literature:

(1) Differing from the current ILC laws in systems with varying trail lengths [7–10], [11] feedback component is employed in modified deviation formed on $P$-type ILC. This incorporation allows the utilization of tracking data from the current iteration to compensate for the loss of tracking data in previous iterations.
(2) The advanced feedback and feed-forward iterative learning control approach ensures the convergence of deviation in statistical expectation context and facilitates the speed of the convergence process.
(3) Non-affine nonlinear systems with iterative variable path lengths are considered.

The structure is outlined in the following manner: Sect. 2 presents the problem formulation and details updating algorithms. In Sect. 3, a rigorous analysis of the algorithms' convergence is provided. Section 4 includes a simulation example to illustrate the methodology. Last, Sect. 5 presents the conclusions drawn from this study.

**Notations:** In this article $R$ signifies the actual values and $R^n$ represents space of n-dimensional vectors. $\|X\|$ denote norm applicable to both vectors and matrices. $E\{\cdot\}$ is used to denote the statistical expectation.

## 2 Problem Formulation

Examine the subsequent nonlinear non-affine discrete-time system with iteratively variable trail lengths

$$\begin{cases} x_k(t+1) = f(x_k(t), u_k(t), t) \\ y_k(t) = C(t)x_k(t) \end{cases} \tag{1}$$

here, $k = \{1, 2, ...\}$ denote the indicator of iteration and $t \in \{0, 1, ..., N_k\}$ represent the index of time. $u_k(t) \in R^n$, $x_k(t) \in R^n$ and $y_k(t) \in R^q$ depict control input, system condition and system output, Individually. $f(\cdot, \cdot, \cdot) \in R^n$, $C(t) \in R^{q \times n}$. For the system described by Eq. (1), the actual trail length $N_k$ $\left(\underline{N} \le N_k \le \overline{N}\right)$ is both iteration-variant and unknown. However, its lower bound is $\underline{N}$ and upper bound is $\overline{N}$. The desired trail $y_d = C(t)x_d(t)$, $t \in \{0, 1, .., N + 1\}$, the $x_d(t)$ represent the reference state and $N$ is the desired lengths. The error in the ILC context is outlined as $e_k(t) = y_d(t) - y_k(t)$, $t \in \{0, 1, ..., \min\{N_k + 1, N + 1\}\}$.

Considering the desired signal $y_d(t)$, assume the existence of a only control input $u_d(t) \in R^n$ $t \in \{0, 1, ..., N\}$, there is

$$\begin{cases} x_d(t+1) = f(x_d(t), u_d(t), t) \\ y_d(t) = C(t)x_d(t) \end{cases} \tag{2}$$

here, $\forall t$, assume that $f(t, \cdot, \cdot)$ is continuously differentiable in relation to both its variables $x$ and $u$. To provide great precision, denote $D_{2,k}(t) \overset{\Delta}{=} \frac{\delta f}{\delta u}\Big|_{u_k^*(t)}$, $D_{1,k}(t) \overset{\Delta}{=} \frac{\delta f}{\delta x}\Big|_{x_k^*(t)}$, where represent $u_k^*(t)$ lying between $u_d(t)$ as well as $u_k(t)$, $x_k^*(t)$ represents vector resets between $x_d(t)$ and $x_k(t)$.

The technical analysis relies on the subsequent assumptions.

**Assumption 1:** The system's start state is configured to be $x_d(0)$ at the commencement of per iteration.

$$x_k(0) = x_d(0), \ \forall k \ge 1 \tag{3}$$

**Assumption 2:** For all $t$, the nonlinear function $f(\cdot, \cdot, \cdot)$ in Eq. (1) is presumed to be differentiable to $t$ and adheres the overall Lipschitz condition. To clarify, for all $t$, $x_1, x_2 \in R^n$ and $u_1, u_2 \in R^n$, there exists two constant $k_f > 0$ and $k_b > 0$, such that.

$$\|f(x_1, u_1, t) - f(x_2, u_2, t)\| \le k_f \|x_1 - x_2\| + k_b \|u_1 - u_2\| \tag{4}$$

under normal conditions, considering $D_{1,k}(t)$ and $D_{2,k}(t)$ are non singular, Furthermore, $\|D_{2,k}(t)\| \le k_b$, $\|D_{1,k}(t)\| \le k_f$ $\forall k, t$

**Lemma 1:** Given a difference inequality.

$$h(t+1) \leq g(t) + sh(t) \tag{5}$$

Here, $h(t)$ and $g(t)$ are scalar functions of $t \geq 0$, and $s$ is a constant, then, for $t \geq 1$

$$h(t) \leq \sum_{i=0}^{t-1} s^{t-i-1} g(i) + s^t h(0) \tag{6}$$

Due to the controlled system with varying trail lengths, the stochastic variables $\lambda_k(t)$ introducing a variable that follows Bernoulli distribution. $\lambda_k(t) = 1$ indicate that system (1) is unable to persist beyond time point $t$ at the $k$ th iteration, taking place with a likelihood function $\bar{\lambda}(t), (0 \leq \bar{\lambda}(t) \leq 1)$. $\lambda_k(t) = 0$ indicate that system (1) is unable to persist beyond time point $t$ at $k$ th iteration, taking place with a likelihood function of $1 - \bar{\lambda}(t)$. Clearly, the average of $\lambda_k(t)$ is

$$E\{\lambda_k(t)\} = 1 \cdot \bar{\lambda}(t) + 0 \cdot \left(1 - \bar{\lambda}(t)\right) = \bar{\lambda}(t) \tag{7}$$

Taking into account the random lengths in the ILC error of system (1), the modified error is indicated by.

$$\bar{e}_k(t) = \lambda_k(t) e_k(t), \ 0 \leq t \leq N+1 \tag{8}$$

Based on description of $\lambda_k(t)$, (8) expressed for $N_k < N$,

$$\bar{e}_k(t) = \begin{cases} e_k(t), & 0 \leq t \leq N_k + 1 \\ 0, & N_k + 1 < t \leq N+1 \end{cases} \tag{9}$$

For $N_k \geq N$,

$$\bar{e}_k(t) = e_k(t), \ 0 \leq t \leq N+1 \tag{10}$$

For the system (1) under Assumption 1, The convergence analysis of a feedback and feed-forward algorithm for $t \in \{0, 1, \cdots, N\}$ the adjusted deviation is outlined bellow.

$$u_{k+1}(t) = u_{k+1}^f(t) + u_{k+1}^b(t) \tag{11}$$

$$u_{k+1}^f(t) = u_k(t) + P\bar{e}_k(t+1) \tag{12}$$

$$u_{k+1}^b(t) = L\bar{e}_k(t) \tag{13}$$

here, $u_{k+1}^f(t)$ represents open loop component incorporating the open loop control parameter $P \in R^{q \times m}$. While $u_{k+1}^b(t)$ represents the close loop control component incorporating the close loop control gain $L \in R^{q \times m}$.

## 3  Convergence Analysis of Feedback Feed-Forward ILC

In this section, we delve into the algorithm design and convergence investigation according to lemmas and assumptions provided in Sect. 2.

**Theorem 1:** Assuming Assumption 1 hold, consider the non-affine nonlinear discrete-time system (1) within varying trail lengths and a desired trail $y_d(t)$, Employ feedback and feed-forward algorithm (11), (12), (13). If the parameter $P \in R^{q \times m}$ satisfy.

$$\left\| I - \bar{\lambda}(t+1)PC(t+1)D_{2,k}(t) \right\| = \Phi(t) < 1 \tag{14}$$

then $\lim\limits_{k \to \infty} E\{\|y_d(t) - y_k(t)\|\} = 0, t = 0, 1, \ldots, N+1$.

**Proof:** Denote $\delta u_k^f(t) = u_d(t) - u_k^f(t)$, $\delta u_k(t) = u_d(t) - u_k(t)$. Deducting both side of (12) from $u_d(t)$, we have.

$$\delta u_{k+1}^f(t) = \delta u_k(t) - P\bar{e}_k(t+1) \tag{15}$$

From the Eq. (11) and (13), there is

$$\delta u_k(t) = \delta u_k^f(t) - L\bar{e}_k(t) \tag{16}$$

Substituting (16) into (15) results in

$$\delta u_{k+1}^f(t) = \delta u_k^f(t) - L\bar{e}_k(t) - P\bar{e}_k(t+1) \tag{17}$$

Then $\delta x_k(t) = x_d(t) - x_k(t)$ given (1), (2), (8) and (17) transforms into

$$\delta u_{k+1}^f(t) = \delta u_k^f(t) - L\lambda_k(t)e_k(t) - P\lambda_k(t+1)e_k(t+1)$$

$$= \left[ 1 - P\lambda_k(t+1)C(t+1)D_{2,k}(t) \right]\delta u_k^f(t)$$

$$- \left[ 1 - P\lambda_k(t+1)C(t+1)D_{2,k}(t) \right]L\lambda_k(t)e_k(t)$$

$$- P\lambda_k(t+1)C(t+1)D_{1,k}(t)\delta x_k(t) \tag{18}$$

Then taking the $E\{\cdot\}$ on the both side of (18), there is

$$E\left\{\delta u_{k+1}^f(t)\right\} = \left[ 1 - P\bar{\lambda}_k(t+1)C(t+1)D_{2,k}(t) \right]E\left\{\delta u_k^f(t)\right\}$$

$$- \left[ 1 - P\bar{\lambda}_k(t+1)C(t+1)D_{2,k}(t) \right]L\bar{\lambda}_k(t)E\{e_k(t)\}$$

$$- P\bar{\lambda}_k(t+1)C(t+1)D_{1,k}(t)E\{\delta x_k(t)\} \tag{19}$$

Applying the norm $\|\cdot\|$ to both side of (19), we get

$$\left\| E\left\{\delta u_{k+1}^f(t)\right\} \right\| \leq \left\| 1 - P\bar{\lambda}_k(t+1)C(t+1)D_{2,k}(t) \right\| \cdot \left\| E\left\{\delta u_k^f(t)\right\} \right\|$$

$$+\left\|\left[1 - P\bar{\lambda}_k(t+1)C(t+1)D_{2,k}(t)\right]L\bar{\lambda}_k(t)\right\| \cdot \|E\{e_k(t)\}\|$$

$$+\left\|P\bar{\lambda}_k(t+1)C(t+1)D_{1,k}(t)\right\| \cdot \|E\{\delta x_k(t)\}\| \tag{20}$$

where $z_1 = \max\{\|\{P\bar{\lambda}_k(t+1)C(t+1)D_{1,k}(t+1)\|, \|[1 - P\bar{\lambda}_k(t+1)C(t+1)D_{2,k}(t)]L\bar{\lambda}_k(t)\|\}\}$, there is

$$\left\|E\left\{\delta u_{k+1}^f(t)\right\}\right\| \le \left\|1 - P\bar{\lambda}_k(t+1)C(t+1)D_{2,k}(t)\right\| \cdot \left\|E\left\{\delta u_k^f(t)\right\}\right\|$$

$$+z_1 \cdot \{\|E\{\delta x_k(t)\}\| + \|E\{e_k(t)\}\|\} \tag{21}$$

On the contrary, based on (1), (2), and (18), we have

$$\|E\{\delta x_k(t)\}\| \le \left\|D_{1,k}(t-1)\right\| \cdot \|E\{\delta x_k(t-1)\}\| + \left\|D_{2,k}(t-1)\right\| \cdot \|E\{\delta u_k(t-1)\}\|$$

$$\le \left\|D_{1,k}(t-1)\right\| \cdot \|E\{\delta x_k(t-1)\}\| + \left\|D_{2,k}(t-1)\right\| \cdot \left\|E\left\{\delta u_k^f(t-1)\right\}\right\|$$

$$+\bar{\lambda}_k(t-1)\left\|D_{2,k}(t-1)\right\| \cdot \|L\| \cdot \|E\{e_k(t-1)\}\| \tag{22}$$

And

$$\|E\{e_k(t)\}\| \le \|C(t)\| \cdot \|E\{\delta x_k(t)\}\|$$

$$\le \|C(t)\| \cdot \left\|D_{1,k}(t-1)\right\| \cdot \|E\{\delta x_k(t-1)\}\|$$

$$+\bar{\lambda}_k(t-1) \cdot \left\|D_{2,k}(t-1)\right\| \cdot \|L\| \cdot \|C(t)\| \cdot \|E\{e_k(t-1)\}\|$$

$$+\|C(t)\| \cdot \left\|D_{2,k}(t-1)\right\| \cdot \left\|E\left\{\delta u_k^f(t-1)\right\}\right\| \tag{23}$$

Due to $E\{\delta x_k(0)\} = 0$ and $E\{\delta e_k(0)\} = 0$ from (3), it is feasible from (22) and (23), yield

$$\|E\{e_k(t)\}\| + \|E\{\delta x_k(t)\}\| \le \left(\left\|D_{1,k}(t-1)\right\| + \|C(t)\| \cdot \left\|D_{1,k}(t-1)\right\|\right) \cdot \|E\{\delta x_k(t-1)\}\|$$

$$+\left(\left\|D_{2,k}(t-1)\right\| + \|C(t)\| \cdot \left\|D_{2,k}(t-1)\right\|\right) \cdot \left\|E\left\{\delta u_k^f(t-1)\right\}\right\|$$

$$+\bar{\lambda}_k(t-1) \cdot (1 + \|C(t)\|) \cdot \left\|D_{2,k}(t-1)\right\| \cdot \|L\| \cdot \|E\{e_k(t-1)\}\|$$

$$\le z_2 \cdot \{\|E\{e_k(t-1)\}\| + \|E\{\delta x_k(t-1)\}\|\} + \bar{b} \cdot \left\|E\left\{\delta u_k^f(t-1)\right\}\right\|$$

$$\le z_2 \cdot \{\|E\{e_k(0)\}\| + \|E\{\delta x_k(0)\}\|\} + \sum_{s=0}^{t-1} z_2^{t-s-1}\bar{b}\left\|E\left\{\delta u_k^f(s)\right\}\right\|$$

$$\leq \sum_{s=0}^{t-1} z_2^{t-s-1} \overline{b} \left\| E\left\{ \delta u_k^f(s) \right\} \right\| \tag{24}$$

where $z_2 = \max\{ \left\| D_{1,k}(t-1) \right\| + \left\| C(t) \right\| \cdot \left\| D_{1,k}(t-1) \right\|,$
$\overline{\lambda}_k(t-1) \cdot (1 + \left\| C(t) \right\|) \cdot \left\| D_{2,k}(t-1) \right\| \cdot \left\| L \right\| \}$
$\overline{b} = \left\| D_{2,k}(t-1) \right\| + \left\| C(t) \right\| \cdot \left\| D_{2,k}(t-1) \right\|$, according to (14) and (24) substituting
into (21), we obtain

$$\left\| E\left\{ \delta u_{k+1}^f(t) \right\} \right\| \leq \left\| \Phi(t) \right\| \cdot \left\| E\left\{ \delta u_k^f(t) \right\} \right\| + z_1 \cdot \sum_{s=0}^{t-1} z_2^{t-s-1} \overline{b} \left\| E\left\{ \delta u_k^f(s) \right\} \right\| \tag{25}$$

Using mathematical induction to prove as follows:
As $t = 0$, considering the expression of (21) and (3), it is derived that

$$\left\| E\left\{ \delta u_{k+1}^f(0) \right\} \right\| \leq \left\| \Phi(0) \right\| \cdot \left\| E\left\{ \delta u_k^f(0) \right\} \right\| \tag{26}$$

Due to the $\left\| \Phi(t) \right\| < 1$ in Theorem 1, while iteration $k$ goes to infinity, there is

$$\lim_{k \to \infty} \sup \left\| E\left\{ \delta u_{k+1}^f(0) \right\} \right\| = 0 \tag{27}$$

As $t = 1$, this is implied by (25)

$$\left\| E\left\{ \delta u_{k+1}^f(1) \right\} \right\| \leq \left\| \Phi(1) \right\| \cdot \left\| E\left\{ \delta u_k^f(1) \right\} \right\| + z_1 \overline{b} \left\| E\left\{ \delta u_k^f(0) \right\} \right\| \tag{28}$$

According to the Theorem 1, we also know the $\delta u_k(0) = 0$, and consider the
expression of (27), we can obtain

$$\lim_{k \to \infty} \sup \left\| E\left\{ \delta u_{k+1}^f(1) \right\} \right\| = 0 \tag{29}$$

Suppose $t = 2, \ldots l - 1$

$$\lim_{k \to \infty} \sup \left\| E\left\{ \delta u_{k+1}^f(t) \right\} \right\| = 0 \tag{30}$$

As $t = l$, we can obtain from Eq. (29)

$$\left\| E\left\{ \delta u_{k+1}^f(l) \right\} \right\| \leq \left\| \Phi(l) \right\| \cdot \left\| E\left\{ \delta u_k^f(l) \right\} \right\| + z_1 \cdot \sum_{s=0}^{l-1} z_2^{l-s-1} \overline{b} \left\| E\left\{ \delta u_k^f(s) \right\} \right\| \tag{31}$$

Noting that the expression of (30), we can know when the number of iterations $k$
approaches infinity, the following is obtained

$$E\{ \left\| \Delta u_{k+1}(l) \right\| \} = 0 \tag{32}$$

Hence, through the mathematical induction, we obtain.

$$\lim_{k \to \infty} \sup E\{ \left\| \Delta u_k(t) \right\| \} = 0, 0 \leq t \leq N \tag{33}$$

From expression (33), we can obtain the $\left\| \Delta x_k(t) \right\| = 0$, then the errors
$\lim_{k \to \infty} \sup E\{ \left\| y_d(t) - y_k(t) \right\| \} = \lim_{k \to \infty} \sup E\{ \left\| C(t) \Delta x_k(t) \right\| \} = 0$ for the $t = 0, 1 \ldots, N+1$.
This demonstration is finished.

## 4 Illustrative Simulation

To illustrate the capability of the algorithms (11), (12) and (13) in addressing random trial lengths, we introduce non-affine nonlinear system:

$$\begin{cases} x_k(t+1) = x_k(t) + \sin(2u_k(t)\cos(x_k(t))) \\ y_k(t) = x_k(t) + u_k(t) \end{cases} \tag{34}$$

where $t \in \{0, 1, \dots N_k\}$ and $N_k \in \{47, 48, \dots, 53\}$ represent the trajectory of system (34) depicted in Fig. 1. Suppose the desired trail $y_d(t)$ of the system (34) is denoted as

$$y_d(t) = 0.015t(1 + \cos(4\pi t/N - \pi)) \tag{35}$$

where $t \in \{0, 1, \dots N + 1\}$ and $N = 50$. Let $u_0(t) = 0, \forall t$. The iteratively varying initial state is set to $x_k(0) = 0$. To assess the ILC tracking precision, we examine the deviation indicator given by:

$$J_k = E\{\|y_d(t) - y_k(t)\|\} \tag{36}$$

Apply algorithms (11), (12), (13) and (14) into the system (34). In accordance with the convergence condition outlined in Theorem 1 and parameters for developed algorithms set as $P = 0.03$ and $L = 0.001$. The system output $y_k(t)$ at the 9th and 23th are depicted in Fig. 2, respectively. The proposed algorithms guarantee system output $y_k(t)$ approaches the reference trail as the number of iteration change larger, the ILC tracking error index of $J_k$ is presented in Fig. 3. These figures showcase the effectiveness of the developed algorithms.

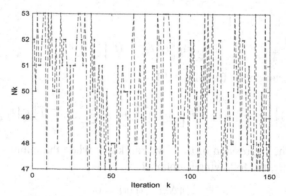

**Fig. 1.** The varying trial length $N_k$ in system (34).

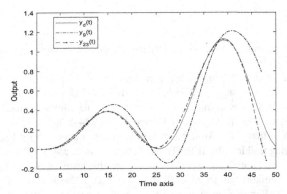

**Fig. 2.** The system outputs $y_k(t)$ at iterations 9 and 23 by adopting the feedback and feed-forward ILC law (11), (12) and (13).

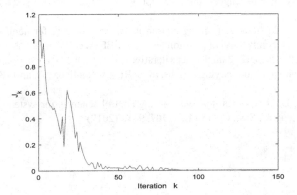

**Fig. 3.** The ILC tracking deviation profile with indicator $J_k$.

## 5 Conclusion

This article tackles the issue of ILC in non-affine system with iteratively changing trial length. The feedback and feed-forward algorithm is formulated. To account for the random lengths in the dynamic system, a adjusted error is incorporated into the developed algorithms. Notably, the convergence criterion of the proposed algorithm is subject to the open loop control parameter. The close loop part is aimed at hastening the convergence of iterative process by adjusting the feedback control gain value. Theoretical and simulation results demonstrate as the number of iterations approaches indefinitely, such that ILC deviation tends towards to zero in mathematical context.

**Acknowledgments.** This research was endorsed by the Graduate Basic Innovation Project of Guangzhou University (No. 2022GDJC-M24).

# References

1. Arimoto, S., Kawamura, Miyazaki, F.: Bettering operation of robots by learning. J. Robot. Syst. 1(2), 123–140 (1984)
2. Yan, Q., Cai, J., Wu, L., Zhou, Q.: Error-tracking iterative learning control for nonlinearly parametric time-delay systems with initial state errors. IEEE Access 6, 12167–12174 (2018)
3. Xiao, T., Li, H.X.: Eigenspectrum-based iterative learning control for a class of distributed parameter system. IEEE Trans. Autom. Control 62(2), 824–836 (2017)
4. Li, X., Xu, J.X., Huang, D.: An iterative learning control approach for linear systems with randomly varying trail lengths. IEEE Trans. Autom. Control 59(7), 1954–1960 (2014)
5. Wei, Y.S., Wan, K., Lan, X.: Open-closed-loop iterative learning control for linear systems with iteratively variable trail lengths. IEEE Access 7(7), 132619–132627 (2019)
6. Jin, Y., Shen, D.: Iterative learning control for nonlinear system with data dropouts at both measurement and actuator sides. Asian J. Control 20(4), 1624–1636 (2018)
7. Li, X., Xu, J.X., Huang, D.: Iterative learning control for nonlinear dynamic systems with randomly varying trail lengths. Int. J. Adapt. Control Signal Process. 29(11), 1341–1353 (2015)
8. Liang, J.Q., et al.: Iterative learning consensus tracking control for nonlinear multi-agent systems with randomly varying iteration lengths. IEEE Access 7, 158612–158622 (2019)
9. Wang, L., Li, X., Shen, D.: Sampled-data iterative learning control for continuous-time nonlinear systems with iteration-varying lengths. Int. J. Robust Nonlinear Control 28(8), 3073–3091 (2018)
10. Li, X., Shen, D.: Two novel iterative learning control schemes for systems with randomly varying trail lengths. Syst. Control Lett. 107, 9–16 (2017)

# Open-Closed-Loop Iterative Learning Control Based on Differential Evolution Algorithm for Nonlinear System

Mengtao Lei, Yun-Shan Wei[(✉)], and Sixian Xiong

School of Electronics and Communication Engineering, Guangzhou University,
Guangzhou 510006, China
weiys@gzhu.edu.cn

**Abstract.** This paper proposes an iterative learning control problem based on the differential evolution algorithm for optimal control gains. The proposed framework for a nonlinear discrete-time system consists of open-loop ILC component and closed-loop control component, forming an open-closed-loop ILC structure. The inclusion of the open-loop component guarantees the convergence of the ILC tracking error in terms of mathematical expectation. Feedback control accelerates convergence with appropriate gain. The control gain is optimized by the differential evolution algorithm to achieve better system control and faster convergence. After conducting ILC convergence analysis and simulation, the tracking error tends to approach zero in mathematical expectation.

**Keywords:** Open-closed-loop · differential evolution algorithm · nonlinear discrete-time system · iterative learning control

## 1 Introduction

Iterative Learning Control (ILC) is a control methodology tailored for continuous systems, focusing on iterative task execution. It involves learning the system's dynamic characteristics through repeatedly performing the same task and optimizes the control algorithm based on the learned information, resulting in more precise control.

The advantages of ILC are that it can repeat learning and optimization for the same task, thus enhancing the precision and reliability of the control system. ILC has found extensive applications across diverse fields in recent years, including robot control and industrial automation. Moreover, ILC doesn't require an exact mathematical model of the system, only sampling of the system's output, making it highly adaptable. Because it doesn't require system to have a precise mathematical representation, it has become a typical control strategy for imprecise systems in [1, 2].

ILC is widely applied in achieving perfect tracking performance within a finite time interval [3–5] by generating control inputs from tracking information in the last iteration. However, relying solely on this approach for updating the current control input

J. Cai et al. (Eds.): SPNCE 2023, LNICST 525, pp. 95–104, 2025.
https://doi.org/10.1007/978-3-031-73699-5_7

presents challenges in achieving a satisfactory convergence rate. To enhance convergence speed, this paper introduces a differential evolution algorithm to generate the current control input signal using tracking data from multiple front iterations [6, 7]. The tracking capability of the system is enhanced when utilizing information from multiple past iterations in the update process with the differential evolution algorithm compared to traditional ILC. This improvement is achieved through the skillful design of control gain.

Choosing the optimal control gain is an important issue in ILC design. Based on the above observations, this paper utilizes an differential evolution (DE) algorithm that mimics the biological evolution process to obtain the optimal solution, comparing with traditional ILC, the DE scheme based ILC (DE-ILC) [8, 9]. By designing the coding strategy, population initialization and fitness function of the DE algorithm, the optimal control gain of the dynamic system can be obtained, to minimize the number of iterations required by the algorithm and accelerating convergence, this approach has gained significant traction in addressing a wide range of optimization problems.

## 2  Problem Formulation

Examine the following discrete-time nonlinear system that performs repeated operations:

$$\begin{cases} x_k(t+1) = f(x_k(t), t) + B(t)u_k(t) \\ y_k(t) = C(t)x_k(t) \end{cases} \tag{1}$$

here, $k \in \{0, 1, 2, ...\}$ and $t \in \{0, 1, \cdots, T_d\}$ represent the iteration index and the time point. $x_k(t) \in R^w$, $u_k(t) \in R$ and $y_k(t) \in R$ denote the state, control input, and output of system (1), separately. $f(\cdot, \cdot) \in R^w$, $B(t) \in R^w$ and $C(t) \in R^{1 \times w}$. The desired trajectory for system (1) is $y_d(t) = C(t)x_d(t)$, $t \in \{0, 1, \cdots, T_d + 1\}$, where $x_d(t)$ is the desired state. For the desired trajectory $y_d(t)$, assume that there exists an only desired input $u_d(t) \in R^w$, $t \in \{0, 1, \cdots, T_d\}$, such that:

$$\begin{cases} x_d(t+1) = f(x_d(t), t) + B(t)u_d(t) \\ y_d(t) = C(t)x_d(t) \end{cases} \tag{2}$$

For this discrete-time system (1), the tracking error can be outlined as $e_k(t) = y_d(t) - y_k(t)$, $t \in \{0, 1, \cdots, T_d + 1\}$.

**Assumption 1.** The starting condition $x_k(0)$ for iterations is subject to random variability, yet its mathematical expectation complies with:

$$E\{\|x_d(0) - x_k(0)\|\} = 0 \tag{3}$$

**Lemma 1.** Give a difference inequality:

$$g(t+1) \le h(t) + sg(t) \tag{4}$$

given that $g(t)$ and $h(t)$ are scalar functions dependent on $t \ge 0$, with $s$ represents a non-negative value, the ensuing result for $t \ge 1$ can be inferred:

$$g(t) \le \sum_{i=0}^{t-1} s^{t-i-1}h(i) + s^t g(0) \tag{5}$$

**Assumption 2.** Presuming the nonlinear function $f(\cdot, \cdot)$ in system (1) exhibits differentiability towards $t$ and maintains global Lipschitz continuity in its first variable, applicable to all instances of $t$ and $\forall \overline{x}(t), \overline{\overline{x}}(t) \in R^w$:

$$\left\| f(\overline{x}(t), t) - f(\overline{\overline{x}}(t), t) \right\| \leq k_f \left\| \overline{x}(t) - \overline{\overline{x}}(t) \right\| \tag{6}$$

where $k_f > 0$ is the Lipschitz constant.

## 3  ILC Design and Convergence Analysis

In this part, we consider the nonlinear discrete-time system (1) based on Assumptions 1–2, a P-type ILC control law is designed for $t \in \{0, 1, \cdots, T_d\}$.

$$u_{k+1}(t) = u_{f,k+1}(t) + u_{b,k+1}(t) \tag{7}$$

$$u_{f,k+1}(t) = u_k(t) + Pe_k(t+1) \tag{8}$$

$$u_{b,k+1}(t) = Le_{k+1}(t) \tag{9}$$

here, $u_{f,k+1}(t)$ denotes P-type ILC element incorporating a open-loop control gain of $P \in R$, while $u_{b,k+1}(t)$ refers to the closed-loop control element utilizing a closed-loop control gain of $L \in R$.

**Theorem 1.** If the control gains $P$ in (11) satisfy:

$$\|1 - PC(t+1)B(t)\| < 1 \tag{10}$$

then $\lim_{k \to \infty} E\{e_k(t)\} = 0$ for $t \in \{0, 1, \cdots T_d + 1\}$.

Defined $\Delta u_{f,k}(t) = u_d(t) - u_{f,k}(t)$, $\Delta u_k(t) = u_d(t) - u_k(t)$, $\Delta x_k(t) = x_d(t) - x_k(t)$. Deducting expression (8) from $u_d(t)$ on both sides, we obtain

$$\Delta u_{f,k+1}(t) = \Delta u_k(t) - Pe_k(t+1) \tag{11}$$

From (1), (2) and (11), we have

$$\Delta u_{f,k+1}(t) = \Delta u_k(t) - PC(t+1)\Delta x_k(t+1)$$

$$= \Delta u_k(t) - PC(t+1)(f(x_d(t), t) - f(x_k(t), t))$$

$$-PC(t+1)B(t)\Delta u_k(t) \tag{12}$$

From (7), (8) and (9), we have

$$\Delta u_k(t) = \Delta u_{f,k}(t) - Le_k(t) \tag{13}$$

Replacing (12) with (13), we obtain

$$\Delta u_{f,k+1}(t) = [1 - PC(t+1)B(t)]\Delta u_k(t) - PC(t+1)(f(x_d(t),t) - f(x_k(t),t))$$

$$= [1 - PC(t+1)B(t)]\Delta u_{f,k}(t) - [1 - PC(t+1)B(t)]Le_k(t)$$

$$-PC(t+1)(f(x_d(t),t) - f(x_k(t),t)) \tag{14}$$

Calculating the norm of both ends of expression (14) results in

$$\left\|\Delta u_{f,k+1}(t)\right\| \le \|[1 - PC(t+1)B(t)]\| \cdot \left\|\Delta u_{f,k}(t)\right\| +$$

$$\|[1 - PC(t+1)B(t)]L\| \cdot \|e_k(t)\| + \|PC(t+1)\| \cdot \|(f(x_d(t),t) - f(x_k(t),t))\| \tag{15}$$

Thus, expression (15) can be transformed into

$$\left\|\Delta u_{f,k+1}(t)\right\| \le \phi\left\|\Delta u_{f,k}(t)\right\| + z_1\|e_k(t)\| + z_1\|\Delta x_k(t)\| \tag{16}$$

here, $\phi = \|1 - PC(t+1)B(t)\|$, $z_1 = \max\{\|[1 - PC(t+1)B(t)]L\|, \|k_f PC(t+1)\|\}$.
According to (1), (2), (4) and (6), we can obtain

$$\|\Delta x_k(t)\| \le k_f\|\Delta x_k(t-1)\| + \|B(t-1)\| \cdot \|\Delta u_k(t-1)\| \tag{17}$$

According to (13) and (17), we obtain

$$\|\Delta x_k(t)\| \le k_f\|\Delta x_k(t-1)\| + \|B(t-1)\| \cdot \left\|\Delta u_{f,k}(t-1)\right\|$$

$$+\|B(t-1)\| \cdot \|L\| \cdot \|e_k(t-1)\| \tag{18}$$

According to (1), (2) and (18), we can obtain

$$\|e_k(t)\| \le \|C(t)\| \cdot \|\Delta x_k(t)\|$$

$$\le \|C(t)\|k_f\|\Delta x_k(t-1)\| + \|C(t)B(t-1)\| \cdot \left\|\Delta u_{f,k}(t-1)\right\|$$

$$+\|C(t)B(t-1)\| \cdot \|L\| \cdot \|e_k(t-1)\| \tag{19}$$

Adding both sides of (18) and (19), we get

$$\|\Delta x_k(t)\| + \|e_k(t)\| \le (k_f + k_f\|C(t)\|)\|\Delta x_k(t-1)\| + (1 + \|C(t)\|)\|B(t-1)\| \cdot \|L\| \cdot \|e_k(t-1)\|$$

$$+(\|B(t-1)\| + \|B(t-1)\| \cdot \|C(t)\|)\left\|\Delta u_{f,k}(t-1)\right\|$$

$$\le z_2(\|\Delta x_k(t-1)\| + \|e_k(t-1)\|) + \bar{b}\left\|\Delta u_{f,k}(t-1)\right\|$$

$$\leq z_2^t(\|\Delta x_k(0)\| + \|e_k(0)\|) + \sum_{s=0}^{t-1} z_2^{t-s-1} \overline{b} \|\Delta u_{f,k}(s)\|$$

$$\leq \sum_{s=0}^{t-1} z_2^{t-s-1} \overline{b} \|\Delta u_{f,k}(s)\| \tag{20}$$

where $z_2 = \max\{k_f + k_f\|C(t)\|, (1 + \|C(t)\|)\|B(t-1)\| \cdot \|L\|\}$ and
$\overline{b} = \|B(t-1)\| + \|B(t-1)\| \cdot \|C(t)\|$.

Substituting (20) into expression (16) and taking the expectation simultaneously, we obtain

$$E\{\|\Delta u_{f,k+1}(t)\|\} \leq E\{\phi\}E\{\|\Delta u_{f,k}(t)\|\} + z_1 \sum_{s=0}^{t-1} z_2^{t-s-1} \overline{b} E\{\|\Delta u_{f,k}(s)\|\} \tag{21}$$

Let $z_3 = \left\|z_1 z_2^{t-s-1} \overline{b}\right\|$, expression (21) can be transformed into

$$E\{\|\Delta u_{f,k+1}(t)\|\} \leq E\{\phi\}E\{\|\Delta u_{f,k}(t)\|\} + z_3 \sum_{s=0}^{t-1} E\{\|\Delta u_{f,k}(s)\|\} \tag{22}$$

Using mathematical induction to prove as follows:

When $t = 0$, we can obtain from expression (22) and under the condition of Assumption 1 that

$$E\{\|\Delta u_{f,k+1}(0)\|\} \leq E\{\phi\}E\{\|\Delta u_{f,k}(0)\|\} \tag{23}$$

When $E\{\phi\} < 1$, as the iterations $k$ tend toward an extremely high number

$$\lim_{k \to \infty} E\{\|\Delta u_{f,k+1}(0)\|\} = 0 \tag{24}$$

When $t = 1$, we can obtain from expression (22) and under the condition of Assumption 1 that

$$E\{\|\Delta u_{f,k+1}(1)\|\} \leq E\{\phi\}E\{\|\Delta u_{f,k}(1)\|\} + z_3 E\{\|\Delta u_{f,k}(0)\|\} \tag{25}$$

Considering expression (24) and Theorem 1, we obtain

$$\lim_{k \to \infty} E\{\|\Delta u_{f,k+1}(1)\|\} = 0 \tag{26}$$

Assuming $t = 2, ..., m - 1$, we have

$$\lim_{k \to \infty} E\{\|\Delta u_{f,k}(t)\|\} = 0 \tag{27}$$

When $t = m$, we can obtain from expression (22) that

$$E\{\|\Delta u_{f,k+1}(m)\|\} \leq E\{\phi\}E\{\|\Delta u_{f,k}(m)\|\} + z_3 \sum_{s=0}^{m-1} E\{\|\Delta u_{f,k}(s)\|\} \tag{28}$$

As the iterations $k$ approaches infinity, we can obtain $\lim\limits_{k\to\infty} E\{\|\Delta u_{f,k+1}(t)\|\} = 0$, so

$$\lim_{k\to\infty} E\{\|\Delta u_{f,k}(t)\|\} = 0 \tag{29}$$

Evidently, this leads to.

$$\lim_{k\to\infty} E\{e_k(t)\} = 0, \ t \in \{0, 1, \cdots, T_d + 1\} \tag{30}$$

This concludes is proved.

## 4 DE-ILC Scheme Design

The proposed method's asymptotic convergence is presented in the third part. It is well known that the convergence performance is greatly influenced by the control gains. In this section, the integration of the DE algorithm into the proposed P-type open-closed-loop ILC law (7) aims to optimize the control gain, thereby minimizing the required iterations for system convergence as cited in [10].

DE refers to an intelligent optimization algorithm that mimics biological evolution to find the best solution. The core concept of DE-ILC can be outlined as follows:

(1) First, set the control gain coefficients in the ILC control law to by $P$ and $L$, initialize them as the initial population $\lambda = \begin{bmatrix} P & L \end{bmatrix}$ and encode them.
(2) According to the convergence condition (10), we get the initial population, without losing the generality, we assume that the initial population is even, and the representation of the variable vector for each individual within population $h$-th is denoted by $\lambda_h = \begin{bmatrix} P_h & L_h \end{bmatrix} \in R^{1\times 2}$, in order to assess the individual dominance in the population, the fitness function $fit_h(\lambda_h) = A - E_h(\lambda_h)$ is introduced, where $A$ is a sufficiently large number, $E_h(\lambda_h) = \sum\limits_{t=0}^{29} |y_d(t) - Y_h(t, \lambda_h)|, (T_d = 29)$.
(3) Then, we adopt a random mutation strategy for the initial population, the mutagenic factor is $0 < F < 1$, generate a new offspring population, calculate its fitness value through the fitness function, screen out the excellent population individuals, and proceed to the next step.
(4) The excellent population individuals screened after mutation are cross-operated, the crossed factor is $0 < CR < 1$, and generate a random number within the range of 0 to 1, and when this number exceeds the crossed factor threshold, a new offspring population is generated.
(5) After the cross-operation is left, the fitness value is calculated through the fitness function, the best population individual is retained, and whether to proceed to the next operation is judged by the termination conditions.
(6) The termination condition within the algorithm relies on both fitness value and tracking error. The algorithm iterates through a hundred population generations, eventually deriving optimal control gains $P$ and $L$ from the most favorable individual generated by DE algorithm. Refer to Fig. 1 for the flowchart illustrating DE-ILC.

## 5   Illustrative Simulation

To assess the efficacy of the suggested DE-ILC approach, let's examine a DC motor drive system governed by the dynamics of the subsequent nonlinear control system:

$$\left(Q_m + \frac{Q_e}{n^2}\right)\ddot{\theta}_m + \left(C_m + \frac{C_e}{n^2}\right)\dot{\theta}_m + \frac{Mgl}{n}\sin\frac{\theta_m}{n} = u \tag{31}$$

here, $\theta_m$ represents motor angle, $Q_m$ stands for motor inertia, $Q_e$ denotes link inertia, $C_m$ signifies motor damping coefficient, $C_e$ represents link damping coefficient, $n$ denotes gear ratio, $u$ stands for motor torque, $M$ represents lumped mass, $g$ symbolizes gravitational acceleration, and $l$ represents the center of mass distance from motion axis.

The system is discretized, and the discrete-time state-space expression of (31) incorporating $x_k^{(1)} = \theta_m$, $x_k^{(2)} = \dot{\theta}_m$ and $y_k = \frac{1}{n}\dot{\theta}_m$ is as follows:

$$\begin{cases} x_k^{(1)}(t+1) = x_k^{(1)}(t) + \Delta x_k^{(2)}(t) \\ x_k^{(2)}(t+1) = -\frac{\Delta Mgl}{n\left(Q_m + Q_e/n^2\right)}\sin\frac{x_k^{(1)}(t)}{n} + \left[1 - \frac{\Delta\left(C_m + C_e/n^2\right)}{Q_m + Q_e/n^2}\right]x_k^{(2)}(t) + \frac{\Delta}{Q_m + Q_e/n^2}u_k(t) \\ y_k(t) = \frac{x_k^{(2)}(t)}{n} \end{cases} \tag{32}$$

here, $\Delta$ is the sampling time. In simulation, let $\Delta = 0.05(s)$, $t \in \{0, 1, \ldots, T_d\}$. Other parameters are set as follows: $Q_m = 0.3$, $Q_e = 0.44$, $M = 0.5$, $g = 9.8$, $C_m = 0.3$, $C_e = 0.25$, $n = 1.6$ and $l = 0.15$ [11].

Within the experimental setup, let $u_0(t) = u_1(t) = 0$, $(0 \le t \le T_d)$ with $T_d = 29$. The designated reference path is denoted as:

$$y_d(t) = \sin\left(\frac{\pi t}{15}\right), \quad (0 \le t \le T_d + 1) \tag{33}$$

The DE-ILC algorithm determines control gains $P$ and $L$ through the DE method, Considering mutagenic factor $F = 0.3$ and crossed factor $CR = 0.7$. Evaluating tracking performance involves defining two tracking indexes, namely the sum absolute error $SE_k$ and total square error $TE_k$ as follows:

$$SE_k = \sum_{t=0}^{30} |e_k(t)| \tag{34}$$

$$TE_k = \sum_{t=0}^{30} [e_k(t)]^2 \tag{35}$$

The DE-ILC is executed in simulation for 10 iterations, and the resultant optimized control gains are tabulated in Table 1.

To assess the convergence speed disparity between DE-ILC and conventional ILC with varying parameters, two distinct cases were chosen for comparison. Case 1: $P = 0.5$, $L = 0.3$. Case 2: $P = 0.6$, $L = 0.2$. Figure 2 displays the corresponding sum absolute error $SE_k$, while Fig. 3 illustrates the total square error $TE_k$ for tracking. Observing these figures reveals that higher control gains $P$ and $L$ are contribute to faster convergence in conventional ILC. Additionally, the proposed DE-ILC method distinctly demonstrates fewer convergence iterations compared to conventional ILC of similar order.

**Table 1.** Optimized control gains achieved by DE-ILC vary at different instances.

| Times | P | L |
|---|---|---|
| 1 | 0.8036 | 0.3032 |
| 2 | 0.8577 | 0.3516 |
| 3 | 0.8655 | 0.3950 |
| 4 | 0.8656 | 0.3706 |
| 5 | 0.8842 | 0.3533 |
| 6 | 0.8679 | 0.3097 |
| 7 | 0.8280 | 0.3105 |
| 8 | 0.8136 | 0.3132 |
| 9 | 0.8455 | 0.3850 |
| 10 | 0.8758 | 0.3823 |
| Average | 0.8507 | 0.3475 |

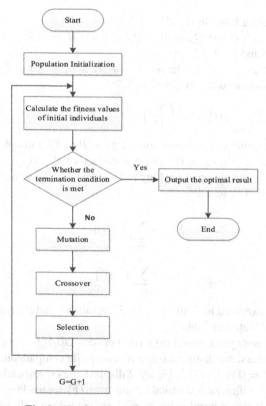

**Fig. 1.** The flowchart of the proposed DE-ILC.

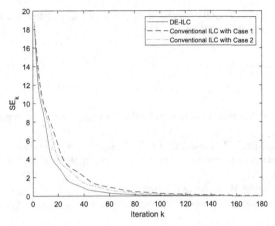

**Fig. 2.** The tracking indexes $SE_k$ at various iterations obtained through DE-ILC and conventional ILC in two distinct cases.

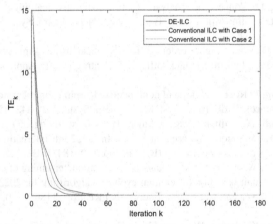

**Fig. 3.** The tracking indexes $TE_k$ at various iterations obtained through DE-ILC and conventional ILC in two distinct cases.

## 6  Conclusion

This study introduces a differential evolution algorithm-based open-closed-loop iterative learning control (ILC) approach. The proposed ILC method utilizes feedback information to adapt the system, ensures stability control through closed-loop regulation, and continuously enhances the control algorithm for error correction during tracking. The convergence process of ILC can be expedited through the adjustment of feedback control gains, guaranteeing system reliability and stability. To achieve the suitable closed-loop control gain, the feedforward and feedback ILC law is enhanced using the differential evolution algorithm. This guarantees rapid convergence while upholding system stability. After conducting theoretical analysis and simulation, the tracking error tends to approach zero in mathematical expectation [12, 13].

**Acknowledgments.** This research received backing from the Graduate Basic Innovation Project of Guangzhou University (No. 2022GDJC-M23).

# References

1. Shen, D., Wang, Y.: Survey on stochastic iterative learning control. J. Process. Control. **24**(12), 64–77 (2014)
2. Dong, J., He, B., Ming, M., Zhang, C., Li, G.: Design of open-closed-loop iterative learning control with variable stiffness for multiple flexible manipulator robot systems. IEEE Access **7**, 23163–23168 (2019)
3. Li, X., Shen, D., Ding, B.: Iterative learning control for output tracking of nonlinear systems with unavailable state information. IEEE Trans. Neural Netw. Learn. Syst. **33**(9), 5085–5092 (2021)
4. Wang, L., Yu, J., Zhang, R., Li, P., Gao, F.: Iterative learning control for multiphase batch processes with asynchronous switching. IEEE Trans. Syst. Man Cybern. Syst. **51**(4), 2536–2549 (2019)
5. Zhang, J., Meng, D.: Convergence analysis of saturated iterative learning control systems with locally Lipschitz nonlinearities. IEEE Trans. Neural Netw. Learn. Syst. **31**(10), 4025–4035 (2019)
6. Wei, Y.S., Li, X.D.: Robust higher-order ILC for non-linear discrete-time systems with varying trail lengths and random initial state shifts. IET Control Theory Appl. **11**(15), 2440–2447 (2017)
7. Meng, D., Zhang, J.: Robust tracking of nonrepetitive learning control systems with iteration-dependent references. IEEE Trans. Syst. Man Cybern. Syst. **51**(2), 842–852 (2018)
8. Yalçin, O., Canli, A., Yilmaz, A.R., Erkmen, B.: Robust tuning of PID controller using differential evolution algorithm based on FPGA. In: 2022 9th International Conference on Electrical and Electronics Engineering (ICEEE), pp. 180–184. IEEE, March 2022
9. Zhang, J., Wu, P., Wang, X., Yu, X., Duan, S.: PID parameter tuning of combined heat and power generation unit based on differential evolution algorithm. In: 2022 7th International Conference on Power and Renewable Energy (ICPRE). pp. 1186–1190. IEEE, September 2022
10. Wei, Y.S., Yang, X., Shang, W., Chen, Y.Y.: Higher-order iterative learning control with optimal control gains based on evolutionary algorithm for nonlinear system. Complexity **2021**, 1–9 (2021)
11. Zhang, Y., Liu, J., Ruan, X.: Iterative learning control for uncertain nonlinear networked control systems with random packet dropout. Int. J. Robust Nonlinear Control **29**(11), 3529–3546 (2019)
12. Zhao, Z., Liu, Z.: Finite-time convergence disturbance rejection control for a flexible Timoshenko manipulator. IEEE/CAA Journal of Automatica Sinica **8**(1), 157–168 (2020)
13. Wan, K., Li, X.D.: Robust iterative learning control of 2-D linear discrete FMMII systems subject to iteration-dependent uncertainties. IEEE Trans. Syst. Man Cybern. Syst. **51**(10), 5949–5961 (2019)

# Overview of Vehicle Edge Computing and Its Security

Shaodong Han⬥, Maojie Wang⬥, and Guihong Chen(✉)⬥

Guangdong Polytechnic Normal University, Guangzhou 510635, China
chenguihong@gpnu.edu.cn

**Abstract.** The Internet of Vehicles (IoV) is a part of the Internet of Things (IoT). With the continuous development of the Internet of Things technology, the Internet of Vehicles technology has also made great progress. However, as more and more vehicles are connected to the Internet of Vehicles, the calculation and transmission of data in the Internet of Vehicles becomes more and more difficult, and at the same time, it is inevitable to face the pressure of data security and privacy protection. In order to solve the above problems, academia and industry have adopted many methods, combining mobile edge computing technology with the Internet of Vehicles to establish a vehicle edge computing network to solve the problems of data computing and transmission. Introducing blockchain technology and federated learning technology into vehicle edge computing. Therefore, the network addresses the issues of data security and privacy protection. Based on these, this paper summarizes the research results of many scholars in related fields, in order to provide reference and reference for subsequent related research.

**Keywords:** Vehicle edge computing · Reinforcement learning · Federated learning

## 1 Introduction

With the rapid growth of the automotive industry, particularly in the field of new energy vehicles, and the advancement of the internet industry with artificial intelligence at its forefront, the market has witnessed the emergence of intelligent connected vehicles, giving rise to a thriving industry. These vehicles are equipped with a range of sensors such as LiDAR, ultrasonic sensors, and cameras, significantly enhancing their perception of the surrounding environment. Additionally, intelligent connected vehicles possess robust communication capabilities, facilitating communication between vehicles, pedestrians, infrastructure,

The work is supported in part by Key Research Projects of Universities in Guangdong Province under Grant 2022ZDZX1011, Guangdong Provincial Natural Science Fund Project under Grant 2023A1515011084 and Doctoral Program Construction Unit Research Capability Enhancement Project at Guangdong Polytechnic Normal University under Grant 22GPNUZDJS27.

J. Cai et al. (Eds.): SPNCE 2023, LNICST 525, pp. 105–121, 2025.
https://doi.org/10.1007/978-3-031-73699-5_8

and servers [50]. Together, these interconnected networks form the Internet of Vehicles (IoV) system, providing convenient transportation solutions. This system has given rise to numerous applications, including in-vehicle entertainment, navigation and positioning, and autonomous driving, resulting in a substantial amount of data generation. Consequently, vehicles must not only process this data in real-time but also transmit and exchange it with the surrounding environment to deliver high-quality applications [39].

However, vehicles encounter several challenges in dealing with and transmitting large volumes of data [29] [20]. Firstly, the onboard computer systems' computational capacity is insufficient to support real-time processing of substantial data. Secondly, the high mobility of vehicles poses significant obstacles to communication with surrounding infrastructure. Lastly, the data transmission process during communication between vehicles and the surrounding infrastructure is inherently vulnerable to security threats, including attacks and data breaches. Addressing these challenges has prompted scholars to propose various solutions.

To address the issue of inadequate computing capabilities in vehicles, researchers have proposed integrating Mobile Edge Computing (MEC) with the Internet of Vehicles (IoV), resulting in a new computing paradigm called Vehicle Edge Computing (VEC) [4]. The VEC architecture, depicted in Fig 1, involves offloading computation tasks from vehicles to edge servers for processing. The computation results are then returned to the vehicles, combined with local computation results, and used to obtain the final outcome. This approach effectively alleviates the computational burden on vehicles, significantly enhancing the efficiency of IoV applications and improving the overall driving experience for users [22,25,34].

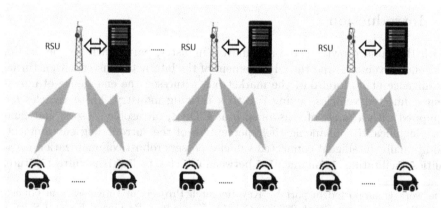

**Fig. 1.** Vehicle edge computing architecture

However, the introduction of vehicle edge computing necessitates careful consideration of the impact of vehicle mobility on communication latency, energy consumption, and communication quality within the IoV. Furthermore, the computation latency and energy consumption of both vehicles and servers during task processing must be taken into account. Only by comprehensively addressing these issues can an efficient system architecture be established, and suitable algorithms be formulated. In practical applications, it is crucial to adopt well-designed computation offloading schemes to minimize communication latency, energy consumption, as well as computation latency and energy consumption. To achieve an optimal computation offloading scheme, researchers have proposed various optimization methods, including those based on Reinforcement Learning (RL) [2].

Addressing the data security challenges in vehicle edge computing, the integration of blockchain technology and Federated Learning (FL) techniques with VEC has garnered significant attention [23]. Blockchain technology, known for its security features such as anonymity and tamper-proof properties of on-chain data, naturally enhances the security of vehicle edge computing [9]. Federated Learning, on the other hand, is an emerging machine learning approach that enables multiple users to collaboratively train a shared model. Participants maintain their data privacy by transmitting only the computed model parameters without sharing their local data [17]. This characteristic aligns with the data security requirements of vehicle edge computing, making it feasible to combine federated learning with VEC to establish a secure IoV system.

At present, research in relevant fields has reached a high level of maturity, with various advanced achievements continually emerging. Our objective is to provide a targeted summary of existing research outcomes to assist researchers in understanding the current state of research in these areas. This paper presents a comprehensive overview of edge computing offloading solutions in vehicular networks based on reinforcement learning. Additionally, we focus on summarizing research solutions that employ blockchain and federated learning for safeguarding the privacy and security of shared vehicular data. This will enable researchers in these domains to quickly grasp the current status and accomplishments of related research, thereby gaining inspiration for advancing their own research and proposing more advanced solutions.

The specific content of this paper is as follows: Sect. 2 will introduce an optimization scheme for vehicle edge computing offloading based on reinforcement learning methods. Section 3 will present a data security solution by integrating vehicle edge computing with blockchain technology. The data security solution combining federated learning and vehicle edge computing will be detailed in Sect. 4. Section 5 will highlight some future research directions for vehicle edge computing. Finally, Sect. 6 will provide a summary of the entire paper.

## 2   Reinforcement Learning-Based Offloading Optimization

In the vehicle edge computing network, the dynamic nature of vehicles in a mobile state during computation offloading tasks significantly impacts the network's topology. This dynamicity introduces variations in communication latency and signal-to-noise ratio, which, in turn, influence the formulation of optimal offloading strategies. Moreover, many tasks have strict time constraints, requiring offloaded computations to be completed within specified deadlines. This entails ensuring that the sum of local computation time on vehicles and the edge server's computation time is less than the task's response time. Furthermore, energy constraints must be considered due to the limited energy resources available in vehicles. Therefore, it is essential to account for energy consumption during communication and computation tasks on vehicles [19].

To obtain an optimal offloading solution, multiple factors need to be considered, including channel bandwidth, signal-to-noise ratio, communication latency, energy consumption, computation latency, energy consumption, as well as vehicle mobility. An optimal solution should minimize communication latency and energy consumption, along with computation latency and energy consumption. Consequently, finding the optimal offloading solution becomes a multi-objective optimization decision problem. In this regard, reinforcement learning methods prove to be one of the most effective approaches for tackling this challenge.

Reinforcement learning, depicted in Fig 2, is a method that enables an intelligent agent to engage in continuous interactions with the environment, gathering experiences and learning the optimal solution to a sequential decision-making

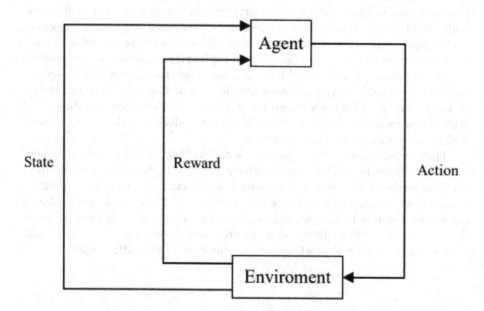

**Fig. 2.** Interactive process of reinforcement learning

**Table 1.** The publication years and main contributions of reinforcement learning based papers

| Paper | Year of publication | Main contributions |
| --- | --- | --- |
| paper[45] | 2020 | Proposing a multi-vehicle user optimization algorithm that integrates deep reinforcement learning with convex optimization. |
| paper[25] | 2019 | Developing a task offloading algorithm for vehicular networking tasks solely using the DQN algorithm. |
| paper[31] | 2023 | Proposing a multi-step reinforcement learning-based vehicle edge computation offloading scheme. |
| paper[22] | 2019 | Abstracting vehicle edge computing offloading and resource allocation as a semi-Markov process and employed both deep reinforcement learning and Q-Learning algorithms to obtain the optimal offloading strategy. |
| paper[28] | 2018 | Proposing a knowledge-driven (KD) offloading decision algorithm. |
| paper[35] | 2021 | Proposing a highly reliable vehiclar edge computing offloading decision network. |
| paper[37] | 2021 | Designing a multi-access vehicular edge computing network utilizing MEC technology. |
| paper[26] | 2020 | Proposing a joint optimization scheme for computation and caching in future 5G vehicular networks. |
| paper[44] | 2021 | Employing digital twin technology to build a virtual model mirroring real vehicle networks, and using a distributed multi-agent reinforcement learning algorithm to obtain the optimal offloading decisions. |
| paper[40] | 2020 | Proposing a deep reinforcement learning-based digital twin service offloading algorithm. |

problem [6]. The determination of vehicle edge computing offloading solutions follows a similar sequential decision-making process. Treating the vehicle as an intelligent agent, it interacts with the environment comprising channel bandwidth, communication latency and energy consumption, computation latency and energy consumption, and signal-to-noise ratio, in order to obtain an optimal offloading solution. To achieve this objective, various non-deep reinforcement learning methods and deep reinforcement learning (DRL) methods can be employed, with DRL methods being widely favored for their superior performance [12,15,32,43]. Besides, in the remainder of this section, we present some of the related papers in detail. The publication years and main contributions of these literatures are shown in Table 1.

Zhang et al. proposed a multi-vehicle user optimization algorithm that integrates deep reinforcement learning with convex optimization [45]. This algorithm utilizes the Deep Q Network (DQN) to make offloading decisions, and then applies the Lagrange multiplier method to allocate the edge server's computing capacity among multiple users, thereby achieving an optimal offloading allocation scheme. Simulation results demonstrate that this approach reduces system latency to only 56% compared to traditional methods. Additionally, deep reinforcement learning methods can also be used independently, delivering satisfactory performance. For example, Ning et al. developed a task offloading algorithm for vehicular networking tasks solely using the DQN algorithm. Performance analysis and experimental results confirm the efficiency and effectiveness of this approach [25]. Han et al. proposed a multi-step reinforcement learning-based vehicle edge computation offloading scheme. They create a two layer VEC architecture, and use an improved algorithm multi-step DQN (MSDQN) to obtain the optimal decision. Simulation results demonstrate that MSDQN-based algorithm can reduce the offloading latency and energy consumption [31].

Liu et al. abstracted vehicle edge computing offloading and resource allocation as a semi-Markov process and employed both deep reinforcement learning and Q-Learning algorithms to obtain the optimal offloading strategy [22]. Experimental results demonstrated that utilizing these algorithms yielded the best offloading strategies, surpassing the efficiency of local computing on vehicles for executing vehicular networking computing tasks. To account for vehicle mobility during the edge computing offloading process, Qi et al. proposed a knowledge-driven (KD) offloading decision algorithm [28]. This algorithm comprehensively considers three major factors: resource requirements, access networks, and vehicle mobility. It utilizes the A3C algorithm for online offloading optimization decision-making. The algorithm incorporates the vehicle's mobility while traveling and accessing different edge computing nodes, leading to varying task computation times. This model is directly applied to the training and learning process of optimal offloading decisions. Simulation experiments demonstrate that the algorithm delivers faster offloading decisions and exhibits strong applicability.

As the number of vehicles in the vehicular network increases, the network's complexity rises, resulting in longer offloading transmission times, higher energy consumption, decreased Quality of Service (QoS), and reduced network reliability. To tackle this challenge, a highly reliable vehicular edge computing offloading decision network has been proposed [35]. This network integrates vehicle edge computing with Software Defined Networking (SDN) to offer a reliable approach for network control and resource management. It encompasses computation, communication, and privacy protection models, and introduces a joint strategy for offloading and resource allocation. The Q-Learning algorithm is employed to explore optimal decisions.

With the continuous advancement of communication technologies, such as 5G, new-generation communication technologies have been applied to vehicular networking. In response, scholars have proposed vehicular edge computing offloading schemes based on 5G networks. Notably, Multi-access Edge Computing (MEC) technology plays a vital role in 5G networks. Wu et al. designed a multi-access vehicular edge computing network utilizing MEC technology [37]. Their approach takes into account multiple tasks concurrency, system computing resource distribution, and network communication bandwidth. They propose a joint optimization algorithm for computation offloading and task migration based on the DQN algorithm. This algorithm effectively reduces task processing latency and device energy consumption compared to traditional methods. It optimizes computation offloading and resource allocation approaches, thereby enhancing system resource utilization.

Ning et al. proposed a joint optimization scheme for computation and caching in future 5G vehicular networks [26]. This scheme takes into account the revenue of Mobile Network Operators (MNOs) and users' usage experience. They designed a joint optimization algorithm based on the Deep Deterministic Policy Gradient (DDPG) algorithm to maximize the profit of MNOs. To address the challenges encountered by vehicular edge computing in real-world environments, some researchers have introduced digital twin technology to create innovative vehicular edge computing networks. Zhang et al. employed digital twin technology to build a virtual model mirroring real vehicle networks, effectively illustrating the connectivity relationships among vehicles. With this model in place, a distributed multi-agent reinforcement learning algorithm is utilized to determine the optimal offloading decisions, minimizing offloading costs. Experimental results demonstrate the superiority of this method over traditional offloading algorithms [44].

To enhance the effectiveness of vehicular edge computing empowered by digital twins, regular updates to the digital twin network of vehicles are crucial for providing improved computing services. However, relying solely on the vehicles' computing capabilities is insufficient to support a wide range of digital twin services. To address this, Xu et al. proposed a deep reinforcement learning-based digital twin service offloading algorithm [40]. This algorithm employs the DQN algorithm to determine the optimal offloading strategy that meets the Quality of Service (QoS) requirements of various digital twin services. Experimental results highlight the effectiveness and applicability of this algorithm in diverse environments.

In this section, we have enumerated various edge computing data offloading solutions for vehicular networks based on reinforcement learning methods, all of which serve to enhance the efficiency of edge computing in vehicular networks. However, vehicular edge computing involves transmitting data in a completely open environment when establishing communication connections, making it highly susceptible to various network attacks that can compromise the security of data transmission and potentially lead to data privacy breaches. To address this issue and ensure the confidentiality, integrity, and availability of vehicular network data, blockchain technology and federated learning techniques can be employed.

## 3    Security Offload Optimization Combined with Blockchain

Ensuring data privacy and security is crucial for the widespread adoption of vehicular edge computing and vehicular networking, which is not addressed in the previous section. However, leveraging blockchain technology can serve as a valuable tool to safeguard the privacy and security of vehicle edge computing data [13].

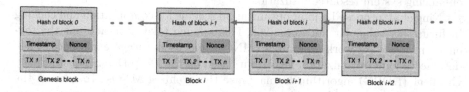

**Fig. 3.** A typical blockchain structure [49]

In 2008, Satoshi Nakamoto published the paper "Bitcoin: A Peer-to-Peer Electronic Cash System," introducing the concept of blockchain [24]. The structure of a typical blockchain is illustrated in Fig 3. Blockchain can be described as an encrypted distributed digital ledger, characterized by decentralization, immutability, traceability, and the participation of multiple parties. It establishes trust among untrusted nodes through consensus mechanisms like Proof-of-Work (PoW) and Proof-of-Stake (PoS), enabling data sharing and peer-to-peer transmission. These properties have led to the widespread adoption of blockchain in environments where data protection is crucial. Vehicular edge computing, as a use case requiring data security and privacy, can leverage blockchain technology for data protection. Scholars have conducted research on this topic and proposed methods to address related issues [1,5,14,36]. Some literatures are listed in detail below, and their publication years and main contributions are shown in the Table 2.

Zhang et al. presented a blockchain-based three-tier security architecture for vehicular edge computing [46]. This architecture consists of the perception layer, edge computing layer, and service layer. The perception layer ensures secure data transmission through the use of blockchain. The edge computing layer provides computing resources and edge cloud services for the perception layer, while the service layer combines traditional cloud storage with blockchain to ensure data security. Zhang et al. introduced a consortium blockchain-based scheme called Data Security Sharing and Storage for Connected Vehicles (DSSCB) [47]. This scheme establishes a decentralized, secure, and reliable database using a consortium blockchain. It employs digital signature technology to ensure the reliability and integrity of transmitted data. Smart contracts are utilized to set conditions for participating nodes during data transmission and storage, and tokens are allocated to vehicles contributing data. Experimental results demonstrate that this method significantly enhances data security compared to traditional approaches. Considering the vulnerability of shared vehicular data to attacks, Singh et al. proposed a blockchain-based trusted data sharing environment [33]. This environment utilizes a blockchain backbone to ensure accuracy and reliability during the transmission of vehicular data.

**Table 2.** The publication years and main contributions of blockchain based papers

| Paper | Year of publication | Main contributions |
|---|---|---|
| paper[46] | 2018 | Presenting a blockchain-based three-tier security architecture for vehicular edge computing. |
| paper[47] | 2019 | Introducing a consortium blockchain-based scheme called Data Security Sharing and Storage for Connected Vehicles. |
| paper[33] | 2017 | Proposing a blockchain-based trusted data sharing environment. |
| paper[3] | 2020 | Proposing a blockchain-driven distributed secure content forwarding and storage framework. |
| paper[30] | 2021 | Developing a blockchain system using the PBFT consensus machanism for offloading and migration of vehicular edge computing services. |
| paper[18] | 2018 | Proposing a secure blockchain system based on the Proof of Work (POW) consensus mechanism for vehicular cloud computing and edge computing. |
| paper[10] | 2018 | Proposing a secure data storage and sharing scheme in a vehicular edge computing network using a consortium blockchain and smart contracts. |
| paper[8] | 2020 | Utilizing the computational resources of parked vehicles for vehicular edge computing and introduce blockchain technology to address security issues in practical applications. |

The combination of vehicular edge computing and blockchain ensures data security during offloading tasks, leveraging reinforcement learning, particularly deep reinforcement learning, to obtain optimal offloading strategies. Once the optimal strategy is determined, data transmission takes place using blockchain technology to preserve data privacy and security.

Building upon this concept, Dai et al. proposed a blockchain-driven distributed secure content forwarding and storage framework. This framework utilizes a deep reinforcement learning algorithm based on DDPG to obtain the optimal allocation scheme. It employs an encrypted blockchain for content storage and forwarding, with a custom consensus mechanism called Proof of Utility (PoU) designed specifically for their scheme. The PoU mechanism achieves consensus on blocks based on the different utilities possessed by nodes executing offloading tasks [3]. In addition to custom consensus mechanisms, traditional consensus mechanisms can also be employed. Ren et al. developed a blockchain system using the PBFT consensus mechanism for offloading and migration of vehicular edge computing services. SDN technology is utilized to partition and manage the vehicular edge computing network, and a deep reinforcement learning algorithm based on A3C is incorporated to obtain an optimal offloading strategy for secure and efficient task offloading and migration [30]. Liu et al. proposed a secure blockchain system based on the Proof of Work (PoW) consensus mechanism for vehicular cloud computing and edge computing. Inspired by blockchain-based virtual currencies, their system introduces data coins and energy coins obtained based on data contribution frequency and energy contribution, respectively, to implement PoW and acquire tokens. Experimental results support the secure realization of vehicular cloud computing and edge computing, demonstrating the effectiveness of their approach [18].

Incorporating smart contracts into vehicular edge computing systems is an essential aspect of leveraging the full potential of blockchain technology. Smart contracts are event-driven, stateful code and algorithm contracts [48]. The following section introduces a vehicular edge computing system that incorporates smart contracts. Kang et al. proposed a secure data storage and sharing scheme in a vehicular edge computing network using a consortium blockchain and smart contracts [10]. This scheme utilizes a consortium blockchain to establish a distributed system for secure management of vehicular data. Smart contracts are employed to achieve secure and efficient data storage and sharing. The Three-weight Subjective Logic (TWSL) model is adopted to select more reliable data sources and enhance data trustworthiness. Huang et al. utilize the computational resources of parked vehicles for vehicular edge computing and introduce blockchain technology to address security issues in practical applications [8]. They establish a distributed vehicular edge computing network using blockchain technology. This network utilizes smart contracts to automate upload tasks, return results, and verify the tasks and results. To obtain the optimal contract, this approach employs a reinforcement learning algorithm based on the Stackelberg game. Security analysis and experimental results demonstrate that the algorithm provides high security and efficiency guarantees.

## 4    Offload Optimization Scheme Combined with Federated Learning

Federated learning is a distributed machine learning approach introduced by Google in 2016 to address the issue of updating models on Android mobile devices locally. It has gained widespread adoption in the field of artificial intelligence research and effectively tackles the problem of "data silos." Data silos refer to the isolation of data owned by different entities due to privacy and confidentiality concerns, resulting in a lack of data sharing [11]. In the context of federated learning, participating users retain their data locally, eliminating the need to upload it to cloud or edge servers during training. Only the locally trained model parameters are uploaded, forming a shared aggregated model when combined with the parameters from other users [42]. These uploaded model parameters are continuously updated to achieve the training objective, breaking down data silos. Additionally, federated learning can be utilized in scenarios that require privacy protection, such as vehicular edge computing, to preserve privacy. By combining vehicular edge computing with federated learning, it becomes possible to establish a robust and privacy-preserving framework for secure vehicular edge computing. This approach allows for the retention of data locally on vehicles, ensuring privacy, while enabling collaborative model training. The general architecture of a vehicle edge federated learning system is illustrated in Fig 4. Many scholars have adopted methods based on federated learning to protect data privacy for vehicle edge computing such as [7,16,21]. Some literatures are

**Table 3.** The publication years and main contributions of federated learning based papers

| Paper | Year of publication | Main contributions |
|---|---|---|
| paper[23] | 2020 | Proposing a blockchain-driven asynchronous federated learing scheme for secure data sharing in the vehicular Internet of Things. |
| paper[27] | 2021 | Proposing a differential privacy-based federated learning scheme for resilient vehicular networks. |
| paper[51] | 2021 | Employing federated learning in 6G-based vehicular network to achieve the aggregation of heterogeneous models. |
| paper[38] | 2021 | Proposing a vehicle selection and resource optimization scheme to select vehicles participate federated learning. |
| paper[41] | 2020 | Proposing a selective model aggregaation algorithm that focuses on a commonly employed task in vehicular networks which is image classification. |

listed in detail below, and their publication years and main contributions are shown in the Table 3.

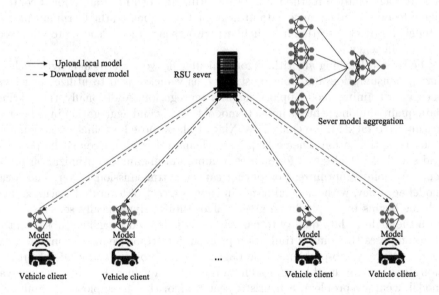

**Fig. 4.** General architecture of vehicle edge federated learning system

Lu et al. proposed a blockchain-driven asynchronous federated learning scheme for secure data sharing in the vehicular Internet of Things [23]. This scheme utilizes a blockchain system, consisting of a confidential privacy blockchain and a local Directed Acyclic Graph (DAG), to enhance the security and reliability of model parameters. The scheme employs a reinforcement learning algorithm based on the actor-critic network to select efficient nodes for establishing an asynchronous federated learning model. Experimental results demonstrate that the scheme achieves high learning accuracy and convergence speed. In addition to integrating with blockchain systems, federated learning algorithms can be combined with other privacy protection methods, such as differential privacy, to further enhance security and privacy. Olowononi et al. proposed a differential privacy-based federated learning scheme for resilient vehicular networks [27]. This scheme combines federated learning and differential privacy to enhance the resilience and attack resistance of vehicular networks. Experimental results show that the scheme improves the resilience, i.e., the ability to withstand attacks, of vehicular networks.

Federated learning, as an emerging technology, finds applications not only in traditional vehicular edge computing environments but also in vehicular edge computing networks based on future wireless communication environments, such as 6G networks. Zhou et al. employed federated learning in 6G-based vehicular networks to achieve the aggregation of heterogeneous models [51]. They designed a novel two-layer federated learning architecture specifically tailored for 6G vehicular networks. This architecture aims to improve learning accuracy while preserving privacy. The authors also developed a multi-layer model selection and aggregation method, effectively utilizing both local and global contextual information to enhance data utilization. Consequently, the learning time for intelligent object detection in vehicular networks is reduced, leading to improved system efficiency.

Federated learning algorithms for vehicular networks face challenges such as energy consumption and time constraints, as vehicles need to utilize their own energy for training, model uploading, and aggregation. Additionally, the varying data quality among vehicles impacts model training and aggregation in federated learning. To tackle these challenges, Xiao et al. proposed a vehicle selection and resource optimization scheme [38]. The scheme takes into account the position and speed of vehicles and formulates a minimum-maximum optimization problem that jointly optimizes computing capacity, transmission power, and local model accuracy, with the goal of minimizing the cost of federated learning. The scheme begins by employing a greedy algorithm to dynamically select vehicles with the highest data quality to participate in federated learning. Subsequently, it decomposes the joint optimization problem into resource allocation and local model accuracy sub-problems. The Lagrange dual problem and gradient projection iterations are used to approximate the optimal values. For solving the local model accuracy problem, a heuristic search algorithm is employed. Simulation results demonstrate that the proposed scheme outperforms other algorithms in terms of balancing learning time and energy consumption, highlighting its effectiveness in addressing the challenges of federated learning in vehicular networks.

To improve the quality of federated learning models, selecting high-quality models for aggregation after local training is a viable approach. Ye et al. proposed a selective model aggregation algorithm that focuses on image classification, a commonly employed task in vehicular networks [41]. The algorithm starts by selecting the "optimal" models for uploading, considering both local image quality and computing capacity. Given the information asymmetry between vehicles and the server, where local data is not uploaded, the algorithm formulates the problem as a two-dimensional contract theory problem. This problem is sequentially solved through relaxation and simplification, employing a greedy algorithm. To evaluate image quality, the algorithm establishes a geometric model that assesses the motion blur level of images, enabling implicit prediction of image quality based on the vehicle's instantaneous speed. Finally, the algorithm constructs a model aggregation scheme based on the FedAvg federated learning algorithm. The proposed algorithm is tested on standard datasets, including MNIST and BelgiumTSC. The results demonstrate that the model aggregation algorithm achieves higher performance, showcasing its effectiveness in improving the quality of federated learning models.

## 5  Future Research Directions

With the widespread adoption of new communication technologies, such as 5G, vehicular edge computing and its security remain active areas of research. In the domains of task offloading and resource allocation, alongside traditional reinforcement learning algorithms, improved algorithms like multi-agent reinforcement learning can be utilized. These algorithms involve multiple agents distributed throughout the network, facilitating better integration with blockchain and federated learning technologies for distributed offloading decisions. While reinforcement learning algorithms ensure the efficiency of computation offloading and resource allocation, offloading methods based on reinforcement learning often suffer from high computational complexity, requiring substantial training time to attain an optimal solution. Thus, a crucial research direction for the future is the design of low-complexity offloading algorithms that meet efficiency requirements.

To address the issue of extended response times in existing blockchain systems, it is crucial to focus on advancing blockchain systems that offer shorter response times, aligning with the task requirements of vehicular edge computing. This advancement would enhance system efficiency while ensuring data security. In the context of blockchain, data security is commonly achieved through a public key encryption system, which involves the establishment of Public Key Infrastructure (PKI) and certificate authorities (CAs). However, this encryption method can introduce computational delays in vehicular edge computing. To reduce data transmission latency, one approach is to position the certificate authorities or registration authorities closer to the vehicles. This enables short-term registrations and improves the efficiency of offloaded computations. Additionally, leveraging smart contracts for certificate registration and issuance can enhance the resilience of the blockchain system against attacks. Therefore, there is significant research potential in designing a secure vehicular edge computing architecture that combines PKI and smart contracts, optimizing system security and efficiency.

In the context of vehicular edge computing, the strong heterogeneity of computational resources and data poses challenges for federated learning algorithms.

To address this, it is important to select federated learning algorithms that excel in handling heterogeneous data as privacy-preserving solutions. This choice enhances overall system efficiency and applicability to meet the requirements of vehicular edge computing data.

Currently, certain federated learning algorithms adopt equal aggregation of model parameters from each client during model aggregation, leading to unnecessary computational and communication overhead that can reduce accuracy and model quality. To mitigate this issue, client-centric model aggregation algorithms can be employed. These algorithms assess the utility of each client based on metrics like data quality and model parameter quality. During aggregation, corresponding model aggregation coefficients are assigned based on the varying utility values of clients. This approach significantly improves the efficiency and accuracy of the algorithm when dealing with heterogeneous data. Therefore, in the integration of federated learning algorithms and vehicular edge computing, it is essential to flexibly design various algorithms that cater to different requirements based on practical application scenarios.

In conclusion, as vehicular networks continue to gain popularity, research in the fields of data security and privacy protection remains highly relevant. These areas play a critical role in ensuring the stability and reliability of vehicular network applications in the long term. This paper presents potential future research directions in vehicle edge computing offloading, data security, and privacy protection. The aim is to offer insights and serve as a reference for future scholars conducting research in these domains.

## 6  Conclusion

This paper focuses on the challenges of offloading decision-making in vehicle edge computing, as well as data security and privacy protection. It begins by summarizing the design of optimal offloading decision-making and resource allocation algorithms using reinforcement learning, with a particular emphasis on deep reinforcement learning. Additionally, it highlights the data security and privacy challenges encountered in edge computing offloading. To mitigate these challenges, the paper provides an overview of data security and privacy protection approaches utilizing blockchain and federated learning methods. Through a review of relevant literature, it presents the current research landscape in this field, identifies existing issues, and outlines future research directions. Overall, the paper offers valuable insights for subsequent studies in this area.

## References

1. Cui, L., et al.: A blockchain-based containerized edge computing platform for the internet of vehicles. IEEE Internet Things J. **8**(4), 2395–2408 (2020)
2. Dai, Y., Xu, D., Maharjan, S., Qiao, G., Zhang, Y.: Artificial intelligence empowered edge computing and caching for internet of vehicles. IEEE Wirel. Commun. **26**(3), 12–18 (2019)

3. Dai, Y., Xu, D., Zhang, K., Maharjan, S., Zhang, Y.: Deep reinforcement learning and permissioned blockchain for content caching in vehicular edge computing and networks. IEEE Trans. Veh. Technol. **69**(4), 4312–4324 (2020)
4. Feng, J., Liu, Z., Wu, C., Ji, Y.: Mobile edge computing for the internet of vehicles: offloading framework and job scheduling. IEEE Veh. Technol. Mag. **14**(1), 28–36 (2018)
5. Firdaus, M., Rahmadika, S., Rhee, K.H.: Decentralized trusted data sharing management on internet of vehicle edge computing (IoVEC) networks using consortium blockchain. Sensors **21**(7), 2410 (2021)
6. François-Lavet, V., Henderson, P., Islam, R., Bellemare, M.G., Pineau, J., et al.: An introduction to deep reinforcement learning. Found. Trends® Mach. Learn. **11**(3-4), 219–354 (2018)
7. Huang, X., Li, P., Yu, R., Wu, Y., Xie, K., Xie, S.: FedParking: a federated learning based parking space estimation with parked vehicle assisted edge computing. IEEE Trans. Veh. Technol. **70**(9), 9355–9368 (2021)
8. Huang, X., Ye, D., Yu, R., Shu, L.: Securing parked vehicle assisted fog computing with blockchain and optimal smart contract design. IEEE/CAA J. Automatica Sinica **7**(2), 426–441 (2020)
9. Jiang, T., Fang, H., Wang, H.: Blockchain-based internet of vehicles: distributed network architecture and performance analysis. IEEE Internet Things J. **6**(3), 4640–4649 (2018)
10. Kang, J., et al.: Blockchain for secure and efficient data sharing in vehicular edge computing and networks. IEEE Internet Things J. **6**(3), 4660–4670 (2018)
11. Kim, J., Ha, H., Chun, B.G., Yoon, S., Cha, S.K.: Collaborative analytics for data silos. In: 2016 IEEE 32nd International Conference on Data Engineering (ICDE), pp. 743–754. IEEE (2016)
12. Kong, X., et al.: Deep reinforcement learning-based energy-efficient edge computing for internet of vehicles. IEEE Trans. Industr. Inf. **18**(9), 6308–6316 (2022)
13. Kumar, S., Velliangiri, S., Karthikeyan, P., Kumari, S., Kumar, S., Khan, M.K.: A survey on the blockchain techniques for the internet of vehicles security. Trans. Emerg. Telecommun. Technol. **35**(4), e4317 (2021)
14. Lang, P., Tian, D., Duan, X., Zhou, J., Sheng, Z., Leung, V.C.: Cooperative computation offloading in blockchain-based vehicular edge computing networks. IEEE Trans. Intell. Veh. **7**(3), 783–798 (2022)
15. Lee, S.S., Lee, S.: Resource allocation for vehicular fog computing using reinforcement learning combined with heuristic information. IEEE Internet Things J. **7**(10), 10450–10464 (2020)
16. Li, C., Zhang, Y., Luo, Y.: A federated learning-based edge caching approach for mobile edge computing-enabled intelligent connected vehicles. IEEE Trans. Intell. Transp. Syst. **24**(3), 3360–3369 (2022)
17. Li, T., Sahu, A.K., Talwalkar, A., Smith, V.: Federated learning: challenges, methods, and future directions. IEEE Signal Process. Mag. **37**(3), 50–60 (2020)
18. Liu, H., Zhang, Y., Yang, T.: Blockchain-enabled security in electric vehicles cloud and edge computing. IEEE Network **32**(3), 78–83 (2018)
19. Liu, L., Chen, C., Pei, Q., Maharjan, S., Zhang, Y.: Vehicular edge computing and networking: a survey. Mob. Netw. Appl. **26**, 1145–1168 (2021)
20. Liu, S., Liu, L., Tang, J., Yu, B., Wang, Y., Shi, W.: Edge computing for autonomous driving: opportunities and challenges. Proc. IEEE **107**(8), 1697–1716 (2019)

21. Liu, S., Yu, J., Deng, X., Wan, S.: FedCPF: an efficient-communication federated learning approach for vehicular edge computing in 6G communication networks. IEEE Trans. Intell. Transp. Syst. **23**(2), 1616–1629 (2021)

22. Liu, Y., Yu, H., Xie, S., Zhang, Y.: Deep reinforcement learning for offloading and resource allocation in vehicle edge computing and networks. IEEE Trans. Veh. Technol. **68**(11), 11158–11168 (2019)

23. Lu, Y., Huang, X., Zhang, K., Maharjan, S., Zhang, Y.: Blockchain empowered asynchronous federated learning for secure data sharing in internet of vehicles. IEEE Trans. Veh. Technol. **69**(4), 4298–4311 (2020)

24. Nakamoto, S.: Bitcoin: a peer-to-peer electronic cash system. Decentralized business review (2008)

25. Ning, Z., Dong, P., Wang, X., Rodrigues, J.J., Xia, F.: Deep reinforcement learning for vehicular edge computing: an intelligent offloading system. ACM Trans. Intell. Syst. Technol. (TIST) **10**(6), 1–24 (2019)

26. Ning, Z., et al.: Joint computing and caching in 5G-envisioned internet of vehicles: a deep reinforcement learning-based traffic control system. IEEE Trans. Intell. Transp. Syst. **22**(8), 5201–5212 (2020)

27. Olowononi, F.O., Rawat, D.B., Liu, C.: Federated learning with differential privacy for resilient vehicular cyber physical systems. In: 2021 IEEE 18th Annual Consumer Communications & Networking Conference (CCNC), pp. 1–5. IEEE (2021)

28. Qi, Q., Ma, Z.: Vehicular edge computing via deep reinforcement learning. arXiv preprint arXiv:1901.04290 (2018)

29. Raza, S., Wang, S., Ahmed, M., Anwar, M.R., et al.: A survey on vehicular edge computing: architecture, applications, technical issues, and future directions. Wirel. Commun. Mob. Comput. **2019**(1), 3159762 (2019)

30. Ren, Y., Chen, X., Guo, S., Guo, S., Xiong, A.: Blockchain-based VEC network trust management: a DRL algorithm for vehicular service offloading and migration. IEEE Trans. Veh. Technol. **70**(8), 8148–8160 (2021)

31. Shaodong, H., Yingqun, C., Guihong, C., Yin, J., Wang, H., Cao, J.: Multi-step reinforcement learning-based offloading for vehicle edge computing. In: 2023 15th International Conference on Advanced Computational Intelligence (ICACI), pp. 1–8. IEEE (2023)

32. Shi, J., Du, J., Wang, J., Wang, J., Yuan, J.: Priority-aware task offloading in vehicular fog computing based on deep reinforcement learning. IEEE Trans. Veh. Technol. **69**(12), 16067–16081 (2020)

33. Singh, M., Kim, S.: Blockchain based intelligent vehicle data sharing framework. arXiv preprint arXiv:1708.09721 (2017)

34. Sun, Y., et al.: Adaptive learning-based task offloading for vehicular edge computing systems. IEEE Trans. Veh. Technol. **68**(4), 3061–3074 (2019)

35. Wang, K., Wang, X., Liu, X.: A high reliable computing offloading strategy using deep reinforcement learning for IoVs in edge computing. J. grid comput. **19**, 1–15 (2021)

36. Wang, S., Ye, D., Huang, X., Yu, R., Wang, Y., Zhang, Y.: Consortium blockchain for secure resource sharing in vehicular edge computing: a contract-based approach. IEEE Trans. Netw. Sci. Eng. **8**(2), 1189–1201 (2020)

37. Wu, Z., Yan, D.: Deep reinforcement learning-based computation offloading for 5G vehicle-aware multi-access edge computing network. China Commun. **18**(11), 26–41 (2021)

38. Xiao, H., Zhao, J., Pei, Q., Feng, J., Liu, L., Shi, W.: Vehicle selection and resource optimization for federated learning in vehicular edge computing. IEEE Trans. Intell. Transp. Syst. **23**(8), 11073–11087 (2021)

39. Xu, W., et al.: Internet of vehicles in big data era. IEEE/CAA J. Automatica Sinica **5**(1), 19–35 (2017)
40. Xu, X., et al.: Service offloading with deep q-network for digital twinning-empowered internet of vehicles in edge computing. IEEE Trans. Industr. Inf. **18**(2), 1414–1423 (2020)
41. Ye, D., Yu, R., Pan, M., Han, Z.: Federated learning in vehicular edge computing: a selective model aggregation approach. IEEE Access **8**, 23920–23935 (2020)
42. Zhang, C., Xie, Y., Bai, H., Yu, B., Li, W., Gao, Y.: A survey on federated learning. Knowl.-Based Syst. **216**, 106775 (2021)
43. Zhang, D., Cao, L., Zhu, H., Zhang, T., Du, J., Jiang, K.: Task offloading method of edge computing in internet of vehicles based on deep reinforcement learning. Clust. Comput. **25**(2), 1175–1187 (2022). https://doi.org/10.1007/s10586-021-03532-9
44. Zhang, K., Cao, J., Zhang, Y.: Adaptive digital twin and multiagent deep reinforcement learning for vehicular edge computing and networks. IEEE Trans. Industr. Inf. **18**(2), 1405–1413 (2021)
45. Zhang, L., Zhou, W., Xia, J., Gao, C., Zhu, F., Fan, C., Ou, J.: DQN-based mobile edge computing for smart internet of vehicle. EURASIP J. Adv. Signal Process. **2022**(1), 1–16 (2022)
46. Zhang, X., Li, R., Cui, B.: A security architecture of vanet based on blockchain and mobile edge computing. In: 2018 1st IEEE International Conference on Hot Information-Centric Networking (HotICN), pp. 258–259. IEEE (2018)
47. Zhang, X., Chen, X.: Data security sharing and storage based on a consortium blockchain in a vehicular ad-hoc network. Ieee Access **7**, 58241–58254 (2019)
48. Zheng, Z., et al.: An overview on smart contracts: challenges, advances and platforms. Futur. Gener. Comput. Syst. **105**, 475–491 (2020)
49. Zheng, Z., Xie, S., Dai, H.N., Chen, X., Wang, H.: Blockchain challenges and opportunities: a survey. Int. J. Web Grid Serv. **14**(4), 352–375 (2018)
50. Zhou, H., Xu, W., Chen, J., Wang, W.: Evolutionary V2X technologies toward the internet of vehicles: challenges and opportunities. Proc. IEEE **108**(2), 308–323 (2020)
51. Zhou, X., Liang, W., She, J., Yan, Z., Kevin, I., Wang, K.: Two-layer federated learning with heterogeneous model aggregation for 6g supported internet of vehicles. IEEE Trans. Veh. Technol. **70**(6), 5308–5317 (2021)

# Multi-party Privacy Preserving Neural Networks

# ConFlow: Contrast Network Flow Improving Class-Imbalanced Learning in Network Intrusion Detection

Lan Liu[1], Pengcheng Wang[1], Jianliang Ruan[1(✉)], Jun Lin[2,3], and Junhan Hu[1]

[1] Guangdong Polytechnic Normal University, Guangzhou 510655, China
ruanjianliang@gpnu.edu.cn
[2] Sun Yat-Sen University, Guangzhou 510006, China
[3] China Electronic Product Reliability and Environmental Testing Research
Institute, Guangzhou 510610, China

**Abstract.** With the increasing complexity and volume of network traffic, accurate detection of malicious network attacks by machine learning-based network intrusion detection systems (NIDSs) remains a challenging task due to imbalanced network traffic. Conventional machine learning algorithms prioritize high overall accuracy without considering class imbalances. To address this issue, we propose ConFlow, a contrastive learning method for network intrusion detection. ConFlow leverages the Dropout layer to obtain two different vector representations of the same traffic, applying supervised contrast loss and cross-entropy loss during training. Experimental results on the ISCX-IDS2012 and CSE-CIC-IDS2017 datasets show that ConFlow outperforms other methods, especially in few-shot learning scenarios, and exhibits high generalization and robustness in real network environments. Our proposed method has significant practical implications for building an intrusion detection system with high accuracy and low false positive rates.

**Keywords:** Cyber security · Network intrusion detection system ·
Deep learning · Class-imbalanced · Contrastive learning

## 1 Introduction

In recent years, the expansion of cyber threats has led to the widespread use of security tools such as firewalls, antivirus software, malware detection, and spam filters to protect networks. However, among these tools, network intrusion detection systems (NIDS) play a critical role in network security. By monitoring network traffic, NIDS can swiftly identify unusual traffic and attack behaviour, thereby improving network security and reliability [1]. It protects network resources such as computers, servers, and data from attacks, destruction,

---

This research is supported by Special focus areas for general universities in Guangdong Province(2022ZDZX1015).

J. Cai et al. (Eds.): SPNCE 2023, LNICST 525, pp. 125–146, 2025.
https://doi.org/10.1007/978-3-031-73699-5_9

unauthorized access, and modification. In doing so, it ensures the availability, confidentiality, and integrity of these resources. NIDS can operate as an expert system based on signature matching, matching suspicious traffic with a predefined signature library of known attacks, or rely on anomaly detection, which measures the difference between observed traffic and trusted baseline traffic.

Currently, traditional machine learning methods are used to detect abnormal traffic through classification, such as support vector machine (SVM), decision tree (DT), random forest (RF), and naïve Bayes. However, the performance of these methods depends on the quality of feature extraction algorithms, and this performance can degrade due to increasingly complex network traffic.

Deep learning, which is an essential branch of machine learning, can mine the latent features of high-dimensional data, transform the problem of network traffic anomaly detection into a classification problem, and enhance the accuracy of intrusion processing through adaptive learning of the difference between normal and abnormal behaviour. Deep learning algorithms such as multi-layer perceptron (MLP), recurrent neural network (RNN), and convolutional neural network (CNN) have been introduced to improve the performance of intrusion detection systems. However, in the real network world, the majority of traffic is normal, and a small number of malicious attacks can be hidden in this large amount of normal traffic, resulting in a highly imbalanced distribution of traffic and a biased classification model towards normal traffic. Despite extensive research on intrusion detection, class imbalance remains an important factor limiting its performance [2].

Recently, supervised contrastive learning has demonstrated good results in representation learning for computer vision (CV) and natural language processing (NLP) [3]. The core idea of supervised contrastive loss is to cluster point clusters of the same class together in the embedding space by effectively utilizing label information while separating samples from different classes [4]. In the context of intrusion detection, the problem can be viewed as separating normal traffic from abnormal traffic.

To build an effective intrusion detection model, the availability of large and well-distributed data is necessary, and the performance may drop significantly when learning on extremely imbalanced or data-starved datasets. However, due to data sparsity, limitations, privacy, and sensitivity, some traffic classes may not have enough data to train a learning model. Therefore, it is essential to establish a network flow feature extraction model and improve network traffic class imbalance learning to develop a network intrusion detection model that can address the real-world traffic environment.

Taking inspiration from the success of supervised contrastive learning in CV and NLP, we introduce it to compare network flows for network intrusion detection. Our goal is to develop a robust and generalizable intrusion detection model that can address the class-imbalanced problem in intrusion detection data. We use supervised contrastive learning to compare network flows by weighting supervised contrastive loss and cross-entropy loss to train the model. Our approach outperforms state-of-the-art baselines on the ISCX-IDS2012 and CIC-IDS2017 datasets. Our contributions are as follows:

(1) Network flow encoder: We design a bidirectional network flow feature extraction encoder that enhances the neural network's representation ability using Gaussian Error Linear Units (GELU), Layer Normalization (LayerNorm), and Skip-connection units in the Multi-Layer Perceptron (MLP). This enables the network to learn to represent network flow data automatically and reduce reliance on feature engineering.

(2) Training framework and loss function: We use the encoder's dropout layer to obtain augmentation data, weigh supervised contrastive loss and cross-entropy loss in the training phase, and directly further mine malicious attacks hidden in normal traffic without requiring additional data augmentation techniques or two-stage training of contrastive learning pre-training and fine-tuning.

(3) Generalization and robustness testing: We explore the performance of our proposed method on few-shot network traffic data with a few labeled samples (10, 100, and 1000) and perform cross-testing on the two datasets to verify ConFlow's generalization and robustness in real network environments.

The remainder of the paper is organized as follows: Sect. 2 introduces the state-of-the-art in advanced network intrusion detection and summarizes related methods for dealing with imbalanced data. Section 3 details our proposed method, and Sect. 4 validates our approach and analyzes the results. Finally, Sect. 5 concludes the paper by summarizing our proposed research method and discussing possible future research directions.

## 2    Related Work

In this section, we summarize the algorithms and research work related to this study.

### 2.1    Intrusion Detection System

With the development of computers and the rapid rise of malware, anomaly-based intrusion detection systems have been proposed to detect unknown malware attacks. The use of machine learning and deep learning has become the mainstream research direction for developing detection models, since it is able to identify variant and unknown threats, compensating for the deficiency of traditional feature and behavior detection methods that detect known attacks only. The technology of threat detection brings forth higher requirements.

Machine learning-based network intrusion detection can be classified into supervised and unsupervised learning. In supervised learning, it can be further classified into generative and discriminative methods according to the modeling algorithm. The generation algorithm aims to learn the distribution of network traffic data from a statistical perspective by reflecting the similarity of the same type of traffic data, such as the Bayesian algorithm [5], Hidden Markov

Model (HMM) [6], and Restricted Boltzmann Machine (RBM) [7]. Meanwhile, the discriminant method can differentiate different traffic data types by learning decision functions or conditional probability distributions as prediction models, such as the K nearest neighbor algorithm (KNN) [8], decision tree (DT) and Support Vector Machine (SVM) [9], logistic regression (LR) [10], and other methods. Unsupervised learning can develop models via dimensionality reduction, clustering, and other methods without relying on network traffic labels. The k-means algorithm is simple and easy to implement, and has been widely adopted in intrusion detection [11]. Hierarchical clustering can discover the hierarchical relationships of classes by calculating the distance between samples and is frequently used for anomaly mining in redundant network traffic [12]. Gaussian Mixture Model (GMM) [13] can learn the probability density function and can identify different types of network traffic with similar distributions; Principal Component Analysis (PCA) [14] is the most commonly used dimensionality reduction method, which can reduce the feature dimension of network traffic and is therefore used in a large number of feature dimension reduction papers.

Over the past decade, deep learning has been extensively employed in intrusion detection models. These methods can generate excellent prediction results by learning the practical features of the data. Network intrusion detection systems based on deep learning mostly exploit supervised and unsupervised learning models to learn the latent features of high-dimensional data. Supervised learning includes autoencoder (AE), deep belief network (DBN), recurrent neural network (RNN), convolutional neural networks (CNN), whereby the network traffic feature data is converted into 1-D sequences, text, or images, and neural networks are utilized for classification [15]. Other researchers employ reinforcement learning for sample selection in the training dataset and to motivate detection results [16], use generative adversarial networks (GAN) for few-class attack generation [17], and utilize Transformers to develop more complex classification models [18]. Unsupervised learning, that is, self-supervised Learning (SSL), creates supervised information through data augmentation and pre-trains large-scale unlabeled network flow, obtaining the features of different network traffic [19].

## 2.2   Imbalanced Learning

Class-imbalanced data can cause the model to learn better on majority class samples but generalize poorly on minor class samples. To address the problem of network imbalance learning, many solutions have been proposed by scholars, which are summarized as follows:

(1) Resampling: Liu et al. proposed oversampling the minority samples (usually malicious) in network traffic [20], while Zuech et al. suggested undersampling the majority samples [21]. However, over-sampling can easily lead to over-fitting of few-class samples, resulting in worse performance on highly imbalanced data. Meanwhile, under-sampling can result in significant information loss of many types, leading to under-fitting. Thus, Bagui et al. combined these two methods to balance the distribution of data types [22].

(2) Data synthesis: Generating "new" data similar to minority samples. The classical method SMOTE and its improvements [13,23,24] arbitrarily select few-class samples, use K nearest neighbors to select similar samples, and generate new samples by linear interpolation of the samples. Other scholars have exploited generative adversarial network framework to create adversarial few-class malicious traffic, improving the model's robustness [25,26].

(3) Reweighting: Assigning different weights to categories of different network traffic. However, the simplest weighting method based on the inverse of the number of categories can be challenging for improving the learning of imbalanced networks since the network traffic distribution is highly skewed. Therefore, some scholars dynamically weight according to the number of "effective" samples to optimize the loss weighting of the classification spacing based on the number of samples [27].

## 2.3   Contrastive Learning

Contrastive learning (CL) is a technique for extracting information from data by constructing positive and negative sample pairs. The core idea behind contrastive learning is to use a contrastive loss function in which the model pulls similar samples closer together, drives dissimilar samples further apart, and compares the representations of similar and dissimilar data.

In recent years, contrastive learning has become popular in computer vision (CV). For example, Chen et al. proposed SimCLR [28], a framework that has been widely adopted in the CV community. SimCLR enhances pairs of images using data augmentation, encodes image representations using an image encoder, maps the image representations to one dimension using a projection head, and calculates the distance between the sample representations using InfoNCE. This approach has achieved a 7% improvement on ImageNet. However, the training process can be time-consuming and computationally intensive due to the need for large batch sizes to ensure contrastive effects. To address this issue, He et al. [29] introduced MoCo (Momentum Contrast), which uses a memory bank to store the representations of previously processed samples. Caron et al. [30] introduced SwAV, a method that clusters various types of samples and distinguishes the clusters of each class. Khosla et al. [4] proposed a supervised contrastive loss that outperforms cross-entropy loss by clustering point clusters belonging to the same class while separating points from different classes in the embedding space.

Recently, contrastive learning has also been applied to natural language processing (NLP). For example, Gunel et al. [31] proposed a new approach that combines supervised contrastive loss and cross-entropy loss with weighting during the fine-tuning stage of the BERT model. Yan et al. [32] proposed ConSERT, a contrastive framework for self-supervised sentence representation transfer that uses contrastive learning to fine-tune BERT in an unsupervised and efficient manner. Gao et al. [33] proposed SimCSE, a simple contrastive learning approach for generating high-quality sentence vectors.

Contrastive learning has also been applied in intrusion detection. For example, Wang et al. [19] proposed a data augmentation strategy for intrusion detection data and an intrusion detection model based on unlabeled self-supervised learning. The proposed model was trained on the unlabeled UNSW-NB15 intrusion detection dataset and achieved excellent performance on all metrics. Similarly, Lopez et al. [34] proposed a scheme that uses a shared embedding space to include labels in the same space as features and performs distance comparisons between features and labels. This approach dramatically reduces the number of pairwise comparisons, improving the model's performance.

# 3   Method

In this section, we propose a network flow encoder and training method for network traffic to improve class-imbalanced learning in NIDS.

## 3.1   Data Preprocessing

Due to data sparsity, data limitations, data privacy, and data sensitivity, we extract features at the network layer (L3). These features only perform statistics on behavioral features and do not require investigation into the data packets in-depth. Network flow division is determined by the seven-tuple network session (source IP address, destination IP address, protocol, source port, destination port, VLAN identifier, tunnel identifier).

We utilized the NFStream [35] tool to parse network packets (PCAP). This tool provides state-of-the-art flow-based statistical feature extraction. It includes both post-mortem statistical features (e.g., min, mean, stddev, and max of packet size and inter-arrival time) and early flow features (e.g., sequence of first n packets sizes, inter-arrival times, and directions). We set time thresholds, such as active timeout and inactive timeout, and performed behavioral statistics and feature extraction for source to destination flows, destination to source flows, and bidirectional flows. The features extracted by NFStream include continuous features and categorical features, with a total of 57 dimensions in Table 1.

**Table 1.** Features of network flow by NFStream(including IP source address to destination flow features (src2dst features), IP destination to source address flow features (dst2src features), and bidirectional flow features (bidirectional features)).

| src2dst features | dst2src features | bidirectional features |
|---|---|---|
| src2dst_duration_ms | dst2src_duration_ms | bidirectional_duration_ms |
| src2dst_packets | dst2src_packets | bidirectional_packets |
| src2dst_bytes | dst2src_bytes | bidirectional_bytes |
| src2dst_syn_packets | dst2src_syn_packets | bidirectional_syn_packets |
| src2dst_cwr_packets | dst2src_cwr_packets | bidirectional_cwr_packets |
| src2dst_ece_packets | dst2src_ece_packets | bidirectional_ece_packets |

continued

**Table 1.** continued

| src2dst features | dst2src features | bidirectional features |
|---|---|---|
| src2dst_urg_packets | dst2src_urg_packets | bidirectional_urg_packets |
| src2dst_ack_packets | dst2src_ack_packets | bidirectional_ack_packets |
| src2dst_psh_packets | dst2src_psh_packets | bidirectional_psh_packets |
| src2dst_rst_packets | dst2src_rst_packets | bidirectional_rst_packets |
| src2dst_fin_packets | dst2src_fin_packets | bidirectional_fin_packets |
| src2dst_min_piat_ms | dst2src_min_piat_ms | bidirectional_min_piat_ms |
| src2dst_mean_piat_ms | dst2src_mean_piat_ms | bidirectional_mean_piat_ms |
| src2dst_stddev_piat_ms | dst2src_stddev_piat_ms | bidirectional_stddev_piat_ms |
| src2dst_max_piat_ms | dst2src_max_piat_ms | bidirectional_max_piat_ms |
| src2dst_min_ps | dst2src_min_ps | bidirectional_min_ps |
| src2dst_mean_ps | dst2src_mean_ps | bidirectional_mean_ps |
| src2dst_stddev_ps | dst2src_stddev_ps | bidirectional_stddev_ps |
| src2dst_max_ps | dst2src_max_ps | bidirectional_max_ps |

### 3.2    Network Flow Encoder

Popular complex network structures, such as CNN and Transformer, have widely demonstrated good performance in computer vision and natural language processing tasks. However, these structures may not be necessary for relatively simple network traffic representation learning. In this study, we propose an architecture that uses MLP and skip-connections as the main components, as shown in Fig. 1, to serve as the representation encoder network for network traffic.

In the proposed network flow feature extraction encoder, we encode categorical features in the input using one-hot encoding and dropout layers, while continuous features are normalized through LayerNorm layers. To enable better information interaction between categorical and continuous features, they are stitched together when inputted to the next neural unit. The main structure of the network includes two Dense Resnet Block (DRB) modules which employ the Skip-connection mechanism to efficiently reduce gradient disappearance and network degradation problems, thus making training easier. After the DRB module, an MLP unit consisting of linear layers, GELU, and Dropout components is utilized to output the representation information extracted by the encoder to a fixed dimension. Finally, the network flow vector obtained by the encoder is mapped to either the classification category dimension or the projection dimension on the unit sphere through a fully connected layer (FC).

The DRB module includes various components such as linear layer, LayerNorm, GELU, and Dropout, which enhance the expressiveness of the network flow embeddings. LayerNorm in the encoder can provide different network features without requiring other data, thus avoiding the issue of mini-batch data distribution in BatchNorm. Additionally, some studies found that BatchNorm can negatively impact network performance, particularly causing information

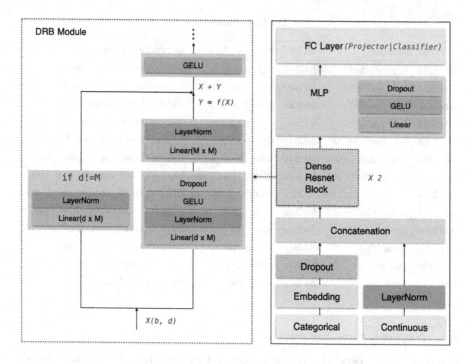

**Fig. 1.** Encoder structure for network flows.

leakage in contrastive learning [36]. Furthermore, GELU (Gaussian Error Linear Unit), which is smoother than ReLU and is utilized by NLP models such as BERT, GPT-3, and ViT, is also adopted in this study to replace the commonly used ReLU activation function.

### 3.3   Training Framework and Loss Function

It is challenging to manually construct data augmentation techniques for network traffic that guarantee semantic invariance. Dropout is commonly utilized to prevent model overfitting in deep learning. SimCSE [33] and R-Drop [37] leverage the randomness of Dropout to rapidly expand data and achieve satisfactory results, as demonstrated on several datasets from different domains. Hence, we employ the "Dropout twice" approach to generate positive samples for supervised contrastive learning. Specifically, a network traffic sample passes through the model twice to obtain different feature vectors of the same input.

However, using Dropout for data augmentation leads to similar positive samples, resulting in feature suppression in the network flow. The deep learning model can not differentiate between sample similarities and class similarities, leading to a bias towards having a large number of normal traffic samples without considering the actual class differences.

Motivated by the success of supervised contrastive learning in CV and NLP, we adopt it to compare network flows. It utilizes sample labels to create new sample pairs to draw samples of the same class closer and away from different classes. By inputting the model twice to obtain different vector representations of the same input and calculating their similarity, we can obtain a similarity matrix with the input's size. We design a supervised contrast loss on this similarity matrix, where the larger the sum of similarity distances of the same type of traffic, the better; and the smaller the sum of similarity distances of different classes, the better.

The architecture of ConFlow is shown in Fig. 2. The first input and output pipeline of network flow are represented as the solid line part, and the second time is represented by the dotted line part. The encoder network maps the traffic to the representation space, where each flow is input to the same encoder twice, yielding a pair of representation vectors. Finally, a 512-dimensional representation vector is obtained using a multilayer perceptron with only one hidden layer. The projection network maps the representation vector to a final vector for loss calculation via a fully connected layer with a dimension of 64. To maximize the similarity between augmentation flow projections and minimize the similarity between different flows, a unit hypersphere is utilized for regularization. The classification network maps the dimensions to the label category dimension using a linear layer.

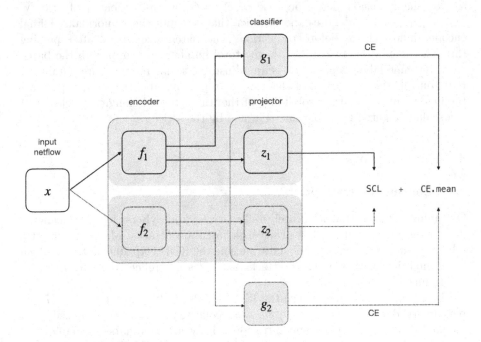

**Fig. 2.** ConFlow's framework.

ConFlow introduces supervised contrastive loss into the standard training method to detect malicious attacks obscured by large volumes of normal traffic. By inputting the model twice, the final loss is calculated based on a weighting of the supervised contrastive loss and the average loss of the two cross-entropies. Additional data augmentation methods are employed, and a two-stage training process is used that includes traditional contrastive learning pre-training followed by fine-tuning.

The loss function used is a weighted cross-entropy (CE) loss with the inclusion of supervised contrastive loss (SCL), which is formulated as follows:

$$\mathscr{L}_{CE} = -\frac{1}{2N}\left(\sum_{i=1}^{N}\sum_{c=1}^{C}y_{i,c}\cdot\log\hat{y}_{i,c'} + \sum_{i=1}^{N}\sum_{c'=1}^{C'}y_{i',c'}\cdot\log\hat{y}_{i',c'}\right) \quad (1)$$

$$\mathscr{L}_{SCL} = \sum_{i=1}^{2N}\frac{-1}{2N_{y_i}-1}\sum_{j=1}^{2N}\mathbb{1}_{i\neq j}\mathbb{1}_{y_i=y_j}\log\frac{\exp\left(z\left(x_i\right)\cdot z\left(x_j\right)/\tau\right)}{\sum_{k=1}^{2N}\mathbb{1}_{i\neq k}\exp\left(z\left(x_i\right)\cdot z\left(x_k\right)/\tau\right)} \quad (2)$$

$$\mathscr{L}_{OSS} = (1-\lambda)\mathscr{L}_{CE} + \lambda\mathscr{L}_{SCL} \quad (3)$$

The canonical definition of the CE loss that we use is given in equation (1). The SCL loss is given in the equation (2). The overall loss is a weighted average of CE and SCL loss, as given in the equation (3).

For the intrusion detection case of class $C$, we use a batch of size $N$, $\{xi, yi\}_{i=1,...N}$. $z(\cdot)$ denotes the encoder that outputs the $l_2$ normalized final encoder hidden layer before projection. The batch size is $2N$ after passing through the encoder twice; $2N_{y_i}$ is the total number of examples in the batch with the same label as $y_i$; $\tau > 0$ is an adjustable scalar temperature parameter that controls the separation of classes; $yi, c$ represent labels and $\hat{y}_i, c$ represents the model output for the probability of the ith example belonging to class $c$; $\lambda$ is a scalar weighted hyperparameter tuned by the setting.

## 4    Experiments

### 4.1    Benchmark Dataset

Obtaining datasets that accurately reflect real-world cyberspace is challenging due to the rarity and secrecy of network intrusion attacks. Many studies still rely on outdated network traffic data, such as the KDD Cup 1999 dataset, which is incompatible with real-world attacks and does not reflect the current cyber environment.

To address this issue, we use the ISCX-IDS2012 [38] and CIC-IDS2017 [39] benchmark datasets. These datasets were collected over nearly a decade and include traffic composition and intrusions. They are modifiable, scalable, and reproducible, making them suitable for our purposes. The ISCX-IDS2012 dataset consists of over 100GiB of labeled network traces, including full packet payloads in PCAP format, and contains DoS, Botnet, Brute force, Infiltration, and normal activities. The CIC-IDS2017 dataset, released by the Canadian Institute for Cybersecurity in late 2017, resembles true real-world data, and includes the most common attacks based on the 2016 McAfee report (DoS, DDoS, Web attack, Brute force, Infiltration, Heart-bleed, Botnet, and Portscan). Table 2 provides a summary of the ISCX-IDS2012 and CIC-IDS2017 intrusion detection evaluation datasets, which cover 7-day and 5-day network activities, respectively.

We extracted features from the ISCX-IDS2012 and CIC-IDS2017 datasets using the NFStream tool. Flows that were idle (no packets received) for more than 15 s were removed, as were activities that lasted longer than 1800 s. We labeled each flow according to its network session seven-tuple and timestamp. The extracted flow data distribution is shown in Table 3, along with the distribution of traffic, which exhibited highly imbalanced bias in the amount of each class. For instance, in the CIC-IDS2017 dataset, the Infiltration attack class was 56032 times more prevalent than benign traffic, posing a challenge for training a model with good generalization.

**Table 2.** Summary of the ISCX-IDS2012 and CIC-IDS2017 datasets(PCAPs).

| Dataset | Date | Description | Size(GiB) |
|---------|------|-------------|-----------|
| ISCX -IDS2012 | 2010-06-11 | Normal, hence no malicious activity | 16.1 |
| | 2010-06-12 | Infiltrating the network from inside and normal activity | 4.22 |
| | 2010-06-13 | Infiltrating the network from inside and normal activity | 3.95 |
| | 2010-06-14 | HTTP denial of service and normal activity | 6.85 |
| | 2010-06-15 | Distributed denial of service using an IRC Botnet | 23.4 |
| | 2010-06-16 | Normal Activity, no malicious activity | 17.6 |
| | 2010-06-17 | Brute force SSH and normal activity | 12.3 |
| CIC-IDS2017 | 2017-07-03 | Normal Activity | 11 |
| | 2017-07-04 | Normal Activity, BForce, SFTP and SSH | 11 |
| | 2017-07-05 | Normal Activity, DoS and Hearbleed Attacks slowloris, Slowhttptest, Hulk and GoldenEye | 13 |
| | 2017-07-06 | Normal Activity, Web and Infiltration Attacks Web BForce, XSS and SQL Inject, Infiltration Dropbox Download and Cool disk | 7.8 |
| | 2017-07-07 | Normal Activity, DDoS LOIT, Botnet ARES, PortScan | 8.3 |

## 4.2   Evaluation Metrics

We employed several evaluation metrics to assess the performance of our experimental model, including Accuracy, Precision, Recall, and F1-measure. These evaluation criteria can effectively evaluate traffic identification, detection rate, and the accuracy of an intrusion detection system.

$$Accuracy = \frac{TP + TN}{TP + TN + FP + FN} \tag{4}$$

$$Precision = \frac{TP}{TP + FP} \tag{5}$$

$$Recall = \frac{TP + TN}{TP + TN + FP + FN} \tag{6}$$

$$F1measure = \frac{2 \times Precision \times Recall}{Precision + Recall} \tag{7}$$

Furthermore, in order to evaluate the performance of the classification model, we included a ROC curve (receiver operating characteristic curve). This graph displays the model's TPR (True Positive Rate) versus its FPR (False Positive Rate) at different classification thresholds. Lowering the classification threshold will increase the number of items classified as positive, subsequently increasing both False Positives and True Positives. The AUC (Area Under the Curve) provides a comprehensive performance assessment across all possible classification thresholds.

**Table 3.** Distribution of ISCX-IDS2012 and CIC-IDS2017 datasets(Imbalanced weight are compared with Benign traffic as a benchmark).

| Dataset | Type | Total | Imbalanced weight |
|---|---|---|---|
| ISCX-IDS2012 | Benign | 2216455 | 1 |
| | Bot | 38288 | 58 |
| | Infiltration | 12467 | 178 |
| | DoS | 5290 | 419 |
| | Brute force | 5011 | 442 |
| CIC-IDS2017 | Benign | 1680963 | 1 |
| | DoS | 179346 | 9 |
| | PortScan | 158946 | 11 |
| | DDoS | 83681 | 20 |
| | Patator | 6953 | 242 |
| | Web Attack | 2005 | 838 |
| | Bot | 1228 | 1369 |
| | Infiltration | 30 | 56032 |

### 4.3  Implementation Details

The experiments detailed in this chapter were performed on an Intel i5-12400F CPU and accelerated using an NVIDIA 3060 GPU. We employed the Adam optimizer with a learning rate of 5e-5 and a dropout rate of 0.3. For contrastive learning, a substantial batch size can ensure the availability of more challenging samples within each batch. This approach can improve the model's capacity to learn and detect a broader range of malicious attacks during training. Thus, for this chapter's experiments, we used a batch size of 16384. Model training was conducted over 500 rounds, with an early stopping threshold of 50 rounds. If the model's performance failed to improve on the validation set after 50 rounds, training would terminate. We randomly sampled 20% of the dataset by traffic category to evaluate the final model's performance on the test set.

## 4.4   Analysis and Results

We conducted a hyperparameter sweep over the range of $\tau \in \{0, 0.1, 0.3, 0.5, 0.7, 0.9, 1.0\}$ and $\lambda \in \{0.03, 0.05, 0.07, 0.1, 0.3, 0.5\}$. When lambda=0, only CE is used to train the model. On the other hand, when $\lambda$ is set to 1, only SCL is used to train the model in two stages. The first stage employs the SCL pre-training model, while the second stage freezes the model's encoder and trains the final classification layer.

Figure 3 displays the results, wherein we observed that the models that displayed the highest F1-measure in the experimental setting predominantly utilized the hyperparameter values of $\tau = 0.05$ and $\lambda = 0.9$.

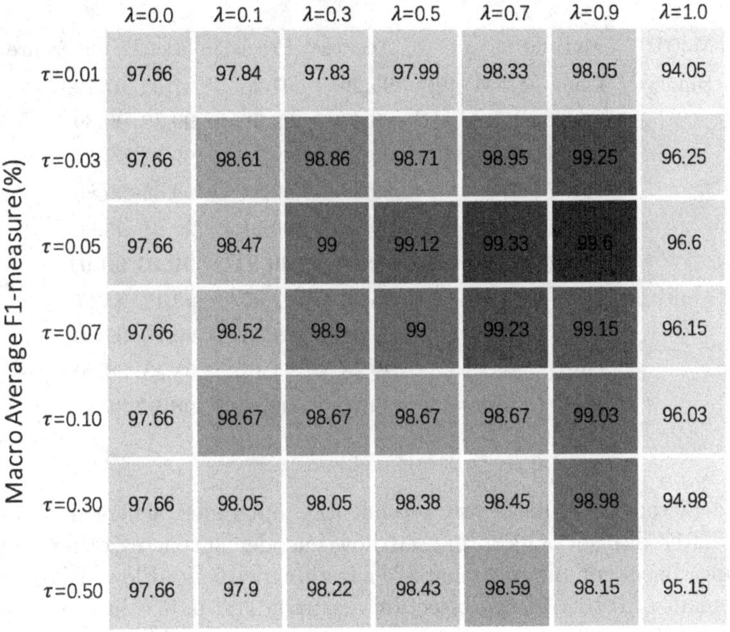

| | $\lambda$=0.0 | $\lambda$=0.1 | $\lambda$=0.3 | $\lambda$=0.5 | $\lambda$=0.7 | $\lambda$=0.9 | $\lambda$=1.0 |
|---|---|---|---|---|---|---|---|
| $\tau$=0.01 | 97.66 | 97.84 | 97.83 | 97.99 | 98.33 | 98.05 | 94.05 |
| $\tau$=0.03 | 97.66 | 98.61 | 98.86 | 98.71 | 98.95 | 99.25 | 96.25 |
| $\tau$=0.05 | 97.66 | 98.47 | 99 | 99.12 | 99.33 | 99.6 | 96.6 |
| $\tau$=0.07 | 97.66 | 98.52 | 98.9 | 99 | 99.23 | 99.15 | 96.15 |
| $\tau$=0.10 | 97.66 | 98.67 | 98.67 | 98.67 | 98.67 | 99.03 | 96.03 |
| $\tau$=0.30 | 97.66 | 98.05 | 98.05 | 98.38 | 98.45 | 98.98 | 94.98 |
| $\tau$=0.50 | 97.66 | 97.9 | 98.22 | 98.43 | 98.59 | 98.15 | 95.15 |

Macro Average F1-measure(%)

**Fig. 3.** The performance visualization with $\tau$ and $\lambda$ combinations of strategies.

The effect of different dropout probabilities p={0.1,0.2,0.3,0.4,0.5} on the performance of the model is explored. As can be seen from Table 4, the highest F1-measure is achieved when the dropout rate is p=0.3, so the probability of the dropout layer of the fixed model in the experiment is p=0.3.

As demonstrated in Table 5, we present the outcomes obtained from the ISCX-IDS2012 dataset. Our proposed flow encoder that has undergone standard CE loss training performs comparably to several baselines. However, post-conducting training with ConFlow, we observed consistent enhancements. The bisection accuracy showed an improvement of 0.73%, and the F1-measure showed an improvement of 0.96%. Notably, in the multiclass task, the F1-measure showed a substantial improvement of 1.4%.

**Table 4.** The performance visualization with $\tau$ and $\lambda$ combinations of strategies.

| p | 0.1 | 0.2 | 0.3 | 0.4 | 0.5 |
|---|---|---|---|---|---|
| F1 | 99.42 | 99.54 | **99.6** | 99.57 | 99.53 |

**Table 5.** Independent test performance metrics of different method on the ISCX-IDS2012 dataset(Accuracy, Precision, and F1-measure are the macro average).

| Metric | Method | Accuracy | Precision | Recall | F1-measure |
|---|---|---|---|---|---|
| Binary | Conv-LSTM [40] | 95.29 | 97.25 | 97.50 | 97.29 |
| | Session-Based [41] | 99.48 | 99.39 | 99.39 | 99.39 |
| | Metric learning [42] | 99.71 | 99.71 | 99.71 | 99.71 |
| | ITSN [43] | 99.88 | 99.83 | 99.85 | 99.83 |
| | Ours(CE) | 99.78 | 99.11 | 98.81 | 98.96 |
| | Ours(ConFlow) | **99.91** | **99.91** | **99.91** | **99.91** |
| Multiclass | DNN-FS [44] | 95.20 | 92.86 | 93.17 | 93.17 |
| | MFVT [?] | 99.88 | 99.86 | 99.75 | 99.80 |
| | Ours(CE) | 99.78 | 98.16 | 98.23 | 98.20 |
| | Ours(ConFlow) | **99.91** | **99.36** | **98.97** | **99.16** |

As depicted in Table 6, we present the outcomes achieved through the CIC-IDS2017 dataset. Our proposed flow encoder surpasses other techniques, exhibiting consistent enhancement after training with ConFlow. We observed an improvement of 0.16% in the bisection accuracy and 0.04% in the F1-measure. Notably, in the multiclass task, the accuracy improved by 0.22%, with a substantial improvement of 1.94% in the F1-measure.

Table 7 displays the few-shot learning outcomes attained on the ISCX-IDS2012 and CIC-IDS2017 datasets, employing 10, 100, 1000, and 10000 labeled

**Table 6.** Independent test performance metrics of different method on the CIC-IDS2017 dataset(Accuracy, Precision, and F1-measure are the macro average).

| Metric | Method | Accuracy | Precision | Recall | F1-measure |
|---|---|---|---|---|---|
| Binary | QDA [45] | 96.00 | 96.60 | 93.20 | 94.40 |
| | RFC [45] | 99.80 | 99.80 | 99.80 | 99.80 |
| | CNN-LSTM [46] | 99.30 | 98.90 | 99.20 | 99.10 |
| | BO-TPE-R [47] | 99.99 | 99.00 | 99.00 | 99.00 |
| | Ours(CE) | 99.83 | 99.89 | 99.95 | 99.92 |
| | Ours(ConFlow) | **99.99** | **99.96** | **99.96** | **99.96** |
| Multiclass | LSTM [48] | 97.84 | 87.42 | 85.82 | 86.61 |
| | TSVM [49] | 83.25 | 84.15 | 91.75 | 87.78 |
| | DBN+ANN [50] | 98.97 | 98.07 | 98.42 | 98.24 |
| | SS-Deep-ID [51] | 99.69 | 92.31 | 96.29 | 94.18 |
| | AE-CGAN-RF [17] | NaN | 98.46 | 93.29 | 95.38 |
| | DNN-FS [44] | 99.73 | 98.05 | 96.68 | 99.58 |
| | Ours(CE) | 99.76 | 99.69 | 99.54 | 97.66 |
| | Ours(ConFlow) | **99.98** | **99.61** | **99.60** | **99.60** |

training examples. As the distribution of network traffic is significantly imbalanced, it is unfeasible to maintain the stratified proportion sampling according to class distribution. Therefore, we randomly selected half of the normal and attack samples from each class. ConFlow exhibited enhanced performance on the test set across all few-shot training sets. In the 10-sample training set, the accuracy rate on the ISCX-IDS2012 dataset improved by 5.47%, with the F1-measure improving by 4.18%. Similarly, in the 100-sample training set, we observed an increase of 5.47% in the accuracy rate and 4.18% in the F1-measure on the ISCX-IDS2012 dataset, whereas on the CIC-IDS2017 dataset, the accuracy rate improved by 1.13%, and the F1-measure improved by 1.26%. However, the improvement was insignificant in the 1000-sample training set, with the accuracy rate on the ISCX-IDS2012 dataset improving by only 0.2%, and the F1-measure improving by 1.19%; on the other hand, the accuracy rate on the CIC-IDS2017 dataset improved by 0.62%, with a 0.95% improvement in the F1-measure. Notably, the performance improvement over CE decreased as the number of labeled examples increased.

We assessed the generalization and robustness of the proposed method through cross-training and testing on two different data generations. Table 8 presents a comparison of the results obtained through the binary classification of CE and ConFlow. The model underwent training on the ISCX-IDS2012 training set, and subsequently, we performed training on the IDS2017 training set, following which we tested the performance on the ISCX-IDS2012 test set. ConFlow imparted improved accuracy and F1-measure values, with a respective increase of 1.31% and 6%. The results indicated that the model trained using the ConFlow technique exhibited enhanced generalization ability and significantly improved robustness compared to CE. In addition, Fig. 4 illustrates the detection performance of the ConFlow method in real scenarios.

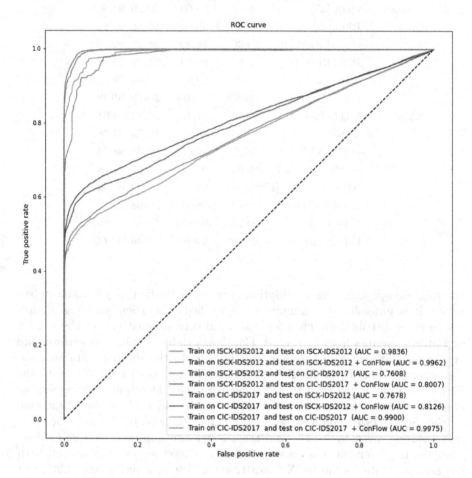

**Fig. 4.** Comparison of ROC curve metric results for cross-training and testing(AUC stands for Area under the ROC Curve).

Figure 5 portrays the loss variation observed during training with CE loss and ConFlow techniques. The figure indicates that training with CE loss transpires an early stop when the training is close to 200 times, and the loss curve is smoother than CE loss during the ConFlow training of 500 times. There was no major fluctuation observed in the curve, and adequate room for further decline persisted. The figure provides an explanation for how the ConFlow method effectively enhances performance. During training, the employment of contrasting network flow can bring similar samples closer and push different samples further

**Table 7.** Independent test performance metrics of different method on the CIC-IDS2017 dataset(Accuracy, Precision, and F1-measure are the macro average).

| Dataset | N | Accuracy | Precision | Recall | F1-measure |
|---|---|---|---|---|---|
| ISCX-IDS2012 | 10+CE | 87.17 | 53.15 | 82.27 | 64.58 |
| | 10+ConFlow | **92.64** | **63.13** | **94.83** | **68.76** |
| | 100+CE | 93.70 | 64.48 | 94.01 | 70.59 |
| | 100+ConFlow | **97.35** | **75.09** | **97.30** | **82.45** |
| | 1000+CE | 98.44 | 81.69 | 98.55 | 88.20 |
| | 1000+ConFlow | **98.64** | **83.31** | **98.55** | **89.39** |
| | full trainset+CE | 99.78 | 97.96 | 97.83 | 97.90 |
| | full trainset+ConFlow | **99.91** | **99.36** | **98.97** | **99.16** |
| CIC-IDS2017 | 10 CE | 95.12 | 92.74 | 93.41 | 93.07 |
| | 10+ConFlow | **96.36** | **94.03** | **94.91** | **94.46** |
| | 100+CE | 97.01 | 96.30 | 95.36 | 95.83 |
| | 100+ConFlow | **98.14** | **97.79** | **96.43** | **97.09** |
| | 1000+CE | 99.15 | 98.72 | 98.68 | 98.70 |
| | 1000+ConFlow | **99.77** | **99.72** | **99.58** | **99.65** |
| | full trainset+CE | 99.83 | 99.89 | 99.95 | 99.92 |
| | full trainset+ConFlow | **99.99** | **99.96** | **99.96** | **99.96** |

away. In comparison with the standard CE loss, this methodology can mine the similarity between hard samples hidden in vast amounts of redundant traffic, without the need for additional data augmentation techniques. Employing the two-stage training approach of contrastive learning pre-training and fine-tuning can enhance class-imbalanced learning concerning network intrusion detection.

In addition, we evaluated the real-time detection for network traffic, and the training throughput could reach up to 96,600 pieces/second during the model training process. The traffic throughput could reach 285,181 pieces/second during the detection model testing process. Therefore, the implementation of the ConFlow approach to detect large-scale network traffic in real-time with high accuracy has significant practical significance.

Comparing the performance of the standard CE loss function trained bidirectional flow encoder designed in this paper evaluation test with some current works, we observed close results, whereas ConFlow demonstrated a significant improvement. Notably, this methodology showed substantial performance improvements during few-sample learning. Finally, we verified the generalization and robustness of ConFlow through cross-training and testing on data from two different generations, thereby effectively reflecting its performance in real network environments. Building an intrusion detection system with high accuracy and low false-positive rates would have far-reaching practical significance.

**Table 8.** Cross training and test on different datasets.

| Test set | Training set | Loss func | Acc | Pre | Recall | F1 |
|---|---|---|---|---|---|---|
| ISCX-IDS2012 | CIC-IDS2017 | CE | 82.26 | 72.93 | 66.18 | 68.33 |
| | | ConFlow | **85.82** | **81.59** | **68.25** | **73.39** |
| | ISCX-IDS2012 | CE | 99.78 | 97.96 | 97.83 | 97.90 |
| | | ConFlow | **99.91** | **99.36** | **98.97** | **99.16** |
| CIC-IDS2017 | ISCX-IDS2012 | CE | 96.93 | 69.83 | 60.52 | 63.50 |
| | | ConFlow | **98.24** | **75.83** | **64.27** | **69.50** |
| | CIC-IDS2017 | CE | 99.83 | 99.89 | 99.95 | 99.92 |
| | | ConFlow | **99.99** | **99.96** | **99.96** | **99.96** |

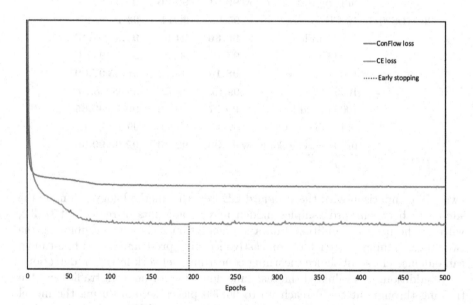

**Fig. 5.** Loss change curve in different loss function in training.

## 5    Conclusion

In real network environments, there exists vast amounts of traffic data, with very little annotated attack activity data, making it challenging to improve class-imbalanced learning in network intrusion detection. To overcome this challenge, we proposed the ConFlow method that contrasts network flow, which obtains different feature vectors using the dropout layer's randomness and the same flow's inputting into the model twice, combined with supervised contrastive learning for model training. Unlike conventional approaches, ConFlow doesn't require the two-stage pre-training and fine-tuning processes, allowing it to mine malicious attacks hidden under a large volume of normal traffic during a single training session. It outperforms state-of-the-art baselines on the ISCX-IDS2012 and CIC-IDS2017 datasets, and its performance in few-shot learning and robust tests reflects its efficacy in real network environments.

Over the past two years, self-supervised learning has emerged as an excellent solution in computer vision and natural language processing, as it doesn't depend on sample labels and can automatically mine feature information from large-scale data. Contrastive learning, which is usually used in data augmentation and other means to construct positive and negative pairs for pre-training, may face challenges in network intrusion detection as positive samples obtained using the dropout layer for data augmentation might be very similar, resulting in feature suppression. Consequently, the model might not be able to distinguish between sample similarity and class similarity, resulting in biases toward having large numbers of normal traffic samples without considering their actual class differences. As a result, we plan to investigate automated feature extraction and data augmentation techniques for network traffic, extending our supervised contrastive learning objective to self-supervised learning, enabling better class-imbalanced learning with fewer labels and label-independent initial feature information. When performing self-supervised learning, an excellent initialization could benefit the model from the pre-training task, eventually learning a more comprehensive representation of network flows.

**Data Availability.** The ISCX-IDS2012 and CIC-IDS2017 datasets used and analysed during this study are available in the Canadian Institute for Cybersecurity datasets repository at https://www.unb.ca/cic/datasets/index.html. The reference code for this study has been made available at https://github.com/AshinWang/ConFlow.

# References

1. Scarfone, K., Mell, P., et al.: Guide to intrusion detection and prevention systems (IDPS). NIST Spec. Publ. **800**, 94 (2007)
2. Molina-Coronado, B., Mori, U., Mendiburu, A., Miguel-Alonso, J.: Survey of network intrusion detection methods from the perspective of the knowledge discovery in databases process. IEEE Trans. Netw. Serv. Manage. **17**, 2451–2479 (2020)
3. Liu, X., et al.: Self-supervised learning: generative or contrastive. IEEE Trans. Knowl. Data Eng. **35**(1), 857–876 (2021)
4. Khosla, P., et al.: Supervised contrastive learning. Adv. Neural. Inf. Process. Syst. **33**, 18661–18673 (2020)
5. Panda, M., Patra, M.R.: Network intrusion detection using naive bayes. Int. J. Comput. Sci. Netw. Secur. **7**, 258–263 (2007)
6. Ariu, D., Tronci, R. & Giacinto, G.: HMMPayl: an intrusion detection system based on Hidden Markov Models. Comput. Secur. **30**, 221–241 (2011). Publisher: Elsevier
7. Seo, S., Park, S., Kim, J.: Improvement of network intrusion detection accuracy by using restricted Boltzmann machine. In: 2016 8th International Conference on Computational Intelligence and Communication Networks (CICN), pp. 413–417. IEEE (2016)

8. Shapoorifard, H., Shamsinejad, P.: Intrusion detection using a novel hybrid method incorporating an improved KNN. Int. J. Comput. Appl. **173**, 5–9 (2017)

9. Mulay, S.A., Devale, P., Garje, G.: Intrusion detection system using support vector machine and decision tree. Int. J. Comput. Appl. **3**, 40–43 (2010)

10. Sapre, S., Ahmadi, P., Islam, K.: A robust comparison of the KDDCup99 and NSL-KDD IoT network intrusion detection datasets through various machine learning algorithms. arXiv preprint arXiv:1912.13204 (2019)

11. Jianliang, M., Haikun, S., Ling, B.: The application on intrusion detection based on k-means cluster algorithm. In: 2009 International Forum on Information Technology and Applications, vol. 1, pp. 150–152. IEEE (2009)

12. Mazarbhuiya, F.A., AlZahrani, M.Y., Georgieva, L.: Anomaly detection using agglomerative hierarchical clustering algorithm. In: International Conference on Information Science and Applications, pp. 475–484. Springer (2018)

13. Zhang, H., Huang, L., Wu, C.Q., Li, Z.: An effective convolutional neural network based on smote and gaussian mixture model for intrusion detection in imbalanced dataset. Comput. Netw. **177**, 107315 (2020)

14. Hadri, A., Chougdali, K., Touahni, R.: A network intrusion detection based on improved nonlinear fuzzy robust PCA. In: 2018 IEEE 5th International Congress on Information Science and Technology (CiSt), pp. 636–641. IEEE (2018)

15. Aldweesh, A., Derhab, A., Emam, A.Z.: Deep learning approaches for anomaly-based intrusion detection systems: a survey, taxonomy, and open issues. Knowl.-Based Syst. **189**, 105124 (2020). Publisher: Elsevier

16. Lopez-Martin, M., Carro, B., Sanchez-Esguevillas, A.: Application of deep reinforcement learning to intrusion detection for supervised problems. Expert Syst. Appl. **141**, 112963 (2020). Publisher: Elsevier

17. Lee, J., Park, K.: AE-CGAN model based high performance network intrusion detection system. Appl. Sci. **9**, 4221 (2019)

18. Kozik, R., Pawlicki, M., Choraś, M.: A new method of hybrid time window embedding with transformer-based traffic data classification in IoT-networked environment. Pattern Anal. Appl. **24**, 1441–1449 (2021). Publisher: Springer

19. Wang, Z., Li, Z., Wang, J., Li, D.: Network intrusion detection model based on improved BYOL self-supervised learning. Secur. Commun. Netw. **2021** (2021)

20. Liu, J., Gao, Y., Hu, F.: A fast network intrusion detection system using adaptive synthetic oversampling and lightGBM. Comput. Secur. **106**, 102289 (2021)

21. Zuech, R., Hancock, J., Khoshgoftaar, T.M.: Detecting web attacks using random undersampling and ensemble learners. J. Big Data **8**(1), 1–20 (2021). https://doi.org/10.1186/s40537-021-00460-8

22. Bagui, S., Li, K.: Resampling imbalanced data for network intrusion detection datasets. J. Big Data **8**(1), 1–41 (2021). https://doi.org/10.1186/s40537-020-00390-x

23. Yulianto, A., Sukarno, P., Suwastika, N.A.: Improving AdaBoost-based intrusion detection system (IDS) performance on CIC IDS 2017 dataset. J. Phys. : Conf. Ser. **1192**, 012018 (2019). IOP Publishing (2019)

24. Ma, X., Shi, W.: AESMOTE: adversarial reinforcement learning with smote for anomaly detection. IEEE Trans. Netw. Sci. Eng. **8**, 943–956 (2021). https://doi.org/10.1109/TNSE.2020.3004312

25. Lin, Z., Shi, Y., Xue, Z.: IDSGAN: generative adversarial networks for attack generation against intrusion detection. arXiv preprint arXiv:1809.02077 (2018)

26. Ding, H., Chen, L., Dong, L., Fu, Z., Cui, X.: Imbalanced data classification: a KNN and generative adversarial networks-based hybrid approach for intrusion detection. Future Gener. Comput. Syst. **131**, 240–254 (2022)

27. Mulyanto, M., Faisal, M., Prakosa, S.W., Leu, J.-S.: Effectiveness of focal loss for minority classification in network intrusion detection systems. Symmetry **13**, 4 (2021)
28. Chen, T., Kornblith, S., Norouzi, M., Hinton, G.: A Simple Framework for Contrastive Learning of Visual Representations. arXiv preprint arXiv:2002.05709 (2020)
29. He, K., Fan, H., Wu, Y., Xie, S., Girshick, R.: Momentum contrast for unsupervised visual representation learning. In: Proceedings of the IEEE/CVF Conference on Computer Vision and Pattern Recognition, pp. 9729–9738 (2020)
30. Caron, M., et al.: Unsupervised learning of visual features by contrasting cluster assignments. In: Proceedings of Advances in Neural Information Processing Systems (NeurIPS) (2020)
31. Gunel, B., Du, J., Conneau, A., Stoyanov, V.: Supervised contrastive learning for pre-trained language model fine-tuning. arXiv preprint arXiv:2011.01403 (2020)
32. Yan, Y., et al.: ConSERT: a contrastive framework for self-supervised sentence representation transfer. arXiv preprint arXiv:2105.11741 (2021)
33. Gao, T., Yao, X., Chen, D.: SimCSE: simple contrastive learning of sentence embeddings. arXiv preprint arXiv:2104.08821 (2021)
34. Lopez-Martin, M., Sanchez-Esguevillas, A., Arribas, J.I., Carro, B.: Supervised contrastive learning over prototype-label embeddings for network intrusion detection. Inf. Fusion **79**, 200–228 (2022)
35. Aouini, Z., Pekar, A.: NFStream: a flexible network data analysis framework. Comput. Netw. **204**, 108719 (2022). https://doi.org/10.1016/j.comnet.2021.108719
36. He, F., Liu, T., Tao, D.: Why resNet works? Residuals generalize. IEEE Trans. Neural Netw. Learn. Syst. **31**, 5349–5362 (2020)
37. Wu, L., et al.: R-drop: regularized dropout for neural networks. Adv. Neural Inf. Process. Syst.**34** (2021)
38. Shiravi, A., Shiravi, H., Tavallaee, M., Ghorbani, A.A.: Toward developing a systematic approach to generate benchmark datasets for intrusion detection. Comput. Secur. **31**, 357–374 (2012)
39. Sharafaldin, I., Lashkari, A.H., Ghorbani, A.A.: Toward generating a new intrusion detection dataset and intrusion traffic characterization. ICISSp **1**, 108–116 (2018)
40. Khan, M.A., Karim, M., Kim, Y., et al.: A scalable and hybrid intrusion detection system based on the convolutional-LSTM network. Symmetry **11**, 583 (2019)
41. Yu, Y., Long, J., Cai, Z.: Session-based network intrusion detection using a deep learning architecture. In: International Conference on Modeling Decisions for Artificial Intelligence, pp. 144–155. Springer (2017)
42. Chen, M., et al.: A network traffic classification model based on metric learning. CMC-Comput. Mater. Continua **64**, 941–959 (2020)
43. Li, M., Han, D., Yin, X., Liu, H., Li, D.: Design and implementation of an anomaly network traffic detection model integrating temporal and spatial features. Secur. Commun. Netw. **2021**, 7045823 (2021)
44. Siddiqi, M.A., Pak, W.: Optimizing filter-based feature selection method flow for intrusion detection system. Electronics **9**, 2114 (2020)
45. Bulavas, V., Marcinkevičius, V., Rumiński, J.: Study of multi-class classification algorithms' performance on highly imbalanced network intrusion datasets. Informatica **32**, 441–475 (2021)
46. Elmrabit, N., Zhou, F., Li, F., Zhou, H.: Evaluation of machine learning algorithms for anomaly detection. In: 2020 International Conference on Cyber Security and Protection of Digital Services (Cyber Security), pp. 1–8. IEEE (2020)

47. Injadat, M., Moubayed, A., Nassif, A.B., Shami, A.: Multi-stage optimized machine learning framework for network intrusion detection. IEEE Trans. Netw. Serv. Manage. **18**, 1803–1816 (2020)

48. Di Mauro, M., Galatro, G., Liotta, A.: Experimental review of neural-based approaches for network intrusion management. IEEE Trans. Netw. Serv. Manage. **17**, 2480–2495 (2020)

49. Wang, X., Wen, J., Alam, S., Jiang, Z., Wu, Y.: Semi-supervised learning combining transductive support vector machine with active learning. Neurocomputing **173**, 1288–1298 (2016)

50. Gamage, S., Samarabandu, J.: Deep learning methods in network intrusion detection: a survey and an objective comparison. J. Netw. Comput. Appl. **169**, 102767 (2020)

51. Abdel-Basset, M., Hawash, H., Chakrabortty, R.K., Ryan, M.J.: Semi-supervised spatiotemporal deep learning for intrusions detection in IoT networks. IEEE Internet Things J. **8**, 12251–12265 (2021)

# Anomaly Detection of Unstable Log Data Based on Contrastive Learning

Lan Liu[1], Zhihao Huang[1], Jun Lin[2,3(✉)], Kangjian He[1], and Zhanfa Hui[1]

[1] Guangdong Polytechnic Normal University, Guangzhou 510655, China
hzhnan@qq.com
[2] Sun Yat–Sen University, Guangzhou 510006, China
[3] China Electronic Product Reliability and Environmental Testing Institute,
Guangzhou 511370, China

**Abstract.** In today's large computer systems, it is almost impossible to locate errors using traditional manual methods in the face of abnormal conditions due to the unprecedented size and complexity of the system. As part of computer resources, log data records every step of the system operation process, making log data a popular method for detecting abnormal system status. However, in actual production environments, normal logs make up most of the log data types, and the log structure is constantly adjusted with each update for maintenance and upgrades. Therefore, overcoming the instability of logs caused by these issues has become a major concern for researchers in the field of log detection. In this paper, we propose a method to improve log instability and enhance model detection accuracy by using contrastive learning in the log vectorization and detection phases. Contrastive learning is used to train the vectorization and diagnostic models by aggregating and distinguishing classes in mathematical space, resulting in a more robust vectorization model and better generalization of the generated template vector data. This also improves the feature extraction ability of the diagnostic model and improves the final anomaly classification results. Experimental results show that our method improves the handling of unstable log data in anomaly detection and outperforms the baseline on HDFS and BGL datasets in terms of experimental performance.

**Keywords:** Anomaly Detection · Log Embedding · Unstable Log Data · Contrastive Learning · Deep Learning

## 1 Introduction

The way of diagnosing systems based on log data has evolved with the development of deep learning techniques in recent years. Before AlexNet [14] technology was proposed, using machine learning to analyze logs was almost the default approach in the academic community. In this context, approaches such as using PCA [30], SVM [16,27], clustering [18], rule-based system detection [2,8,23,32], and pattern recognition-based analysis methodss [19,29] were developed, amongothers. As deep learning gained popularity in industry and academia

© ICST Institute for Computer Sciences, Social Informatics and Telecommunications Engineering 2025
Published by Springer Nature Switzerland AG 2025. All Rights Reserved
J. Cai et al. (Eds.): SPNCE 2023, LNICST 525, pp. 147–160, 2025.
https://doi.org/10.1007/978-3-031-73699-5_10

due to its powerful feature extraction capabilities in space and time, more researchers began to explore using log data in a deep learning approach for diagnosing system states. Logs are generated sequentially over time and thus exhibit a high degree of correlation with each other in the temporal dimension. This makes techniques like RNN [4,21,22,33] and BERT [7], which are powerful at capturing features in the temporal space, well-suited for uncovering deep temporal features between logs and log sequences to determine the current system state. These techniques have achieved experimental results that far surpass those of machine learning.

Although log data is a valuable resource for recording system states, in practice the model's performance can be impacted by the instability of logs. The instability of log data manifests in two main ways: (1) Since the normal state of the system is much more common than the abnormal state in real-world environments, a small amount of abnormal data is often hidden among a large amount of normal data, resulting in an imbalance between categories. (2) Due to system maintenance and upgrades, the log template format changes, which can confuse the running detection model with unfamiliar log templates. Despite extensive research and progress in the field of log detection, the problem of log instability remains an important factor limiting the performance of log detection.

In recent years, pre-trained language models and contrastive learning have achieved good results in computer vision (CV) and natural language processing (NLP) respectively. In many well-known pre-trained models, researchers have adopted the transformer architecture [26], which allows for simultaneous observation of moments on either side of a moment in time. The BERT model, designed using the transformer architecture, has a larger number of parameters than other neural networks, allowing for a richer learning process during pre-training. Sentence-BERT [24], proposed by Nils Reimers and Iryna Gurevych, aims to train a generalized linguistic embedding model, using the model to vectorize character sentences in the form of vectors. This approach has achieved good results in terms of speed and accuracy. The core idea of the contrastive loss function, proposed in the context of contrastive learning, is to spatially partition different samples such that samples of the same kind are aggregated and samples of different categories are separated in the embedding space. This makes contrastive learning well-suited for classification tasks. With the efforts of academic researchers, contrastive learning-based techniques have achieved excellent results on both supervised [1,13] and unsupervised tasks [5,6,31].

We expect system state detection models to have high detection accuracy, be able to handle unstable log data, and exhibit high robustness. Building on the previously proposed problem, this work proposes the following two contributions as a solution to the problem.

(1) To address the problem of accuracy degradation caused by the model's difficulty in dealing with unknown template types introduced by the development and maintenance process, we propose a Bert-based log template embedding model. We obtain positive example samples in contrastive learning by two random dropouts, and finally update the model parameters in an unsuper-

vised way to obtain semantically more abstract and more generalized vector data.

(2) In the log data detection phase, we propose a novel detection model that learns the system state information implicit in the log data and infers the current system state information accordingly. The model uses LSTM and CNN modules in parallel to capture temporal and attentional information, respectively, and the results of both modules are early fused before input to the MLP projection.

The rest of this paper is organized as follows: Sect. 2 presents the current state of research on system detection models based on log data and summarizes related methods for handling unstable logs. Section 3 describes our proposed method in detail. Section 4 compares and validates the related algorithms, and analyzes and discusses the results. Section 5 is the conclusion section, which summarizes the research methods proposed in this paper and discusses potential future research directions.

## 2 Related Work

In this section, we summarize the algorithms and research work related to this study.

### 2.1 Log Anomaly Detection

Over the past few years, the popularity of deep learning has allowed it to start replacing traditional statistical and rule-based machine learning in log detection. Most of these methods use neural networks to learn feature information in log sequences to determine the current state of the system and have achieved good prediction results in practice. Lu et al. [20] used convolutional neural networks (CNNs) to extract feature information from log data by convolution, which improved the accuracy of prediction results. The DeepLog model proposed by Du et al. [4] used the LSTM model, which is better at capturing timing information, compared to CNNs, and split the log information into two parts, log keys and log variables, to be modeled separately, which effectively improved the effectiveness of the detection model compared to other published methods. Meng et al. [22] proposed a novel log vectorization approach to address the shortcomings of previous studies on log preprocessing, which more fully exploits the semantic information of log data, and the model shows stronger robustness in processing than previous approaches when facing unfamiliar logs. Wang et al. [28] proposed a multiscale detection model that uses CNNs for feature extraction of both global and local information and combines features at multiple scales to complement the expressiveness of feature information. Guo et al. proposed a novel training approach based on the idea of DeepLog by taking advantage of the transformer's ability to simultaneously take into account information from each time period, which improved the detection accuracy of the model. [7]

## 2.2  Unstable Log Data

In practice, logs evolve as the system is maintained and updated, so they are not static, and we can assume that the vast majority of environments have far more normal states than abnormal states, which creates an imbalance in log data in terms of categories. Although many works have achieved good results in experiments, this is often based on a closed-world assumption, which is often affected by unstable log data in real environments. Therefore, Zhang et al.'s LogRobust [33] proposes a novel vectorization technique that effectively mitigates the negative effects of sentence structure and character transformations by mapping log data onto the data space. The vectorization scheme is further refined in the LogAnomaly [22] method proposed by Meng et al. by introducing "template2vec", which takes into account the synonyms and antonyms of the characters in the log, making the generated vectors more robust, and also uses the word Term Frequency-Inverse Document Frequency (TF-IDF) method to assign weights to different characters to balance their influence on the final results, ultimately achieving higher accuracy. In terms of both accuracy and robustness, the final results are excellent. In solving the class imbalance problem of log data in a practical environment, Shayan et al. proposed a detection model based on a Siamese network, which is effective for similarity learning and can learn from both anomalous and non-anomalous data without relying on balanced training data, achieving good results in dealing with the class imbalance of log data [9].

## 3  Method

In this section, we propose a Bert-based Embedding model for log data and a novel detection model to improve the problem of unstable log data in log detection systems.

### 3.1  Data Pre-processing

Raw log data is typically unstructured. In order to convert log data into a form that can be easily processed by the model, we use the Drain method [10] to pre-process log data and convert unstructured text into structured text. Drain uses a fixed-depth parse tree that encodes parsing rules specifically designed to guide the parsing of log data. It is worth noting that although Drain's performance is excellent and demonstrates its capability in log parsing, some noise will inevitably still be introduced into the parsing results during the parsing process. However, our approach is sufficient to handle this problem.

Drain is an online log parsing method based on a fixed-depth tree. When a new raw log message arrives, Drain preprocesses it using simple regular expressions based on domain knowledge. Drain then searches for log groups (i.e., leaf nodes of the tree) according to special design rules encoded in the nodes inside the tree. If a suitable log group is found, the log message is matched to a log event stored in that log group. Otherwise, a new log group is created based on the log message.

## 3.2  BERT-Based Embedding Model

This method of vectorizing log data is based on the BERT model [3], which can grasp the semantics globally compared to Word2ver's vectorization method.BERT benefits from the Transformer architecture, which can take into account the character information at each point in time when processing sentence information, making the quantized sentences characterize stronger abstract information. It has stronger robustness and generalization ability when facing unstable log data.

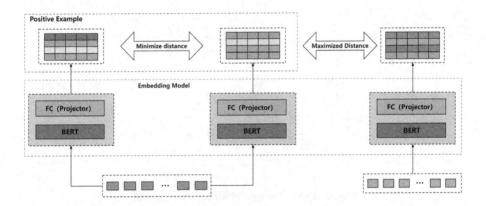

**Fig. 1.** Embedding model training framework

To train the model, we use an unsupervised contrast learning method to fine-tune a pre-trained BERT model. A fully connected layer is attached to the output of the BERT model for vector projection. The structure and training process of the model are shown in Fig. 1. The log data is first input to the BERT model, and the first CLS sentence vector is taken as the vector representation of the global data. The data is then input to the fully connected layer to obtain the projection of the data on the vector space. By using two random dropouts, different positive examples of the same example are obtained. In the loss training, unsupervised contrastive learning is used to calculate the loss of the results, to minimize the distance between positive examples of samples in the vector space, while maximizing the distance between negative samples. This guides the model to update its parameters according to the loss results, so that the vector generated by the final model has a stronger degree of aggregation within the category and a more obvious distinction between different categories, resulting in stronger generalization in the results.

## 3.3  Detection Model Based on Log Data

For log data, it is difficult to manually augment the data while ensuring semantic invariance. In SimCSE [5] and R-Drop [17], we use a method that doesn't involve manual processing, but rather leverages the properties of neural networks to perform data augmentation. This method uses the properties of randomly deactivated neurons in Dropout to augment a piece of data, and it produces good results. Therefore, we also use a simple "Dropout twice" method to construct a supervised contrastive learning method for positive samples. The samples are passed through the feature extraction model twice to obtain different feature vectors for the same input.

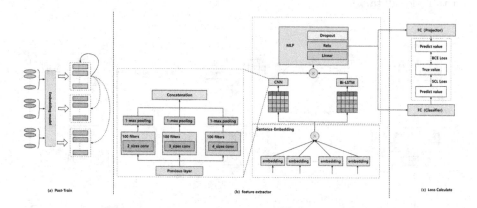

**Fig. 2.** Detection model structure diagram

In this section, we propose a novel model for log data detection. The architecture of the model is shown in Fig. 2, and the whole model consists of three major parts, which are log template embedding, feature extraction of vector information, and loss calculation during the training update stage. The information on log template vectorization can be know in detail from Sect. 3.2. For the feature extraction of vector information, we use Long Short Term Memory Network (LSTM) [12] and Convolutional Neural Network (CNN) [15] in parallel, LSTM has the advantage of capturing the temporal sequence of long sequence information, which can uncover the implicit semantic expressions hidden between the sequence information, while CNN model has the advantage of giving different attentions to uncover the key information, and the output of these two models is The outputs of these two models are ealry fused and the fused results are fed into a Multilayer Perceptron (MLP) to obtain two semantically consistent vectors with different expressions using the randomness of dropout in the MLP. The role of the projection network is to map the feature-extracted vectors into final vectors for loss computation. In this paper, the projection network uses a 256-dimensional fully-connected layer, uses a unit hypersphere for vectorization. And the classification network will map the dimensionality to the number of label categories through a fully connected layer.The final model parameters will be updated based on the Supervised Contrastive Learning(SCL) loss values and Binary Cross Entropy(BCE) loss values on the projection and classification layers.

---

**Algorithm 1:** Anomaly detection model training

**input** : A batch T, which contains the log sequence $x_i$ and its corresponding label $y_i$, uses $e(\cdot)$ to represent the function of the embedding layer, $f(\cdot)$ to represent the function of the projection calculation, and $g(\cdot)$ to represent the function of the classification calculation

**output**: Updated anomaly detection model

1  **foreach** $(x_i, y_i) \in T$ **do**
2      Vectorize the log sequence $E(x_i) = e_i$;
3      Input $e_i$ twice to the feature extraction model and to the projection and classification layers, respectively, using $f^*(\cdot)$ and $g^*(\cdot)$ to represent the computational process when the sample is input to the model a second time;
4      Data is output from the projection layer:$f(e_i) = f_i, f^*(e_i) = f_i^*$;
5      Data is output from the classification layer:$g(e_i) = g_i, g^*(e_i) = g_i^*$;
6      **if** $y_i == 1$ **then**
7          $\ell_{BCE} = (f_i, 1)\, and\, (f_i^*, 1)$;
8          $\ell_{SCL} = (g_i, g_i^*, g_{j \neq i}, 1)$;
9          $\ell = \lambda \ell_{BCE} + (1 - \lambda)\, \ell_{SCL}$;
10     **end**
11     **if** $y_i == 0$ **then**
12         $\ell_{BCE} = (f_i, 0)\, and\, (f_i^*, 0)$;
13         $\ell_{SCL} = (g_i, g_i^*, g_{j \neq i}, 0)$;
14         $\ell = \lambda \ell_{BCE} + (1 - \lambda)\, \ell_{SCL}$;
15     **end**
16     Update anomaly detection models using loss functions;
17 **end**

---

### 3.4  Loss Function

For the training of the embedding model, we use an Unsupervised Contrastive Learning approach. We represent the log sequences as $\{x_i\}_i^m$. Simultaneous use $x_i$ and $x_i^+$ to represent different samples between the same positive cases. Think of $z$ as the random mask used by the embedding model in random dropot. We treat equation $h_i^z = f_\theta(x_i, z)$ as the vector result obtained by the model when processing the log sequence $x_i$ and the random mask $z$. For the same sequence, we input it into the model twice and use different random masks to get two different vectorization results. In a batch of m log sequences, the loss function will be expressed as the following eq. (1),$\tau > 0$ is an adjustable scalar temperature parameter that controls the separation of classes;

$$\ell_{CL} = -\log \frac{e^{\text{sim}\left(\mathbf{h}_i^{z_i}, \mathbf{h}_i^{z_i'}\right)/\tau}}{\sum_{j=1}^{m} e^{\text{sim}\left(\mathbf{h}_i^{z_i}, \mathbf{h}_j^{z_j'}\right)/\tau}} \tag{1}$$

The BCE loss function in Eq. (2) calculates the cross-entropy loss for each sample in the batch. The cross-entropy loss is commonly used for binary classification tasks, where the goal is to predict the probability that a sample belongs to the positive class. In this case, the BCE loss function is applied to both the original sample $x_i$ and its corresponding positive example $x_i^+$.

The SCL loss function in Eq. (3) uses supervised contrastive learning to calculate the loss for each sample in the batch. Supervised contrastive learning is a technique used to improve the representation learning of a model by contrasting the features of similar and dissimilar samples. In this case, the SCL loss function compares the features of each sample with those of every other sample in the batch, and applies a log loss to the contrastive terms.

The total loss is the weighted average of the BCE and SCL loss functions, where the weight of each loss is determined by the hyperparameter $\lambda$. By setting $\lambda$ to different values, it is possible to adjust the relative importance of the BCE and SCL loss functions in the final loss calculation.

$$\ell_{BCE} = \frac{1}{2N} \sum_i - \left[ y_i \cdot \log(p_i) + (1 - y_i) \cdot \log(1 - p_i) + \right.$$

$$\left. y_i^+ \cdot \log(p_i) + \left(1 - y_i^+\right) \cdot \log(1 - p_i) \right] \quad (2)$$

$$\ell_{SCL} = \sum_{i=1}^{2N} - \left[ \frac{1}{2N_{y_i} - 1} \sum_{j=1}^{2N} \mathbf{1}_{i \neq j} \mathbf{1}_{y_i = y_j} \cdot \right.$$

$$\left. \log \frac{\exp\left(f\left(x_i\right) \cdot f\left(x_j\right) / \tau\right)}{\sum_{k=1}^{2N} \mathbf{1}_{i \neq k} \exp\left(f\left(x_i\right) \cdot f\left(x_k\right) / \tau\right)} \right] \quad (3)$$

$$\ell = (1 - \lambda)\mathcal{L}_{BCE} + \lambda\mathcal{L}_{SCL} \quad (4)$$

## 4    Experiments

### 4.1    Benchmark Dataset

In this thesis, we use the log data provided by the open-source loghub project [11] for our experiments. Loghub is a well-known dataset for system anomaly detection based on log data, and has been used by many seminal and groundbreaking works in the field.

Loghub provides 17 real-world log datasets collected from a variety of systems, including distributed systems, supercomputers, operating systems, mobile systems, server applications, and standalone software. In our experiments, we use two of these datasets, HDFS and BGL, as the data for our experiments.

The BGL dataset is generated by the Blue Gene/L supercomputer and consists of 4,747,963 logs, each of which has been manually labeled as normal or abnormal. The HDFS dataset contains 11,175,629 logs collected from over 200 Amazon EC2 nodes. The dataset includes 575,061 log blocks, of which 16,838 blocks have been labeled as abnormal by Hadoop domain experts.

In this experiment, we use Drain [10] to parse the logs. Drain is a fast and accurate parser that can parse logs in a streaming and timely manner. To improve

**Table 1.** Details of the datasets.

| Datasets | Description | #Durain | #Messages |
|----------|-------------|---------|-----------|
| HDFS | Hadoop distributed file system | 38.7 h | 11,175,629 |
| BGL | BlueGene/L Supercomputer log | 7 months | 4,747,963 |

its performance, Drain uses a fixed-depth parse tree with specially designed parsing rules. This allows it to achieve both high accuracy and fast parsing speeds, making it a superior choice compared to other parsers.

**Table 2.** Details of the processed datasets.

| Datasets | #Log Template | #Log Sequence | #Sequence Anomaly |
|----------|---------------|---------------|-------------------|
| HDFS | 48 | 575061 | 16838 |
| BGL | 1000 | 37315 | 3018 |

For the HDFS logs, we vectorized all of the templates and used them to build our diagnostic system. However, to test the robustness of the system, we only used 100 of the 1000 available templates for BGL logs. The remaining 900 templates were vectorized using a vectorization model, and their similarity to the selected 100 templates was measured using cosine similarity. The categories of the unfamiliar templates were then matched to the most similar ones among the selected templates. This allowed us to evaluate the performance of the diagnostic system on both familiar and unfamiliar templates.

## 4.2 Evaluation Criteria

We use Prediction, Recall, and F1-measure to evaluate the performance of the experimental model. These evaluation criteria reflect the performance of the model for detecting the system state.

$$\text{Precision} = \frac{TP}{TP + FP} \tag{5}$$

$$\text{Recall} = \frac{TP}{TP + FN} \tag{6}$$

$$F1 \text{ measure} = \frac{2 \times \text{Precision} \times \text{Recall}}{\text{Precision} + \text{Recall}} \tag{7}$$

## 4.3 Implementation Details

We used 80% of the dataset for training our model and 20% for testing the results. We trained the model using the Adam optimizer with a learning rate of 1e-2, a uniform batch size of 1024, and a dropout of 0.3 for a total of 500 epochs. We selected Deeplog [4], LogRobust [33], CNNLog [20], LogBERT [7], LogCluster [25], and LogAnomaly [22] as the baseline models for comparison.

## 4.4    Evaluation of The Overall Performance

In this section, we compare our method with the baseline method on both the HDFS and BGL datasets. Additionally, in our proposed method, we compare the use of the Contrastive loss with versions using only the BCE loss and a mixed loss of BCE and SCL to verify the effectiveness of the Contrastive loss.

**Table 3.** Independent test performance metrics of different methods on the dataset (Precision, Recll, and F1-measure)

| Datasets | Method | Precision | Recall | F1-measure |
|----------|--------|-----------|--------|------------|
| HDFS | LogCluster | 0.87 | 0.74 | 0.80 |
|  | LogBERT | 0.87 | 0.78 | 0.82 |
|  | Deeplog | 0.95 | 0.96 | 0.96 |
|  | LogRobust | 0.98 | 1.00 | 0.99 |
|  | LogAnomaly | 0.96 | 0.94 | 0.95 |
|  | CNNLog | 0.97 | 0.99 | 0.98 |
|  | Ours(BCE) | **0.99** | 0.96 | 0.98 |
|  | Ours(SCL+BCE) | **0.99** | 0.99 | **0.99** |
| BGL | LogCluster | 0.42 | 0.87 | 0.57 |
|  | LogBERT | 0.89 | 0.92 | 0.90 |
|  | Deeplog | 0.90 | 0.96 | 0.93 |
|  | LogAnomaly | 0.97 | 0.94 | 0.96 |
|  | Ours(BCE) | **0.97** | 0.93 | 0.94 |
|  | Ours(SCL+BCE) | **0.97** | 0.94 | **0.96** |

**Performance on Log Anomaly Detection.** In Table 3, we can see that on the HDFS dataset, our method using SCL+BCE achieves the best F1 score, while using only BCE yields the best precision. SCL+BCE performs slightly worse than BCE in terms of recall and F1. On the BGL dataset, our method using SCL+BCE achieves the best F1 and precision scores, while the method using only BCE performs slightly worse in terms of both recall and F1. It should be noted that for the BGL template data, we only used one-tenth of it for training and prediction. Despite this, our model still achieved the best results, demonstrating its robustness in low-quality data environments.

## 4.5    Visualization Contribution of Contrastive Learning to Category Clustering

Figures 3, 4, and 5 show images of the BGL data projected by the projection layer and then reduced in dimension using PCA. Figure 3 shows the results of training our model using only the BCE method, while Figs. 4 and 5 show the results of training our model using the BCE+SCL method with different temperature hyperparameters. In Fig. 4, $\tau$ was set to 0.09, and in Fig. 5, $\tau$ was set to 0.2.

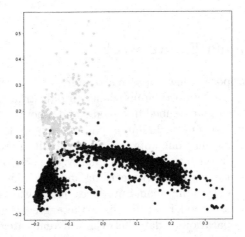

**Fig. 3.** Vector projection map using only the BCE loss function

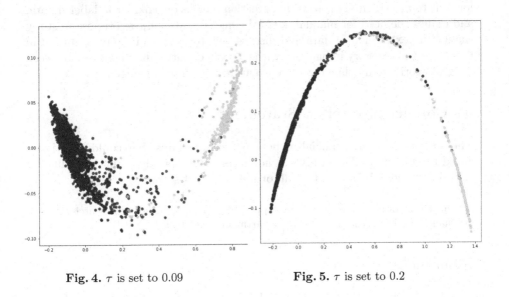

**Fig. 4.** $\tau$ is set to 0.09                    **Fig. 5.** $\tau$ is set to 0.2

**Projection Results.** It can be seen that when using only the BCE method, the normal and abnormal data are less tightly clustered in spatial distribution, and similar data are more severely separated from each other. In contrast, when using the contrastive loss function, the data is more densely clustered within the same category and more clearly separated between different categories. In Figs. 4 and 5, where $\tau$ is set to 0.09 and 0.2, respectively, it can be seen that using a larger temperature hyperparameter results in better clustering and separation of the data.

## 5　Conclusion and Future Work

In this paper, we propose a new approach to address the common challenges of log template updates and data type imbalance in industrial environments. Our approach uses a log template embedding model and a novel log detection model based on contrastive learning techniques. Through experiments on HDFS and BGL datasets, we show that our approach yields small improvements over the baseline, while being robust to poor data quality. We attribute the success of our approach to the use of contrastive learning and data augmentation through simple dropout. The embedding model produces data with stronger generalization, while the detection model benefits from the aggregation of data between categories and the separation of data between different categories, resulting in improved detection accuracy.

In future work, we plan to explore the potential of extending our model from supervised to self-supervised and unsupervised settings. Another area of interest for us is to investigate how to train detection models on small or unlabeled data, and reduce the need for manual data labeling. To this end, we propose to study the feature extraction of data and discuss how to improve its representation in the context of category imbalance, with the goal of better distinguishing between data categories and achieving more accurate judgments of system status.

## 6　Conflict of Interest Statement

The authors have no financial or personal relationships that could have influenced the research. This study did not receive any specific grant from funding agencies in the public, commercial, or not-for-profit sectors.

**Acknowledgments.** This work was supported in part by Scientific Research Projects of Guangdong Provincial Education Department (No. 2022ZDZX1015).

## References

1. Chen, T., Kornblith, S., Norouzi, M., Hinton, G.: A simple framework for contrastive learning of visual representations. In: International Conference on Machine Learning, pp. 1597–1607. PMLR (2020)
2. Cinque, M., Cotroneo, D., Pecchia, A.: Event logs for the analysis of software failures: a rule-based approach. IEEE Trans. Software Eng. **39**(6), 806–821 (2012)

3. Devlin, J., Chang, M.W., Lee, K., Toutanova, K.: BERT: pre-training of deep bidirectional transformers for language understanding. ArXiv preprint arxiv: abs/1810.04805 (2019)
4. Du, M., Li, F., Zheng, G., Srikumar, V.: DeepLog: anomaly detection and diagnosis from system logs through deep learning. In: Proceedings of the 2017 ACM SIGSAC Conference on Computer and Communications Security, pp. 1285–1298 (2017)
5. Gao, T., Yao, X., Chen, D.: SimCSE: simple contrastive learning of sentence embeddings. arXiv preprint arXiv:2104.08821 (2021)
6. Giorgi, J., Nitski, O., Wang, B., Bader, G.: DeCLUTR: deep contrastive learning for unsupervised textual representations. arXiv preprint arXiv:2006.03659 (2020)
7. Guo, H., Yuan, S., Wu, X.: LogBERT: log anomaly detection via BERT. In: 2021 International Joint Conference on Neural Networks (IJCNN), pp. 1–8 (2021)
8. Hansen, S.E., Atkins, E.T.: Automated system monitoring and notification with swatch. In: LISA, vol. 93, pp. 145–152. Monterey, CA (1993)
9. Hashemi, S., Mäntylä, M.: Detecting anomalies in software execution logs with siamese network. ArXiv preprint arxiv: abs/2102.01452 (2021)
10. He, P., Zhu, J., Zheng, Z., Lyu, M.R.: Drain: an online log parsing approach with fixed depth tree. In: 2017 IEEE International Conference on Web Services (ICWS), pp. 33–40 (2017)
11. He, S., Zhu, J., He, P., Lyu, M.R.: Loghub: a large collection of system log datasets towards automated log analytics. ArXiv preprint arxiv: abs/2008.06448 (2020)
12. Hochreiter, S., Schmidhuber, J.: Long short-term memory. Neural Comput. **9**, 1735–1780 (1997)
13. Khosla, P., et al.: Supervised contrastive learning. Adv. Neural. Inf. Process. Syst. **33**, 18661–18673 (2020)
14. Krizhevsky, A., Sutskever, I., Hinton, G.E.: ImageNet classification with deep convolutional neural networks. Commun. ACM **60**, 84–90 (2012)
15. LeCun, Y., Bottou, L., Bengio, Y., Haffner, P.: Gradient-based learning applied to document recognition. Proc. IEEE **86**, 2278–2324 (1998)
16. Li, K.L., Huang, H.K., Tian, S.F., Xu, W.: Improving one-class SVM for anomaly detection. In: Proceedings of the 2003 International Conference on Machine Learning and Cybernetics (IEEE Cat. No. 03EX693), vol. 5, pp. 3077–3081. IEEE (2003)
17. Liang, X., et al.: R-drop: regularized dropout for neural networks. In: NeurIPS (2021)
18. Lin, Q., Zhang, H., Lou, J.G., Zhang, Y., Chen, X.: Log clustering based problem identification for online service systems. In: Proceedings of the 38th International Conference on Software Engineering Companion, pp. 102–111 (2016)
19. Lou, J.G., Fu, Q., Yang, S., Xu, Y., Li, J.: Mining invariants from console logs for system problem detection. In: 2010 USENIX Annual Technical Conference (USENIX ATC 10) (2010)
20. Lu, S., Wei, X., Li, Y., Wang, L.: Detecting anomaly in big data system logs using convolutional neural network. In: 2018 IEEE 16th Intl Conf on Dependable, Autonomic and Secure Computing, 16th Intl Conf on Pervasive Intelligence and Computing, 4th Intl Conf on Big Data Intelligence and Computing and Cyber Science and Technology Congress(DASC/PiCom/DataCom/CyberSciTech), pp. 151–158 (2018)
21. Malhotra, P., Ramakrishnan, A., Anand, G., Vig, L., Agarwal, P., Shroff, G.: LSTM-based encoder-decoder for multi-sensor anomaly detection. arXiv preprint arXiv:1607.00148 (2016)
22. Meng, W., et al.: Loganomaly: unsupervised detection of sequential and quantitative anomalies in unstructured logs. In: IJCAI, vol. 19, pp. 4739–4745 (2019)

23. Prewett, J.E.: Analyzing cluster log files using logsurfer. In: Proceedings of the 4th Annual Conference on Linux Clusters. Citeseer (2003)
24. Reimers, N., Gurevych, I.: Sentence-BERT: sentence embeddings using siamese BERT-networks. arXiv preprint arXiv:1908.10084 (2019)
25. Vaarandi, R., Pihelgas, M.: Logcluster - a data clustering and pattern mining algorithm for event logs. In: 2015 11th International Conference on Network and Service Management (CNSM), pp. 1–7 (2015). https://doi.org/10.1109/CNSM.2015.7367331
26. Vaswani, A., et al.: Attention is all you need. ArXiv preprint arxiv: abs/1706.03762 (2017)
27. Wang, Y., Wong, J., Miner, A.: Anomaly intrusion detection using one class SVM. In: Proceedings from the Fifth Annual IEEE SMC Information Assurance Workshop, 2004, pp. 358–364. IEEE (2004)
28. Wang, Z., Chen, Z., Ni, J., Liu, H., Chen, H., Tang, J.: Multi-scale one-class recurrent neural networks for discrete event sequence anomaly detection. In: Proceedings of the 27th ACM SIGKDD Conference on Knowledge Discovery & Data Mining (2021)
29. Xu, W., Huang, L., Fox, A., Patterson, D., Jordan, M.: Online system problem detection by mining patterns of console logs. In: 2009 ninth IEEE International Conference on Data Mining, pp. 588–597. IEEE (2009)
30. Xu, W., Huang, L., Fox, A., Patterson, D., Jordan, M.I.: Detecting large-scale system problems by mining console logs. In: Proceedings of the ACM SIGOPS 22nd Symposium on Operating Systems Principles, pp. 117–132 (2009)
31. Yan, Y., Li, R., Wang, S., Zhang, F., Wu, W., Xu, W.: ConSERT: a contrastive framework for self-supervised sentence representation transfer. arXiv preprint arXiv:2105.11741 (2021)
32. Yen, T.F., et al.: Beehive: large-scale log analysis for detecting suspicious activity in enterprise networks. In: Proceedings of the 29th Annual Computer Security Applications Conference, pp. 199–208 (2013)
33. Zhang, X., et al.: Robust log-based anomaly detection on unstable log data. In: Proceedings of the 2019 27th ACM Joint Meeting on European Software Engineering Conference and Symposium on the Foundations of Software Engineering, pp. 807–817 (2019)

# An Integration-Enhanced ZNN Approach for Chaotic Combination Synchronization with External Disturbances*

Chenfu Yi$^{(\boxtimes)}$, Mingdong Zhu, Jingjing Chen, and Jinghui Peng

School of Cyber Security, Guangdong Polytechnic Normal University,
510635 Guangzhou, China
chenfuyi@gpnu.edu.cn

**Abstract.** Robust combination synchronization has garnered extensive attention within the domains of science and engineering, particularly in the realm of secure communication in recent years. In contrast to conventional single master-single slave system, the introduction of multiple variables and intricate combination methods in combination synchronization significantly increases the complexity of decryption, boosting the confidentiality and security of signal transmission. However, due to the ubiquity of time-varying external interference, the synchronization results of ordinary methods are not ideal or may even be divergent. In view of these challenges, this paper proposes the integration-enhanced zeroing neural network (IEZNN) model and its associated controller to achieve robust combination synchronization of chaotic systems. Theoretical research fully substantiate the effectiveness of the proposed IEZNN approach and its related controller. Additionally, the numerical findings show that, in comparison to the conventional zeroing neural network (CZNN) method, the controller designed by IEZNN model have remarkable anti-interference performance in the presence of external time-varying disturbances.

**Keywords:** Zeroing neural network · Chaotic combination synchronization · Chaotic systems · External disturbances · Robustness

---

This work was supported by the special Projects in National Key Research and Development Program of China (2018YFB1802200, 2019YFB1804403), GPNU Foundation (2022SDKYA029), the Key Areas of Guangdong Province (2019B010118001), National Natural Science Foundation of China (61972104, 61902080, 62002072, 61702120), Science and Technology Project in Guangzhou (201803010081), Foshan Science and Technology Innovation Project, China (2018IT100283), Guangzhou Key Laboratory (202102100006) and Science and Technology Program of Guangzhou, China (202002020035), Industry-University-Research Innovation Fund for Chinese Universities (2021FNA04010), the Programs for Foundations of Jiangxi Province of China (20192BBG70050, GJJ180749), the GPNU Foundation (2022SDKYA029), the Education Department of Guangdong Province under Grant 2021KTSCX063.

© ICST Institute for Computer Sciences, Social Informatics and Telecommunications Engineering 2025
Published by Springer Nature Switzerland AG 2025. All Rights Reserved
J. Cai et al. (Eds.): SPNCE 2023, LNICST 525, pp. 161–174, 2025.
https://doi.org/10.1007/978-3-031-73699-5_11

# 1 Introduction

At the end of the 20th century, Pecora and Carroll [12] accomplished a watershed moment when they realized the synchronization control of chaotic systems, kicking off chaotic synchronization research. The concept of chaotic synchronization refers to the process of achieving consistency between two or more chaotic systems by modifying specific motion characteristics while under the influence of coupling or external forces. It is extensively applied in a variety of domains, including secure communication [5,7], biomedicine [10], power electronics [4], signal processing [8], and economics [6]. For instance, Vaseghi et al. [17] used the adaptive sliding mode control method for chaos synchronization and applied it to secure communication in wireless sensor networks. Additionally, Lin et al. [11] have achieved significant breakthroughs in the field of secure communication, attaining chaos synchronization with the aid of controllers created utilizing brain-limited neural networks.

However, when employed for secure communication, the conventional single master-single salve system synchronous control architecture is relatively straightforward and easily cracked. Therefore, Sun et al. [16] achieved combination synchronization between two master systems and two slave systems based on the Lyapunov stability theorem and adaptive control. For the purpose of using combination synchronization in secure communication, the transmission signal can be split into several pieces and loaded into various master systems. Alternatively, time can be divided into various intervals, and signals from those intervals can be loaded into various master systems. [13]. In addition, chaotic combination synchronization has an advantage over the conventional single master-single slave system due to the use of numerous variables and sophisticated combination techniques. Decrypting becomes increasingly challenging because it requires access to essential state variables and their corresponding combination techniques. Therefore, compared to earlier transmission techniques, using combination synchronization for signal transmission improves confidentiality.

It is worth noting that there are numerous control strategies that can effectively address the issue of chaotic combination synchronization. Specifically, the lyapunov stability theorem and adaptive control technology [14,16], the active backstepping design method [13], and the sliding mode control technology [15]. Moreover, Li et al. [9] used the conventional zeroing neural network (CZNN) to construct a straightforward chaotic synchronization controller while taking parameter disturbances, model uncertainty, and outside disturbances into consideration.

While the aforementioned methods, such as the CZNN method, have found widely use in practical engineering, research on the robustness of the CZNN method in chaotic combination synchronization is still in its early stages. Proverbially, chaotic systems inevitably encounter some external disturbances, such as bias errors, interactions with environment, electromagnetic interference in circuit systems, and noise during signal transmission [3]. These time-varying external disturbances may affect the stability and accuracy of the relevant controllers for synchronizing chaotic systems, which can result in the failure of the synchronization process. [2]. To accomplish chaotic combination synchronization in practical applications, effective and reliable approaches to suppress time-varying external disturbances are therefore urgently needed.

In order to mitigate external noise interference during the synchronization procedure, unlike the research based on the CZNN approach [9] or research foucusing on rate of convergence [1], this article uses the IEZNN model and devises a corresponding controller to achieve robust combination synchronization of chaotic systems in the presence of time-varying external disturbances. Moreover, the usefulness and superiority of the IEZNN model and its associated controller in practical applications are further confirmed by numerical experiments that include three examples of combination synchronization.

The remainder of this essay is organized as follows. In Sect. 2, the IEZNN model and its associated controller are described, together with a preliminary formula for the synchronization problem between two chaotic systems under the impact of time-variant external disturbances. Besides, some lemmas are presented in Sect. 3. In Sect. 4, simulation experiments were carried out using three examples of combination synchronization in the presence of time-varying external noise, and the IEZNN model was compared with the CZNN model. The complete material is summarized in Sect. 4.1. Before wrapping up this introduction, the letter's main contributions are given below.

i) Differing from traditional single master-single salve system synchronization, chaotic combination synchronization exhibits greater confidentiality in secure communication owing to its multiple variables and complex combination methods.
ii) This article proposes the IEZNN model and designs associated controller to synchronize chaotic systems in the presence of time-varying external disturbances, overcoming the shortcomings of traditional techniques that fall to attain synchronization.
iii) Under the influence of external disturbances, the effectiveness and superiority of the IEZNN model and its associated controller in practical applications are validated through numerical research that include three examples of chaotic combination synchronization.

## 2   Preliminary and Approaches

In this section,the expression of the synchronisation issue between master and slave chaotic systems with noise is introduced. Moreover, the relevant synchronous controller designed with IEZNN model is proposed.

### 2.1   Synchronization of Chaotic Systems

Chaos synchronization refers to the consistency and stability of the trajectories of the master chaotic system and the slave chaotic system. In the presence of external noise influences, the differential equation of the master chaotic system can be defined as:

$$\begin{cases} \dot{y}_{m1}(t) = z_{m1}(y_{m1}(t)) + \beta_1, \\ \dot{y}_{m2}(t) = z_{m2}(y_{m2}(t)) + \beta_2, \\ \dot{y}_{m3}(t) = z_{m3}(y_{m3}(t)) + \beta_3, \end{cases} \tag{1}$$

where $y_m(t) = [y_{m1}(t), y_{m2}(t), \cdots, y_{mn}(t)] \in \mathbb{R}^n$ is the state vector of the master chaotic system; $z_m(\cdot) : \mathbb{R}^n \to \mathbb{R}^m$ represents the nonlinear-mapping function and $\beta$ stands for the external noise and acting during synchronization. Similarly, the general expression for the chaotic system with controller input can be expressed as follows:

$$\begin{cases} \dot{y}_{s1}(t) = z_{s1}(y_{s1}(t)) + u_1(t), \\ \dot{y}_{s2}(t) = z_{s2}(y_{s2}(t)) + u_2(t), \\ \dot{y}_{s3}(t) = z_{s3}(y_{s3}(t)) + u_3(t), \end{cases} \tag{2}$$

where $y_s(t) = [y_{s1}(t), y_{s2}(t), \cdots, y_{sn}(t)] \in \mathbb{R}^n$ denotes the state vector of the slave chaotic system; $z_s(\cdot) : \mathbb{R}^n \to \mathbb{R}^m$ stands for the nonlinear-mapping function and $u(t) = [u_1(t), u_2(t), \cdots, u_n(t)]^T \in \mathbb{R}^n$ represents controller and acts on the synchronization process.

Complete synchronization is the earliest proposed method in chaotic synchronization. Under the control of a controller, two chaotic systems with distinct initial conditions gradually converge in their trajectories amidst external noise interference. Therefore, the controller's design should guarantee that the slave system can follow the master system, ultimately achieving synchronization. In other words, let the error expression $\varepsilon(t) = y_m(t) - y_s(t)$ approaches to 0.

## 2.2 Controller Design

With the objective of achieving chaotic synchronization and accelerate convergence time, this paper presents an IEZNN-based controller to mitigate external noise during the synchronization process. The specific design steps are delineated as follows.

To attain the stated objective, the controller must fulfill the subsequent conditions:

$$\begin{cases} \lim\limits_{t \to \infty} |y_{m1}(t) - y_{s1}(t)| = 0, \\ \lim\limits_{t \to \infty} |y_{m2}(t) - y_{s2}(t)| = 0, \\ \lim\limits_{t \to \infty} |y_{m3}(t) - y_{s3}(t)| = 0, \end{cases} \tag{3}$$

As was previously noted, the goal is to make the problem's error converge to 0 and to some extent muffle outside noise. Using the IEZNN design technique, we create the corresponding error function and design formula. Taking time-varying matrix inversion problem $A(t)X(t) = I$ as an example, the design procedure of IEZNN to solve this problem is outlined below:

1) To make the right side of the equation equal to 0, we can obtain the following equation: $A(t)X(t) - I = 0$.

2) An errot function $E(t) = A(t)X(t) - I$ can be constructed and it is the core design of the ZNN

3) To make the equation hold, the error function must tend to 0. One design formula $\dot{E}(t) = -\gamma E(t) - \lambda \int_0^t E(\delta)d\delta$ can be designed to ensure $E(t)$ converge to 0. Besides, $\gamma > 0$ and $\lambda > 0$ are employed to regulate the convergence rate of the IEZNN model.

Inspired by the aforementioned IEZNN design process, the error function for the complete synchronization problem can be conceived to

$$\begin{cases} \varepsilon_1(t) = y_{m1}(t) - y_{s1}(t), \\ \varepsilon_2(t) = y_{m2}(t) - y_{s2}(t), \\ \varepsilon_3(t) = y_{m3}(t) - y_{s3}(t), \end{cases} \tag{4}$$

For the purpose of achieving finite-time convergence for each component of the error function $\varepsilon(t)$, give the following IEZNN design formulation:

$$\dot{\varepsilon}_i(t) = -\gamma \varepsilon_i(t) - \lambda \int_0^t \varepsilon_i(\delta)d\delta \tag{5}$$

Considering the existence of external noise interference, the design of the IEZNN model is:

$$\dot{\varepsilon}_i(t) = -\gamma \varepsilon_i(t) - \lambda \int_0^t \varepsilon_i(\delta)d\delta + \beta_i \tag{6}$$

With the derivation of Eq.(4), we can obtain

$$\begin{cases} \dot{\varepsilon}_1(t) = \dot{y}_{m1}(t) - \dot{y}_{s1}(t), \\ \dot{\varepsilon}_2(t) = \dot{y}_{m2}(t) - \dot{y}_{s2}(t), \\ \dot{\varepsilon}_3(t) = \dot{y}_{m3}(t) - \dot{y}_{s3}(t), \end{cases} \tag{7}$$

then put Eqs.(1) and (2) into Eq.(7) and it will evolve into

$$\begin{cases} \dot{\varepsilon}_1(t) = z_{m1}(y_{m1}(t)) + \beta_1 - z_{s1}(y_{s1}(t)) - u_1(t), \\ \dot{\varepsilon}_2(t) = z_{m2}(y_{m2}(t)) + \beta_2 - z_{s2}(y_{s2}(t)) - u_2(t), \\ \dot{\varepsilon}_3(t) = z_{m3}(y_{m3}(t)) + \beta_3 - z_{s3}(y_{s3}(t)) - u_3(t). \end{cases} \tag{8}$$

Utilizing Eqs.(6) and (8), the controller for the IEZNN model can be derived, and its expression is:

$$u_i(t) = z_{mi}(y_{mi}(t)) - z_{si}(y_{si}(t)) + \gamma \varepsilon_i(t) + \lambda \int_0^t \varepsilon_i(\delta)d\delta \tag{9}$$

## 3  Performance Analysis

Two lemmas about the IEZNN technique are offered in this subsection, showing their ability to synchronize chaotic systems even in the presence of external time-varying disturbances.

**Lemma 1.** *In the context of multiple chaotic systems, starting from distinct initial state* $y_m(0) \neq y_s(0)$, *with initial error* $\varepsilon(t) \neq 0$, *the tajectory of the salve system's state vector* $y_s(t)$ *will synchronize with the trajectory of the master system's state vector* $y_m(t)$ *at time* $t \geq 0$ *with external noise if it satisfies*

$$\lim_{t \to \infty} |y_m^i(t) - y_s^i(t)| \leq \xi, i = 1, 2, \cdots, n, \tag{10}$$

*for the arbitrary small* $\xi > 0$.

**Lemma 2.** *Assuming that the chaotic system is affected by an additive disturbance* $\beta_i$, *and regulation parameters* $\gamma > 0$ *and* $\lambda > 0$, *the slave system starting from different initial position* $y_m(0) \neq y_s(0)$, *the IEZNN model is capable of achieving finite-time convergence when* $y_m(t)$ *converges to* $y_s(t)$ *within a finite-time interval* $T_f$.

## 4    Illustrative Verification

This chapter demonstrates the superiority of the IEZNN model through numerous simulation examples, including the one master chaotic system with three slave chaotic systems, two master chaotic systems with two slave chaotic systems, and three master chaotic systems with one slave chaotic system. To further illustrate the robustness of the IEZNN model, four types of noise are introduced as follows:

1) Constant noise, which is expressed as $\beta_i = c$.
2) Exponential noise, as a representative of dynamical bounded vanishing noise, which is formulated as $\beta_i = \beta_m' \exp(-(1+t)) + c$.
3) Random noise, which is an uniform random noise in $[-\beta_m, \beta_m]$.
4) Sinusoidal noise, as a representative of periodic noise, which is described as $\beta_i = \sin(\beta_m' + c)$, where $c$ is a constant vector, $\beta_m$ represents the upper bound of $\beta_i$, and $\beta_m'$ denotes the upper bound of the gradient of $\beta_i$.

For the purpose of demonstrating the capability to resist external interference of the IEZNN model, we utilize the CZNN model for comparative analysis. Therefore, we can obtain the controller designed by the CZNN method is:

$$u_i(t) = z_{mi}(y_{mi}(t)) - z_{si}(y_{si}(t)) + \lambda \varepsilon_i(t) \tag{11}$$

with parameter $\lambda \geq 0$.

### 4.1    Synchronisation Examples

Considering the following four chaotic systems, the expression for the Chen chaotic system is:

$$\begin{cases} \dot{x}_1(t) = a_1(y_1(t) - x_1(t)), \\ \dot{y}_1(t) = -a_2 x_1(t) + a_3 y_1(t) - x_1(t) z_1(t), \\ \dot{z}_1(t) = -a_4 z_1(t) + x_1(t) y_1(t), \end{cases} \tag{12}$$

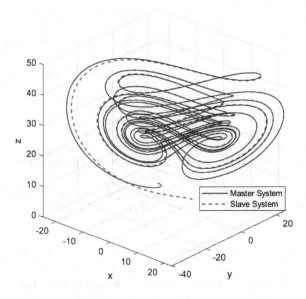

**Fig. 1.** Three-dimensional synchronization trajectory synthesized by IEZNN model (6) for systems (16) and (17) without noise.

with $a_1 = 35, a_2 = 7, a_3 = 28, a_4 = 3$. The improved Lü chaotic system is expressed as:

$$\begin{cases} \dot{x}_2(t) = b_1(y_2(t) - x_2(t) + y_2(t)z_2(t)), \\ \dot{y}_2(t) = b_2 y_2(t) - x_2(t)z_2(t), \\ \dot{z}_2(t) = -b_3 z_2(t) + x_2(t)y_2(t), \end{cases} \tag{13}$$

with $b_1 = 35, b_2 = 14, b_3 = 5$. The Lü chaotic system is expressed as:

$$\begin{cases} \dot{x}_3(t) = c_1(y_3(t) - x_3(t)), \\ \dot{y}_3(t) = c_2 y_3(t) - x_3(t)z_3(t), \\ \dot{z}_3(t) = -c_3 z_3(t) + x_3(t)y_3(t), \end{cases} \tag{14}$$

with $c_1 = 36, c_2 = 20, c_3 = 3$. The Zhou chaotic system is expressed as:

$$\begin{cases} \dot{x}_4(t) = d_1(y_4(t) - x_4(t)), \\ \dot{y}_4(t) = d_2 x_4(t) - x_4(t)z_4(t), \\ \dot{z}_4(t) = -d_3 z_4(t) + x_4(t)y_4(t), \end{cases} \tag{15}$$

with $d_1 = 10, d_2 = 16, d_3 = 1$.

In this section, we have successively selected the synchronization between one master three salve chaotic systems, the synchronization between two master two salve chaotic systems, and the synchronization between three master one salve chaotic systems. Set the synchronization time to 10 s. In addition, adjust the parameters $\lambda = 5$ and $\gamma = 5$.

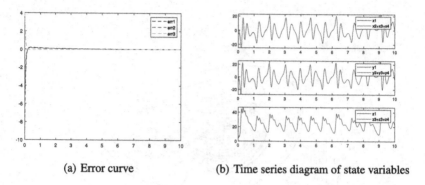

(a) Error curve            (b) Time series diagram of state variables

**Fig. 2.** The error curve and time series diagram of state variables during the combination synchronization process between systems (16) and (17) without noise.

For this type of synchronization, we first set the initial values of these four systems as (-6, 3, 7), (1, 1, 1), (1, 1, 1), and (1, 1, 1) respectively. The system (12) is designated as the master chaotic system. Under the conditions of additional disturbances, its expression can be represented as:

$$\begin{cases} \dot{x}_1(t) = a_1(y_1(t) - x_1(t)) + \beta_1, \\ \dot{y}_1(t) = -a_2 x_1(t) + a_3 y_1(t) - x_1(t)z_1(t) + \beta_2, \\ \dot{z}_1(t) = -a_4 z_1(t) + x_1(t)y_1(t) + \beta_3, \end{cases} \quad (16)$$

at the same time, the sum of the remaining three chaotic systems is considered as the slave system. Therefore, the expression for the slave chaotic system with controller input is:

$$\begin{cases} \dot{x}_2(t) = b_1(y_2(t) - x_2(t) + y_2(t)z_2(t) + c_1(y_3(t) \\ \qquad - x_3(t)) + d_1(y_4(t) - x_4(t)) + u_1, \\ \dot{y}_2(t) = b_2 y_2(t) - x_2(t)z_2(t) + c_2 y_3(t) - x_3(t) \\ \qquad z_3(t) + d_2 x_4(t) - x_4(t)z_4(t) + u_2, \\ \dot{z}_2(t) = -b_3 z_2(t) + x_2(t)y_2(t) + -c_3 z_3(t) + \\ \qquad x_3(t)y_3(t) + -d_3 z_4(t) + x_4(t)y_4(t) + u_3, \end{cases} \quad (17)$$

The corresponding synchronous simulation results for two nonidentical chaotic systems (16) and (17) using the proposed IEZNN model are depicted in the figure. Specifically, Fig. 1 illustrates the synchronization between systems (16) and (17) in a three-dimensional space without noise in real-time. It can be observed that the two systems quickly synchronize and achieve consistent trajectories at different initial values. Moreover, as shown in Fig. 2(a), the synchronization error between systems (16) and (17) approaches zero. Figure 2(b) displays the state variable curves of the two systems over time, demonstrating a rapid convergence and overlap of their state variable trajectories.

**Synchronization Between Two Master Two Salve Chaotic Systems.**
For this particular form of synchronization, we first set the initial values of these
four systems as (8, 5, -7), (1, 1, 1), (1, 1, 1), and (1, 1, 1) respectively. The
summation of the two systems (12) and (13) is considered as the master chaotic
system. With the existence of additional disturbances, it can be articulated as:

$$\begin{cases} \dot{x}_1(t) = a_1(y_1(t) - x_1(t)) + b_1(y_2(t) - x_2(t) + y_2(t)z_2(t)) + \beta_1, \\ \dot{y}_1(t) = -a_2x_1(t) + a_3y_1(t) - x_1(t)z_1(t) + b_2y_2(t) - x_2(t)z_2(t) + \beta_2, \\ \dot{z}_1(t) = -a_4z_1(t) + x_1(t)y_1(t) + -b_3z_2(t) + x_2(t)y_2(t) + \beta_3, \end{cases} \quad (18)$$

after adding the controller input into the sum of systems (14) and (15), the slave
chaotic system can be formulated as follows:

$$\begin{cases} \dot{x}_2(t) = c_1(y_3(t) - x_3(t)) + d_1(y_4(t) - x_4(t)) + u_1, \\ \dot{y}_2(t) = c_2y_3(t) - x_3(t)z_3(t) + d_2x_4(t) - x_4(t)z_4(t) + u_2, \\ \dot{z}_2(t) = -c_3z_3(t) + x_3(t)y_3(t) + -d_3z_4(t) + x_4(t)y_4(t) + u_3, \end{cases} \quad (19)$$

In the absence of noise interference, Fig. 3 depicts the synchronization between
two distinct chaotic systems (18) and (19) using the proposed IEZNN model in
three-dimensional space. It is obvious that even if the initial values are different,
these two systems can quickly synchronize and achieve consistent trajectories.
Furthermore, as shown in Fig. 4(a), the synchronization error between systems
(18) and (19) converges to zero. Figure 4(b) displays the state variable curves
for the two systems over time, and their state variable change curves quickly
overlap.

**Synchronization Between Three Master One Salve Chaotic Systems.**
For this type of synchronization, we first set the initial values of these four
systems as (9, 7, 5), (1, 1, 1), (1, 1, 1), and (1, 1, 1) respectively. The aggregate
of the three systems (12), (13), and (14) is considered the master chaotic system.
When subjected to extra disturbances, its representation can be articulated as
follows:

$$\begin{cases} \dot{x}_1(t) = a_1(y_1(t) - x_1(t)) + b_1(y_2(t) - x_2(t) \\ \qquad\quad + y_2(t)z_2(t)) + c_1(y_3(t) - x_3(t)) + \beta_1, \\ \dot{y}_1(t) = -a_2x_1(t) + a_3y_1(t) - x_1(t)z_1(t) \\ \qquad\quad + b_2y_2(t) - x_2(t)z_2(t) + c_2y_3(t) \\ \qquad\quad - x_3(t)z_3(t) + \beta_2, \\ \dot{z}_1(t) = -a_4z_1(t) + x_1(t)y_1(t) + -b_3z_2(t) + \\ \qquad\quad x_2(t)y_2(t) + -c_3z_3(t) + x_3(t)y_3(t) + \beta_3, \end{cases} \quad (20)$$

simultaneously, upon incorporating the controller input into the system
described by equation (15), the formulation for the chaotic behavior of the slave
system can be exhibited as:

$$\begin{cases} \dot{x}_2(t) = d_1(y_4(t) - x_4(t)) + u_1, \\ \dot{y}_2(t) = d_2x_4(t) - x_4(t)z_4(t) + u_2, \\ \dot{z}_2(t) = -d_3z_4(t) + x_4(t)y_4(t) + u_3, \end{cases} \quad (21)$$

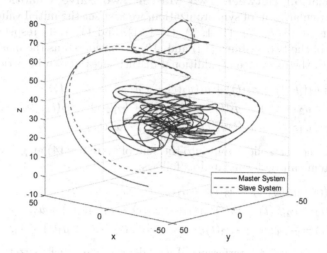

**Fig. 3.** Three-dimensional synchronization trajectory synthesized by IEZNN model (6) for systems (18) and (19) without noise.

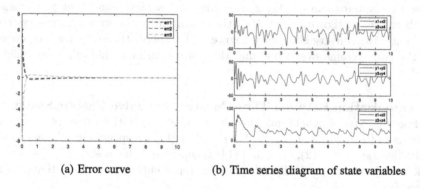

(a) Error curve                    (b) Time series diagram of state variables

**Fig. 4.** The error curve and time series diagram of state variables during the combined synchronization process between systems (18) and (19) without noise.

Excluding external perturbations, the real-time synchronous simulation results for two nonidentical chaotic systems (20) and (21) in a three-dimensional space, employing the proposed IEZNN model, are depicted in Fig. 5. As shown, the two systems quickly synchronize and achieve consistent trajectories at different initial values. Furthermore, as seen in Fig. 6(a), the synchronization error between systems (20) and (21) tends to 0, achieving convergence. Figure 6(b) displays the curves of each state variable of the two systems over time, with their state variable change curves rapidly overlapping.

The above experimental results show that the IEZNN model is effective in solving combination synchronization problems.

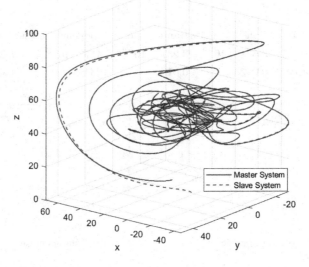

**Fig. 5.** The three-dimensional synchronization trajectory generated by the IEZNN model (6) for systems (20) and (21) is illustrated in the absence of noise.

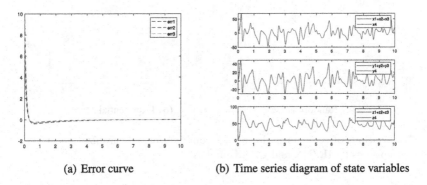

(a) Error curve                    (b) Time series diagram of state variables

**Fig. 6.** The error curve and time series diagram of state variables during the combined synchronization process between systems (20) and (21) without noise.

## Comparsion with CZNN Model

Without sacrificing generality, take the combination synchronization of two master two salve systems as an example. In this section, we substantiate that the IEZNN model has better performance than the previous CZNN model. Under the same external interference, we conducted combination synchronization experiments employing distinct controllers generated by these two divergent models. And the experimental results are compared and further elaborated. As delineated in Table 1, both the IEZNN and CZNN models exhibit the capability of achieving finite-time convergence without noise. However, when there exist external disturbances, the IEZNN model accomplishes finite-time convergence,

**Table 1.** Convergence performance of IEZNN model and CZNN model under different noise disturbances.

| noise | Non-noise | Constant noise | Random noise | Exponential noise | Sinusoidal noise |
|---|---|---|---|---|---|
| IEZNN | $3.418 \times 10^{-3}$ | $3.678 \times 10^{-3}$ | $3.237 \times 10^{-3}$ | $3.477 \times 10^{-3}$ | $9.435 \times 10^{-3}$ |
| CZNN | $8.165 \times 10^{-15}$ | 0.6928 | 0.0185 | 0.0346 | 0.3449 |

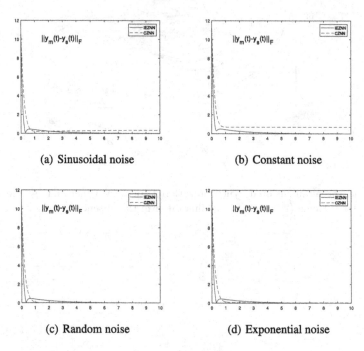

(a) Sinusoidal noise                    (b) Constant noise

(c) Random noise                    (d) Exponential noise

**Fig. 7.** Variations of error norm during the combination synchronization process with different noise using IEZNN and CZNN models.

while the CZNN model is not particularly ideal. This discrepancy signifies the CZNN model's inability to attain combination synchronization under such circumstances. Moreover, as shown in Fig. 7, the IEZNN model exhibits better convergence performance when exposed to various external noise compared with the CZNN model.

## 5    Conclusion

With the aim of enhancing signal confidentiality during transmission, this paper proposes the IEZNN model and its associated controller for achieving chaotic combination synchronization under the influence of external time-varying noise interference. Theoretical scrutiny reveals the IEZNN model's efficiency in mitigating the impact of external time-varying interference, leading to synchronization errors tend to zero. Contrast this with the CZNN technique, which is prone to external noise interruptions, leading to unsuccessful convergence to zero or even divergence in synchronization results. Furthermore, numerical results show that the IEZNN model outperforms the CZNN approach in terms of anti-interference performance when faced with external time-varying noise.

# References

1. Chen, D., Li, S., Wu, Q.: Rejecting chaotic disturbances using a super-exponential-zeroing neurodynamic approach for synchronization of chaotic sensor systems. Sensors **19**(1), 74 (2018)
2. Chen, D., Zhang, Y.: Robust zeroing neural-dynamics and its time-varying disturbances suppression model applied to mobile robot manipulators. IEEE Trans. Neural Netw. Learn. Syst. **29**(9), 4385–4397 (2017)
3. Chen, D., Zhang, Y., Li, S.: Tracking control of robot manipulators with unknown models: a Jacobian-matrix-adaption method. IEEE Trans. Industr. Inf. **14**(7), 3044–3053 (2017)
4. Chen, Q., Ren, X., Na, J.: Robust finite-time chaos synchronization of uncertain permanent magnet synchronous motors. ISA Trans. **58**, 262–269 (2015)
5. Feki, M.: An adaptive chaos synchronization scheme applied to secure communication. Chaos, Solitons Fractals **18**(1), 141–148 (2003)
6. Jajarmi, A., Hajipour, M., Baleanu, D.: New aspects of the adaptive synchronization and hyperchaos suppression of a financial model. Chaos, Solitons Fractals **99**, 285–296 (2017)
7. Kwon, O., Park, J.H., Lee, S.: Secure communication based on chaotic synchronization via interval time-varying delay feedback control. Nonlinear Dyn. **63**, 239–252 (2011)
8. Li, G., Zhang, B.: A novel weak signal detection method via chaotic synchronization using chua's circuit. IEEE Trans. Industr. Electron. **64**(3), 2255–2265 (2016)
9. Li, J., Mao, M., Zhang, Y.: Simpler ZD-achieving controller for chaotic systems synchronization with parameter perturbation, model uncertainty and external disturbance as compared with other controllers. Optik **131**, 364–373 (2017)
10. Liao, T.L., Chen, H.C., Peng, C.Y., Hou, Y.Y.: Chaos-based secure communications in biomedical information application. Electronics **10**(3), 359 (2021)
11. Lin, C.M., Pham, D.H., Huynh, T.T.: Synchronization of chaotic system using a brain-imitated neural network controller and its applications for secure communications. IEEE Access **9**, 75923–75944 (2021)
12. Pecora, L.M., Carroll, T.L.: Synchronization in chaotic systems. Phys. Rev. Lett. **64**(8), 821 (1990)
13. Runzi, L., Yinglan, W., Shucheng, D.: Combination synchronization of three classic chaotic systems using active backstepping design. Chaos: Interdisc. J. Nonlinear Sci. **21**(4) (2011)
14. Sun, J., Cui, G., Wang, Y., Shen, Y.: Combination complex synchronization of three chaotic complex systems. Nonlinear Dyn. **79**, 953–965 (2015)
15. Sun, J., Shen, Y., Wang, X., Chen, J.: Finite-time combination-combination synchronization of four different chaotic systems with unknown parameters via sliding mode control. Nonlinear Dyn. **76**, 383–397 (2014)

174    C. Yi et al.

16. Sun, J., Shen, Y., Zhang, G., Xu, C., Cui, G.: Combination-combination synchronization among four identical or different chaotic systems. Nonlinear Dyn. **73**,
1211–1222 (2013)
17. Vaseghi, B., Pourmina, M.A., Mobayen, S.: Secure communication in wireless sensor networks based on chaos synchronization using adaptive sliding mode control. Nonlinear Dyn. **89**(3), 1689–1704 (2017). https://doi.org/10.1007/s11071-
017-3543-9

# A Lightweight Anomaly Detection Method for Industrial Processes Based on Event Correlation Behavior

Jianzhen Luo⑩, Yan Cai(✉)⑩, Jun Cai⑩, and Wanhan Fang⑩

Guangdong Polytechnic Normal University, Guangzhou, Guangdong, China
luojz@gpnu.edu.cn, 1744409360@qq.com

**Abstract.** In recent years, the industrial Internet has faced severe threats of production process attacks. By injecting malicious commands or data into the application layer protocols, the attackers change the industrial control flow and disrupt the normal production process, leading to equipment failures and even production accidents. From a network perspective, the traffic of production process attacks does not violate the syntax of communication protocols. However, from the industrial system point of view, the production process attack violates some restrictive rules or physical laws of the industrial production process. This paper proposes a lightweight industrial process anomaly detection method based on event-associated behavior for the characteristics of industrial production process attacks, adopts HsMM with low model complexity to model the state data of field devices in the industrial production process, analyzes the temporal behavioral evolution law of the production process, constructs the temporal behavioral model of the production equipment, and then constructs a lightweight production process anomaly detection method based on behavioral offset.

**Keywords:** Anomaly detection · Behavioral profiling · Industrial security · Hidden semi-Markov model (HsMM)

## 1 Introduction

With the accelerated integration of new-generation information technologies such as cloud computing, artificial intelligence, and the Internet of Things(IoT) with manufacturing technologies, industrial control systems(ICS) have shifted from closed and independent to open and shared, from standalone to interconnected, and from automated to intelligent. Open and interactive industrial environments pose security risks to devices, networks, controls, and data. In industrial production, there are production process attacks that disrupt normal production processes by injecting malicious commands or data into application layer protocols, altering the industrial control flow, and causing production accidents. Therefore, there is an urgent need to apply anomaly detection(AD) methods to monitor the safe operation of systems [1].

© ICST Institute for Computer Sciences, Social Informatics and Telecommunications Engineering 2025
Published by Springer Nature Switzerland AG 2025. All Rights Reserved
J. Cai et al. (Eds.): SPNCE 2023, LNICST 525, pp. 175–187, 2025.
https://doi.org/10.1007/978-3-031-73699-5_12

Anomaly detection refers to the detection of patterns in data that do not conform to expected behavior. Exceptions themselves can have a positive or negative nature, depending on their context and interpretation. The importance of anomaly detection is due to the transformation of anomalies in data into important actionable information in various application fields. Correctly detecting such abnormal information enables decision makers to take action on the system in order to fully respond, avoid, or correct situations related to it [2].

During industrial anomaly detection, attackers can inject malicious instructions into the application layer to alter device configuration information, thereby disrupting normal industrial production processes. For example, "Stuxnet" uses highly complex malicious code and multiple zero day vulnerabilities as attack weapons, targeting uranium centrifuges, thereby changing the centrifuge speed and causing overpressure to cause batch damage to the centrifuges [3]. Due to the fact that malicious instructions do not violate the syntax of communication protocols and do not differ from normal communication modes, such attacks often cannot be judged based on industrial control protocol specifications or network traffic characteristics [4].

Therefore, this paper proposes a lightweight industrial process anomaly detection method based on event-related behavior for the characteristics of industrial production process attack. The HsMM model [5] with low model complexity is used to establish a normal sensor time series data model to describe the normal dynamic changes of field equipment state data in the industrial production process and analyze the law of state transfer in the production process. When detecting, the real-time collected sensor data are input into the model, and whether there is any abnormality is judged by calculating the absolute fluctuation derivative of the average entropy. At the same time, this paper also proposes a segmentation algorithm with the time series trend change point as the cut point to describe the equipment state in an intuitive and feasible way. Our major contributions in this paper include the following:

1. A production process event characterization and mining method is proposed to differentiate production event states based on the trends of time series influence factors, which can accurately detect production process attacks that violate the restriction rules or physical laws of industrial production processes.
2. An event-based data-driven industrial production process modeling approach is proposed to construct a time-series behavioral model of production equipment by simplifying the production process events into a hidden semi-Markov process.
3. A lightweight industrial process anomaly detection method based on event-related behaviors is proposed to detect anomalies in industrial processes efficiently, lightly and in real time.

The rest of the paper is organized as follows. Section 2 provides a brief overview of recent related work. Section 3 describes the details of the selected model and the anomaly detection method. Section 4 elucidates the implementation of the anomaly detection method and the results of the experiments with.

Finally, Sect. 5 summarizes the work of this paper and indicates future research directions.

## 2   Related Work

Industrial control system anomaly detection techniques are methods used to detect and identify anomalous behavior or events in an industrial control system [6]. Depending on the principle, they can be categorized as mechanism-driven and data-driven.

### 2.1   Mechanism-Driven Anomaly Detection

Mechanism-driven anomaly detection is an approach based on the working principle and physical model of a system, which describes the characteristics and behaviors of a system under normal operating conditions by building a mechanism model of the system based on its working principle, components and interrelationships. It can provide in-depth understanding and detailed analysis of the system state, and can respond quickly when abnormal events occur.

Astillo [7] proposed a distributed anomaly detection method based on the physical state of heterogeneous embedded IoT nodes, which can identify the misbehavior of heterogeneous embedded IoT nodes in a closed-loop smart greenhouse agricultural system. Yang [8] proposed an anomaly detection of an IoT system based on the fingerprinting of the physical state of the registers, which adopts a Boolean logic to represent the IoT system controller of each register physical state and generates a device fingerprint based on a deterministic finite automata model, thus realizing active detection and passive monitoring based on device fingerprints. He [9] modeled the supercharger efficiency as a key indicator using a thermodynamic mechanism approach, and proposed a hybrid driving model based on thermodynamic mechanism and data. Lv [10] analyzed the device physical state in real time based on the The physical state of the device analyzes the trustworthiness of the device in real time, and implements an industrial control system attack defense and monitoring system based on the trustworthiness of the device. Xie [11] propose a PLC malware detection method based on model checking, which utilizes Satisfaction Mode Theory(SMT) constraints to model the PLC system and generates detection rules based on the Invariant Extraction and Rule Design modes.

Mechanism-driven approaches typically identify anomalies based on known system workings and behavioral patterns. Emerging, unknown anomalies may not be accurately detected, thus requiring constant updating of the rule set to maintain detection capabilities for the latest attack methods.

### 2.2   Data-Driven Anomaly Detection

Data-driven anomaly detection is an approach to detecting and recognizing anomalies based on data analysis and statistical methods [12]. It does not rely on a working or physical model of the system, but rather describes the distribution of normal data by modeling the normal data of the system. The data-driven anomaly detection approach does not rely on a deep understanding and modeling of the system and is suitable for systems that are complex and difficult to model accurately. It automatically learns the characteristics of normal data and performs anomaly detection when there are deviations from normal behavior.

Zolanvari [13] used a machine learning algorithm model to analyze network traffic features to detect attacks such as backdoor, command injection, and SQL injection. ANNIE [14] proposed an intelligent anomaly detection extensive deep clustering(ODC) algorithm for network traffic analysis and optimization by combining AutoEncoder and BIRCH clustering algorithms for detecting known and unknown malicious network traffic. Nguyen [15] use a federated learning approach to cluster unlabeled network traffic data to construct behavioral profiles for specific device types to detect anomalies. Matouek [16] use a probabilistic automaton to create normal profiles of the communication patterns of an industrial control system to identify the application layer of the industrial Internet of security attacks and unknown threats. Akpinar [17] propose an EtherCAT network anomaly detection technique to detect device-level periodicity and its offset stateby using protocol-specified operations and fields.

In recent years, anomaly detection in industrial control systems is often combined with machine learning algorithmic models. Compared with the lightweight production process anomaly detection method based on HsMM proposed in this paper, deep learning-based anomaly detection techniques are able to automatically learn feature representations and adapt to data in different domains, but they usually require a large amount of labeled data and a large amount of computational resources for training and inference, and they cannot be used to detect new types of attacks. Deep learning models are considered black-box models and it is difficult to explain their decision-making process and anomaly detection results.

## 3    Proposed Model

Production process attacks can often be manifested in abnormal fluctuations of data over time. HsMM is able to capture temporality and state transitions in time-series data to better reflect the dynamic changes of data.

Therefore, this paper constructs a transfer model of state based on HsMM. As shown in Fig. 1, the whole architecture is divided into four modules in total. In the preprocessing stage, the sensor temporal sequences are smoothed and cut, and then the feature extraction of sub-sequences is carried out, and then the sequences are subjected to DBSCAN clustering, so as to obtain the cluster corresponding to each sub-sequence. During training, based on the obtained state sequences as well as the set of sub-sequences, the subsequence state transfer process is mapped to the HsMM process with variable duration, and the parameters of the normal timing behavior model are updated by an unsupervised parameter estimation algorithm. Finally, the average logarithmic entropy is calculated based on the observed signals to do abnormal behavior detection.

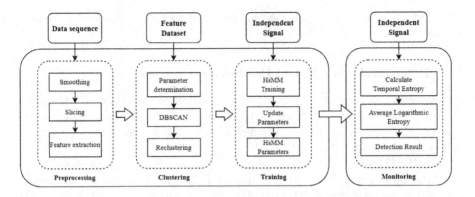

**Fig. 1.** Monitoring architecture: Abnormal detection of industrial control systems based on production behavior.

### 3.1 Event Characterization and Mining

Prior to modeling individual sensor data, preprocessing and clustering of the data is required in order to improve the quality and usability of the data to better suit the subsequent analysis and modeling tasks. Among the preprocessing there are three steps: data smoothing, data cutting and feature selection and transformation.

In order to make the data smoother and more reliable, the time series are smoothed using the Savitzky-Golay filter to obtain a data series that retains the trend of the data and has less noise, and then cut to obtain multiple subseries using the trend change point of the series as the cut point. The subseries obtained by cutting often have a single trend: increasing, decreasing or flat, for this characteristic, we choose to use the $< k, average, width >$ as a set of eigenvalues of the subsequence, where $k$ represents the average slope of the subsequence, and $average$ and $width$ represent the mean and length of the subsequence, respectively, to obtain the feature matrix.

DBSCAN is a clustering algorithm based on densely connected regions, which is usually suitable for datasets where the number of clusters cannot be determined in advance and are of low dimensionality, so DBSCAN is chosen for clustering here. By DBSCAN clustering algorithm, the subsequences are divided into different classes, but such clustering algorithms are still not able to cluster the sequences according to the curvilinear trend very well and are unable to represent the continuity of the state.

Therefore, it is necessary to perform another clustering to classify the fuzzy classes into normal classes, and at the same time, the subsequences in each class are split according to the positive and negative slopes, and the neighboring similar classes are merged to obtain the final sequence class. The observation sequences collected by any sensor are segmented according to the trend of parameter changes, theoretically, the subsequences in each class after clustering have similar trends and change intervals, so in the training process, each class is regarded as a state and the average eigenvalue of each class is taken as the state feature.

## 3.2 Behavioral Modeling of Production Processes

Throughout the production process, the variation of the observed parameters of the sensors can be considered as a Hidden Semi-Markov process, where the clusters and sequence lengths obtained in the previous stage are the implied states and state durations of the HsMM.

The HsMM allows the underlying process to be a Semi-Markov chain, where the duration or dwell time of each state is variable [18]. The number of observations generated in state $j$ is determined by the state duration $d = \{0, 1, 2, \ldots, D\}$. Let the set of states be $S_j = \{1, 2, \ldots, n\}$, $p_j(d)$ represents the probability of the duration distribution of state j, and $o_{t_1:t_2}$ denotes the sequence of observations within the moments $t_1$ to moment $t_2$.

Given the HsMM model $\lambda \triangleq (\pi, A, B, P)$, where the initial state probability is $\pi$, $A$ represents the state transfer probability matrix, $B$ denotes the probability distribution matrix of the sequence emitted from the current state, and the probability matrix of the sequence duration distribution is denoted as $P$, as follows:

$$a_{(i,d')(j,d)} = Pr[S_{[t+1:t+d]} = j | S_{[t-d'+1:t]} = i]$$

$$= a_{ij}p_j(d) \tag{1}$$

$$b_j(o_{t_1:t_2}) = Pr[o_{t_1:t_2} | S_{[t_1:t_2]} = j] \tag{2}$$

Since there are many unknowns and uncertainties in the actual production process, a limited test data set cannot accurately reflect the complexity and diversity of the real environment. Therefore, to avoid the situation of being too absolute, the following definitions are made.

**Definition 1.** *Events that do not occur in the test data are considered to be small probability events and are assigned a sufficiently small, but not zero, value at the corresponding position in the probability matrix.*

**Definition 2.** *The ratio of the distances between the observed sequence feature points and the state feature points is regarded as the similarity between the two, and $b_j(d)$ is obtained on this basis.*

**Definition 3.** *The state duration distribution is assumed to be an equal probability event, i.e. , $p_j(d) = \dfrac{Occurrence_{[d-step:d]}}{Occurrence_{[1:T]}}$, where step denotes the time unit, and $T$ is the total duration.*

On the basis of (1) and (2), the parameter estimation of HsMM can be accomplished by Forward-Backward Algorithms. The forward and backward variables are defined as follows.

$$\alpha_t(j) \triangleq Pr[S_t] = j, o_{1:t}|\lambda]$$

$$= \sum_{\substack{i \in S \backslash \{j\} \\ d \in D}} \alpha_{t-d}(i) \cdot a_{ij} \cdot p_j(d) \cdot b_j(o_{t-d:t}) \tag{3}$$

$$\beta_t(j) \triangleq Pr[o_{t+1:T}|S_t] = j, \lambda]$$

$$= \sum_{\substack{i \in S \backslash \{j\} \\ d' \in D}} a_{ji} \cdot p_i(d') \cdot b_i(o_{t:t+d}) \cdot \beta_{t+d'}(i, d') \tag{4}$$

In the initialization phase of the model, set $\pi = (\frac{1}{n}, \frac{1}{n}, \dots, \frac{1}{n})$, and statistical methods and similarity comparisons can be obtained for $A$, $P$, $B$. To iterate over the model parameters, three probability functions are defined:

$$\eta_t(j, d) \triangleq Pr[S_{[t-d:t]} = j, o_{1:T}|\lambda]$$

$$= \sum_{d \in D} \sum_{i \in S \backslash \{j\}} \alpha_{t-d}(j) \cdot a_{ij} \cdot p_j(d) \cdot b_j(o_{t-d:t}) \cdot \beta_t(j) \tag{5}$$

$$\xi_t(i, j) \triangleq Pr[S_t] = i, S_{t+d]} = j, o_{1:T}|\lambda]$$

$$= \sum_{d' \in D} \sum_{d \in D} \alpha_t(i) \cdot a_{ij} \cdot p_j(d) \cdot b_j(o_{t:t+d}) \cdot \beta_{t+d}(j) \tag{6}$$

$$\gamma_t(j) \triangleq Pr[o_1^T, q_t = j]$$

$$= \gamma_{t+1}(j) + \sum_{i \in S \backslash \{j\}} [\xi_t(j, i) - \xi_t(i, j)] \tag{7}$$

Then, the model is iteratively optimized using the EM algorithm and the parameters are updated with the following equations:

$$\hat{\pi}_j = \gamma_0(j) / \sum_j \gamma_0(j) \tag{8}$$

$$\hat{a}_{ij} = \sum_t \xi_t(i, j) / \sum_{j \neq i} \sum_t \xi_t(i, j) \tag{9}$$

$$\hat{p}_j(d) = \sum_t \eta_t(j, d) / \sum_d \sum_t \eta_t(j, d) \tag{10}$$

The EM algorithm estimates the values of the model parameters and the values of the missing data based on the training data, then re-estimates the parameter values based on the estimated missing data plus the previously observed data, and then iterates repeatedly until the final convergence, thus obtaining the trained HsMM model parameters.

### 3.3   Production Process Anomaly Detection

Entropy is a concept that measures the uncertainty of information and is often used to measure the degree of chaos or disorder in a data set [19]. Anomalous data

182     J. Luo et al.

may cause the distribution of a dataset to become more uneven and disordered, thus giving it a relatively high entropy value. Although entropy can be used as a measure of data anomalies, there may be limitations in using entropy alone for anomaly detection.

Absolute Difference is a commonly used statistic to measure the degree of difference between each data point in a data set and its mean. By looking at the change in the derivative of the absolute difference, when anomalous line segments are usually characterized by sharp changes or unusual spikes in the derivative. Therefore, the absolute mean difference of average logarithmic entropy (ALE) is further obtained. Assuming that the current observed sequence is $o_{t-d:t}$, the Absolute difference in entropy(ADE) of the observed sequence is calculated according to the following equation:

$$ALE_t = \ln(Pr[o_1^t|\lambda])/t$$
$$= \ln(\sum_{j \in S} \alpha_t(j))/t \tag{11}$$

$$ADE_t = \left| \frac{ALE_t}{\sum_{t \in T} ALE_t} \right| \tag{12}$$

In order to determine the abnormality more quickly and accurately, the middle interval of the normal data set is taken after modeling, and $ADE_{normal}$ is obtained according to the formula (12), which is used to determine the threshold to determine whether the data is abnormal or not.

In real industrial production, when one device is attacked, it may have an impact on the operational status of the whole system. For example, if the attack results in the tampering or interruption of the control signal of one device, it may cause other devices to fail to operate normally. Therefore, indirect attacks need to be considered when detecting them. If the data of other devices is abnormal immediately after the attack, it may be a direct effect, and if there is a certain time delay or time interval, it may be an indirect effect.

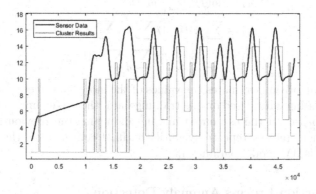

**Fig. 2.** Clustering effect: SWaT sensor LIT101.

# 4   Experiments

## 4.1   Implemention

The Safe Water Treatment (SWaT) system is a simulation and experimentation platform in the field of Industrial Internet. The test bed was monitored by 25 different types of sensors to monitor the operation of the equipment, and data sets were generated after seven days of operation under normal operating conditions and four days of operation under continuous or intermittent attack conditions. During this period, 36 different attacks were executed by outsiders. In many of the attacks, the attackers manipulated data received from other components, forcing the receiving component to misbehave.

This experiment was trained using normal data generated during the first 7 d of SWaT. In order for the sequence to contain as many attack signals as possible, while ensuring reliable detection accuracy. The time unit in the experiment is chosen to be 10 s, and different sensors correspond to different state maximum durations $D$. The length of the sequence was chosen to be 120 s. First, the observations of the time series are clustered to obtain the implied states under the HsMM model. The states clustered by different sensors are different, and the number of states of the sensors in the test is generally between 4 and 22. The clustering effect of the selected sensors LIT101 is shown in Fig. 2, and the number of clusters is 15.

**Table 1.** Detection Result: When the amplification factor is 1.65, the detection status of sensor LIT101 is shown, where the bold serial number represents the sensor that has been directly attacked.

| Sensor | TP | FP | FN | Sensor | TP | FP | FN |
|--------|----|----|----|--------|----|----|----|
| 1 | 0 | 0 | 0 | 14 | 138 | 29 | 0 |
| **2** | 12 | 0 | 0 | **15** | 17 | 2 | 0 |
| 3 | 0 | 7 | 0 | 16 | 0 | 1 | 0 |
| **4** | 2 | 0 | 0 | **17** | 22 | 1 | 0 |
| 5 | 0 | 0 | 0 | 18 | 51 | 0 | 0 |
| 6 | 0 | 0 | 0 | **19** | 20 | 0 | 0 |
| **7** | 5 | 0 | 0 | 20 | 14 | 0 | 0 |
| 8 | 0 | 0 | 0 | 21 | 10 | 0 | 0 |
| **9** | 9 | 0 | 0 | 22 | 15 | 0 | 0 |
| 10 | 0 | 0 | 0 | 23 | 12 | 1 | 0 |
| **11** | 24 | 5 | 0 | 24 | 10 | 1 | 0 |
| **12** | 14 | 0 | 0 | 25 | 0 | 0 | 0 |
| **13** | 14 | 1 | 0 | | | | |

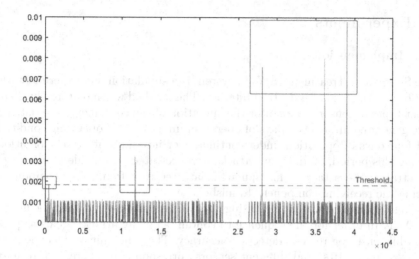

**Fig. 3.** ADE sequence: SWaT sensor LIT101 as an example.

Then, training takes the form of iterative training. The training set is cut into a number of subsets of length 3000, with every 50 subsets as a group. Each group of subsets is trained directly, and the corresponding $\eta, \xi, \gamma$ are found by the formula (5)(6)(7), respectively. After in-group sequence training, the three parameters obtained are averaged, and then the HsMM model parameters are updated and inputted into the next training group. Finally, the anomaly detection model based on production behavioral features is obtained through iterative training.

### 4.2  Results and Analysis

Detecting attacks through the model is essentially a multiple classification problem, and the detection results can be categorized into 4 classes:False Positive(FN), False Negative(TN), True Negative(FP), TruePositive(TP). Based on the above four statistical results, the performance metrics *Precision*, *Recall*, and $F1$ are defined to evaluate the model. The above three metrics are in the range of $(0,1)$, the closer to 1 means the better the detection performance of the model, and the closer to 0 means the worse the detection performance of the model. During detection, if there is an overlap between the detected attack time period and the real attack time period, it is considered correct, and when there is an attack time period that is not judged at all, the attack is considered to be ignored or unrecognized.

For anomaly detection, the average entropy derivative of three consecutive sequences is obtained according to the formula (12), where $t = 360$. In order to avoid that the threshold is set too low, which leads to the normal but slightly deviating from the average sequence being misjudged as abnormal, the threshold

**Table 2.** Comparison of Techniques Against SWaT Dataset [20]

| Technique | Precision | Recall | F1 Score |
|---|---|---|---|
| CNN(8 layers) | N/A | N/A | 0.861 |
| DNN | 0.98 | 0.68 | 0.8 |
| One Class SVM | 0.92 | 0.69 | 0.79 |
| PCA | 0.2492 | 0.2163 | 0.23 |
| MADGAN | 0.9897 | 0.6374 | 0.77 |
| ABATegaussian(log-entry based) | 0.95 | 0.63 | 0.76 |
| ABATegaussian(attack-window based) | 0.95 | 0.95 | 0.95 |
| AE | 0.7263 | 0.5263 | 0.61 |
| TABOR | 0.86 | 0.788 | 0.82 |
| HsMM-ADE | 0.8901 | 1 | 0.9419 |

needs to be appropriately enlarged. After several validation experiments, the best detection performance is achieved when the amplification factor is 1.65.

Table 1 describes the detection results of the 25 sensors. A sensor under direct attack will detect multiple small intervals within an attack interval at the same time. At this time, the ADE of LIT101 is shown in Fig. 3. A total of 5 direct attacks were made on LIT101, and it can be seen from the figure that a total of 5 time intervals exceeded the threshold, which roughly coincided with the time period when the device was attacked.

Table 2 reports the precision, recall, and $F1$ values for different techniques and the technique proposed in this paper. This method achieves 100% recall while also maintaining high precision and $F1$. Meanwhile, this part will discuss its performance in the following aspects.

1. **Adaptability and Interpretability:** In different scenarios, the HsMM model parameters can be adjusted so that the model has different sensitivities to different anomalies and adapts to more diverse environments. Meanwhile, HsMM can provide predictions and explanations for the moments when anomalies occur. By extrapolating the HsMM, the state and the duration of the state at each moment can be obtained, and the cause and duration of the anomaly can be explained.
2. **Computational Complexity:** In the training phase, $O((D + N)TNIKJ)$ of computation is required, where $N$ is the number of states in HsMM, $D$ is the maximum time the states last, $T$ is the length of training samples, $I$ is the number of sequences contained in each set of samples, $K$ is the number of groups, and $J$ is the number of iterations. In the experiment, the time unit is 10, $T = 300$, $I = 50$, $K = 7$, $J$ is about 5. Due to the large cutting accuracy, the number of states is between 4 and 22, while $D$ is kept around 160. With MATLAB, training is typically completed in about 2 to 8 hours per sensor. In the detection phase, the computation mainly focuses on the ADE of the observations with a computational complexity of about

$O(DNT)$. Experiments show that anomaly detection takes about 0.0028 s per 120 s sampling period.

## 5  Conclusion

In this paper, we propose a HsMM-based method for detecting behavioral anomalies in industrial equipment. It uses the historical data of industrial equipment to abstract the normal operating state transfer into a Hidden Semi-Markov process, and then uses the average entropy derivative of the observations to carry out the anomalies that exist in the time period. The test results of the SWaT dataset show that the detection recall for direct attacks reaches 100%, and the $F1$ scores reaches 94%, which indicates that this method is effective in detecting the attacks on the industrial production process. Where the decrease in precision mainly comes from the impact of indirect attacks, when a device is attacked, other devices in the same system may be affected, and this impact arrives at different times, making it difficult to limit it according to the same criteria. Therefore, in future plans, the addition of a neural network structure to the current architecture will be considered in order to analyze the interdependence of the devices from a systemic point of view, and thus to better distinguish indirect attacks.

**Acknowledgement.** Thanks for the support of the Key Project of Guangdong Provincial Department of Education (No. 2021ZDZX1031).

## References

1. Chandola, V., et al.: Anomaly detection: a survey. ACM Compute. Surv. **41**, 15:1–15:58 (2009)
2. Martí, L., Sanchez-Pi, N., Molina, J.M., Garcia, A.C.B.: Anomaly detection based on sensor data in petroleum industry applications. Sensors **15**, 2774–2797 (2015). https://doi.org/10.3390/s150202774
3. Langner, R.: Stuxnet: dissecting a cyberwarfare weapon. IEEE Secur. Priv. **9**, 49–51 (2011)
4. Zhang, W., et al.: A survey of network intrusion detection methods for industrial control systems(2019)
5. Yu, S.-Z., Kobayashi, H.: An efficient forward-backward algorithm for an explicit duration hidden Markov model. IEEE Signal Process. Lett. **10**(1), 11–14 (2003)
6. Injadat, M., Salo, F., Nassif, A.B., Essex, A., Shami, A.: Bayesian optimization with machine learning algorithms towards anomaly detection. In: 2018 IEEE global communications conference (GLOBECOM), pp. 1–6 (Dec 2018)
7. Astillo, P., Kim, J., Sharma, V., et al.: SGF-MD: behaviorrulespecification-based distributed misbehavior detection of embedded iot devices in a closed-loop smart greenhouse farming system. IEEE Access **8**, 196235–196252 (2020)
8. Yang, K., Li, Q., Lin, X., Chen, X., Sun, L.: iFinger: intrusion detection in industrial control systems via register-based fingerprinting. IEEE J. Sel. Areas Commun. **38**(5), 955–967 (2020)

9. He, X.: Thermodynamic mechanism and data hybrid driven model based marine diesel engine turbocharger anomaly detection with performance analysis. In: CAA Symposium on Fault Detection, Supervision and Safety for Technical Processes (SAFEPROCESS) (2019), pp. 477–482 (2019)

10. Lv, Z., Han, Y., Singh, A., Manogaran, G., Lv. H.: Trustworthiness in industrial IoT systems based on artificial intelligence. IEEE Trans. Ind. Inf. **17**(2), 1496–1504 (2021)

11. Xie, Y., et al.: A malware detection method using satisfiability modulo theory model checking for the programmable logic controller system. Concurrency Comput. : Pract. Experience 34(16), e5724 (2020): n. pag

12. Hua, F., Peng, X., Ruoyan, X.: KLS-A: a full-life-time anomaly detection method. In: 2020 International Conference on Artificial Intelligence and Computer Engineering (ICAICE), Beijing, China, 2020, pp. 489–493 (2020). https://doi.org/10.1109/ICAICE51518.2020.00101

13. Zolanvari, M., Teixeira, M.A., Gupta, L., et al.: Machine learning based network vulnerability analysis of industrial internet of things. IEEE Internet Things J. **6**(4), 6822–6834 (2019)

14. Roselin, A.G., Nanda, P., Nepal, S., He, X.: Intelligent anomaly detection for large network traffic with optimized deep clustering (ODC) algorithm. IEEE Access **9**, 47243–47251 (2021). https://doi.org/10.1109/ACCESS.2021.3068172

15. Nguyen, T.D., Marchal, S., Miettinen, M., et al.: DÏoT: a federated self-learning anomaly detection system for IoT. In: IEEE 39th International Conference on Distributed Computing Systems (ICDCS), pp. 756–767. IEEE (2019)

16. Matouek, P., Ryav, O., Grégr, M., et al.: Flow based monitoring of ICS communication in the smart grid. J. Inf. Secur. Appl. **54**, 102535 (2020)

17. Akpinar, K., Ozcelik, I.: Methodology to determine the device-level periodicity for anomaly detection in EtherCAT-based industrial control networks. IEEE Trans. Netw. Serv. Manag. **18**(2) 2308–2319 (2021)

18. Yu, S.: Hidden semi-Markov models. Artif. Intell. **174**, 215–243 (2010)

19. Xie, Y., Shunzheng, Yu.: Monitoring the application-layer DDoS attacks for popular websites. IEEE/ACM Trans. Network. **17**, 15–25 (2009)

20. Narayanan, S.N., Joshi, A., Bose, R.: ABATe: automatic behavioral abstraction technique to detect anomalies in smart cyber-physical systems. IEEE Trans. Dependable Secure Comput. 19(3), 1673–1686 (2022). https://doi.org/10.1109/TDSC.2020.3034331

# A Novel Polar Code-Based Key Encapsulation Mechanism with Non-permutation Equivalent Public Key

Huiling Zhang[1], Zhiqiang Lin[1], Jingang Liu[2,3(✉)], and Haixiong Zhou[4]

[1] School of Mathematics and Information Science, Guangzhou University, Guangzhou 510006, People's Republic of China
[2] School of Mathematics and Systems Science, Guangdong Normal University of Technology, Guangzhou 510665, People's Republic of China
liujingang@gpnu.edu.cn
[3] Henan Key Laboratory of Network Cryptography, Zhengzhou 450001, People's Republic of China
[4] Guangzhou Chinagdn Security Technology Co., Ltd., Guangzhou 510640, People's Republic of China

**Abstract.** Code-based cryptography is one of the post-quantum cryptography techniques which is able to resist attacks from quantum computers. This paper proposes a novel key encapsulation mechanism (KEM) based on polar codes. As the basic technology of 5G communication, polar codes have efficient encoding and decoding procedures, thus can improve the efficiency of a code-based cryptosystem. We apply polar codes to a variant of the McEliece public-key encryption scheme in which the codes of the public key and secret key are non-permutation equivalent. Then we construct the KEM protocol by Fujisaki-Okamoto transformation method. This KEM is indistinguishably secure from a chosen ciphertext attack. The public key size of the proposed KEM is smaller than that of the Classic McEliece KEM in NIST PQC standardization process, under the same security level.

**Keywords:** Public-key cryptography · Post-quantum cryptography · Polar code · Key encapsulation mechanism

## 1 Introduction

Cryptography is an essential foundation of information security technology. However, with the rapid development of quantum computers, public-key cryptosystems such as RSA, ElGamal and ECC, have suffered from potentially catastrophic attacks. This fact impels cryptographic researchers to find new cryptographic primitives which can resist quantum attacks, i.e., the post-quantum cryptography (PQC) [5, 19, 23]. In December 2016, the National Institute of Standards and Technology (NIST) has launched a PQC standardization project [9],

© ICST Institute for Computer Sciences, Social Informatics and Telecommunications Engineering 2025
Published by Springer Nature Switzerland AG 2025. All Rights Reserved
J. Cai et al. (Eds.): SPNCE 2023, LNICST 525, pp. 188–201, 2025.
https://doi.org/10.1007/978-3-031-73699-5_13

in order to call for cryptosystems that are secure for both quantum and classical computers, and compatible with existing communication protocols and networks. The scope of the cryptosystems includes key-encapsulation mechanisms, public-key encryption schemes, and digital signature schemes. After three rounds of rigorous selection, four standard algorithms were chosen: CRYSTALS-Kyber, CRYSTALS-Dilithium, Falcon, and SPHINCS+ [1,7]. In addition, there are four alternative algorithms that have been preserved: BIKE, Classic-McEliece, and HQC, SIKE. In Europe, as early as 2015, the PQCRYPTO project has been launched and has put forward relevant standardization proposals [14]. In 2018, Chinese Association for Cryptologic Research (CACR) initiated a national cryptographic algorithm design competition. The submitted algorithms are encouraged to be PQC algorithms. Unsurprisingly, the winning public key algorithms that were eventually announced in January 2020 are all quantum-resistant [8].

Key encapsulation mechanism (KEM) is a protocol that uses asymmetric cryptographic algorithms to realize secure exchange of the symmetric keys between two parties of a session. KEM is able to improve the problem of limiting the space of plaintexts in the process of using public key encryption. It is one of the effective ways to solve the problems of key distribution and key management in large-scale networks. Code-based KEM is an important part of the post-quantum cryptography. In 1978, Berlekamp et al. proved that the decoding problem of a general linear code is NP-complete. In the same year, Robert J. McEliece utilized this difficult problem and proposed the McEliece public-key cryptosystem [16]. It is based on Goppa codes, with very fast speed of encryption and decryption. During more than four decades, this scheme has withstood various cryptographic attacks and analyses, and no serious security vulnerabilities have been found. However, the main defect is that its public key size is too large comparing with RSA or ECC, and has not been widely used. For PQC's demand, Classic-McEliece, a code-based KEM which adopts the McEliece public-key cryptosystem as its basic framework [12], has entered the 4th round of the NIST PQC standardization project. In addition, two candidate schemes of the 4th round, BIKE and HQC, are also code-based KEMs. The construction of the BIKE scheme is based on the proposed cyclic medium-density parity-check codes, while the construction of the HQC scheme is based on the problem of decoding difficulty of random cyclic codes on the Hamming metric.

In 2009, Arikan discovered polar codes [2], which is the only code currently available that can reach the Shannon capacity. Polar codes use a low-complexity decoding algorithm, Arikan's successive elimination decoder, to obtain the capacity of any symmetric binary discrete memoryless channel (B-DMC). They have better decoding and error correction capabilities than the Goppa codes used by Classic-McEliece, thus can be applied to reduce the size of the public key. Moreover, since polar codes are the basic codes for 5G wireless communication systems with good performance and low complexity, the polar code-based cryptosystems can be highly integrated with the booming 5G network communication systems.

In 2014, two variants of the McEliece public-key encryption scheme based on polar codes were presented [13,20]. In 2016, Bardet et al. proposed a structural attack by using minimum weight codewords [4]. This attack attempts to solve the code equivalence problem for polar codes, which may have an impact on the security of this class of cryptosystems. In [15] Liu et al. combine the idea of RLCE scheme [21] and introduce a first polar code-based KEM. By inserting random columns to the secret code generator matrix, this KEM scheme can resist against the code equivalent attacks. In 2022, Reza et al. follow the framework of [13] and present a KEM based on polar codes, called KEM-PC [12]. They avoid the code equivalent attacks by exploiting a special kind of random subcodes of polar codes instead of the original form in [12].

**Our Contribution.** In this paper, we propose a novel polar code-based KEM which can be immune to code equivalence attacks. The fundamental public-key encryption of the KEM scheme is a variant of McEliece cryptosystem proposed by Baldi et al. [3]. It exhibits the property that the public-key codes are non-permutation equivalent to the code used as the secret codes. We apply the Fujisaki-Okamoto transformation under the random oracle machine model and construct the KEM protocol. Comparing with the Classic-McEliece KEM in the NIST PQC standardization project, our scheme has the following advantages:

Firstly, the generator matrix of the polar codes can be more flexibly selected, with a wider range of choices, which helps to avoid possible attacks against the fixed generator matrix in a code-based cryptosystem. Secondly, the lower encoding and decoding complexity ($\mathcal{O}(n\log n)$) of the polar codes can increase the speed of the system. Thirdly, the non-permutation property of the encryption process is able to the resistance to the code equivalence attacks.

## 2    Preliminaries

In this section, we briefly introduce some basic background of polar codes and key-encapsulation mechanism. We denote vectors by lower-case bold letters and matrices by upper-case bold letters throughout this paper, e.g., vector $\mathbf{m}$ and matrix $\mathbf{A}$.

### 2.1    Polar Codes

Polar codes are a class of linear codes proposed by E. Arikan [2] in 2009 based on the phenomenon of channel polar. They are the first channel codes that can be proved theoretically to reach the capacity of any binary input discrete memoryless symmetric channel, and have low encoding and decoding complexity and determinacy.

Suppose $\{W : X \to Y\}$ is a channel with input $X = \{0,1\}^n$ and output $Y = \{0,1\}^n$, respectively. The transition probability of the channel $W$ is defined by $\{W(y|x), x \in X, y \in Y\}$. Polar codes have two important parameters, i.e., $I(W)$ and $Z(W)$. $I(W) \in [0,1]$ is used as a measure of the symmetric mutual information among input and output of channel $W$, when $W$ is a binary memoryless symmetric (BMS) channel. $Z(W) \in [0,1]$ is known as the Bhattacharyya parameter of the channel $W$, which can be used as a criterion for reliability measure. The computational formulas for $I(W)$ and $Z(W)$ is as follows:

$$I(W) \triangleq \sum_{y \in Y} \sum_{x \in X} \frac{1}{2} W(y|x) \log \frac{2W(y|x)}{W(y|0) + W(y|1)},$$

$$Z(W) \triangleq \sum_{y \in Y} \sqrt{W(y|0)W(y|1)}.$$

If $W$ is a binary erasure channel with determination probability $\varepsilon$, denoted by $\mathrm{BEC}(\varepsilon)$, then we have $Z(W) = \varepsilon$ and $I(W) = 1 - Z(W) = 1 - \varepsilon$. When the value of the channel $Z(W) \in [0,1]$ is smaller, it indicates that this channel is more reliable. The basic idea of polar codes is to transmit data only in channels where $Z(W)$ is close to 0.

Polar codes essentially are a class of binary linear codes, and thus can be encoded by a generator matrix: $\mathbf{x}^n = \mathbf{u}^n \mathbf{G}^n$, where the generator matrix is $\mathbf{G}_n = \mathbf{B}_n \mathbf{F}^{\otimes}$, and $\mathbf{B}_n$ is a sorting matrix to accomplish the inverse order bit by bit. $\mathbf{F}^{\otimes}$ denotes that the matrix $\mathbf{F}$ undergoes $n$ times the operation of Kronecker product and the recursion is:

$$\mathbf{F}^{\otimes 1} = \mathbf{F} = \begin{bmatrix} 1 & 0 \\ 1 & 1 \end{bmatrix},$$

$$\mathbf{F}^{\otimes n} = \mathbf{F} \otimes \mathbf{F}^{\otimes n-1}.$$

The main process of polar code encoding can be briefly summarized as follows: 1) reliability estimation, 2) bit mixing, 3) construct the generation matrix, 4) matrix multiplication calculation, 5) output coding. Serial offset decoding based on log-likelihood ratio (LLR) can be used for polar code decoding because LLR is a sufficient statistic of the received signal in the binary input channel, which is numerically stable, and LLR decoding [2] is also used in practical systems. In addition, all decoding algorithms for polar codes have a certain bit error ratio. It will impact on the decryption of the KEM. We will discuss the decryption failure in detail in Subsect. 3.1.

### 2.2 Key Encapsulation Mechanism

A key encapsulation mechanism consists of four probabilistic polynomial time algorithms, i.e., KEM = (Setup, KeyGen, Encaps, Dncaps), as follows:

- KEM.Setup($\lambda$) $\rightarrow$ $pp$: A trusted authority runs the Setup algorithm, which takes as input a security parameter $\lambda$ and outputs the global public parameters $pp$.
- KEM.KeyGen($pp$) $\rightarrow$ ($\mathbf{pk}, \mathbf{sk}$): The user runs the key generation algorithm, which outputs a key pair ($\mathbf{pk}, \mathbf{sk}$) with the public parameters $pp$ as input. The public key $\mathbf{pk}$ is released while the private key $\mathbf{sk}$ is kept secret to the user.

- KEM.Encaps($pp, \mathbf{pk}$) → ($\mathbf{c}, \mathbf{k}$): An encapsulator runs the encapsulation algorithm and outputs a ciphertext $\mathbf{c} \in \mathcal{C}$ and a key $\mathbf{k} \in \mathcal{K}$ using the public key $\mathbf{pk}$ and the public parameters $pp$ as inputs. The ciphertext $\mathbf{c}$ is publicly broadcast and the encapsulation key $\mathbf{k}$ is kept secret to the encapsulator. Here $\mathcal{C}$ is the ciphertext space and $\mathcal{K}$ is the key space.
- KEM.Decaps($pp, \mathbf{sk}, \mathbf{c}$) → ($\mathbf{k} \vee \perp$): A decapsulator runs the decapsulation algorithm with the key $\mathbf{sk}$, the ciphertext $\mathbf{c}$ and the public parameters $pp$ as input and the key $\mathbf{k}$ or $\perp$ as output, Where $\perp$ is the symbol for decapsulation failure.

If for any security parameters $\lambda$, $pp$, ($\mathbf{pk}, \mathbf{sk}$) and ($\mathbf{c}, \mathbf{k}$), the probability of decapsulation failure is satisfied:

$$Pr[KEM.Decaps(pp, \mathbf{sk}, \mathbf{c}) \neq \mathbf{k}] \leq \delta,$$

then the KEM is said to be $\delta$-correct. The KEM is correct if $\delta = 0$.

### 2.3   IND-CCA Security for Key Encapsulation Mechanisms

A key encapsulation mechanism where an attacker cannot obtain any information about the key even if he has access to the decryption mechanism to decrypt any ciphertext of his choice, which is said to be indistinguishably secure from a chosen ciphertext attack (IND-CCA).

Let $\mathcal{A}$ be an adversary and let $\Pi$ = (Gen,Encaps,Decaps) be a KEM with key length $k$. Consider the following IND-CCA experiment $KEM_{\mathcal{A},\Pi}^{ind-cca}(\lambda)$ and the experiment $KEM_{\mathcal{A},\Pi}^{ind-cca}(\lambda)$ is visualized as in Fig. 1.

- Gen($1^\lambda$) is run to get the key pair ($\mathbf{pk}, \mathbf{sk}$), and Encaps$_{\mathbf{pk}}(1^\lambda)$ is run to generate ($\mathbf{k}, \mathbf{c}$).
- Choose a uniform bit $b \in \{0, 1\}$. If $b = 0$ set $\hat{\mathbf{k}} = \mathbf{k}$. If $b = 1$, then choose a uniform $\hat{\mathbf{k}} \in \{0, 1\}^k$.
- $\mathcal{A}$ is given ($\mathbf{pk}, \mathbf{c}, \hat{\mathbf{k}}$) and access to an oracle $\mathcal{O}_{Dcaps(\cdot)}$, but may not request decapsulation of $\mathbf{c}$ itself.
- $\mathcal{A}$ outputs a bit $b'$. The output of the experiment $KEM_{\mathcal{A},\Pi}^{ind-cca}(\lambda)$ is defined to be 1 if $b' = b$; otherwise, it is defined to be 0.

**Definition 1.** *A KEM $\Pi$ is IND-CCA secure if for all probabilistic polynomialtime adversaries $\mathcal{A}$ there is negligible function negl such that*

$$Pr[KEM_{\mathcal{A},\Pi}^{ind-cca}(\lambda) = 1] \leq \tfrac{1}{2} + negl(\lambda).$$

## 3   Polar Codes Based Key Encapsulation Mechanism

In this section, we first construct a public key algorithm based on polar codes, then the KEM is obtained by using the Fujisaki-Okamoto transformation.

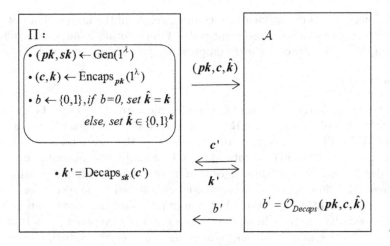

**Fig. 1.** Flowchart of experimental $\text{KEM}_{\mathcal{A},\Pi}^{ind-cca}(\lambda)$

### 3.1 A Variant of McEliece Public Key Cryptosystem Based on Polar Codes

In 2016, Baldi proposed a variant of McEliece cryptosystem, which replaces the permutation matrix in the public key with a dense matrix, thus the relationship between the public and private keys no longer permutational equivalent [3]. This scheme can resist to the code equivalence attacks. We apply polar code to this public-key scheme, and the construction is as follows.

- **Key Generation**

Choose an $[n,k]$ polar code, construct a $k \times n$ generating matrix $\mathbf{G}$, and then randomly choose a $k \times k$ non-singular matrix $\mathbf{S}$ and an $n \times n$ dense transformation matrix $\mathbf{Q}$. Let the public key be $\mathbf{G}_{pub} = \mathbf{S}^{-1}\mathbf{G}\mathbf{Q}^{-1}$ and $\mathbf{a}$, and the private key be $(\mathbf{S}, \mathbf{G}, \mathbf{Q})$, where $\mathbf{Q} = \mathbf{R} + \mathbf{T}$ and $\mathbf{a}$ are constructed as follows:
The matrix $\mathbf{R}$ is an $n \times n$ dense matrix, such that $\mathbf{a}_i, \mathbf{b}_i (1 \leq i \leq 2)$ are matrices defined on $\mathbb{F}_2$ whose size are $1 \times n$. In particular, define $\mathbf{a} = \mathbf{a}_1 + \mathbf{a}_2$ and the matrix $\mathbf{R}$ is denoted by

$$\mathbf{R} = \begin{pmatrix} \mathbf{a} \\ \mathbf{0} \end{pmatrix}^T \cdot \begin{pmatrix} \mathbf{b}_1 \\ \mathbf{b}_2 \end{pmatrix}.$$

The matrix $\mathbf{T}$ is an $n \times n$ non-singular matrix with average row-column weights $\mu(1 < \mu < 2)$.

- **Encryption**

To encrypt a plaintext $\mathbf{m} \in \mathbb{F}_2^k$, in addition to the use of a public key, a randomly selected error vector $\mathbf{e} = (\mathbf{e}_1, \mathbf{e}_2, \cdots, \mathbf{e}_n)$ with Hamming weight $t_{pub} = \lfloor \frac{t}{\mu} \rfloor$ is required, where $\mu$ is the average row-column weight of the matrix $\mathbf{T}$ and $t$ is the error-correcting capacity of the polar codes. On the other hand, $\mathbf{e}$ is required to satisfy $\mathbf{a} \cdot \mathbf{e}^T = \mathbf{0}$. The ciphertext computation procedure is $\mathbf{c} = \mathbf{mG}_{pub} + \mathbf{e}$.

- **Decryption**

In order to decode the ciphertext $\mathbf{c}$, we first calculate $\mathbf{cQ} = \mathbf{mS}^{-1}\mathbf{G} + \mathbf{eQ}$, i.e., $\mathbf{cQ} = \mathbf{mS}^{-1}G + \mathbf{eR} + \mathbf{eT}$. Since $\mathbf{R} = \mathbf{a}^T \cdot \mathbf{b}_1$ and $\mathbf{a} \cdot \mathbf{e}^T = \mathbf{0}$, then $\mathbf{eR} = \mathbf{e} \cdot \mathbf{a}^T \cdot \mathbf{b}_1 = \mathbf{0}$. Also, $\mathcal{W}_H(\mathbf{eT}) \leq t$ since the average weight of the rows and columns of the matrix $\mathbf{T}$ is $\mu$. Thus, $\mathbf{cQ} = \mathbf{mS}^{-1}\mathbf{G} + \mathbf{eT}$. Finally, the plaintext $\mathbf{m}$ can be decoded using the SC decoding algorithm [2] or other decoding algorithms.

Classic-McEliece based on Goppa codes considered to be secure for one-way chosen plaintext attack (OW-CPA) when appropriate parameters are adopted [16]. The security analyses in [3] and Subsect. 3.4 of this paper show that there is no new effective attack for our polar codes based cryptosystem. Hence it can also be considered as OW-CPA security.

## 3.2    Construction of the Key Encapsulation Mechanism

We show how to use the Fujisaki-Okamoto transformations to construct a polar code based KEM [11].

Let $\mathcal{G}, \mathcal{H}, \mathcal{K}$ and $\mathcal{L}$ be hash functions. The KEM is described by three algorithms: KeyGen for key generation, Encaps for encapsulation and Decaps for decapsulation.

---

**Algorithm 1.** KeyGen

---

**Input:** Security parameter $\lambda$.
**Output:** Public key **pk** and secret key **sk**.
1: Choose an $[n, k]$ polar code, construct a $k \times n$ generating matrix $\mathbf{G}$.
2: Randomly choose a $k \times k$ non-singular matrix $\mathbf{S}$ and an $n \times n$ dense transformation matrix $\mathbf{Q}$, where $\mathbf{Q} = \mathbf{R} + \mathbf{T}$. (Matrix construction omitted, the same as **Key Generation** 3.1)
3: **return**    secret key $\mathbf{sk} = (\mathbf{S}, \mathbf{G}, \mathbf{Q})$ and public key $\mathbf{pk} = (\mathbf{S}^{-1}\mathbf{GQ}^{-1}, \mathbf{a})$. (The construction of $\mathbf{a}$ is omitted and is the same as for **Key Generation** 3.1)

---

Unlike Goppa codes, the decoding algorithm of polar codes exists error probability, which will lead to the decryption failure of the polar code-based public-key cryptosystem. The decapsulation failure rate (DFR) can be estimated by the method of [10], which is depended on the Bhattacharyya parameter $Z(W)$ and the code parameters $[n, k, t]$. The parameters selected in Subsect. 3.4 can ensure that the DFR in our scheme is no more than $2^{-15}$ according to [10].

To further reduce the probability of the decapsulation failure, Algorithm 4 adopts parallel encryption operations, that is, $P$ error vectors $\mathbf{e}_i$ are generated simultaneously, corresponding to $P$ ciphertexts $\mathbf{c}_i$. The decapsulation can be

---

**Algorithm 2.** Encaps

---

**Input:** Public key $\mathbf{pk}$ and $\mathbf{s} \leftarrow seed \in \{0,1\}^k$.
**Output:** The key $\mathbf{k}$ and key encapsulation $\mathbf{c} = (\mathbf{c}_1, \mathbf{c}_2, \cdots, \mathbf{c}_P)$.
1: **for** $i = 1$ to $P$ **do**
2:    Let $\mathbf{e}_i = \mathcal{G}(\mathbf{s}||i).//$ see algorithm 4.
3:    Compute $\mathbf{x}_i = \mathbf{s} + \mathcal{H}(\mathbf{e}_i||i)$.
4:    Compute $\mathbf{c}_i = Enc_{\mathbf{pk}}(\mathbf{x}_i, \mathbf{e}_i)$.
5: **end for**
6: Compute $\mathbf{k} = \mathcal{K}(\mathbf{s})$.
7: **return** the key $\mathbf{k}$ and key encapsulation $\mathbf{c} = (\mathbf{c}_1, \mathbf{c}_2, \cdots, \mathbf{c}_P)$.

---

**Algorithm 3.** Decaps

---

**Input:** Secret key $\mathbf{sk}$, public key $\mathbf{pk}$, and encapsulation $\mathbf{c} = (\mathbf{c}_1, \mathbf{c}_2, \cdots, \mathbf{c}_P)$.
**Output:** The key $\mathbf{k} := \mathcal{K}(\mathbf{s}^*)$ or decapsulation failure " $\perp$ ".
1: **for** $i = 1$ to $P$ **do**
2:    Run $(\mathbf{x}_i^*, \mathbf{e}_i^*) \leftarrow \text{Dec}(\mathbf{sk}, \mathbf{c}_i)$.
3:    **if** $\text{Dec}(\mathbf{sk}, \mathbf{c}_i)$ successfully decoded for the first time **then**
4:       Set used index $j = i$.
5:       **if** $\text{Dec}(\mathbf{sk}, \mathbf{c}_i)$ failed to decode for $i = 1$ to $P$ **then**
6:          Return decapsulation failure " $\perp$ ".
7:       **end if**
8:    **end if**
9:    Compute $\mathbf{s}^* = \mathbf{x}_i^* + \mathcal{H}(\mathbf{e}_i^*||i)$.
10:    Compute $\mathbf{e}_i^{**} = \mathcal{G}(\mathbf{s}^*||i)$, $\mathbf{x}_i^{**} = \mathbf{s}^* + \mathcal{H}(\mathbf{e}_i^{**}||i)$ and $\mathbf{c}_i^{**}=Enc_{\mathbf{pk}}(\mathbf{x}^{**}, \mathbf{e}^{**})$.
11: **end for**
12: **if** $\mathbf{c}_i = \mathbf{c}_i^{**}$ for all $i = 1, 2, \cdots, P$ **then**
13:    Return $\mathbf{k} := \mathcal{K}(\mathbf{s}^*)$.
14: **else**
15:    Return decapsulation failure " $\perp$ ".
16: **end if**

---

**Algorithm 4.** Error vector $\mathbf{e}$ generation

---

**Input:** A binary seed vector $\mathbf{s} \leftarrow seed \in \{0,1\}^k$, integers $n$ and $t_{pub} = \lfloor \frac{t}{\mu} \rfloor$.
**Output:** A binary error vector $\mathbf{e} = (\mathbf{e}_1, \mathbf{e}_2, \cdots, \mathbf{e}_n)$ of length $n$ and weight $t_{pub}$.
1: Set $\mathbf{e} \leftarrow 1^{t_{pub}}||0^{n-t_{pub}}$.
2: **for** $i = 1$ to $P$ **do**
3:    $j \leftarrow \mathcal{F}(\mathbf{s})mod(n - i)$: Truncate $\mathcal{L}(s)$ to a string with $q$ bytes and $q > n$. Convert the string with $q$ bytes to an integer $Z$.
4:    **if** $Z > 2^{8q} - (2^{8q}mod(n - i))$ **then**
5:       Go back step 3.
6:    **else**
7:       Return $j = Zmod(n - i)$.
8:    **end if**
9: **end for**
10: Switch the $\mathbf{e}_i$ and $\mathbf{e}_{i+j}$ positions in $\mathbf{e}$.
11: **return** $\mathbf{e} = (\mathbf{e}_1, \mathbf{e}_2, \cdots, \mathbf{e}_n)$.

completed as long as one of the $c_i$ is decrypted correctly. Therefore we can control the failure rate to a desired range. For instance, to provide security levels $\mathbf{k} := 128, 192, 256$, we can choose $P = 9, 13, 18$, respectively. Thus, our KEM protocol achieves the desired negligible target DFR value $2^{135}, 2^{195}, 2^{270}$.

### 3.3   Proof of IND-CCA Secure

We now prove that our proposed polar code-based KEM is IND-CCA secure under the random oracle model.

**Theorem 1.** *If the public-key scheme described in Subsect. 3.1 is OW-CPA secure, and if $\mathcal{G}, \mathcal{H}, \mathcal{R}$ can be used as a random oracle machine, then the polar code-based key encapsulation mechanism proposed in this section is IND-CCA secure.*

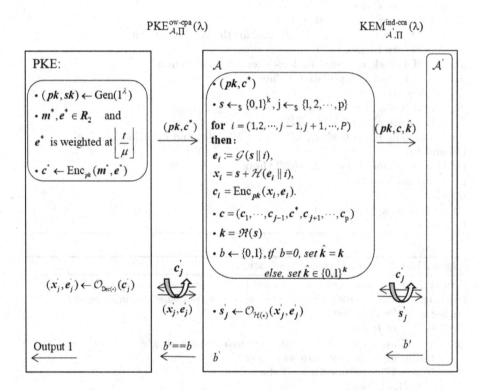

**Fig. 2.** Visualization of the IND-CCA Security Reduction Experiment

*Proof.* A visualization of the proof is shown in Fig. 2.

In the $\text{PKE}_{A,\Pi}^{ow-cpa}(\lambda)$ experiment. The public-key encryption scheme generates a key pair $(\mathbf{pk}, \mathbf{sk})$, encrypts the plaintext $\mathbf{m}^*$ to generate the ciphertext $\mathbf{c}^*$, and sends $(\mathbf{pk}, \mathbf{c}^*)$ to the adversary $\mathcal{A}$, who is essentially acted as a KEM. Adversary $\mathcal{A}$ randomly selects a seed $\mathbf{s}$ of length $k$, and in turn, for all $i = 1, 2, ..., P$, generates $\mathbf{e}_i$, $\mathbf{x}_i$, and $\mathbf{c}_i$, respectively, by the hash function. A random index $j$ is chosen, and the adversary replaces the position of $\mathbf{c}_j$ with $\mathbf{c}^*$. Finally, the adversary A obtains $\mathbf{c} = (\mathbf{c}_1, \cdots, \mathbf{c}_{j-1}, \mathbf{c}^*, \mathbf{c}_{j+1}, \cdots, \mathbf{c}_P)$ and the key $\mathbf{k} = \mathcal{K}(s)$. Choose a bit $b \in \{0, 1\}$, and if $b = 0$, let $\hat{\mathbf{k}} = \mathbf{k}$; else, let $\hat{\mathbf{k}} \in \{0, 1\}^{\mathbf{k}}$. Finally, adversary $\mathcal{A}$ provides $(\mathbf{pk}, \mathbf{c}, \hat{\mathbf{k}})$ to adversary $\mathcal{A}'$.

In the $\mathrm{PKE}_{\mathcal{A}', \Pi}^{ind-cca}(\lambda)$ experiment. Adversary $\mathcal{A}'$ receives $(\mathbf{pk}, \mathbf{c}, \hat{\mathbf{k}})$ and accesses the oracle, which generates a new ciphertext $\mathbf{c}_j'$ using the public key. Then, it sends the newly generated ciphertext $\mathbf{c}_j'$ to the public key encryption algorithm in the $\mathrm{PKE}_{\mathcal{A}, \Pi}^{ow-cpa}(\lambda)$ experiment. The decryption oracle responds to $\mathbf{c}_j'$ by returning $(\mathbf{x}_j', \mathbf{e}_j')$. Adversary $\mathcal{A}$ accesses the decryption oracle $\mathcal{O}_{\mathcal{H}(\cdot)}$ with $(\mathbf{x}_j', \mathbf{e}_j')$ and provides the corresponding seed $\mathbf{s}_j'$, which is then returned to adversary $\mathcal{A}'$. The process of sending $\mathbf{c}_j'$ and receiving the corresponding seed $\mathbf{s}_j'$ can be repeated multiple times. Eventually, adversary $\mathcal{A}'$ outputs a bit $b'$ based on the data comparison. If $b = b'$, the $\mathrm{PKE}_{\mathcal{A}, \Pi}^{ow-cpa}(\lambda)$ experiment outputs 1; otherwise, it outputs 0.

Assuming that the constructed key encapsulation mechanism is not IND-CCA secure, there exists a probabilistic polynomial time adversary $\mathcal{A}'$ such that $\Pr[\mathrm{KEM}_{\mathcal{A}', \Pi}^{ind-cca}(\lambda) = 1] = \frac{1}{2} + \varepsilon$, with $\varepsilon$ is a non-negligible function. Whereas the public-key encryption scheme is OW-CPA secure, and the probability that a probabilistic polynomial time adversary breaks it is $\Pr[\mathrm{PKE}_{\mathcal{A}, \Pi}^{ow-cpa}(\lambda) = 1] = \frac{1}{2} + negl(\lambda)$, where $negl(\lambda)$ is a negligible function. It is evident that the success of the key encapsulation mechanism adversary $\mathcal{A}'$ implies the success of the public-key encryption scheme adversary $\mathcal{A}$ among the experimentally viewable security protocols in Fig. 2. However, the probability of success for $\mathcal{A}'$, which is $\frac{1}{2} + \varepsilon$, is not equal to the probability of success for $\mathcal{A}$, which is $\frac{1}{2} + negl(\lambda)$. Therefore, there is a contradiction, and the assumption is not valid.

### 3.4 Security Analysis

According to Theorem 1, the security of the polar code-based KEM is totally depended on the public-key cryptosystem in Subsect. 3.1. We will discuss the possible attacks against the public-key cryptosystem, and illustrate that it is OW-CPA secure. Finally, we give the suggested parameters for the scheme.

- **Key recover attacks**

The adversary attempts to obtain the private key $(\mathbf{S}, \mathbf{G}, \mathbf{Q})$ from the public key $\mathbf{G}_{pub} = \mathbf{S}^{-1} \mathbf{G} \mathbf{Q}^{-1}$ by exhaustively guessing $\mathbf{S}$ and $\mathbf{Q}$. The invertible matrix $\mathbf{S}$ has a total of $\Pi_{i=1}^{k}(2^k - 2^{i-1}) > 2^{k^2-2}$ on $\mathbb{F}_2$. As for the private key $\mathbf{Q}$, without considering the structural attack, the adversary can only treat it as a random $n \times n$ matrix, so $\mathbf{Q}$ has a total of $\Pi_{i=1}^{n}(2^n - 2^{i-1}) > 2^{n^2-2}$ on $\mathbb{F}_2$. It is obviously that the brute force attack is invalid.

In the design of the public-key cryptosystem, we disclose $\mathbf{a}$, which is part of the private key $\mathbf{Q}$. This vulnerability is discussed in detail in [3]. The adversary can first calculate the parity check matrix $\mathbf{H}_{pub}$ of the public key $\mathbf{G}_{pub}$, and let $\mathbf{H}' = (\mathbf{H}_{pub}, \mathbf{a})$. Then according to the constraints $\mathbf{a} \cdot \mathbf{e}^T = \mathbf{0}$, the adversary is able to obtain an equivalent subcode with respect to the private key $\mathbf{G}$, and construct distinguishers through the code equivalent attack [22]. However, the above vulnerability is no longer available when we apply polar codes. Polar codes has a large Hull as well as a group of equivalence codes, thus can avoid the code equivalent attack.

Recently, Bardet et al. introduced a very effective structural attack [20] on the McEliece cryptosystem based on polar codes [4]. They manage to determine the structure of the minimum weight codeword of the original polar codes. Then the code equivalence problem for polar codes with respect to decreasing monomial codes is solved. However, the authors in [4] point out that this attack is very specific and applies only to the original McEliece scheme [20] used polar codes. It is impracticable for our proposed public-key cryptosystem. Notice that the scheme in this paper is of non-permutation, and the generator matrices are of randomly chosen. The codes of the private key are no longer equivalent to the original polar codes. Therefore, our proposed public-key cryptosystem is able to avoid key recovery attacks.

- **Message decoding attacks**

The idea of the message decoding attacks is to recover private messages from ciphertexts. It is an important issue in code-based cryptography. This problem is directly related to the hardness of generic decoding for linear code. One famous message decoding attack is the information set decoding (ISD) algorithm. The ISD algorithm decodes a random $[n, k, t]$ linear code by searching for a number of information sets such that positions are all out of the information sets. It does not depend on any structural properties of the code. Hence, the ISD algorithm is used to measure the choosing of the parameters. If the parameters of the public-key cryptosystem are well selected, the adversary cannot recover the error vector from the ciphertext and public keys, thus the cryptosystem is of OW-CPA secure. The general form of the ISD algorithm is shown as following [18]:

---

**Algorithm 5.** General form of the ISD algorithm

---

**Input:** Matrix $\mathbf{G} \in \mathbb{F}_2^{k \times n}$, received ciphertext $\mathbf{c} \in \mathbb{F}_2^n$ and weight parameter $t$.
**Output:** Message $\mathbf{m} \in \mathbb{F}_2^k$.
  1: Select a random subset $\Gamma \in \{1, 2, \cdots, n\}$.
  2: Compute $\mathbf{x} = \mathbf{x}_\Gamma \mathbf{G}_\Gamma$.
  3: **if** $\mathcal{W}_H(\mathbf{c} + \mathbf{x}\mathbf{G}) \leq t$ **then**
  4:     Set back $\mathbf{x}$.
  5: **else**
  6:     Return to step 1.
  7: **end if**

---

In this paper, we use an optimized version of the ISD algorithms, i.e., the Stern's algorithm [6,17] to compute a rough approximation of the security level. In fact, most of the NIST PQCRYPTO code-based submissions utilize this complexity computation tool to determine the security level of their proposals.

According to Stern's algorithm, we provide the suggested parameters in Table 1 for our proposed scheme, with the three most relevant standard security levels, $\mathbf{k} := 128, 192, 256$.

**Table 1.** Suggested Security Parameter Selection.

| Security level | $[n, k, t]$ | Public Key(KB) | Private Key(KB) | Ciphertext (KB) | ISD Attack Overhead |
|---|---|---|---|---|---|
| 128 | $[2^{10}, 700, 70]$ | 27.69 | 59.81 | 0.125 | $\mathcal{O}(2^{133.82})$ |
| 192 | $[2^{11}, 1400, 110]$ | 110.74 | 239.26 | 0.25 | $\mathcal{O}(2^{195.49})$ |
| 256 | $[2^{12}, 2295, 205]$ | 504.55 | 642.95 | 0.5 | $\mathcal{O}(2^{262.47})$ |

Table 2 lists the public key, private key, and ciphertext parameters of the Goppa-based Classic-McEliece KEM scheme in the NIST PQC standardization project.

**Table 2.** Classic-McEliece Program Parameters.

| Security level | Public Key(KB) | Private Key(KB) | Ciphertext (KB) |
|---|---|---|---|
| 128 | 225 | 6.3 | 0.125 |
| 192 | 511.88 | 13.25 | 0.19 |
| 256 | 1326 | 13.75 | 0.23 |

Observing from the comparison of Table 1 and Table 2, it can indicate that the size of the ciphertexts are similar between the Classic-McEliece scheme and our scheme. The public key size in our scheme is significantly shorter, which will improve the communication efficiency of the cryptosystem. However, It is also noted that the private key size of our scheme is larger than that of the Classic-McEliece scheme. This is due to the fact that Goppa codes can be generated in polynomial form, while polar codes do not have this property.

## 4 Conclusion

In this paper, a secure and efficient key encapsulation mechanism is constructed by taking advantage of the qualities of flexible structure and fast decoding speed of polar codes. We first apply polar codes to a variant of the McEliece cryptosystem with non-permutation property, which is able to resist the code equivalent attacks. Then we use the Fujisaki-Okamoto transformation and construct the polar code-based KEM. To reduce the probability of the decapsulation failure, parallel encryption operations are employed in the proposed KEM, hence we can obtain a negligible security level without changing the parameters.

The IND-CCA secure proof to our proposed KEM is presented under the random oracle model. The proof indicates that the security of the KEM is depended on the OW-CPA secure of the public-key cryptosystem in Subsect. 3.1. We analyze the security of the proposed public-key cryptosystem for the resistance of key recovery attacks and message recovery attacks, and declare it is OW-CPA secure. Finally, we give suggested parameters according to the NIST PQC standardization project standard. Comparing with the Classic-McEliece KEM, our scheme is able to significantly shorten the size of the public key. Furthermore, since polar codes are the basic code of 5G communication, our scheme is expected to be developed into a PQC standard algorithm under the new era of information and communication technology.

**Acknowledgements.** This work is supported in part by the National Key Research and Development Program of China (Grant No. 2021YFB3100200), Henan Key Laboratory of Network Cryptography Technology (LNCT2021-A01) and Guangzhou basic and applied basic research project (No. 202201011213).

# References

1. Announcing Four Candidates to be Standardized, Plus Fourth Round Candidates. https://csrc.nist.gov/News/2022/pqc-candidates-to-be-stand
2. Arikan, E.: Channel polarization: a method for constructing capacity-achieving codes for symmetric binary-input memoryless channels. IEEE Trans. Inf. Theory **55**(7), 3051–3073 (2009)
3. Baldi, M., et al.: Enhanced public key security for the McEliece cryptosystem. J. Cryptol. **29**, 1–27 (2016)
4. Bardet, M., Chaulet, J., Dragoi, V., Otmani, A., Tillich, J.-P.: Cryptanalysis of the McEliece public key cryptosystem based on polar codes. In: Takagi, T. (ed.) PQCrypto 2016. LNCS, vol. 9606, pp. 118–143. Springer, Cham (2016). https://doi.org/10.1007/978-3-319-29360-8_9
5. Bernstein, D.J.: Introduction to post-quantum cryptography. In: Post-Quantum Cryptography, pp. 1–14. Springer, Heidelberg (2009)
6. Bernstein, D.J., Lange, T., Peters, C.: Attacking and defending the McEliece cryptosystem. In: Buchmann, J., Ding, J. (eds.) PQCrypto 2008. LNCS, vol. 5299, pp. 31–46. Springer, Heidelberg (2008). https://doi.org/10.1007/978-3-540-88403-3_3
7. Boutin, C.: NIST announces first four quantum-resistant cryptographic algorithms. In: National Institute of Standards and Technology (2022)
8. CACR: Chinese national cryptographic algorithm design competition (in Chinese). https://www.cacrnet.org.cn/site/content/854.html
9. Chen, L., et al.: Report on post-quantum cryptography, vol. 12. US Department of Commerce, National Institute of Standards and Technology (2016)
10. Dragoi, V.: Algebraic approach for the study of algorithmic problems coming from cryptography and the theory of error correcting codes. Ph.D. thesis. Université de Rouen, France (2017)

11. Eiichiro et al.: Secure integration of asymmetric and symmetric encryption schemes. J. Cryptol. **26**(1), 80–101 (2013)
12. Hooshmand, R., Khoshfekr, M.: Key encapsulation mechanism based on polar codes. IET Commun. **16**, 2438–2447 (2022)
13. Hooshmand, R., et al.: Reducing the key length of McEliece cryptosystem using polar codes. In: 2014 11th International ISC Conference on Information Security and Cryptology, pp. 104–108. IEEE (2014)
14. Lange, T.: PQCRYPTO Project in the EU. In: NIST Workshop on Cybersecurity in a Post-Quantum World (2015)
15. Liu, J., et al.: polarRLCE: a new code-based cryptosystem using polar codes. Secur. Commun. Netw. 2019(2), 1–10 (2019)
16. McEliece, R.J.: A public-key cryptosystem based on algebraic. In: Coding Thv, vol. 4244, pp. 114–116 (1978)
17. Peters, C.: Information-set decoding for linear codes over Fq. In: Sendrier, N. (ed.) PQCrypto 2010. LNCS, vol. 6061, pp. 81–94. Springer, Heidelberg (2010). https://doi.org/10.1007/978-3-642-12929-2_7
18. Prange, E.: The use of information sets in decoding cyclic codes. IRE Trans. Inf. Theory **8**(5), 5–9 (1962)
19. Shor, P.W.: Polynomial time algorithms for discrete logarithms and factoring on a quantum computer. In: Adleman, L.M., Huang, M.-D. (eds.) ANTS 1994. LNCS, vol. 877, pp. 289–289. Springer, Heidelberg (1994). https://doi.org/10.1007/3-540-58691-1_68
20. Shrestha, S.R., Kim, Y.S.: New McEliece cryptosystem based on polar codes as a candidate for post-quantum cryptography. In: International Symposium on Communications & Information Technologies, pp. 368–372 (2014)
21. Wang, Y.: Quantum resistant random linear code based public key encryption scheme RLCE. In: 2016 IEEE International Symposium on Information Theory (ISIT), pp. 2519–2523. IEEE (2016)
22. Wieschebrink, C.: Cryptanalysis of the niederreiter public key scheme based on GRS subcodes. In: Sendrier, N. (ed.) PQCrypto 2010. LNCS, vol. 6061, pp. 61–72. Springer, Heidelberg (2010). https://doi.org/10.1007/978-3-642-12929-2_5
23. Zhang, H., et al.: Review on cyberspace security. SCIENTIA SINICA Informationis **46**(2), 125–164 (2016)

# Two-Stage Multi-lingual Speech Emotion Recognition for Multi-lingual Emotional Speech Synthesis

Xin Huang[1], Zuqiang Zeng[1], Chenjing Sun[1], and Jichen Yang[2(✉)]

[1] School of Electronics and Information Engineering,South China Normal University, Foshan 528225, China
[2] School of Cyber Security, Guangdong Polytechnic Normal University, Guangzhou 510665, China
nisonyoung@163.com

**Abstract.** In multi-lingual emotional speech synthesis, it is difficult to incorporate suitable emotional expressions in the synthesis process due to the differences between the emotional expressions of different linguals. In order to extract better emotional expressions of different linguals to assist the multi-lingual emotional speech synthesis, this paper conducts research on multi-lingual speech emotion recognition. In the current study of multi-lingual speech emotion recognition (SER), the combining method (TCM) and multi-task method (TMM) are the popular methods. However, good performance can't be obtained, the reason is that TCM doesn't consider the emotional difference of different linguals and it is not easy to train the good emotion recognition model and good language recognition model at the same time for TMM. In order to settle the issue, a two-stage multi-lingual SER method is proposed in this paper, wherein language recognition is to recognize the language type at the first stage, and then emotion recognition is applied at the second stage. In addition, wav2vec 2.0 is used as the input while ResNet18 is selected as the model for language recognition and emotion recognition respectively. The experimental results show that the proposed method can work on multi-lingual SER, meanwhile, the proposed method performs better than TCM and TMM.

**Keywords:** Speech emotion recognition · Multi-lingual · Emotional speech synthesis

## 1 Introduction

In recent years, the performance of text-to-speech (TTS) systems in terms of quality and naturalness of synthesized speech has improved significantly [1,2]. With globalization, bilinguals and polyglots are becoming a common trend in today's world, which makes speech communication more complex. In response to this trend, the performance of speech analysis tools such as emotional speech

J. Cai et al. (Eds.): SPNCE 2023, LNICST 525, pp. 202–211, 2025.
https://doi.org/10.1007/978-3-031-73699-5_14

synthesis needs to be further improved in terms of multi-lingual. However, due to the large differences between the emotional expressions of different linguals, the challenge of multi-lingual emotional speech synthesis is that it is difficult to incorporate emotional expressions suitable for various linguals in the synthesis process. A well-performing multi-lingual speech emotion recognition (SER) system can extract the emotion expressions from different linguals, which enables the multi-lingual emotional speech synthesis system to incorporate the emotion expressions containing the matching emotions during the speech synthesis, and thus improves the performance of the multi-lingual emotional speech synthesis system. Therefore, this paper is aimed at multi-lingual SER.

SER has been an important research topic in the field of speech signal processing. The goal of SER is to accurately recognize the emotion type for the input speech utterance under the trained model, where the model is trained by using training data and corresponding emotion labels. Many methods have been proposed for single-lingual SER. For example, the accuracy of emotion recognition can be improved by optimizing the structure of a single model after feature extraction of the audio information [3]. Optimized neural networks can also be used to recognize emotions in a single language [4]. In the multi-lingual emotion recognition task, different features of speech information are used to recognize and classify. For example, combining features such as formant peaks, intensity and pitch can improve the accuracy of emotion recognition [5].

To date, there have been two methods for multi-lingual SER: the combining method (TCM) [6] and the multi-task method (TMM) [7,8]. TCM trains the model by combing different-lingual training data with the same emotion as a type, which borrows the method of single-lingual SER for multi-lingual SER. While TMM regards the multi-lingual SER as two tasks, one is language recognition and the other is emotion recognition, in other words, the language recognition and emotion recognition models are trained at the same time.

Since TCM does not take into account the emotion differences of different linguals in multi-lingual SER, it usually fails to obtain good performance as in [6]. Theoretically speaking, TMM can obtain good performance if the emotion recognition model and the language recognition model are successfully trained in the training stage. However, it is not easy to train a good emotion recognition model and a good language recognition model at the same time, for example, it is very difficult to assign suitable weights to the loss function for different tasks.

There is a general belief that it is easier to train one model than to train two models at the same time using the same training data. In this regard, in order to address the multi-lingual SER issues, a two-stage multi-lingual SER method is proposed in this paper. It consists of two stages: the first stage is to recognize language while the second stage is to recognize emotion. Compared with TMM, we can see that both the proposed method and TMM regard multi-lingual SER as two tasks.

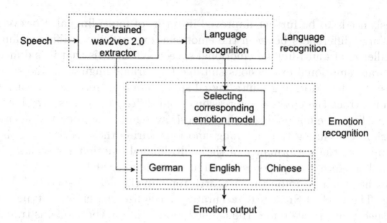

**Fig. 1.** The framework of the proposed two-stage multi-lingual SER.

## 2   Proposed Method

Figure 1 is the framework of the proposed two-stage multi-lingual SER method. From Fig. 1, it can be seen that the proposed two-stage multi-lingual SER consists of two parts: language recognition and emotion recognition, wherein language recognition is at the first stage while emotion recognition is at the second stage. Note that wav2vec 2.0 is used as the input for language recognition and emotion recognition because it is a well-known self-supervised representation and it has more useful information than some commonly used features.

In order to recognize the language type of the input speech signal, a language recognition model must be trained in advance. To do so, a three-class corresponding German, English and Chinese classifier is trained. Once the model training is finished, the language type of the input signal can be recognized under the model.

On the basis of language recognition, the corresponding emotion recognition model is selected to recognize emotion with wav2vec 2.0 of the input speech. To this end, three emotion recognition models (German, English and Chinese) are trained on their own training data and corresponding emotion labels respectively.

In the following, the two main models in the two-stage multi-lingual SER approach are described in detail, which are the pre-trained wav2vec 2.0 emotion representation extraction model and the recognition model used for both language and emotion recognition.

### 2.1   Pre-trained Wav2vec 2.0 Emotion Representation Extraction Model

As shown in Fig. 2, the pre-trained wav2vec 2.0 model consists of a multilayer convolutional feature encoder, a Transformer and a quantization module [9]. Where the multilayer convolutional feature encoder $f : X \rightarrow Z$ takes the raw

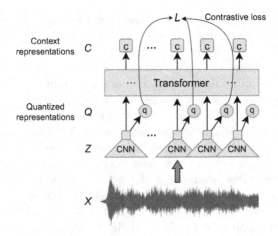

**Fig. 2.** The architecture of pre-trained W2V2 model.

audio $X$ as input and outputs the latent speech representations $z_1, \ldots, z_T$ with time step $T$. The Transformer $g : Z \to C$ takes the latent speech representation $Z$ as input, captures the global information of the sequence, and extracts the contextual representations $c_1, \ldots, c_T$ of the sequence. The quantization module $Z \to Q$ also takes the latent speech representation $Z$ as input, discretizes it into $q_t$ and outputs it. The outputs $C$ and $Q$ of the Transformer and the quantization module are used as inputs for the contrastive loss.

The feature encoder processes the input signal into low-level features, which consists of a temporal convolution, a layer normalization and a GELU activation function. The raw waveform input to the encoder is normalized to zero mean and unit variance.

Transformer extracts contextual representations in low-level features, it uses a convolutional layer as relative positional embedding, and captures global information using self-attention mechanisms.

Quantization module discretizes the low-level features into a finite set of speech representations through product quantization. The product quantization operation makes the features more robust and less susceptible to a small number of perturbations by splitting the infinite spatial space of feature representations into finite codebooks.

## 2.2 Recognition Model

ResNet18 is used to train the language recognition model and emotion recognition model in this work. The reason behind this is that ResNet18 has good performance in the task of classification. Residual network (ResNet) was proposed by Microsoft Research in 2015 [10]. The problem solved by this network is that as the depth of the network becomes deeper and deeper, the problem of network 'degradation' becomes obvious, that is, as the number of layers of the network increases, the accuracy of the model begins to saturate, and then rapidly degrades. ResNet describes the training degradation problem and new solutions in detail on the ImageNet dataset.

The overall structure of ResNet consists of a number of residual units and bottleneck residual units, each of which contains a number of residual blocks. The input of the whole network is a picture, which undergoes multi-layer convolution operation and outputs a vector with corresponding class probabilities for classification tasks. With the increase of network depth, ordinary networks show higher training errors, while residual networks appear to be very easy to optimize. As the number of layers of the network increases, the residual network can easily achieve better accuracy, and the accuracy will be higher than the previous network. ResNet was originally intended for image recognition work. Neural network also has a good effect on SER [11]. In this paper, we modify ResNet to make it applicable to SER and classification [12]. Therefore, ResNet also has a good effect on voice information processing.

## 3   Database Introduction

The German speech data used in this paper is EMO-DB, a German emotional speech database consisting of recordings from ten actors (five males and five females) simulating seven target emotions [13], which are anger, neutral, fear, boredom, happiness, sadness and disgust, respectively.

The Chinese and English speech data used in the experiment were taken from the emotion speech database (ESD) [14], which consists of parallel phrases recorded by 10 native speakers for Chinese and English, respectively. These phrases covered five emotion categories, which are angry, happy, neutral, sad and surprise, respectively. Here, we call the Chinese part and English part in ESD as ESD-Chi and ESD-Eng, respectively.

Considering angry, happy, sad and neutral types appear in EMO-DB, ESD-Chi and ESD-Eng respectively. Thus, the four types of emotion in the three databases are selected to evaluate the proposed two-stage multi-lingual SER. The utterance number of each emotion type in the training, test and eva subsets of the three databases are given in Table 1.

## 4   Experimental Setup

The experimental deployment in this study was conducted using the Pytorch platform. The weighted accuracy (WA) and the unweighted accuracy (UA) are used as the evaluation metrics. The pre-trained wav2vec 2.0 model XLSR-53 is used in the experiment because it was trained on multi-lingual data [15].

After wav2vec 2.0 is extracted by the pre-trained model, three-class language recognition model is trained based on ResNet18, in the same way, ResNet18 is also trained to train emotion recognition models using the training data of EMO-DB, ESD-Chi and ESD-Eng respectively.

**Table 1.** The utterance number of each emotion type in the training, test and eva subsets of the three databases.

| Database | Subset | Angry | Happy | Sad | Neutral |
|---|---|---|---|---|---|
| ESD-Chi | Training | 3000 | 3000 | 3000 | 3000 |
| | Test | 300 | 300 | 300 | 300 |
| | Eva | 200 | 200 | 200 | 200 |
| ESD-Eng | Training | 3000 | 3000 | 3000 | 3000 |
| | Test | 300 | 300 | 300 | 300 |
| | Eva | 200 | 200 | 200 | 200 |
| EMO-DB | Training | 84 | 49 | 42 | 49 |
| | Test | 12 | 7 | 6 | 7 |
| | Eva | 24 | 14 | 12 | 14 |

## 5   Experimental Results and Analysis

Table 2 reports the experimental results on the three databases using the proposed two-stage multi-lingual SER method in terms of accuracy, UA and WA. Accuracy is used to calculate every emotion recognition accuracy in every database while UA and WA are used to evaluate all emotion recognition accuracy in one database.

**Table 2.** Experimental results on the three databases using the proposed two-stage multi-lingual SER method in terms of accuracy (%), UA (%) and WA (%).

| Database | Accuracy | | | | UA | WA |
|---|---|---|---|---|---|---|
| | Angry | Happy | Sad | Neutral | | |
| ESD-Chi | 94 | 98.5 | 96 | 99 | 96.87 | 96.87 |
| ESD-Eng | 96.5 | 84.5 | 87.5 | 92 | 90.12 | 90.12 |
| EMO-DB | 79.2 | 64.3 | 91.7 | 85.7 | 79.71 | 79.68 |
| All | 94.07 | 91 | 91.26 | 94.99 | 92.83 | 92.84 |

From Table 2, two conclusions can be drawn:

- The proposed two-stage multi-lingual SER on ESD-Chi performs better than that on ESD-Eng and that on EMO-DB in terms of UA and WA. In which, the result on EMO-DB gives the worst performance, the reason may be that there is not so much training data in EMO-DB.
- The proposed two-stage multi-lingual SER is able to recognize most of the emotion types in ESD-Chi in terms of accuracy while unable to recognize angry and happy types in EMO-DB, the reason is the same as mentioned above.

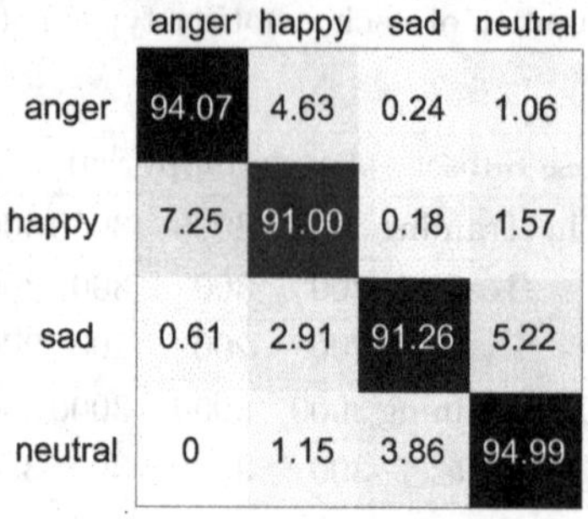

| | anger | happy | sad | neutral |
|---|---|---|---|---|
| anger | 94.07 | 4.63 | 0.24 | 1.06 |
| happy | 7.25 | 91.00 | 0.18 | 1.57 |
| sad | 0.61 | 2.91 | 91.26 | 5.22 |
| neutral | 0 | 1.15 | 3.86 | 94.99 |

**Fig. 3.** Multi-lingual: Confusion matrix of the two-stage multi-lingual SER with UA of 92.83% and WA of 92.84% on multi-lingual data.

## 5.1   Confusion Matrix Analysis

Confusion matrix can clearly show the recognition effect of this paper's system on different emotions when inputting multi-lingual data. As shown in Fig. 3, the proposed system can achieve more than 90% recognition effect for each emotion, with the best recognition ability for anger and neutral emotions, and a slightly worse recognition ability for happy and sad emotions.

## 5.2   Comparison with Commonly Used Features

In this section, we would like to compare different inputs for the proposed two-stage multi-lingual SER. Commonly used features such as MFCC [16] and WavLM [17] are selected here. Table 3 gives the experimental results comparison between wav2vec 2.0 and commonly used features on the three databases in terms of UA and WA.

**Table 3.** Experimental results comparison between wav2vec 2.0 and commonly used features such as MFCC and WavLM in terms of UA (%) and WA (%).

| Features | UA | WA |
|---|---|---|
| MFCC | 78.26 | 78.28 |
| WavLM | 85.21 | 85.26 |
| wav2vec2.0 | 92.83 | 92.84 |

As shown in Table 3, the proposed system with wav2vec 2.0 as the input significantly outperforms MFCC and WavLM in terms of UA and WA, which means that wav2vec 2.0 is more suitable for the task of multi-lingual SER. The reason may be that there is more emotion information in wav2vec 2.0 than that in MFCC and WavLM.

## 5.3   Comparison with State-of-the-Art Methods

To better validate the effectiveness of our proposed method, it is compared with state-of-the-art methods such as TCM and TMM. Wav2vec 2.0 is used as the input for both TCM and TMM, which is the same as the proposed method. Comparison results are given in Table 4.

From Table 4, it can be found that the proposed method performs better than TCM and TMM. Furthermore, TCM gives the worst performance. It means that the proposed method can correctly recognize more emotion types in multi-lingual SER. The reason is that TCM does not take into account the emotion differences between different linguals in multi-lingual SER. And it is not easy for TMM to train a good emotion recognition model and a good language recognition model at the same time.

**Table 4.** Comparison with state-of-the-art methods on the three databases in terms of UA (%) and WA (%).

| Methods | UA | WA |
|---|---|---|
| TCM | 89.66 | 89.67 |
| TMM | 91.37 | 91.38 |
| The proposed method (Ours) | 92.83 | 92.84 |

# 6   Conclusion

In order to improve the performance of the multi-lingual emotional speech synthesis system, this paper investigates its underlying multi-lingual SER. In order to address the issues of multi-lingual SER, a two-stage multi-lingual SER method is proposed, which consists of two stages, the first stage is to recognize the language and the second stage is to recognize emotion. In addition, wav2vec 2.0 is used as the input while ResNet18 is selected as the model for both language recognition and emotion recognition. The experimental results show that the proposed method can work on multi-lingual SER, meanwhile, the proposed method performs better than state-of-the-art methods such as TCM and TMM. This means that the multi-lingual emotional speech synthesis system can achieve better performance by using the emotional representations extracted from the multi-lingual SER system in this paper as inputs in the final synthesis phase.

**Acknowledgments.** This work was supported by NSFC(62001173, 62171188). The authors gratefully acknowledge the support of 2022 Guangdong Hong Kong-Macao Greater Bay Area Exchange Programs of South China Normal University (SCNU).

# References

1. Wang, Y., Skerry-Ryan, R.J., Stanton, D., et al.: Tacotron: towards end-to-end speech synthesis. In: Proceedings of Interspeech 2017, pp. 4006–4010 (2017)
2. Lei, Y., Yang, S., Wang, X., Xie, L.: MsEmoTTS: multi-scale emotion transfer, prediction, and control for emotional speech synthesis. IEEE/ACM Trans. Audio Speech Lang. Process. **30**, 853–864 (2022)
3. Zayene, B., Jlassi, C., Arous, N.: 3D convolutional recurrent global neural network for speech emotion recognition. In: 2020 5th International Conference on Advanced Technologies for Signal and Image Processing (ATSIP), Sousse, Tunisia, pp. 1–5 (2020)
4. Kong, Q., Cao, Y., Iqbal, T., et al.: PANNs: large-scale pretrained audio neural networks for audio pattern recognition. IEEE/ACM Trans. Audio Speech Lang. Process. **28**, 2880–2894 (2020)
5. Meftah, A., Alotaibi, Y., Selouani, S.-A.: Emotional speech recognition: a multilingual perspective. In: 2016 International Conference on Bio-engineering for Smart Technologies (BioSMART), Dubai, United Arab Emirates, pp. 1–4 (2016)
6. Yadav, A., Vishwakarma, D.K.: A multilingual framework of CNN and Bi-LSTM for emotion classification. In: 2020 11th International Conference on Computing, Communication and Networking Technologies (ICCCNT), Kharagpur, India, pp. 1–6 (2020)
7. Sharma, M.: Multi-lingual multi-task speech emotion recognition using wav2vec 2.0. In: ICASSP 2022 - 2022 IEEE International Conference on Acoustics, Speech and Signal Processing (ICASSP), Singapore, pp. 6907–6911 (2022)
8. Yue, P., Qu, L., Zheng, S., Li, T.: Multi-task learning for speech emotion and emotion intensity recognition. In: 2022 Asia-Pacific Signal and Information Processing Association Annual Summit and Conference (APSIPA ASC), Chiang Mai, Thailand, pp. 1232–1237 (2022)
9. Baevski, A., Zhou, Y., Mohamed, A., Auli, M.: wav2vec 2.0: a framework for self-supervised learning of speech representations. In: Advances in Neural Information Processing Systems, vol. 33, pp. 12449–12460 (2020)
10. He, K., Zhang, X., Ren, S., Sun, J.: Deep residual learning for image recognition. In: 2016 IEEE Conference on Computer Vision and Pattern Recognition (CVPR), Las Vegas, NV, USA, pp. 770–778 (2016)
11. Qayyum, A.B.A., Arefeen, A., Shahnaz, C.: Convolutional neural network (CNN) based speech-emotion recognition. In: 2019 IEEE International Conference on Signal Processing, Information, Communication & Systems (SPICSCON), Dhaka, Bangladesh, pp. 122–125 (2019)
12. Zhang, Z., Zhang, X., Guo, M., et al.: A multilingual framework based on pre-training model for speech emotion recognition. In: 2021 Asia-Pacific Signal and Information Processing Association Annual Summit and Conference (APSIPA ASC), Tokyo, Japan, pp. 750–755 (2021)
13. Burkhardt, F., Paeschke, A., Rolfes, M., et al.: A database of German emotional speech. In: Proceedings of Interspeech 2005, pp. 1517–1520 (2005)
14. Zhou, K., Sisman, B., Liu, R., Li, H.: Emotional voice conversion: theory, databases and ESD. Speech Commun. **137**, 1–18 (2022)
15. Conneau, A., Baevski, A., Collobert, R., et al.: Unsupervised cross-lingual representation learning for speech recognition. In: Proceedings of Interspeech 2021, pp. 2426–2430 (2021)

16. Latif, S., Rana, R., Khalifa, S., et al.: Survey of deep representation learning for speech emotion recognition. IEEE Trans. Affect. Comput. **14**(2), 1634–1654 (2021)
17. Chen, S., Wang, C., Chen, Z., et al.: WavLM: large-scale self-supervised pre-training for full stack speech processing. IEEE J. Sel. Top. Signal Process. **16**(6), 1505–1518 (2022)

# EncoderMU: Machine Unlearning in Contrastive Learning

Zixin Wang[1], Bing Mi[2], and Kongyang Chen[1,3]($\boxtimes$)

[1] Institute of Artificial Intelligence and Blockchain, Guangzhou University, Guangzhou, China
kychen@gzhu.edu.cn
[2] Guangdong University of Finance and Economics, Guangzhou, China
[3] Pazhou Lab, Guangzhou, China

**Abstract.** Machine unlearning is a complex process that necessitates the model to diminish the influence of the training data while keeping the loss of accuracy to a minimum. Despite the numerous studies on machine unlearning in recent years, the majority of them have primarily focused on supervised learning models, leaving research on contrastive learning models relatively underexplored. With the conviction that self-supervised learning harbors a promising potential, surpassing or rivaling that of supervised learning, we set out to investigate methods for machine unlearning centered around contrastive learning models. In this study, we introduce a novel gradient constraint-based approach for training the model to effectively achieve machine unlearning. Our method only necessitates a minimal number of training epochs and the identification of the data slated for unlearning. Remarkably, our approach demonstrates proficient performance not only on contrastive learning models but also on supervised learning models, showcasing its versatility and adaptability in various learning paradigms.

**Keywords:** Machine Unlearning · Contrastive Learning · Distributed Learning

## 1 Introduction

In contemporary society, artificial intelligence (AI) has become increasingly pervasive, with numerous AI applications leveraging machine learning models. AI has permeated various aspects of human society, encompassing learning, work, and daily life. However, model privacy has emerged as a significant concern, as models may inadvertently expose individual users' privacy. For example, membership inference attacks capitalize on the discrepancies between training and non-training data predictions to infer whether specific data were utilized for model training, thereby exposing privacy risks. Additional challenges to model privacy and security include backdoor attacks and model adversarial attacks.

© ICST Institute for Computer Sciences, Social Informatics and Telecommunications Engineering 2025
Published by Springer Nature Switzerland AG 2025. All Rights Reserved
J. Cai et al. (Eds.): SPNCE 2023, LNICST 525, pp. 212–223, 2025.
https://doi.org/10.1007/978-3-031-73699-5_15

Moreover, privacy regulations such as the European General Data Protection Regulation (GDPR) [8] afford users the right to request the deletion of their personal data from learning models, a component of the right to be forgotten. The Protection of Personal Information Act (APPI) [3] and Canada's proposed Consumer Privacy Protection Act (CPPA) [6], both mandate the deletion of private information. Erasing data from learning models is a challenging task requiring the selective reversal of the learning process. In the absence of targeted methods, the sole option is retraining the model, a costly and feasible approach only when the original data remains accessible. As a remedial measure, researchers like Cao and Yang, and Bourtoule et al. [2, 4] have proposed machine unlearning methods. These techniques partially reverse the learning process, facilitating the retrospective deletion of specific data points, mitigating privacy breaches, and addressing user deletion requests. Yan et al. [10] and Ga et al. [9] introduced an approximate unlearning method, achieving effects akin to retraining with minimal additional training.

Nonetheless, these methods exhibit limitations, chiefly their dependence on supervised learning for machine unlearning. Research on contrastive and self-supervised learning remains relatively limited [5]. In this study, we present a novel gradient penalty-based machine unlearning method, enabling approximate unlearning by modifying the loss during model training. This approach requires minimal training to effectuate machine unlearning for designated data while ensuring that the model can forget specified data without a substantial loss in accuracy (generally within 10%). Our method is simple, efficient, and highly adaptable, demonstrating commendable performance on both supervised and contrastive learning models.

## 2 Related Work

The premise of machine unlearning [7] is to enable a model to completely forget the influence of specified data, with the main idea being to directly remove the data to be forgotten from the entire model training process. Based on this concept, two directions for machine unlearning have emerged: complete unlearning and approximate unlearning.

Complete unlearning entails retraining the entire model. SISA [2] (Sliceable Incremental and Selective Aggregation) is an early method for machine unlearning. The core idea of SISA is to split the original dataset into multiple independent subsets, which do not share information during training. These independent subsets are then incrementally trained by slicing and partitioning the data. Incremental training implies that the model trains on each data slice and updates the model parameters after each training session, allowing the model to gradually adapt to all sliced datasets. Finally, an ensemble method is used to combine these models. One ensemble approach calculates the output vector for each model, averages these output vectors, and selects the maximum value from the mean vector as the final classification result. The advantage of this method is that it can achieve complete unlearning of the data to be forgotten.

However, its drawbacks are that it requires adopting a specific framework, which may not be compatible with existing models and training frameworks used by most companies, and the loss of model accuracy due to the ensemble method can be substantial, greatly impacting the model's performance.

Due to these drawbacks, approximate unlearning has been considered as an alternative. Approximate unlearning does not require the model to achieve the same effect as with non-trained data; it only needs to be close. Moreover, it can be achieved by training the existing model for a small number of iterations. This approach not only saves a significant amount of training resources but also preserves the model's original performance to the greatest extent. PUMA [9] (Private Update via Model Approximation) is a method for implementing approximate unlearning. Its goal is to remove the influence of training data while maintaining minimal changes in model performance. PUMA achieves this primarily by generating synthetic data and fine-tuning the model using this data. However, one drawback is that generating perturbation data with activation values similar to the forgotten samples in the model can be challenging. This process may require complex optimization methods, such as gradient matching, thereby increasing computational complexity.

The method proposed in this paper is also an approximate unlearning approach. However, the key difference is that our method can be applied to both supervised learning and contrastive learning models, making it a versatile solution for a wider range of applications.

## 3   Gradient Penalty-Based Unlearning Method

In this section, we will specify the details of our unlearning method, and the source of inspiration for our method.

### 3.1   Gradient Penalty

Our approach is inspired by WGAN [1], in which the generator needs to compute gradient_penalty as a loss to ensure the stability of the model training. The gradient penalty ensures that the gradient of the discriminator remains appropriate during training by interpolating between the real and generated samples and requiring the gradient of the interpolated points to be close to 1 in magnitude. This gradient penalty term will be added to the loss function of the discriminator to ensure the stability of the training process. By using the gradient penalty, WGAN-GP has better stability in training the game process between the generator and the discriminator, and reduces the risk of gradient disappearance and pattern collapse problems. The following is the flow chart of the algorithm for the penalty term.

Through our investigation, we have discovered that by treating real samples as trained samples and fake samples as non-trained samples, the gradient penalty loss can bring the model's prediction confidence for both trained and non-trained data closer together. This, in turn, renders the trained and non-trained data indistinguishable. The core component of this function hinges on generating interpolated data between trained and non-member data, followed by computing the respective gradients and calculating the penalty value. Below is the formula for calculating the penalty value.

$$\text{gradient\_penalty} = \frac{1}{N} \sum_{i=1}^{N} \left( \|\nabla_{\mathbf{z}_i} D(\mathbf{z}_i)\|_2 - 1 \right)^2 \tag{1}$$

However, this approach presents a notable limitation. While it successfully brings the model's prediction confidence for both member and non-member data closer together, it does so by mutually converging the predictions. In other words, the predictions for non-trained data are also altered, eventually causing the trained and non-trained data to aggregate at a central point between the two. Although this process reduces the probability distribution of the model's output prediction confidence for trained data, it concurrently increases the output prediction confidence for non-member data. This outcome is not desirable; ideally, the model should treat predictions for trained data as if it were untrained, while maintaining the non-trained data predictions unchanged (Figs. 1 and 2).

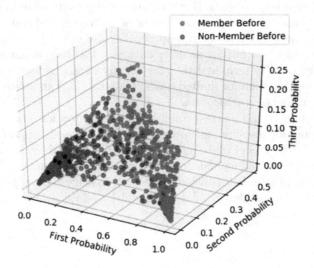

**Fig. 1.** Before gradient penalty

## 3.2   Our Objectives

Due to the aforementioned issue, our primary focus in subsequent research is to identify a loss function or a specific technique capable of reducing the model's prediction confidence for data. Although L2 regularization can mitigate the extent of overfitting in the model, it fails to alleviate the disparity between

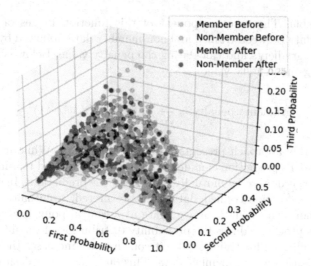

**Fig. 2.** After gradient penalty

member and non-member data. However, since the penalty term in WGAN can reduce the difference in prediction outputs between trained and non-trained data, we propose a combination of the two approaches. By calculating the average L2 norm of the model's output for member data as a loss component and combining it with the penalty term and the member data training loss, we can create a composite loss function for limited model training. This approach enables the targeted unlearning of specific data.

With this understanding, we establish the foundation for our study on contrastive learning for machine unlearning, focusing primarily on two objectives. First, to enable the model to defend against membership inference attacks, the model's output prediction confidence for member and non-member data should be nearly identical or indistinguishable. Second, to achieve data unlearning, the model's prediction confidence for data should be relatively low, or the uncertainty should be considerably high.

### 3.3 Our Method

To accomplish these two objectives, we employ the WGAN gradient penalty term as a loss function for machine unlearning training, ensuring that the model's prediction confidence for member and non-member data is nearly indistinguishable. Subsequently, we calculate the L2 norm of the model's encoder prediction output for member data as a loss function for machine unlearning training, aiming to reduce the model's prediction confidence for data. Finally, we incorporate the model's training loss for member data as a constraint term during the machine unlearning training process to maintain the model's accuracy.

Our proposed method is capable of rendering member and non-member data predictions indistinguishable while maintaining a minimal loss in model accuracy (at most approximately 10%). This approach is applicable to both contrastive learning models and supervised models. For contrastive learning models, we first extract the model's encoder, then perform unlearning based on the encoder's prediction output for the data. Our method requires only a simple modification to the training loss function, and demands a relatively low number of training epochs (approximately 10). The general form of our loss function is as follows:

$$\mathcal{L} = \alpha \cdot L_{\text{MEMtrain}} + \beta \cdot L_{\text{GP}} + \gamma \cdot L_{\text{Norm}} \tag{2}$$

The loss function is composed of three distinct components. The first component corresponds to the training loss of the data to be forgotten within the model. This element primarily serves to prevent model collapse during the unlearning process. In our experiments, omitting this component resulted in significant losses in model accuracy. The second component is the gradient constraint term from WGAN, which, in its original form, stabilizes model training by preventing gradient explosion and vanishing. However, our research has discovered that this function can also facilitate convergence in prediction output confidence for both member and non-member data. The third component involves computing the L2 norm of the model's prediction output, aimed at reducing the prediction confidence. Although the second component can induce convergence in prediction confidence, it tends to elevate the confidence for non-member data predictions. Therefore, we strive to lower the model's prediction confidence for all data.

## 4 Experiments

### 4.1 Experimental Settings

**DataSets:** We conducted experiments on the SVHN, CIFAR10, CIFAR100 data sets. The distribution of the datasets is shown in Table 1

**Table 1.** Datasets description

| Datasets | Shape | Classes | Training data | Testing data |
|----------|-------|---------|---------------|--------------|
| CIFAR-10 | $32 \times 32 \times 3$ | 10 | 50,000 | 10,000 |
| CIFAR-100 | $32 \times 32 \times 3$ | 100 | 50,000 | 10,000 |
| SVHN | $32 \times 32 \times 3$ | 10 | 73,257 | 26,032 |

**Experimental Details:** We implemented the series of attacks described above using PyTorch in Python 3.7. Our computational resources included 4 NVIDIA V100 GPUs. To control variables, we conducted experiments using a combination of 10,000 training data and 10,000 test data samples. During contrastive learning model training, we trained the model for 1,600 epochs to induce overfitting, using the Adam optimizer with a learning rate of 0.01.

Common methods for evaluating encoder performance include linear evaluation and weighted KNN evaluation. Linear evaluation measures the quality of feature representations extracted by the encoder when trained with a linear model. Weighted KNN evaluation involves comparing feature representations' cosine similarity and classifying them using a weighted voting k-nearest neighbors method. During the training process, we monitored performance using weighted KNN evaluation and tested the final performance with linear evaluation.

For the experiments, the baseline amount of data to be forgotten was 2,000 out of 10,000 training data samples, which corresponds to 20% of the data. We conducted additional comparative experiments by varying the number of forgotten data samples. The supervised learning model used a ResNet architecture, while the contrastive learning model employed MoCo. The number of epochs required for unlearning training was 10. We also conducted ablation experiments to demonstrate the importance of loss selection in our method.

**Evaluation Metrics:** Membership inference attacks primarily evaluate classifiers; therefore, our evaluation metrics include accuracy, precision, recall, and AUC.

1. Accuracy: Accuracy is the proportion of samples that the classification model correctly predicts relative to the total number of samples. It is calculated using the following formula: Accuracy is suitable for balanced classes; however, in imbalanced class situations, it may not accurately reflect model performance.
2. Precision: Precision is the proportion of true positive samples among all samples predicted as positive by the model. It is calculated using the following formula: Precision reflects the reliability of the model when predicting positive classes.
3. Recall: Recall is the proportion of true positive samples that the model correctly predicts as positive among all actual positive samples. It is calculated using the following formula: Recall reflects the extent to which the model covers the detection of positive classes.
4. AUC (Area Under Curve): AUC represents the area under the Receiver Operating Characteristic (ROC) curve. The ROC curve is drawn based on the true positive rate (TPR) and false positive rate (FPR) at different thresholds. AUC values range from 0 to 1, with a perfect classifier having an AUC of 1 and a random classifier having an AUC of approximately 0.5. AUC is a comprehensive performance metric that can reflect the model's classification ability in imbalanced class situations.

### 4.2 Experimental Results

We first use our machine unlearning method for the self-supervised comparison learning model, and then we use the method of that ENcoderMI paper to perform membership inference attacks on the model, and then record the change in the success rate of the membership attacks before and after performing machine unlearning, as shown in the following Tables 2 and 3.

**Table 2.** Contrast Machine unlearning performance before Unlearning.

| Dataset | Before Unlearning | | | |
|---|---|---|---|---|
| | model_acc | mia_acc | mia_rec | mia_pre |
| cifar10 | 70% | 87% | 87% | 88% |
| cifar100 | 32% | 92% | 92% | 92% |
| svhn | 76% | 86% | 87% | 86% |

**Table 3.** Contrast Machine unlearning performance after Unlearning.

| Dataset | After Unlearning | | | |
|---|---|---|---|---|
| | model_acc | mia_acc | mia_rec | mia_pre |
| cifar10 | 60% | 51% | 52% | 52% |
| cifar100 | 25% | 51% | 51% | 51% |
| svhn | 73% | 51% | 51% | 51% |

From the above table, we can see that our method is able to be member inference attack completely invalid, while it can keep the accuracy loss of the model not too high to some extent. To further demonstrate the feasibility of our method, we experimented with different models for moco, simclr and byol, and the experimental results are shown in the following Table 4.

**Table 4.** Performance of different models on CIFAR-10

| Model | ACC_bef | ACC_af | MIA_bef | MIA_af |
|---|---|---|---|---|
| MoCo | 70% | 60% | 90% | 50% |
| SimCLR | 66% | 60% | 70% | 50% |
| BYOL | 55% | 49% | 70% | 50% |

To investigate whether our method truly achieves unlearning or approximates the effect of unlearning, we will employ three approaches to study the model. The first approach is based on our observation that, although contrastive models do not require labels during the training process, the output probabilities obtained using their encoders to predict data exhibit high prediction confidence. This difference in prediction confidence is one of the core components in supervised membership inference attacks. Thus, it suggests that an overfitted self-supervised contrastive learning model can also be targeted by supervised membership inference attacks. Our implementation confirms this, with the inference success rate being similar to that of the EncoderMI method. However, our primary focus here is on prediction confidence.

The difference in prediction confidence between training and non-training data is mainly manifested in the model's prediction probability distribution for

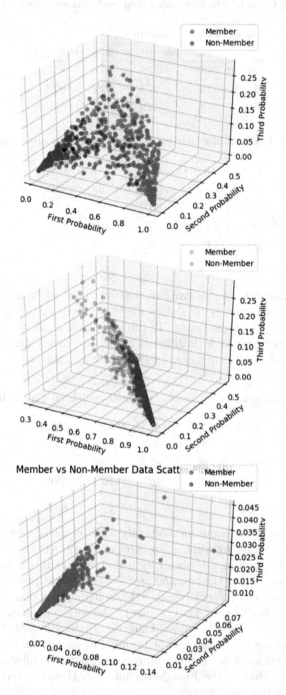

**Fig. 3.** The distribution of the predicted data probabilities before unlearning.

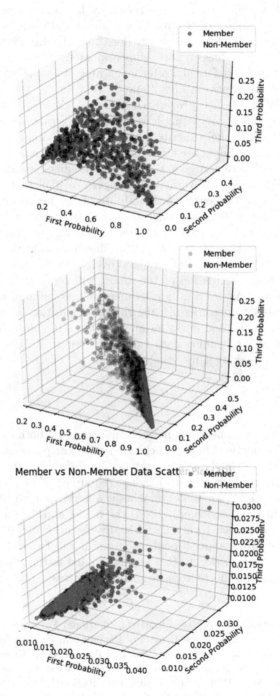

**Fig. 4.** The distribution of the predicted data probabilities after unlearning.

non-training data, which tends to be relatively flat and uniform. In contrast, the prediction probability distribution for training data exhibits an extremely skewed distribution. The following figure illustrates the distribution of the top-3 prediction confidence values in three-dimensional space for an overfitted contrastive learning model before and after unlearning, with respect to training and non-training data, as shown in Figs. 3 and 4.

There are various forms of overfitting, and as shown in the figure above, all three distributions of overfitting have close success rates of inference attacks on their members, but their distributions of top3 probability values for team-trained and non-trained data are quite different. The explanation we give here is that the model will have a large variation in its prediction ability or prediction confidence as the degree of overfitting changes. We believe that this may be due to a decrease in the generalization ability of the model and the fact that the internal parameters of the model are tuned to fit the training data more easily as the team training data are trained in depth. We found that when a smaller learning rate is used, the overfitting distribution of the model changes in the direction of the most lateral graph above. When we increase the learning rate, the overfitting distribution of the model will be as shown in the middle of the figure above. As we continue to increase the learning rate, the model overfitting distribution becomes like the rightmost position in the upper panel. Using our forgetting method works for all three types of unlearning, i.e., making the distribution of the training data vary as if it were the distribution of the non-training data, making it indistinguishable.

## 5   Conclusion

We propose a machine unlearning method that supports both contrastive learning models and supervised models, achieving excellent performance levels. Our approach effectively defends against membership inference attacks (MIAs) and protects user privacy. Moreover, it does not require complex preprocessing, nor does it rely on specific frameworks, making it a fairly generalizable method. To implement our method, one simply needs the model and the data to be forgotten, making the approach highly user-friendly. Additionally, our method does not demand extensive computational resources; it can be achieved with just a few training epochs. However, further evaluation and testing, such as examining the model's unlearning effects from various perspectives, remain areas for future research.

**Acknowledgments.** This work is supported by National Natural Science Foundation of China (No. 61802383), Research Project of Pazhou Lab for Excellent Young Scholars (No. PZL2021KF0024), Guangzhou Basic and Applied Basic Research Foundation (No. 202201010330, No. 202201020162), Guangdong Philosophy and Social Science Planning Project (No. GD19YYJ02), Guangdong Regional Joint Fund Project (No. 2022A1515110157), and Research on the Supporting Technologies of the Metaverse in Cultural Media (No. PT252022039).

# References

1. Arjovsky, M., Chintala, S., Bottou, L.: Wasserstein generative adversarial networks. In: International Conference on Machine Learning, pp. 214–223. PMLR (2017)
2. Bourtoule, L., et al.: Machine unlearning. In: 2021 IEEE Symposium on Security and Privacy (SP), pp. 141–159. IEEE (2021)
3. Cao, Y., Yang, M.: Legal regulation of big data killing:-from the perspective of "personal information protection law. J. Educ. Humanit. Soc. Sci. **7**, 233–241 (2023)
4. Chen, K., Huang, Y., Wang, Y., Zhang, X., Mi, B., Wang, Y.: Privacy preserving machine unlearning for smart cities. Ann. Telecommun. **79**(1), 61–72 (2023)
5. Chen, T., Kornblith, S., Norouzi, M., Hinton, G.: Simclr: a simple framework for contrastive learning of visual representations. In: Proceedings of the 37th International Conference on Machine Learning, pp. 1597–1607 (2020)
6. Mayfield, M.: Talk data to me: why michigan should adopt a comprehensive data protection statute. Wayne St. UJ Bus. L. **6**, 1 (2023)
7. Nguyen, T.T., Huynh, T.T., Nguyen, P.L., Liew, A.W.C., Yin, H., Nguyen, Q.V.H.: A survey of machine unlearning. arXiv preprint arXiv:2209.02299 (2022)
8. Politou, E., Alepis, E., Patsakis, C.: Forgetting personal data and revoking consent under the GDPR: challenges and proposed solutions. J. Cybersecur. **4**(1), tyy001 (2018)
9. Wu, G., Hashemi, M., Srinivasa, C.: Puma: performance unchanged model augmentation for training data removal. In: Proceedings of the AAAI Conference on Artificial Intelligence, vol. 36, pp. 8675–8682 (2022)
10. Yan, H., Li, X., Guo, Z., Li, H., Li, F., Lin, X.: Arcane: an efficient architecture for exact machine unlearning. In: Proceedings of the Thirty-First International Joint Conference on Artificial Intelligence, IJCAI-22, pp. 4006–4013 (2022)

# NoCrypto: A Web Mining Behavior Detection Method Based on RGB Images

Hui Wang[1]📙, Yu Zhang[1]📙, Xiaoming Pan[2](✉)📙, and Weiyi Huang[1]📙

[1] Guangdong Polytechnic Normal University, GuangZhou 510665,
GuangDong, China
bullzhangyu@gpnu.edu.cn
[2] Zhejiang Electronic Information Products Inspection and Research Institute (Key
Laboratory of Information Security of Zhejiang Province), HangZhou 310007,
ZheJiang, China
pxm@zdjy.org.cn

**Abstract.** In recent years, there has been a growing prevalence of mining web pages using the new web technology of WebAssembly (WASM), resulting in the unauthorized exploitation of user resources. However, existing detection methods have shown limited ability to counter obfuscation techniques and have exhibited low detection efficiency. To address these issues, this paper proposes a novel static detection method based on the visualization of WASM modules. The proposed method involves instantiating the binary files of the WASM mining operations within web pages. These binary files are then combined with the information of local entropy and global entropy, resulting in the visualization of RGB images. Compared to grayscale images, RGB images retain more of the original file information. After training and learning the image features using a convolutional neural network (CNN), the model achieves an impressive accuracy rate of 99.18% when tested on real-world web pages. This accuracy is approximately 2% higher than that of existing visualization-based detection methods. Moreover, the model exhibits a shorter execution time. The proposed NoCrypto method demonstrates quick execution speed and accurate detection.

**Keywords:** Web mining · WebAssembly (WASM) · RGB visualization detection · CNN model

## 1 Introduction

Since the introduction of WebAssembly (WASM) technology in March 2017 [1], it has gained attention due to its capabilities as a low-level bytecode language that enables faster transmission, parsing, and execution of programs. Unfortunately, hackers have also taken notice of these advantages. They have begun utilizing this new web technology to mine memory-constrained cryptocurrencies, such as Monero. This new form of mining reached its peak by the end of 2017.

J. Cai et al. (Eds.): SPNCE 2023, LNICST 525, pp. 224–236, 2025.
https://doi.org/10.1007/978-3-031-73699-5_16

According to a research paper [2], it was found that among the top one million websites ranked by Alexa, one out of every 600 sites used WebAssembly. Furthermore, one-third of these sites spent more than 75% of their time executing WebAssembly instead of JavaScript code. Mining websites accounted for 32% of the sites using WebAssembly. Consequently, this shift has prompted a transition in mining detectors from focusing on JavaScript to addressing WebAssembly.

In order to detect mining websites based on WebAssembly (WASM) technology and protect computer users' computational resources from unauthorized usage, researchers from both domestic and international backgrounds have conducted studies on web mining behaviors, yielding significant achievements [3]. Existing detection techniques can be mainly categorized into three types: rule-based detection, machine learning-based detection, and deep learning-based detection.

Rule-based detection techniques for WebAssembly-based mining websites involve extracting the WASM modules used for mining and converting them into WAT (WebAssembly Text) format. From the WAT format, the bytecode or opcode instructions are extracted and matched against semantic signatures based on the counts of these instructions. This approach aims to detect mining activities based on the semantics of WASM bytecode or opcode instructions. However, the effectiveness of this detection technique is limited when faced with new generation mining viruses that employ common obfuscation techniques such as code obfuscation, one-click encryption, throttling evasion, and URL obfuscation. These techniques make it challenging for the rule-based detection method to deobfuscate the mining scripts effectively. Additionally, the bytecode and opcode of new mining scripts may differ from the previously defined instructions, rendering this detection method ineffective against obfuscated mining scripts and new types of mining scripts.

Machine learning based detection technique by applying the principle that the WASM module will be called multiple times during the execution of the mining website, the number of Wasm modules in the stack function is used as a numerical feature to identify the mining behavior, and the detection is carried out by fusing multiple features through the method of machine learning, which requires a certain amount of running overhead due to the use of dynamic analysis.

In response to the above mentioned problems of poor anti-obfuscation ability, low recognition rate of new mining scripts, and dynamic analysis requiring some running overhead, deep learning methods are beginning to be used. Deep learning based detection techniques combine deep learning with visualization methods to convert the binary file form of the WASM module into an image, and then use the deep learning model to identify it, this method has a strong anti-obfuscation ability, has a high recognition rate of all kinds of mining scripts, and belongs to the static analysis, which doesn't require a great running overhead. However, the existing deep learning detection methods convert WASM into grayscale images through the B2M grayscaling algorithm, and the information enriched in the grayscale image and the clarity of the image contour are not as good as the RGB image, and the detection accuracy is still to be improved.

The RGB visualization method proposed in this paper generates images with clearer contours, images generated by different mining scripts are more similar, the degree of differentiation between them and non-mining scripts is greater, and the final detection effect is better than the grayscale method.

This paper's detection method offers several advantages compared to existing techniques:

- In terms of image visual analysis, the proposed method introduces a novel approach for visualizing binary files as RGB images. By combining local entropy and global entropy, it effectively retains a greater amount of local and global feature information. This technique enhances the representation of the binary files, allowing for more comprehensive analysis and detection of mining behaviors. The utilization of both local and global entropy ensures that important characteristics of the files are preserved in the resulting RGB images.
- This paper presents a method for visualizing mining-related WebAssembly (WASM) features to achieve mining web page detection. Compared to existing grayscale-based methods for WASM feature extraction, the proposed method provides clearer image textures. Furthermore, the visual distinction between benign and malicious images is more prominent in terms of image contours. As a result, the overall performance of the proposed method is superior, offering improved accuracy and reliability in distinguishing between mining and non-mining web pages.
- The proposed method is characterized by its simplicity, as it eliminates the requirement for operators to possess domain-specific knowledge in the field of mining websites. Once the model is trained, the method only requires the input of a website URL for detection. This greatly reduces the analysis complexity, while simultaneously improving the speed and efficiency of the analysis process. As a result, the method offers a user-friendly and time-saving approach for detecting mining web pages.

## 2   Related Work

This paper focuses on bytecode characterization of WASM files. In the rule set based mining web page detection technique, Konoth [4] et al. converted the WASM module used for mining by extracting it from a website into WAT text format, which contains assembly bytecode. They used a debugger to convert the WASM into linear assembly byte code, followed by semantic signature matching, and finally a machine learning classification algorithm to obtain a 93.78% detection rate. Wang [5] et al. analyzed to reveal the distribution of WASM instructions executed by the mining scripts, which were used at runtime to differentiate between mining and non-mining activities. The semantic signature matching of WASM bytecode instruction counts can detect whether WASM is mining or not with 98% accuracy. This technique performs semantic signature matching after manually creating a rule set by reading bytecode instructions from the WAT text format [6–9]. In machine learning based mining webpage detection techniques,

Outguard [10], MinerAlert [11], etc. by combining the presence of WASM module as one of the mining behavioral characteristics combined with performance analysis of the hybrid detection method, the use of Random Forest detection model ultimately obtains an accuracy rate of 99.59%.

Unlike the above detection methods for WASM assembly byte codes or instruction opcodes, the paper MINOS [12], which was made public in 2021, achieves the combination of benign WASM and malicious WASM visualization and deep learning detection by grayscaling the extracted WASM binaries into images with the help of the deep learning model CNN, which is the beginning of the combination of the field of mining webpage detection with deep learning model combination, finally the method achieved 98.97% detection rate, but its detection rate and the stability of the model still need to be improved.

The main shortcomings of current detection methods are:

- JS script-based detectors fail to detect WASM code;
- Existing WASM detectors are susceptible to obfuscation techniques;
- For the emergence of a new generation of mining scripts based on the WASM module, the existing WASM detectors are ineffective in detecting them.

In order to solve the above problems, based on the premise that the visual representations of different types of mining scripts are similar and differ greatly from those of benign scripts, this paper proposes a new visualization method for mining webpage detection based on the mining features of WASM binaries, i.e., the RGB visualization method that combines the local entropy and global entropy with the purpose of improving the recognition and detection rate of novel mining webpages.

## 3   NoCrypto

As shown in Fig. 1, the method consists of three parts: collection of WASM samples, sample RGB visualization, and training and detection of image classification models.

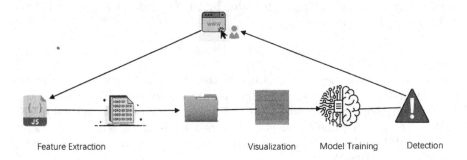

Feature Extraction                    Visualization    Model Training    Detection

**Fig. 1.** Design diagram of NoCrypto method flow

## 3.1    WASM Sample Collection

The sample collection method utilized in this paper draws inspiration from the approach described in [2]. A script written in Node.js is used to automatically collect WASM binary files when users browse the web. These files are then downloaded and stored in a specified folder. The method leverages Puppeteer, a Node.js library that allows communication with and manipulation/control of Google Chrome through an advanced API and DevTools protocol. The code wraps instances of JavaScript functions such as WebAssembly. InstantiateStreaming, and records the binary files of the modules to the Node.js backend.

## 3.2    WASM Sample RGB Visualization

A WASM module binary consists of a series of hexadecimal numbers. This vector of hexadecimal values can be modified and converted to an image. In such a conversion, the WASM binary is first converted to a vector of 8-bit unsigned integers (UINT8) and then reshaped into a one-dimensional array. This reshaped array is then divided by 255 in order to represent each integer as a pixel with a value ranging from 0 to 255 (0 is black and 255 is white). These pixel values together form the WASM module binary representation of the red channel of the RGB image; the one-dimensional array is transformed into a two-dimensional matrix, and 60 times the local entropy of each value is used as a representation of the green channel of the RGB image, with the local entropy calculated using the specific formula below:

$$H\_local = -60 * n/9 * log2(n/9) \tag{1}$$

where n is the frequency of each value in the sub-matrix, the formula represents multiplying the probability of each value in the sub-matrix (n/9) with its corresponding amount of information (-log2(n/9)), and then summing all the values within the sub-matrix to obtain the value of local entropy H_local.

To represent each numerical value of the global entropy as the blue channel in the RGB image, we multiply the value by 60. The calculation process of the global entropy is as follows:

$$L\_local = -60 * n/N * log2(n/N) \tag{2}$$

where n is the frequency of each value in the two-dimensional matrix and the total number of values in the two-dimensional matrix is N. The formula represents multiplying the probability of each value in the two-dimensional matrix (n/N) with its corresponding amount of information (-log2(n/N)), and then summing up all the values within the two-dimensional matrix to obtain the value of global entropy H_local.

The R, G, and B values mentioned above can be mapped to the three channels to form an RGB image. An example of the binary to image conversion for malicious and benign web pages is illustrated in Fig. 2. From Fig. 2, it can be observed that the binary files used for cryptocurrency mining exhibit striking visual similarity when converted to grayscale images. This similarity arises from their utilization of hashing algorithms to implement proof-of-work (PoW) schemes, resulting in similar syntactic and semantic features. On the other hand, the images representing malicious WASM binary files differ from those associated with benign web pages.

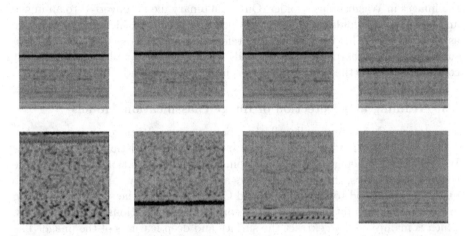

**Fig. 2.** The first line represents the RGB image obtained by visualizing the WASM binary file in a mining web page. The second line represents the RGB image obtained by visualizing the WASM binary file in a benign web page.

The visualization process is implemented using a recursive function written in python3, the implementation details are described in Algorithm 1. The module first reads all the WASM binaries under the folder, and in lines 2–3 the while loop checks every second if the destination folder of the extracted WASM binaries is empty. In lines 4–7, once the binary file is collected and added to the folder, it is opened and prepared for further preprocessing. In line 5, the folder Wasm_images is declared, which will store the converted images. Line 6 ensures that if a site loads more than one Wasm module, each downloaded module will be accessed in each iteration of the for loop and preprocessed. In lines 8–15, the binary file byte stream is converted into a two-dimensional matrix of relatively similar length and width g. In line 11, the file is converted into an array of unsigned integers, and in lines 13–14, the file is deleted from the directory after the array has been reshaped and the file has been closed so that, once the function is executed, it does not preprocess the same module repeatedly. In lines 16–20, the values of the three channels are obtained and sequentially output as an RGB image. In line 17, each value of the 2D matrix is used as the red channel value, in line 18, 60 times the local entropy value of each value of the 2D matrix is used as the green channel value, the sliding window is set to 3*3 size, in line 19, 60 times the global entropy value of each value of the 2D matrix is used as the blue channel value, in line 20, the RGB image object is created, and in line 21, the RGB image is Save the RGB image to the specified folder. In lines 22–26 reshape the image obtained above to a specified size of 100*100 and save it to a folder, in line 22 convert the data type of the variable image to an 8-bit unsigned integer type, in line 23 reshape the variable image to an image of size 100*100 by using the double interpolation algorithm, store all the obtained images of the same size h to the Wasm_images folder and lines 25–26 detect all the images in Wasm_images folder. Once the binary file is converted to an image and added to this folder, the detector() function is called which takes the image as an argument. This function will be referenced and discussed in the following subsections the preprocess function ends with a recursive call, ensuring that it continues to check the directory for new input every second (Table 1).

### 3.3    Training and Detection of Image Classification Models

The detector() function will call the above processed image as input to the CNN model. The model is pre-trained on a dataset consisting of 55 malicious WASMs and 424 benign WASMs after binary data visualization. A total of three convolutional layers, three pooling layers and their two fully connected layers are used in this method to form the trained CNN model and the structure is shown in Fig. 3. The convolutional layer is the core of the convolutional neural network, which is mainly used to extract the surface and deep features of the image. The number and size of convolution kernels of the first convolutional layer used in the present invention are 20,3*3, the second layer is 50,3*3, and the third layer is 100,3*3. The pooling layer is mainly used for feature selection and downsampling of the image. The pooling layer used in the present invention has a size of 2*2 and a step size of 2. The features are fed into the fully connected layer after feature extraction and feature selection through the convolutional layer and the pooling layer. The role of the fully connected layer is mainly to reduce the influence of the spatial location of the image on the features and to classify the samples. In this invention, two fully connected layers are used, 1*256,1*2 respectively, and finally softmax is used to output the classification of the image. In addition, in this method, the output of each layer is nonlinearly transformed by Relu function.

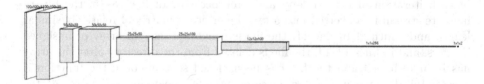

**Fig. 3.** CNN model architecture diagram

The trained model is used to detect random web pages in the real world. Access the web page url thus extracting the WASM binary file from the web page,

Table 1. Wasm module visualization methodology

| Algorithm 1: Wasm module visualization methodology |
| --- |
| 1    **def** preprocess(): |
| 2        **while** len(Wasm directory) == 0 do |
| 3            time.sleep(1) |
| 4        **if** len(Wasm directory)! = 0 then |
| 5            Wasm_images → [] |
| 6            **for** file in Wasm directory do |
| 7                f → open(file) |
| 8                ln → getSize(file) |
| 9                width → math.pow(ln, 0.5) |
| 10               rem → ln%width |
| 11               a → array(B) |
| 12               a.fromfile(f, ln  rem) |
| 13               f.close() |
| 14               os.remove(file) |
| 15               g → reshape(len(a)/width), width) |
| 16               rgb_image→np.zeros(len(a)/width, width, 3) |
| 17               rgb_image[:,:,0]→ g |
| 18               rgb_image[i, j, 1] → int(local_entropy * 60) |
| 19               rgb_image[:,:,2] → int(global_entropy * 60) |
| 20               image → Image.fromarray(rgb_image) |
| 21               image.save(output_path) |
| 22               image→ np.uint8(image) |
| 23               h → Image.fromarray(image).resize((100, 100)) |
| 24               h.save(Wasm_images) |
| 25           detector(Wasm images) |
| 26   **return** preprocess() |

convert the WASM file into an RGB image as per the visualization in the previous section and feed it into the trained model, if the mining web page detection model classifies the WASM binary file as malicious then the user is informed that the web page they are currently accessing is mining cryptocurrencies using their computational resources and they are advised to close the webpage, thereby terminating any mining processes running in the background. However, if the binary is classified as benign, the detection module performs no action, the user continues to browse the page, and the collection module continues to check the instantiation of the WASM module in the web page.

## 4    Performance Evaluation

To evaluate the effectiveness of the NoCrypto method, we conducted experiments on two different datasets, which include WASM binary files and web pages used for mining attack detection. The first dataset consists of WASM binary files used to train the NoCrypto model. The second dataset comprises real-world internet web pages that utilize WASM. Below, we provide a detailed description of each dataset, followed by an explanation of the metrics used in our evaluation:

Training dataset: the dataset used to train the WASM detector consists of 55 malicious and 424 benign WASM binaries obtained from a large number of studies and resources. A large portion of the dataset consists of binaries collected and used by studies in the literature: MinerRay [13], Minesweeper [4]. The remaining binaries were collected manually using resources such as the MadeWithWasm [14] website, the webassembly-examples-main [15] project, etc. A breakdown of the number of binaries collected from each resource, including the distribution of benign and malicious samples, can be found in Table 2 below. This is followed by a brief description of the other resources and how binaries were collected from each.

**Table 2.** Description of the training data set

|                              | Benign WASM | Malware WASM |
| ---------------------------- | ----------- | ------------ |
| MinerRay                     | 141         | 21           |
| Minesweeper                  | 4           | 34           |
| Made with Wasm               | 263         | 0            |
| Webassembly-examples-main    | 16          | 0            |

MadeWithWASM: Made With WebAssembly is a site that showcases applications, projects, and websites that use WebAssembly. By accessing the projects on the site, access is made using Chrome DevTools, which downloads the WASM module in WAT text format and converts it to a binary file using WABT. Note that when checked with Chrome DevTools, not all use cases and websites listed on MadeWithWASM instantiated the WASM module. At this point download all the WASM modules by accessing all the files for the project from the github site and add them to the dataset of benign WASM samples.

Webassembly-examples-main: This is a github project containing web files that use WASM.

Test dataset: this dataset consists of real websites, both benign and encrypted, which use WebAssembly technology. The source of this dataset is Tranco [16].

Tranco is a public top-level domain ranking dataset based on Alexa rankings for measuring and analyzing the most popular websites on the Internet. It provides a list of millions of domains, ranked by their number of visits and traffic. We extracted 123 wasm binaries from the top 100,000 ranked pages on the Tranco website. 119 of them are benign,4 are malicious.

In order to label the real dataset we have used certain criteria to label the real samples and the criteria used are as follows:

(1) The obtained wasm binary file is converted to WAT text format by using the WABT tool to check whether the hash function exists in the WAT file.
(2) Since the size of the WASM binary of the game/application is significantly larger than the WASM binary of the malicious application, the size of the extracted WASM binary was tagged by checking the size of the website.

Classification Accuracy Metrics: To evaluate the accuracy of NoCrypto, we selected a number of accuracy metrics. Using the training dataset, we evaluated the performance of NoCrypto by calculating its overall accuracy, learning curve (loss vs. number of calendar elements), and ROC curve (true positive rate vs. false positive rate). The NoCrypto framework is further evaluated by testing the field dataset using metrics such as accuracy, precision, recall and F1 score.

### 4.1 Performance of NoCrypto Detection Methods on Training Set

NoCrypto's performance on the training dataset is evaluated based on a number of metrics, including accuracy, optimization loss, true positive rate, and false positive rate. The dataset is divided into a training set and a test set using an 80/20 split. In Fig. 4(a), it can be seen that the model converges to 100% accuracy on the test set. The optimization learning curve in Fig. 4(b) shows that after about 30 epochs, both the training and testing losses drop to a stable point. This suggests that the model is neither over nor underfitting and therefore can be effectively generalized. Figure 4(c) shows the model performance of the detector. The F1 Score, Recall and Precision are all equal and their values are converging to 100%, which means that the model performs very well when combining Precision and Recall, effectively identifying positive examples and excluding negative ones with very few false predictions.

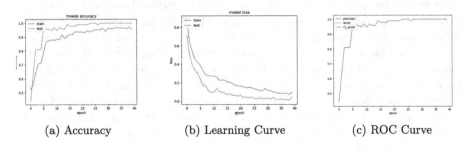

(a) Accuracy      (b) Learning Curve      (c) ROC Curve

**Fig. 4.** Model Training Performance Metrics

## 4.2 Performance of NoCrypto Detection Methods On a Test Set

The performance evaluation metrics on the test set are the same as the training set, by scanning the top 100,000 websites ranked by Tranco website, 389 WASM binaries are obtained, some web pages use the same WASM module, a total of 123 WASM binaries are obtained after de-emphasis, a total of 119 WASM binaries are generated by manually executing each web page tagging the 123 files, 119 benign web pages, 4 malicious web pages, and 10 tests finally obtain an average of 99.18% accuracy, 1 benign sample is incorrectly identified as malicious, and 4 malicious web pages are generated as WASM binary files and 4 WASM binary files generated by malicious web pages, 10 tests were performed finally obtaining an average accuracy of 99.18%, 1 benign sample was incorrectly identified as malicious and all 4 malicious web pages were correctly identified. Table 3 shows other calculated accuracy metrics that illustrate the performance of the NoCrypto system for this dataset.

**Table 3.** Performance of the NoCrypto system on the test set

| Evaluation indicators | Accuracy | Precision | Recall | F1 Score |
|---|---|---|---|---|
| NoCrypto | 99.18% | 99.18% | 99.18% | 99.18% |
| MINOS | 96.88% | 96.88% | 96.88% | 96.88% |

In order to verify the classification performance of the method in this paper, we compare it with the latest visualization-based mining webpage detection method that also uses the above dataset. The accuracy of the above dataset tested by the grayscaling method mentioned in this MINOS [12] paper reaches only 96.88%, which also shows that the visualization method in our detection method is more effective and the detection model is more robust.

## 4.3 Performance of the NoCrypto Assay in Confounded Samples

To evaluate the robustness of NoCrypto against adversarial evasion, we collected WASM mining obfuscation samples from publicly available papers that employ function name obfuscation, which obfuscates a varying number of function names in source and header files. Figure 5 shows a grayscale image representation of the mining samples. As shown in the figure, the resultant binaries of mining have very similar grayscale image representations, despite blurring different numbers of function names in the mining code. To evaluate the robustness of NoCrypto to the blurred mining samples shown in Fig. 5, we sent the samples to NoCrypto and observed that NoCrypto was able to detect all blurred binaries regardless of the level or degree of blurring.

**Fig. 5.** RGB image after visualization of WASM mining samples with increasing degree of confusion

## 5   Conclusions

Due to the increasing prevalence of mining web pages utilizing new WebAssembly (WASM) technology, traditional static detection methods are prone to interference from obfuscation techniques, while dynamic detection techniques require significant computational resources. In this paper, we propose a novel static detection method that visualizes WASM binary files as RGB images and utilizes a CNN network model for detection and recognition. This method achieves excellent results, demonstrating a certain degree of resistance to obfuscation techniques, fast execution speed, and minimal resource consumption during operation. In the future, we plan to incorporate a detection method for mining web pages based on JavaScript (JS) scripts. Ultimately, we aim to develop a browser extension for Google Chrome that detects mining websites. This extension will provide users with a comprehensive solution to identify and protect against the unauthorized utilization of their computing resources for mining activities. The extension will be designed for widespread adoption and usage.

**Acknowledgment.** This work is supported by the National Natural Science Foundation of China under Grant No. 61862022, 62172182; the Natural Science Foundation of Guangdong under Grant No. 2023A1515011084; the Key Scientific Research Platforms and Projects of Guangdong under Grant No. 2022ZDZX1022; the Talent fund of Guangdong Polytechnic Normal University under Grant No. 99166990223; the Doctoral Program Establishment and Construction of Scientific Research Capacity Improvement Project of Guangdong Polytechnic Normal University under Grant No. 22GPNUZDJS27; the fund of Key Laboratory of Information Security of Zhejiang Province under Grant No. KF202306.

## References

1. Lehmann, D., Pradel, M.: Wasabi: a framework for dynamically analyzing webassembly. In: Proceedings of the Twenty-Fourth International Conference on Architectural Support for Programming Languages and Operating Systems, pp. 1045–1058. Association for Computing Machinery, NY, United States (2019)
2. Musch, M., Wressnegger, C., Johns, M., Rieck, K.: New kid on the web: a study on the prevalence of WebAssembly in the wild. In: Perdisci, R., Maurice, C., Giacinto, G., Almgren, M. (eds.) DIMVA 2019. LNCS, vol. 11543, pp. 23–42. Springer, Cham (2019). https://doi.org/10.1007/978-3-030-22038-9_2

3. Tekiner, E., Acar, A., Uluagac, A.S., Kirda, E., Selcuk, A.A.: SoK: cryptojacking malware. In: 2021 IEEE European Symposium on Security and Privacy, pp. 120–139. IEEE, Piscataway, NJ (2021)

4. Konoth, R.K., et al.: Minesweeper: an in-depth look into drive-by cryptocurrency mining and its defense. In: Proceedings of the 2018 ACM SIGSAC Conference on Computer and Communications Security, pp. 1714–1730. Association for Computing Machinery, NY, United States (2018)

5. Wang, W., Ferrell, B., Xu, X., Hamlen, K.W., Hao, S.: SEISMIC: secure in-lined script monitors for interrupting cryptojacks. In: Lopez, J., Zhou, J., Soriano, M. (eds.) ESORICS 2018. LNCS, vol. 11099, pp. 122–142. Springer, Cham (2018). https://doi.org/10.1007/978-3-319-98989-1_7

6. Bian, W., Meng, W., Zhang, M.: Minethrottle: defending against wasm in-browser cryptojacking. In: Proceedings of the Web Conference 2020, pp. 3112–3118. Association for Computing Machinery, NY, United States (2020)

7. Yu, G., Yang, G., Li, T., Han, X., Guan, S., Zhang, J., Gu, G.: MinerGate: a novel generic and accurate defense solution against web based cryptocurrency mining attacks. In: Lu, W., et al. (eds.) CNCERT 2020. CCIS, vol. 1299, pp. 50–70. Springer, Singapore (2020). https://doi.org/10.1007/978-981-33-4922-3_5

8. Bian, W., Meng, W., Wang, Y.: Poster: detecting webassembly-based cryptocurrency mining. In: Proceedings of the 2019 ACM SIGSAC Conference on Computer and Communications Security, pp. 2685–2687. Association for Computing Machinery, NY, United States (2019)

9. Rüth, J., Zimmermann, T., Wolsing, K., Hohlfeld, O.: Digging into browser-based crypto mining. In: Proceedings of the Internet Measurement Conference 2018, pp. 70–76. Association for Computing Machinery, NY, United States (2018)

10. Kharraz, A., et al.: Outguard: detecting in-browser covert cryptocurrency mining in the wild. In: The World Wide Web Conference, pp. 840–852. Association for Computing Machinery, NY, United States (2019)

11. Tommasi, F., Catalano, C., Corvaglia, U., Taurino, I.: MinerAlert: an hybrid approach for web mining detection. J. Comput. Virol. Hacking Tech. 18(4), 333–346 (2022)

12. Naseem, F.N., Aris, A., Babun, L., Tekiner, E., Uluagac, A.S.: MINOS: a lightweight real-time cryptojacking detection system. In: NDSS. At: Virtual (2021). https://doi.org/10.14722/ndss.2021.24444

13. Romano, A., Zheng, Y., Wang, W.: Minerray: semantics-aware analysis for ever-evolving cryptojacking detection. In: Proceedings of the 35th IEEE/ACM International Conference on Automated Software Engineering, pp. 1129–1140. Association for Computing Machinery, NY, United States (2020)

14. Made With Webassembly. https://madewithwebassembly.com/. Accessed 21 Mar 2023

15. Webassembly-examples-main. https://github.com/mdn/webassembly-examples/. Accessed 01 Apr 2023

16. Pochat, V.L., Van Goethem, T., Tajalizadehkhoob, S., Korczyński, M., Joosen, W.: Tranco: a research-oriented top sites ranking hardened against manipulation. In: arXiv preprint arXiv:1806.01156 (2018)

# Security and Privacy Steganography and Forensics

# Image Copy-Move Forgery Detection in the Social Media Based on a Prior Density Clustering and the Point Density

Cong Lin[1,3]($\boxtimes$) (iD), Hai Yang[2], Ke Huang[2], Yufeng Wu[1], Yamin Wen[1,3], and Yuqiao Deng[1]

[1] Applied Laboratory of Dig Data and Education Statistics, School of Statistics and Mathematics, Guangdong University of Finance and Economics, Guangzhou 510320, China
`lincong0310@gmail.com`
[2] School of Information, Guangdong University of Finance and Economics, Guangzhou 510320, China
[3] Guangdong Provincial Key Laboratory of Information Security Technology, Sun Yat-sen University, Guangzhou 51006, China

**Abstract.** Copy-move forgery is one common image manipulation technique. Many images are compressed by the social media, but most of the existing copy-move forgery detection schemes are proposed to deal with the uncompressed version of images. To handle this problem, in this paper, a copy-move forgery detection scheme for social media is proposed based on the point density and a prior density clustering. Firstly, the concept of "point density" is proposed, and it is combined with feature extraction to improve the extraction effect. Secondly, the hierarchical matching is adopted, and the keypoints are grouped according to the pixel value. Thirdly, a prior-based density clustering is proposed, called prior-DBSCAN. In this scheme, the matching pairs are divided into start points and end points for clustering, respectively, and the prior region of each cluster is obtained. Then, the clustering with the new cluster radius is performed. Finally, an iterative localization technique is used to obtain the final localization results. Considering the compression of images during their transmission through the social media, the proposed scheme is made more suitable for real-world scenarios. The experimental results demonstrate that the proposed scheme based on a prior density clustering and the point density, which is better and more robust than the state-of-the-art schemes on publicly available datasets.

Supported by Characteristic Innovation Project of Regular Institutions of Higher Learning of Guangdong Province (Natural Science) (2022KTSCX041); Basic and Applied Basic Research Project of Guangzhou Science and Technology Program (202102080316); Opening Project of Guangdong Province Key Laboratory of Information Security Technology (No. 2020B1212060078); Science and Technology Program of Guangzhou Haizhu District (海科工商信计2022-45).

**Keywords:** Multimedia forensics · Image forensics · Copy-move forgery · Density clustering · Point density

# 1 Introduction

With the increasing popularity of chat tools and image editing software, people can freely publish modified images on the Internet through simple operations and extremely low costs, which has caused serious social integrity problems. Therefore, it is necessary to study digital image forgery detection. The main forgery schemes are splicing, inpainting and copy-move. Image copy-move forgery refers to one or several parts of an image are copied and pasted into another region of the same image. At present, many excellent CMFD schemes have been proposed. Most of them can be divided into three categories: block-based schemes, keypoint-based schemes and deep learning-based schemes.

The main idea of block-based schemes is to divide the image into several overlapping rectangular blocks or circular blocks, and features are extracted from each block for matching. The main difference among the block-based schemes is the block features. Fridrich et al. [10] proposed to use Discrete Cosine Transform (DCT) as the block feature, the blur moment invariants were proposed by Mahdian et al. [19], Muhammad et al. [21] chose to use Discrete Wavelet Transform (DWT) as the features, Ryu et al. [26,27] proposed to use the Zernike moment feature, Li et al. [15] used Polar Cosine Transform (PCT) as the block feature, Qin et al. [25] introduced the features of radial harmonic Fourier moments, Lai et al. [13] introduced the features of Exponential-Fourier moments, and Emam et al. [9] proposed to use Polar Complex Exponential Transform (PCET) as the block features, Meena et al. [20] proposed the scheme of using Tetrolet transform. Wang et al. [34] used a scheme combining PCET with Singular Value Decomposition (SVD). The above block-based schemes have shown certain robustness under various attack schemes. However, the image is divided into many pixel blocks, it brings high computational complexity. In order to solve this problem, a new forgery detection scheme based on improved PatchMatch was proposed by Cozzolino et al. [8], and the efficiency of the algorithm was greatly improved. In summary, the block-based schemes robustness is poor for large-scale geometric transformations, such as rotation and scaling. Based on this, the keypoint-based schemes were proposed and became another research hotspot.

The basic steps of the keypoint-based schemes include feature extraction, matching, clustering and post-processing. For feature extraction, the Scale-Invariant Feature Transform (SIFT) algorithm is widely used as features in [2,14,24,31]. To obtain sufficient and uniform SIFT keypoints, Li et al. [14] introduced to reduce the contrast threshold and resize the input image, Gan et al. [11] designed an improved SIFT structure with inherent scale invariance and removed the contrast threshold, and Wang et al. [31] proposed strategies to normalize images and remove contrast thresholding. In addition, SURF [28,29], KAZE [36], and LIOP [5,16,18] are also adopted as CMFD features. For feature matching, Pan et al. [24] introduced a 2-Nearest Neighbor (2NN) matching

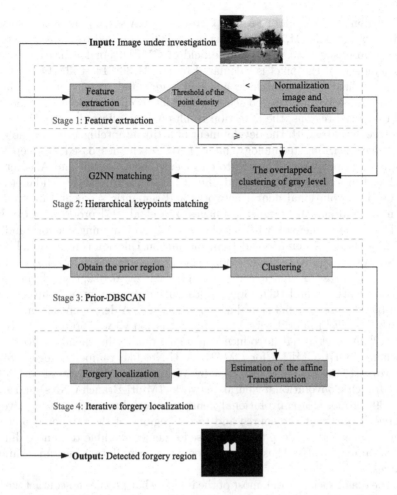

**Fig. 1.** Framework of the proposed copy-move forgery detection scheme.

method. However, this method cannot handle the case of multiple matching points. Therefore, Amerini et al. [2] proposed the generalized 2-nearest neighbor (G2NN) method. Subsequently, the reverse G2NN (RG2NN) method was proposed by Wang et al. [32]. The double matching approach was used in [18,31]. Li et al. [14] designed a hierarchical matching strategy, and magnitude hierarchical matching was adopted by Niu et al. [23] for feature matching. A Feature Label Matching (FLM) method was proposed by Gan et al. [11]. To detect possible duplicate regions, keypoint clustering is adopted by many keypoint-based schemes. The agglomerative hierarchical clustering was used in [2]. Afterwards, Amerini et al. [3] adopted the JLinkage algorithm [30] and Lyu et al. [18] proposed to use DBSCAN to classify matching points. Yang et al. [37] proposed a grid-based and cluster-based two-stage filtering scheme. For post-processing, to estimate the geometric transformation between the original region and the forged region, the RANdom SAmple Consensus (RANSAC) algorithm is used in the work of [2,14,18,24,36,38]. Wang et al. [33] proposed to apply Progressive sample Consensus (PROSAC) in the field of CMFD. For localization, correlation coefficient of the pixel is calculated by [18,24,36]. Li et al. [14] performed forgery localization by matching adjacent segmented regions of keypoints. In summary, most keypoint-based schemes extract too few keypoints in smooth or small tampered regions, the detection results will be affected.

In recent years, with the development of artificial intelligence and the maturity of deep learning technology, many CMFD schemes based on deep learning have been proposed. The end-to-end Dense-InceptionNet and AR-Net were introduced by Zhong et al. [40] and Zhu et al. [41], respectively. Jindal et al. [1] used deep convolutional neural networks and semantic segmentation to detect copy-move and splicing tampered images. Liu et al. [17] proposed a two-stage CMFD scheme framework with backbone self deep matching network and Proposal SuperGlue. An end-to-end High-Resolution Dilation convolutional Attention Network (HRDA-Net) detection scheme was proposed by Zhu et al. [42] to handle the case of multiple tampering. Nazir et al. [22] used DenseNet-41 to extract features, and then forgery localization was performed through mask region-based convolutional neural network (RCNN). A deep convolutional neural network (VI-NET) hybrid with VGG and inception v3 was proposed by Kumar et al. [12]. Aria et al. [4] introduced an image quality-independent deep learning scheme (QDL-CMFD) for CMFD. A U-Net-like tampered region related framework (UCM-Net) was proposed by Weng et al. [35]. Barni et al. [6] used Multi-Branch Convolutional Neural Networks (Multi-Branch CNNs) and Zhang et al. [39] proposed a convolutional neural network-based generative adversarial network to detect the source and target regions of the tampered image. In summary, most of the deep learning-based schemes are able to handle different types of tampering. But those schemes require a lot of data, time and computing resources.

In the era of social media, most of the images that people can contact with are compressed by the social media. The original version of the image is often dealt with by the previous schemes. Therefore, the detection of images compressed by social media has more theoretical value and practical significance. In this paper, a novel copy-move forgery detection scheme for social media is proposed. The main contributions of this paper are as follows:

1) The concept of "point density" is proposed. Combining "point density" with feature extraction, the effect of feature extraction is improved;
2) The concept of "prior" is proposed. The approximate region of the tampering target is obtained by using "prior", resulting in an enhancement of keypoints clustering and the forgery localization effectiveness;
3) A novel density clustering algorithm is proposed, which is called prior-DBSCAN. The prior region with arbitrary shape is fitted by a circle of equal area, thus, the clustering effect is enhanced, the grouping of keypoints and the filtering of false matches are improved effectively.

The remainder of this paper is organized as follows. Section 2 describes the proposed scheme in detail; Sect. 3 shows the experimental results of copy-move forgery detection; Finally, a brief summary is made in Sect. 4.

(a)                                          (b)

**Fig. 2.** Keypoints detection: (a) The SIFT under common setting.(b) The SIFT by combining the point density.

## 2 Proposed Scheme

This section describes the proposed copy-move forgery detection scheme in detail. Figure 1 shows the framework of the proposed scheme. First, the SIFT feature are extracted from the input image, and the better effect is obtained by combining the point density with feature extraction. Then, the extracted keypoints are grouped by the gray values, and the keypoints in different groups are matched. Subsequently, a prior-DBSCAN method is proposed. The prior region of each cluster is obtained by clustering the matching pairs, and then clustering combined with prior region is performed. The possible tampered regions are obtained and mismatched pairs are removed. Finally, the iterative forgery localization method is used to detect the forgery region from the input image.

### 2.1 Feature Extraction

Since the SIFT feature is invariant to scaling, rotation and translation, and has good robustness to illumination changes and affine transformations. Similar to many existing copy-move forgery detection schemes, the SIFT is adopted for detecting keypoints with corresponding interest regions.

The number of keypoints is closely related to the detection performance. The sufficiency of the number of keypoints should not only be determined by their quantity, but also combined with the image size for comprehensive evaluated. Therefore, in this paper, the concept of "point density" is introduced to measure whether the number of extracted keypoints is sufficient or not. The definition of "point density" $\rho$ is as follows:

$$\rho = \frac{n}{N_I \times M_I} \tag{1}$$

where $n$ means the number of the SIFT keypoints; $N_I \times M_I$ is the resolution for the input image $I$. Image point density denotes the number of keypoints per unit area. By using the point density, the interest region in the image can be selected, the real region and the forged region can be distinguished. For the keypoint-based on CMFD scheme, not only the total number of keypoints is sufficient, but also enough keypoints can be contained in the critical area. However, with the development of social media, a large number of images will be compressed and transmitted through social network channels. After the image is compressed by social media, the resolution is reduced and the number of keypoints extracted is decreased. In order to balance the efficiency and performance of the proposed scheme, if Eq. (2) is satisfied, the image resolution will be increased:

$$(n \leqslant N_p) \cup (\rho \leqslant T_\rho) \tag{2}$$

where $N_p = 10000$ and $T_\rho = 0.005$ in our implementation. For images that do not satisfy Eq. (2), it means that the number of keypoints is sufficient.

Combining point density with feature extraction, $n$ keypoints $\{k_1, k_2, \ldots, k_n\}$ are generated for the given image $I$, where $k = (x, y, \sigma, \theta)$, $x$, $y$ are the coordinates of the keypoint, $\sigma$, $\theta$ are the scale and direction of the keypoint, respectively. The descriptor corresponding to each keypoint is $\{f_1, f_2, \ldots, f_n\}$, where $f$ is a 128-dimensional vector. Two examples of the keypoint detection using SIFT features extracted under common settings and combined point density are shown in Fig. 2. As can be seen that, after combining the point density, the keypoints are more uniformly and densely distributed in the image, the number is increased, so that the copy-move regions can be covered by extracted keypoints.

## 2.2   Keypoint Hierarchical Matching

In the copy-move forgery detection scenario, the gray value between the corresponding positions of the tampered object will be the same or similar. Based on this, in this paper, the keypoints are grouped by their gray values [14], and matched over each group. After the keypoints are grouped, the number of keypoints in each group is reduced, which speeds up the matching process of keypoints.

Suppose that $n$ keypoints are extracted, for each keypoint $k_i$, the Euclidean distance between it and the remaining $(n-1)$ keypoints are calculated. Denote vector $D = \{d_1, d_2, \ldots, d_{n-1}\}$ as the Euclidean distances in an increasing order. Then the keypoint $k_i$ is matched if and only if:

$$d_1/d_2 < T_d \tag{3}$$

where the threshold $T_d$ is fixed to 0.6. If Eq. (3) is satisfied, the keypoint corresponding to the minimum Euclidean distance $d_1$ is considered as the matching point of $k_i$. This is the traditional 2NN matching method. Since copy-move forgery may happen that the same region is cloned repeatedly, a keypoint can be matched to multiple keypoints. Therefore, in this paper, the G2NN matching method proposed by Amerini et al. [2] is adopted. Multiple matching points of the keypoint $k_i$ can be found only if:

$$d_j/d_{j+1} < T_d, j \in (2, \ldots, n-2) \tag{4}$$

is satisfied. Increase the value of $j$ until the Eq. (4) is not satisfied, then the keypoints corresponding to $\{d_1, d_2, \ldots, d_{j-1}\}$ are the matching points of $k_i$.

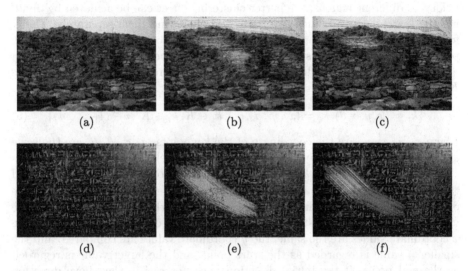

(a)          (b)          (c)

(d)          (e)          (f)

**Fig. 3.** The results after matching and clustering. Column 1: The input images. Column 2: The results after feature matching. Column 3: The results after clustering.

The iterative operation is performed on all keypoints, and a set of each keypoint and its corresponding matching points is obtained. The second column of Fig. 3 shows that the matching of the two images. The results show that there are some keypoints of mismatching outside the region with high density of matching pairs. If the matching pairs obtained in this step is directly used for forgery localization, the localization accuracy will be affected. Therefore, the following clustering step will be used to reduce false matching, and improve localization efficiency and localization accuracy.

## 2.3   Prior-DBSCAN

After keypoints matching, the density of matching keypoints in the tampered regions is often significantly greater than other mismatched regions. Therefore, to identify possible tampered regions, density clustering is performed after matching. Density-Based Spatial Clustering of Applications with Noise (DBSCAN) is a representative density clustering algorithm. It has the advantages of being insensitive to noisy data and can cluster dense datasets of any shape. However, the traditional DBSCAN has the disadvantages that it is difficult to distinguish the regions that are close to each other and sensitive to parameters.

To overcome the shortcomings of the DBSCAN algorithm. In this section, a new density clustering algorithm called Prior-DBSCAN is proposed. First, the prior region is obtained by each cluster after an adaptive radius clustering; Second, the prior region is fitted and the clustering is executed again.

**Obtain the Prior Region.** Considering that the matching keypoints should belong to different regions, the better clustering effect can be achieved by dividing the matching points into two parts and clustering them separately. Therefore, a unified direction for the matching pairs is obtained, and the matching pairs are divided into the start points and the end points to cluster separately. Suppose $m$ pairs of matching keypoints $(K, K')$ are detected, the keypoints $K = \{k_1, k_2, \ldots, k_m\}$, $K' = \{k'_1, k'_2, \ldots, k'_m\}$ and

$$\{k_i = (x, y, \sigma, \theta), k'_i = (x', y', \sigma', \theta'), k_i \in K, k'_i \in K', i \in (1, \ldots, m)\} \quad (5)$$

where $x_i, y_i, x'_i, y'_i$ are the coordinate of the keypoints, $\sigma_i, \sigma'_i, \theta_i, \theta'_i$ are the scale and direction information of the keypoints, respectively. In this paper, the direction of matched pair $< k_i, k'_i >$ is specified from $k_i$ to $k'_i$, the start point $k_i$ and the end point $k'_i$ of the matching keypoints are determined by the coordinate of the keypoint. In a matching pair, the keypoint with the smaller $x$ coordinate value is considered as the start point, and the larger one is the end point. If the $x$ coordinate values are the same, the $y$ coordinate values are compared, and the smaller $y$ value is regarded as the start point, and the larger value is regarded as the end point. If the initial direction does not satisfy the above direction conditions, the exchange is performed:

$$\{swap(k_i, k'_i) | (x_i > x'_i) \cup (x_i = x'_i, y_i > y'_i), k_i \in K, k'_i \in K'\} \quad (6)$$

where the $swap(k_i, k'_i)$ means to exchange keypoint $k_i$ and $k'_i$. Finally, the direction of each matching pair is adjusted.

The results of density clustering are affected by the clustering radius. If a fixed radius is used for all images, it is not satisfactory for clustering effects of some image. Therefore, an adaptive clustering radius is selected for each image, which reduces the objective preferences, and improves the accuracy and robustness of the DBSCAN results.

The adaptive clustering radius is determined by the mean of the Euclidean distance between the matching points:

$$R = \alpha \cdot aver(\sum_{i=1}^{m} \sqrt{(x_i - x'_i)^2 + (y_i - y'_i)^2}) \quad (7)$$

where $m$ is the number of the matching keypoints, $x_i, x'_i, y_i, y'_i$ are the coordinates of the two matching keypoints, $aver(\cdot)$ refers to mean distance between matching points, $\alpha = 1/10$ in our implementation. After the adaptive clustering radius is obtained, the clustering is performed on the start point set $Z$ and the end point set $Z'$, and the clusters with more than 4 points are selected:

$$C = DBSCAN(Z, R)$$
$$and \quad C' = DBSCAN(Z', R) \tag{8}$$

where $C$ is clustering result of the start point set $Z$, denoted as $C = (c_1, \ldots, c_p)$, $C'$ is clustering result of the end point set $Z'$, denoted as $C' = (c'_1, \ldots, c'_q)$. After clustering, the number of clusters at both ends may be different. It is necessary to find the matching cluster according to the number of matching keypoints in the two clusters. If the number of matching keypoints between the two clusters is more than 4 pairs, then the two clusters are considered to be matched clusters. In order to intuitively identify the matching clusters, in the following sections, the matching results of each cluster are uniformly represented by $C = (c_1, \ldots, c_s)$, $C' = (c'_1, \ldots, c'_s)$, and there are $s$ matching clusters in total.

Figure 3 shows the effect after clustering. The images in the second column contains many irregular matching pairs. The red points represent the start points, and the blue points represent the end points. The direction of the matching pairs is red to blue. After clustering, the effect of filtering the wrong matching pairs can be achieved. The results are shown in the third column. The connecting lines of different colors represent different matching clusters after clustering.

After the adaptively selected clustering radius is used for clustering, and $s$ pairs of matching clusters are obtained. The prior region of each cluster can be obtained according to the matching keypoints in each cluster. Suppose $k_0 = (x_0, y_0, \sigma_0, \theta_0)$ is a keypoint in cluster $c_1$, then the region $s_0$ composed of the keypoint:

$$s_0 = \{(x, y) | \sqrt{(x - x_0)^2 + (y - y_0)^2} \leqslant \beta\sigma_0, (x, y) \in S\} \tag{9}$$

where $s_0$ is a circular region centered at $(x_0, y_0)$, $S$ is the set of all pixels of the whole image, $(x, y)$ is the coordinates of the pixels in $S$, $(x_0, y_0)$ are the coordinates of the $k_0$; $\sigma_0, \theta_0$ are the scale and direction of $k_0$ respectively, $\beta = 14$ in our implementation. The prior region of cluster $c_1$ is obtained by superimposing the circular region corresponding to each keypoint in $c_1$. According to the Eq. (9), each cluster in $C$, $C'$ is selected for the same calculation. The prior region corresponding to each cluster are obtained.

**Clustering.** After the previous step, $s$ pairs of matching clusters and their corresponding prior regions have been obtained. Considering that there may be multiple pairs tampered regions in a forgery image, and the distribution of keypoints of tampered regions in an image may also be different. To optimize the matching pairs, in this section, a circle is used to fit the prior region to obtain the new cluster radius, and the clustering is performed again according to the new radius to obtain a more accurate tampering region.

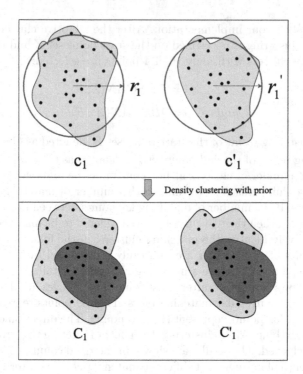

**Fig. 4.** The Prior-DBSCAN procedure. The yellow region indicates the prior region after clustering. The red circle is the fitting circle corresponding to the yellow region. The blue region represents the region after the prior-DBSCAN. (Color figure online)

Firstly, for each cluster, a circle is adopted to fitting with the prior region, denote $Ac$ as the area of the circle, $Ap$ as the area of the prior region, where $Ac = Ap$. The circle radius $r$ can be represented as:

$$r = \sqrt{Ac/\pi} \tag{10}$$

Then, the new cluster radius is:

$$R' = \gamma r \tag{11}$$

where $\gamma = 1/3$ in our implementation.

As shown in Fig. 4, the clusters $c_1, c_1'$ are a pair of matching clusters, and the keypoints in them are one-to-one matching. First, the keypoints in clusters $c_1, c_1'$ are used to obtain the respective prior regions (yellow regions), and according to Eq. (10), the circles (red circles) can be obtained respectively. Then, in the cluster $c_1, c_1'$, a central keypoint (the center point of all keypoints contained in the cluster $c_1, c_1'$) is selected as the start point. According to the circle radius $r_1$ and $r_1'$, the cluster radius $R_1$ and $R_1'$ can be obtained by Eq. (11). The density clustering is performed, and the new clusters $C_1, C_1'$ can be obtained (points within the blue region).

### 2.4   Iterative Forgery Localization

In this section, an iterative localization method is used to locate the forgery image.

Step 1): Estimation of affine matrix;

Step 2): Correlation coefficients are used for forgery localization.

**Table 1.** Precision, Recall, and $F_1$ Scores (%) for Translation on FAU Dataset.

| Methods | Precision | Recall | $F_1$ |
|---|---|---|---|
| Cozzolino [8] | **58.22** | 51.73 | 52.91 |
| Li [14] | 48.59 | 32.34 | 37.22 |
| Lyu [18] | 13.78 | 2.75 | 4.07 |
| Proposed | 55.72 | **63.44** | **55.56** |

**Table 2.** Precision, Recall, and $F_1$ Scores (%) for Translation on MICC-F600 Dataset.

| Methods | Precision | Recall | $F_1$ |
|---|---|---|---|
| Cozzolino [8] | **60.25** | 53.34 | 54.84 |
| Li [14] | 53.52 | 35.91 | 41.19 |
| Lyu [18] | 16.86 | 3.64 | 5.29 |
| Proposed | 57.59 | **64.47** | **56.63** |

**Estimation of Affine Transform.** The affine matrix $H$ is defined as follows:

$$\begin{pmatrix} x' \\ y' \\ 1 \end{pmatrix} = H \begin{pmatrix} x \\ y \\ 1 \end{pmatrix}, H = \begin{pmatrix} t_{11} & t_{12} & t_x \\ t_{21} & t_{22} & t_y \\ 0 & 0 & 1 \end{pmatrix} \tag{12}$$

where $(x, y)$, $(x', y')$ is the coordinates of keypoints and points after affine transformation, $t_{11}, t_{12}, t_{21}, t_{22}$ is the rotation and scaling parameter, $t_x, t_y$ is the translation parameter.

To obtain a unique solution to the transform parameters, at least 3 matched pairs are required to calculate the affine matrix $H$. However, the obtained results are inaccurate due to the mismatched keypoints. To obtain a more accurate affine matrix, we employ the RANSAC algorithm to select inliers and remove outliers:

1) Randomly select more than 3 matching pairs that are not collinear from a pair of matching clusters, and an affine matrix is calculated;

2) Select a matching pair $(k, k')$ in the matching cluster successively. If the following conditions are satisfied:

$$\|Hk - k'\|_2^2 \leqslant T_1 \tag{13}$$

where $T_1 = 9$, the matching pair is regarded as the inlier corresponding to the affine matrix, otherwise it is regarded as the outlier. Then the number of inliers corresponding to the affine matrix is recorded;

3) Steps 1) and 2) are repeated $Q$ times ($Q = 50$ in our implementation), and the affine matrix corresponding to the largest number of inliers is selected as the optimal affine matrix;

4) If there are multiple affine matrices obtained in step 3). Then, according to the Eq. (14), an affine matrix is selected as the optimal affine matrix:

$$H = \arg \min_H \sum_{i=1}^{n} \|k'_i - Hk_i\|_2^2 \tag{14}$$

where $n$ is the number of inliers, $(k_i, k'_i)$ is the inlier of the affine matrix.

**Forgery Localization.** It is assumed that there is a pair of duplicated regions $(S_1, S_2)$, and the affine transformation matrix between the two regions is obtained, which satisfies the following:

$$S_1 \xrightarrow{H} S_2 \tag{15}$$

where $H$ is the affine matrix from region $S_1$ to $S_2$, Select a pixel $e$ in $S_1$ successively, and it is matched to $e^*$ through the affine transformation $H$:

$$e^* = He, e \in S_1 \tag{16}$$

Let $\Omega_1$ as the $5 \times 5$ pixels neighbor field centered at $e$, $\Omega_2$ as the $5 \times 5$ pixels neighbor field centered at $e^*$. The correlation coefficient between two pixels is computed as:

$$C_e = \frac{\sum_{p \in \Omega_1, q \in \Omega_2} I(p)I(q)}{[\sum_{p \in \Omega_1} I^2(p)][\sum_{q \in \Omega_2} I^2(q)]} \tag{17}$$

where $I(\cdot)$ refers to the gray value, $p$ is the pixel of $\Omega_1$, $q$ is the pixel of $\Omega_2$.

After calculating the correlation coefficient of each pixel in a pair of duplicated regions, then the forgery localization is performed. Firstly, all the pixel values of the image are set to 0. If $C_e \geqslant T_2$ ($T_2 = 0.5$ in our implementation), the pixel value corresponding to the pixel $e$ is set to 1. In this way, until all the pixels in the region are processed. The binary image can be obtained.

The same operation is performed on all matching clusters, and the binary images obtained from each matching cluster are merged. The preliminary localization result is obtained. Then the obtained localization result is post-processed, such as removing small regions, filling with the internal region and other morphological operations. Finally, the localization result of the input image is obtained.

In order to obtain the more accurate results, our scheme choose to perform $N$ iterations of the two steps ($N = 10$ in our implementation). Then $N$ binary images are merged to get the final results.

## 3    Experimental Results

In this section, the proposed scheme will be evaluated through experiments. The operating system of the PC running the algorithm is Microsoft Windows10, the PC used for testing has Intel i5-4200H CPU and 8 GB RAM, and the software is MATLAB 2021a.

**Table 3.** Precision, Recall, and $F_1$ Scores (%) for Scale on MICC-F600 Dataset.

| Methods | $Precision$ | $Recall$ | $F_1$ |
|---|---|---|---|
| Cozzolino [8] | 55.60 | 43.37 | 46.00 |
| Li [14] | 31.69 | 16.70 | 20.44 |
| Lyu [18] | 4.91 | 0.80 | 1.38 |
| Proposed | **62.50** | **55.63** | **53.45** |

**Table 4.** Precision, Recall, and $F_1$ Scores (%) for Multiple Copy-Move on MICC-F600 Dataset.

| Methods | $Precision$ | $Recall$ | $F_1$ |
|---|---|---|---|
| Cozzolino [8] | 51.52 | 37.66 | 42.33 |
| Li [14] | 38.18 | 18.27 | 22.66 |
| Lyu [18] | 19.27 | 4.39 | 6.28 |
| Proposed | **52.23** | **61.24** | **53.62** |

### 3.1    Datasets and Evaluation Criteria

Two public copy-move forgery test datasets, i.e., FAU [7] and MICC-F600 [3] are used to demonstrate the effectiveness of the proposed scheme.

The FAU is built by Christlein et al. [7]. This dataset consists of 48 original images and 1440 tampered images which include a variety of tampering types:

**Table 5.** Precision, Recall, and $F_1$ Scores(%) for Rotation on MICC-F600 Dataset.

| Methods | $Precision$ | $Recall$ | $F_1$ |
|---|---|---|---|
| Cozzolino [8] | 56.80 | 50.24 | 51.96 |
| Li [14] | 57.73 | 38.26 | 43.74 |
| Lyu [18] | 12.22 | 1.52 | 2.42 |
| Proposed | **63.48** | **59.87** | **55.80** |

**Table 6.** Precision, Recall, and $F_1$ Scores(%) for Comprehensive Results on MICC-F600 Dataset.

| Methods | Precision | Recall | $F_1$ |
|---|---|---|---|
| Cozzolino [8] | 56.05 | 46.15 | 48.78 |
| Li [14] | 45.28 | 27.29 | 32.01 |
| Lyu [18] | 13.32 | 2.59 | 3.84 |
| Proposed | **58.95** | **60.30** | **54.88** |

240 rotated images with a rotation angle range of $[0 : 0.02 : 0.1]$; 240 images are added with 5 different level of noise, and the range of added noise is $[0° : 2° : 10°]$; 432 JPEG compressed images with a quality factor range of $[20 : 10 : 100]$; 480 images are scaled by different scales, the range is $[0.91 : 0.02 : 1.09]$; There are also 48 images with plain copy-move forgery, this form of tampering means that only a simple copy-move operation is used on the tampered region. All images are of high quality, with an average resolution of $3000 \times 2300$.

The MICC-F600 was proposed by Amerini et al. [3]. This dataset consists of 600 images in total, of which 440 are original images and 160 are tampered images. The image resolution of the dataset ranges from $800 \times 533$ to $3888 \times 2592$. The tampered image is obtained from 40 basic images through the following 4 operations:

- **Translation:** The target region in the image is copied once and moved to another location in the image;
- **Rotation:** Rotate the duplicated region of the image by 30°;
- **Multiple:** Copy the target region in the image two or three times and move them to other location of the image;
- **Scale:** The duplicated region of the image is rotated by 30° and scale by 120%.

Nowadays, social media has become an indispensable tool to obtain information in human life. In order to save network resource, images transmitted on social media are often compressed, so most of the images that people contact at ordinary times are not the original version of the images. In this case, it is necessary to propose a CMFD scheme to detect images compressed by social media. Therefore, in our experiment, 48 plain copy tampered images of FAU and 160 tampered images of MICC-F600 are compressed by WeChat, and then the performance of the proposed scheme is tested. After compression, the average resolution of the dataset is about $800 \times 500$.

To evaluate the performance of the proposed scheme, *recall*, *precision* and $F_1$ scores are calculated at the pixel level to evaluate performance of the proposed scheme. They are calculated as:

$$precision = \frac{TP}{TP + FP} \tag{18}$$

$$recall = \frac{TP}{TP + FN} \tag{19}$$

$$F_1 = \frac{2 * precision * recall}{precision + recall} \tag{20}$$

where $TP$ is the True Positive, which represents the number of correctly detected tampered pixels. $FP$ is the False Positive, which are the number of falsely detected true pixels. $FN$ is the False Negative, which represents the number of undetected tampered pixels. $F_1$ score is the comprehensive evaluation of the *precision* and the *recall*.

### 3.2  Comparison Results and Analysis

In order to verify the effectiveness of the proposed scheme, it is compared with some state-of-the-art CMFD schemes. The schemes are proposed by Cozzolino et al. [8], Li et al. [14] and Lyu et al. [18].

**Experimental Results Under Plain Copy-Move.** Tables 1 and 2 show the results of our scheme and several other schemes on two datasets. From the table, it can be seen that on FAU and MICC-F600 datasets, the *recall* and $F_1$ scores of our scheme are the best, and the $F_1$ score are 2.65% and 1.79% higher than those of the second best schemes on FAU and MICC-F600 datasets respectively. This indicates that the proposed scheme is better than those of the other schemes. The scheme is proposed by Cozzolino [8] has the highest *precision* and second in $F_1$ score and *recall*.

One of the main reasons why the $F_1$ score of the proposed scheme is better than other schemes may be that our scheme combines point density in the feature extraction stage, the sufficient keypoints are extracted. Another main reason is that this scheme optimizes the matching keypoints by using prior-DBSCAN combined with prior regions, which reduces the keypoints of mismatching. Finally, the localization accuracy is improved.

**Experimental Results Under Different Transforms.** In this subsection, the performance of the proposed scheme is tested with images under different transforms, which are more challenging than the plain copy tampered images. Overall, the *precision*, *recall* value and $F_1$ value of our scheme are higher than those of the other three schemes. It shows that the detection performance of the proposed scheme is better than that of the other three schemes.

Table 3 shows that the proposed scheme obtains the best detection results for scaled tampered images on MICC-F600 dataset. As you can see from the table, the *precision*, *recall* and $F_1$ score of the proposed scheme are 6.90%, 12.26% and 7.45% higher than those of the second best scheme. It indicates that our scheme is robust to scaling attacks. Table 4 shows the detection results for images where the target region is copied multiple times on the MICC-F600 dataset. From the data in the Table 4, the proposed scheme obtained the best

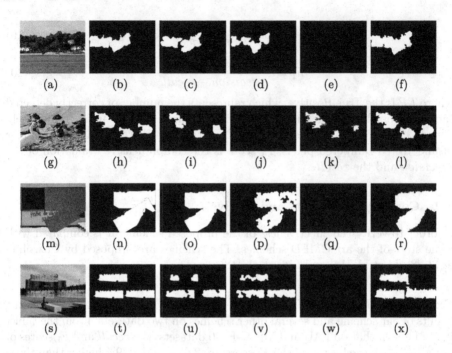

**Fig. 5.** Some challenging examples of copy-move forgery detection. From the first column to the last: the forged images, the ground-truth masks, the corresponding detection results by Cozzolino [8], by Li [14], by Lyu [18] and by our proposed scheme.

result. The *precision*, *recall* and $F_1$ score of the proposed scheme are 0.71%, 23.58%, 11.29% higher than those of the second best scheme. Table 5 shows the detection results of rotated tampered images on MICC-F600 dataset. It can be seen from the experimental results in the table that the *precision*, *recall* and $F_1$ score obtained by our scheme are the highest among several schemes, reaching to 63.48%, 59.87% and 55.80% respectively, which are 5.75%, 9.63%, 3.84% higher than those of the second best scheme. The results show that the proposed scheme is robust to rotation attacks. Table 6 shows the overall detection results of each scheme on MICC-F600 dataset. The proposed scheme obtains the best results. The *precision*, *recall* and $F_1$ score of the proposed scheme are 2.90%, 14.15%, 6.10% higher than those of the second best scheme. It shows that the proposed scheme has significant advantages in detecting images processed by the social media. The experimental results of the Lyu's scheme are relatively bad. The reasons are as follows. First, the Difference of Gaussians (DoG) keypoints and LIOP descriptors are extracted from the input image, then the Delaunay triangles are obtained and matched. Second, expanded triangle set are used to match again. Third, after the images are processed by social media, the results of feature extraction and feature matching of this scheme are not ideal. Then the forgery detection results of Lyu's are bad.

**Performance of Challenging Copy-Move Forgery Detection.** In this Section, some challenging copy-move forgery detection examples are shown in Fig. 5. In this figure, Fig. 5(a) are scaled tampered image, Fig. 5(g) and Fig. 5(s) are copied multiple times images, and Fig. 5(m) is a rotated tampered image.

As can be expected, the tampered region detected by Cozzolino in the third image is roughly the same as its ground-truth mask, and the tampered region of the other images is great different from the ground-truth mask. In the second image, no tampered regions were detected by Li. Lyu did not detect tampered regions in the first, third and fourth images, and in the second images, the detected tampered regions were relatively small. In contrast, the proposed scheme in this paper detects tampered regions in all four images, and the difference of tampered regions are relatively small compared with the ground-truth masks. As we can see, the robustness of the proposed scheme is the best, and good detection results are still achieved under those challenging conditions.

## 4    Conclusion

The existing schemes cannot effectively solve the problem that copy-move forgery images are processed by the social media. In order to solve this problem, a CMFD scheme based on the point density and the prior-DBSCAN is proposed. First of all, the concept of the point density is proposed. Considering that images transmitted through the social media are generally compressed. This paper measures the point density of the input image, and normalizes the image to get enough keypoints. Then, the keypoints are grouped by the pixel value to optimize the matching speed. Secondly, a novel prior-DBSCAN is proposed in this paper, a unified direction is appointed to matching pairs, and they are divided into starting points and ending points for DBSCAN. Then the corresponding prior region is obtained for each cluster after clustering. The prior region is fitted by a circle, the area of the circle is equal to that of the prior region, and the new clustering radius is obtained. The clustering is performed again to optimize the clustering effect. Finally, tampered regions are iteratively located by computing multiple affine matrices of the matched clusters. Experiments on public datasets show that the proposed scheme performs better than state-of-the-art schemes, under various challenging conditions, such as translation, scale, rotation, etc.

## References

1. Abhishek, Jindal, N.: Copy move and splicing forgery detection using deep convolution neural network, and semantic segmentation. Multimedia Tools Appl. **80**(3), 3571–3599 (2021)
2. Amerini, I., Ballan, L., Caldelli, R., Bimbo, A.D., Serra, G.: A SIFT-based forensic method for copy-move attack detection and transformation recovery. IEEE Trans. Inf. Forensics Secur. **6**(3), 1099–1110 (2011)
3. Amerini, I., Ballan, L., Caldelli, R., Del Bimbo, A., Del Tongo, L., Serra, G.: Copy-move forgery detection and localization by means of robust clustering with J-Linkage. Signal Process. Image Commun. **28**(6), 659–669 (2013)

4. Aria, M., Hashemzadeh, M., Farajzadeh, N.: QDL-CMFD: a quality-independent and deep learning-based copy-move image forgery detection method. Neurocomputing **511**, 213–236 (2022)

5. Aydın, Y.: A new copy-move forgery detection method using LIOP. J. Vis. Commun. Image Represent. **89**, 103661 (2022)

6. Barni, M., Phan, Q.T., Tondi, B.: Copy move source-target disambiguation through Multi-Branch CNNs. IEEE Trans. Inf. Forensics Secur. **16**, 1825–1840 (2020)

7. Christlein, V., Riess, C., Jordan, J., Riess, C., Angelopoulou, E.: An evaluation of popular copy-move forgery detection approaches. IEEE Trans. Inf. Forensics Secur. **7**(6), 1841–1854 (2012)

8. Cozzolino, D., Poggi, G., Verdoliva, L.: Efficient dense-field copy-move forgery detection. IEEE Trans. Inf. Forensics Secur. **10**(11), 2284–2297 (2015)

9. Emam, M., Han, Q., Niu, X.: PCET based copy-move forgery detection in images under geometric transforms. Multimedia Tools Appl. **75**(18), 11513–11527 (2016)

10. Fridrich, J., Soukal, D., Lukáš, J.: Detection of copy-move forgery in digital images. In: Proceeding of Digital Forensic Research Workshop (DFRW), pp. 19–23. Cleveland, OH, USA (2003)

11. Gan, Y., Zhong, J., Vong, C.: A novel copy-move forgery detection algorithm via feature label matching and hierarchical segmentation filtering. Inf. Process. Manag. **59**(1), 102783 (2022)

12. Kumar, S., Gupta, S.K., Kaur, M., Gupta, U.: VI-NET: a hybrid deep convolutional neural network using VGG and inception V3 model for copy-move forgery classification. J. Vis. Commun. Image Represent. **89**, 103644 (2022)

13. Lai, Y., Huang, T., Jiang, R.: Image region copy-move of forgery detection based on exponential-fourier moments. J. Image Graph. **20**(9), 1212–1221 (2015)

14. Li, Y., Zhou, J.: Fast and effective image copy-move forgery detection via hierarchical feature point matching. IEEE Trans. Inf. Forensics Secur. **14**(5), 1307–1322 (2019)

15. Li, Y.: Image copy-move forgery detection based on polar cosine transform and approximate nearest neighbor searching. Forensic Sci. Int. **224**(1–3), 59–67 (2013)

16. Lin, C., et al.: Copy-move forgery detection using combined features and transitive matching. Multimedia Tools Appl. **78**(21), 30081–30096 (2019)

17. Liu, Y., Xia, C., Zhu, X., Xu, S.: Two-stage copy-move forgery detection with self deep matching and proposal superglue. IEEE Trans. Image Process. **31**, 541–555 (2021)

18. . Lyu, Q., Luo, J., Liu, K., Yin, X., Liu, J., Lu, W.: Copy move forgery detection based on double matching. J. Vis. Commun. Image Represent. **76**(1), 103057 (2021)

19. Mahdian, B., Saic, S.: Detection of copy-move forgery using a method based on blur moment invariants. Forensic Sci. Int. **171**(2), 180–189 (2007)

20. Meena, K.B., Tyagi, V.: A copy-move image forgery detection technique based on tetrolet transform. J. Inf. Secur. Appl. **52**, 102481 (2020)

21. Muhammad, G., Hussain, M., Bebis, G.: Passive copy move image forgery detection using undecimated dyadic wavelet transform. Digit. Investig. **9**(1), 49–57 (2012)

22. Nazir, T., Nawaz, M., Masood, M., Javed, A.: Copy move forgery detection and segmentation using improved mask region-based convolution network (RCNN). Appl. Soft Comput. **131**, 109778 (2022)

23. Niu, P.P., Wang, C., Chen, W., Yang, H., Wang, X.: Fast and effective keypoint-based image copy-move forgery detection using complex-valued moment invariants. J. Vis. Commun. Image Represent. **77**, 103068 (2021)

24. Pan, X., Lyu, S.: Region duplication detection using image feature matching. IEEE Trans. Inf. Forensics Secur. **5**(4), 857–867 (2010)

25. Qin, J., Li, F., Xiang, L., Yin, C.: Detection of image region copy-move forgery using radial harmonic Fourier moments. J. Image Graph. **18**(8), 919–923 (2013)
26. Ryu, S.J., Kirchner, M., Lee, M.J., Lee, H.K.: Rotation invariant localization of duplicated image regions based on Zernike moments. IEEE Trans. Inf. Forensics Secur. **8**(8), 1355–1370 (2013)
27. Ryu, S.-J., Lee, M.-J., Lee, H.-K.: Detection of copy-rotate-move forgery using Zernike moments. In: Böhme, R., Fong, P.W.L., Safavi-Naini, R. (eds.) IH 2010. LNCS, vol. 6387, pp. 51–65. Springer, Heidelberg (2010). https://doi.org/10.1007/978-3-642-16435-4_5
28. Shivakumar, B., Baboo, S.S.: Detection of region duplication forgery in digital images using SURF. Int. J. Comput. Sci. Issues (IJCSI) **8**(4), 199–205 (2011)
29. Silva, E., Carvalho, T., Ferreira, A., Rocha, A.: Going deeper into copy-move forgery detection: exploring image telltales via multi-scale analysis and voting processes. J. Vis. Commun. Image Represent. **29**, 16–32 (2015)
30. Toldo, R., Fusiello, A.: Robust multiple structures estimation with J-linkage. In: Forsyth, D., Torr, P., Zisserman, A. (eds.) ECCV 2008. LNCS, vol. 5302, pp. 537–547. Springer, Heidelberg (2008). https://doi.org/10.1007/978-3-540-88682-2_41
31. Wang, C., Huang, Z., Qi, S., Yu, Y., Shen, G., Zhang, Y.: Shrinking the semantic gap: spatial pooling of local moment invariants for copy-move forgery detection. IEEE Trans. Inf. Forensics Secur. **18**, 1064–1079 (2023)
32. Wang, X.Y., Li, S., Liu, Y.N., Niu, Y., Yang, H.Y., Zhou, Z.L.: A new keypoint-based copy-move forgery detection for small smooth regions. Multimedia Tools Appl. **76**(22), 23353–23382 (2017)
33. Wang, X., Chen, W., Niu, P., Yang, H.: Image copy-move forgery detection based on dynamic threshold with dense points. J. Vis. Commun. Image Represent. **89**, 103658 (2022)
34. Wang, Y., Kang, X., Chen, Y.: Robust and accurate detection of image copy-move forgery using PCET-SVD and histogram of block similarity measures. J. Inf. Secur. Appl. **54**, 102536 (2020)
35. Weng, S., Zhu, T., Zhang, T., Zhang, C.: UCM-Net: a U-Net-like tampered-region-related framework for copy-move forgery detection. IEEE Trans. Multimedia 1–14 (2023)
36. Yang, F., Li, J., Lu, W., Weng, J.: Copy-move forgery detection based on hybrid features. Eng. Appl. Artif. Intell. **59**, 73–83 (2017)
37. Yang, J., Liang, Z., Gan, Y., Zhong, J.: A novel copy-move forgery detection algorithm via two-stage filtering. Digit. Signal Process. **113**, 103032 (2021)
38. Zandi, M., Mahmoudi-Aznaveh, A., Talebpour, A.: Iterative copy-move forgery detection based on a new interest point detector. IEEE Trans. Inf. Forensics Secur. **11**(11), 2499–2512 (2016)
39. Zhang, Y., et al.: CNN-Transformer based generative adversarial network for copy-move source/target distinguishment. IEEE Trans. Circuits Syst. Video Technol. **33**(5), 2019–2032 (2022)
40. Zhong, J.L., Pun, C.M.: An end-to-end dense-InceptionNet for image copy-move forgery detection. IEEE Trans. Inf. Forensics Secur. **15**, 2134–2146 (2019)
41. Zhu, Y., Chen, C., Yan, G., Guo, Y., Dong, Y.: AR-Net: adaptive attention and residual refinement network for copy-move forgery detection. IEEE Trans. Industr. Inf. **16**(10), 6714–6723 (2020)
42. Zhu, Y., Yu, Y., Guo, Y.: HRDA-Net: image multiple manipulation detection and location algorithm in real scene. J. Commun. **43**(1), 217–226 (2022)

# Detection of Speech Spoofing Based on Dense Convolutional Network

Yong Wang[1], Xiaozong Chen[1](✉), Yifang Chen[1], and Shunsi Zhang[2]

[1] Guangdong Polytechnic Normal University, Guangzhou 510000, China
xiaozong_chan@163.com
[2] Guangzhou Quwan Network Technology Co., Ltd., Guangzhou 510627, China

**Abstract.** In recent years, the rapid development of voice synthesis technologies has led to an increasing concern about the abuse of fake human voices for malicious purposes, such as deepfake audio, spam calls and social engineering attacks. This paper proposes a novel deep learning-based model to effectively identify counterfeit human voices generated by various voice synthesis algorithms. The proposed model employs a combination of Dense-Style Network to capture both spectral and temporal features of human speech. The model is extensively evaluated on ASVspoof 2019 datasets. The experimental results indicate that our model achieves competitive performance compared to existing methods and has a certain degree of anti-compression ability. In addition, anti-compression research was conducted to investigate the recognition performance of the model in response to compressed speech. Our findings pave the way for further research in combating against the misuse of artificially generated human voices and sound authenticity verification in general.

**Keywords:** Dense-Style Network · ASVspoof 2019 · anti-compression

## 1 Introduction

Speech spoofing [1] refers to the use of specific methods to alter the sound of one's voice, leading individuals or systems to misjudge the speaker's identity and achieve a deceptive effect. Speech spoofing can be categorized into two types: mechanical spoofing and electronic spoofing [2]. The first type involves physical means such as manipulating organs of the human body, covering the mouth, or pinching the nose to alter the voice. This type is known as mechanical speech spoofing [3]. Although this form of spoofing can achieve certain results, its effectiveness is limited by the language skills of the speaker.

Electronic spoofing refers to the manipulation of a speaker's original voice using electronic devices or voice processing software. In comparison to mechanical spoofing, electronic spoofing utilizes electronic devices and built-in algorithms to modify the temporal or spectral characteristics of the voice, resulting in a more natural-sounding spoofing. Through various algorithms, digital tools are used to process speech with the aim of disguising the voice, ensuring that the altered voice does not raise suspicion.

J. Cai et al. (Eds.): SPNCE 2023, LNICST 525, pp. 258–267, 2025.
https://doi.org/10.1007/978-3-031-73699-5_18

Compared to mechanical speech spoofing, electronic spoofing poses greater risks, thus in this study we focus on researching the detection of electronic spoofing, collectively referred to as speech spoofing. Currently, there are several typical forms of speech spoofing, including Voice Conversion (VC) [4, 5], Speech Synthesis (SS) [6, 7], Voice Redubbing [8, 9], and Voice Transformation (VT) [10, 11].

Existing research has shown that speech spoofing poses a threat to Automatic Speaker Verification (ASV) systems [12–14]. Attackers can utilize speech spoofing techniques to forge others' voiceprints or speech samples, thereby deceiving identity authentication through ASV systems. Currently, research on ASV systems primarily focuses on two aspects: feature parameter extraction and pattern recognition. Feature parameter extraction involves analyzing and processing the speech signal to remove irrelevant information for speaker identification, obtaining essential characteristics representing individuals within the speech signal. Pattern recognition, on the other hand, classifies the extracted feature vectors to determine whether the current speaker is a known individual. Pattern recognition is one of the core technologies in ASV systems and includes designing and training classifiers. Commonly used classifiers include Gaussian Mixture Models (GMM), Support Vector Machines (SVM), and Deep Neural Networks (DNN). As a gateway safeguarding people's privacy, the security of ASV systems is crucial for ensuring privacy protection.

There are various methods related to speech spoofing. In terms of detection models, Korsh et al. [17] designed a DNN-deep neural network structure that enables the learning of speech features and classification models together. Dinkel et al. [18] proposed a deep model for spoofing detection based on raw waveforms, eliminating the need for any preprocessing or post-processing of data, making training and evaluation a streamlined process that consumes less time compared to other neural network-based methods. Liu et al. [19] introduced an end-to-end anti-spoofing model composed entirely of one-dimensional convolutional neural networks, specifically for detecting speech spoofing under noisy conditions. Huang et al. [20] proposed a novel model based on segment-wise linear filterbank features, combining the advantages of CNN and RNN, which outperforms traditional GMM models and exhibits better resistance to overfitting. Gong et al. [21] presented a new neural network-based model for replay attack detection, utilizing both spectral and spatial information from multi-channel audio, significantly improving the performance of replay attack detection. In terms of speech features, Chen et al. [22] discovered through experiments that the number of minimum value MDCT coefficients in fake audio is fewer than in genuine audio. Therefore, Renza [23] and Ghobadi [24] applied watermarks on audio using MDCT characteristics to aid in identifying the forged sections within the audio. Sathya et al. [25] used Cosine-Normalized Phase based Cepstral Coefficient (CNPCC) features to enhance the detection of deceptive speech. Das et al. [26] proposed an improved version of $\gamma$-frequency cepstral coefficients to enhance the performance of spoofing detection. Alzantot et al. [27] designed a network model based on deep residual networks that combines three different speech features. Zhan et al. [28] introduced a fragment-based approach for detecting deceptive speech, combining a constant Q cepstral coefficient-based method with a constant Q cepstral coefficient-based speech segment extraction method to improve the robustness of embedded systems based on speech authentication.

In terms of classifiers, Tian et al. [29] proposed a time-domain CNN-based classifier and investigated spoofing detection based on unit selection. Zhe et al. [30] proposed the use of an ensemble classifier set, including multiple Gaussian Mixture Model (GMM)-based classifiers, as well as two new GMM average super-vector Gradient Boosting Decision Tree (GSV-GBDT) and GSV-Random Forest (GSV-RF) classifiers. La et al. [31] employed a linear kernel SVM classifier to classify the extracted i-vector advanced feature representations. Cui et al. [32] introduced a backend classifier based on dense convolution and short connections, combining popular features such as constant Q cepstral coefficients with Linear Frequency Cepstral Coefficients (LFCC), thereby improving fusion performance. Sun et al. [33] constructed a novel joint voice detector based on gamma-tone frequency cepstral coefficient features, combining self-attention residual networks and light gradient boosting machines. This classifier avoids overfitting, has low computational complexity, replaces traditional fully connected layer classifiers, and effectively discriminates between genuine and deceptive sounds.

In this paper, we don't use any front-end feature. The raw voice data been processed will feed to the network directly. For back-end classification, we refer to the excellent DenseNet and design a DNN with a DenseNet-style architecture.

## 2  Proposed Model

This paper aims to address security issues caused by speech spoofing. The goal is to establish a model for detecting speech spoofing and classify whether the speech is original or manipulated. It is generally believed that deeper networks perform better, but in the case of speech spoofing detection, spoofed speech often only undergoes minor modifications on genuine speech. If the network is too deep, the features of spoofed speech may be lost [34]. Therefore, we should avoid using excessively deep networks.

### 2.1  Model Structure

We constructed a dense convolutional neural network. The input of this model is all processed 6 s speech data. The network structure is shown in Fig. 1.

The network has a total of 49 layers, with 971,890 model parameters. The input tensor size of the speech data is $1 \times 96000$ (which means channels $\times$ sample rates). The DenseNet-style blocks are used, as shown in Fig. 2.

Each block consists of 10 layers, including a $1 \times 3$ convolutional layer, batch normalization layer, and ReLu activation layer, each of which is repeated twice for a total of 6 layers. This is followed by a $1 \times 3$ convolutional layer, batch normalization layer, and finally a $1 \times 1$ convolutional layer for the input data of the block. The outputs of these two layers are concatenated together and passed through the final ReLu activation layer. The specific network parameters in the entire network structure are shown in Table 1.

### 2.2  Model Training Strategy

The raw speech data of ASVspoof 2019 vary in length, and preprocessing of the dataset is necessary to ensure a uniform tensor input size for the model. Additionally, the ratio

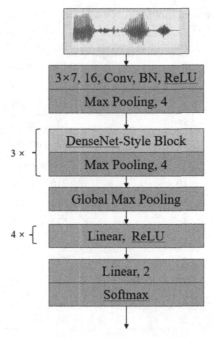

**Fig. 1.** Model Struct

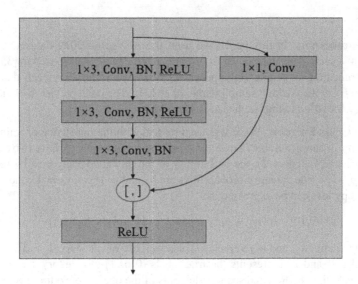

**Fig. 2.** DenseNet-Style Block

of genuine speech data to spoofed speech data in the original dataset is unbalanced, and measures should be taken to address this imbalance. The model training includes the following strategies.

**Table 1.** Detailed parameters of each layer of the network model.

| Layer | Number of layers | Input Size | Output Size |
|---|---|---|---|
| 3×7 Conv, BN, ReLU | 3 | $1 \times 96000$ | $16 \times 96000$ |
| Max Pooling 4 | 1 | $16 \times 96000$ | $16 \times 24000$ |
| DenseNet-Style Block | 10 | $16 \times 24000$ | $64 \times 24000$ |
| Max Pooling 4 | 1 | $64 \times 24000$ | $64 \times 6000$ |
| DenseNet-Style Block | 10 | $64 \times 6000$ | $256 \times 6000$ |
| Max Pooling 4 | 1 | $256 \times 6000$ | $256 \times 1500$ |
| DenseNet-Style Block | 10 | $256 \times 1500$ | $512 \times 1500$ |
| Max Pooling 4 | 1 | $512 \times 1500$ | $512 \times 375$ |
| Global Max Pooling | 1 | $512 \times 375$ | $512 \times 1$ |
| flatten | 1 | $512 \times 1$ | 512 |
| Linear, ReLU | 2 | 512 | 256 |
| Linear, ReLU | 2 | 256 | 128 |
| Linear, ReLU | 2 | 128 | 64 |
| Linear, ReLU | 2 | 64 | 32 |
| Linear | 1 | 32 | 2 |
| Softmax | 1 | 2 | 2 |

**Data Preprocessing.** In this paper, we used the ASVspoof 2019 dataset. Since the duration of speech in the dataset varies, we adopted the method proposed in [35], which involves truncating or duplicating speech data to ensure that all speech data have a duration of 6 s, with a default sampling rate of 16 kHz. The input precision of the feature vectors is $9.6 \times 10^4$, and the batch size is set to 32.

**Weighted Cross Entropy.** WCE was used to deal with the imbalance of training data caused by the different number of true and false voices. Assuming we have two categories (Category 1 and Category 2), the probability of the predicted categories by the model is $p_1$ and $p_2$. The true category probabilities are $y_1$ and $y_2$ ($y_1 + y_2 = 1$), the weighted Cross entropy loss can be expressed as:

$$WCE = [w_1 \times y_1 \times \log(p_1) + w_2 \times y_2 \times \log(p_2)] \tag{1}$$

Among them, w1 and $w_2$ represents the weights of category 1 and category 2, respectively, $y_1$ and $y_2$ represents the true labels (0 or 1) of category 1 and category 2, respectively, i.e. the first and second elements of the one hot encoding vector, $p_1$ and $p_2$ represents the probabilities of category 1 and category 2 predicted by the model, which are transformed by the SoftMax function, Log represents the Natural logarithm

The Adam optimizer with a Learning rate of 0.95 is selected for model training, and the model parameters with the lowest Equal Error Rate (EER) are selected from 100 epochs in the validation set to test the test set each time.

# 3   Result

## 3.1   Corpus

The speech data in the LA subset of the ASVspoof 2019 database is entirely derived from the VCTK corpus. The VCTK corpus consists of authentic speech from 107 speakers, including 46 males and 61 females. All the authentic speech samples were recorded using the same recording configuration without any channel or background noise interference. The authentic speech samples in the LA subset are directly selected from the VCTK corpus. The spoofed speech samples in the dataset are generated by applying various speech synthesis and voice conversion techniques to these authentic speech samples. The sampling rate for all the speech data is 16 kHz.

The LA dataset is divided into three subsets: the training set, the development set, and the evaluation set. Both the training set and the development set include spoofed speech samples generated using six identical speech synthesis and voice conversion techniques. These six techniques represent known attack types and can be used to train and adjust the synthetic speech detection system. In contrast, the evaluation set includes spoofed speech samples generated using two of the aforementioned known attacks and eleven additional speech synthesis and voice conversion techniques that differ from the six known attacks. These eleven techniques represent unknown attack types that the system may encounter.

## 3.2   Equal Error Rate

The Equal Error Rate (EER) can be used to evaluate the performance of an authentication speaker recognition system. False acceptance rate (FAR) represents the probability of incorrectly accepting a non-matching sample as a match without proper authorization. False rejection rate (FRR) represents the probability of incorrectly rejecting a matching sample as a non-match. Calculate the FAR and FRR for a range of possible thresholds and plot the Detection Error Tradeoff (DET) curve, which shows the relationship between them. EER corresponds to the point on the DET curve where the false acceptance rate equals the false rejection rate in terms of error rate.

EER is the threshold at which the false acceptance rate equals the false rejection rate. In other words, the EER is the error rate achieved when the false acceptance rate and false rejection rate are equal. The EER provides an intuitive and comparable measure of performance for authentication or speaker recognition systems in balancing error rates. A lower EER corresponds to better performance.

## 3.3   Main Result

After preprocessing the data, it was fed into the network. After 100 epochs of training, the model's loss curve, as shown in Fig. 3, was obtained. From the loss curve, it can be observed that the loss gradually decreases smoothly with an increasing number of training epochs. The decreasing slope indicates that the training effectiveness of the model is improving gradually. This smooth decreasing trend suggests that as the number of training epochs increases, the model reduces prediction errors and captures the patterns and features within the data. The decreasing slope also suggests that the model is approaching convergence. We achieved the optimal results, as shown in Table 2 finally.

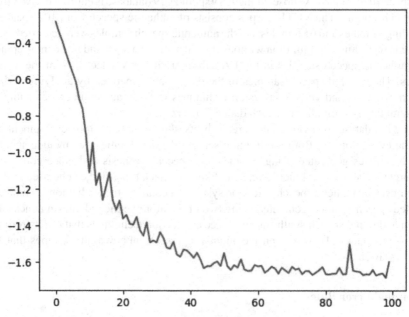

**Fig. 3.** Loss (Logarithm Base 10 Scale) Curve of 100 epochs

From the table, it can be seen that the EER of our model's results are significantly better than the baseline, as well as outperforming results [37–39], and approaching the results of [40]. However, our model's parameters are much smaller than theirs. Even though the model parameters of [35] are fewer than ours, our EER is lower than theirs.

**Table 2.** EER (%) between the proposed model and state-of-art method

| Method | Params | Dev | Eval |
|---|---|---|---|
| Baseline CQCC+GMM [36] | - | 2.71 | 8.09 |
| 8 Features+MLP [37] | - | 0 | 4.13 |
| Spec+CQCC+ResNet+SE [38] | 5.80 M | 0 | 6.7 |
| Spec+VGG+SincNet [39] | >4.32 M | 0 | 8.01 |
| 3 Features+CNN [40] | 30.6 M | 0 | 1.86 |
| CQT+Res2Net+SE [35] | 0.92 M | 0.43 | 2.5 |
| Dense-Style Net | 0.97 M | 0.71 | 1.98 |

### 3.4 Anti-compression Research

Compressing audio is widely used in everyday internet connections, making it necessary for models to have good anti-compression performance. In this study, we compressed the dataset with 16:1 MP3 compression and repeated the experimental steps mentioned above. The resulting EER results are shown in Table 3.

**Table 3.** EER (%) between the uncompressed and compressed models.

|                | Dev  | Eval |
|----------------|------|------|
| No Compressed  | 0.71 | 1.98 |
| Compressed     | 1.66 | 3.34 |

## 4  Conclusion

In this paper, we addressed the problem of spoof speech detection using deep learning. Our research aimed to lower the EER while reducing the computational complexity.We made several significant contributions in this study. Firstly, we proposed a Dense-Style convolutional neural network architecture that incorporates attention mechanisms to enhance feature selection and improve classification performance. Furthermore, we conducted Anti-Compression studies to analyze the impact of compression in our model.

In conclusion, the results indicate that our model has a lower EER compared to the existing state-of-the-art model. Moreover, our model performs better even though it has fewer parameters and lower complexity than the models that outperform ours. In terms of compression resistance, the research findings demonstrate that our model exhibits a certain level of resistance to 16:1 MP3 compression.

**Acknowledgement.** I would like to express my heartfelt gratitude to all those who have supported and assisted me throughout the process of completing this research. First and foremost, I would like to thank my advisor, Professor Yong Wang, for providing me with invaluable guidance and advice throughout the entire research process. Additionally, I would like to extend my thanks to the resources and support provided by the university, which have given me the necessary conditions and environment to conduct this research. I sincerely appreciate each and every person who has contributed to my research work. Without your support and assistance, I would not have been able to accomplish this study. Thank you very much!

## References

1. Perrot, P., Aversano, G., Chollet, G.: Voice disguise and automatic detection: review and perspectives. Prog. Nonlinear Speech Process., 101–117 (2007)
2. Lau, Y.W., Wagner, M., Tran, D.: Vulnerability of speaker verification to voice mimicking. In: Proceedings of 2004 International Symposium on Intelligent Multimedia, Video and Speech Processing, 2004, pp. 145–148. IEEE (2004)

3. Zhang, C., Li, B., Chen, S., et al.: Acoustic analysis of whispery voice disguise in Mandarin Chinese. In: Proceedings of the Interspeech, pp. 1413–1416 (2018)
4. Stylianou, Y., Cappé, O., Moulines, E.: Continuous probabilistic transform for voice conversion. IEEE Trans. Speech Audio Process. **6**(2), 131–142 (1998)
5. Erro, D., Navas, E., Hernaez, I.: Parametric voice conversion based on bilinear frequency warping plus amplitude scaling. IEEE Trans. Audio Speech Lang. Process. **21**(3), 556–566 (2012)
6. Tokuda, K., Nankaku, Y., Toda, T., et al.: Speech synthesis based on hidden markov models. Proc. IEEE **101**(5), 1234–1252 (2013)
7. Yamagishi, J., Kobayashi, T., Nakano, Y., et al.: Analysis of speaker adaptation algorithms for HMM-based speech synthesis and a constrained SMAPLR adaptation algorithm. IEEE Trans. Audio Speech Lang. Process. **17**(1), 66–83 (2009)
8. Shang, W, Stevenson, M.: Score normalization in playback attack detection. In: Proceedings of the 2010 IEEE International Conference on Acoustics, Speech and Signal Processing, pp. 1678–1681. IEEE (2010)
9. Villalba, J., Lleida, E.: Detecting replay attacks from far-field recordings on speaker verification systems. In: Vielhauer, C., Dittmann, J., Drygajlo, A., Juul, N.C., Fairhurst, M.C. (eds.) Biometrics and ID Management. BioID 2011. Lecture Notes in Computer Science, vol. 6583, pp. 274–285. Springer, Heidelberg (2011). https://doi.org/10.1007/978-3-642-19530-3_25
10. Perrot, P., Chollet, G.: The question of disguised voice. J. Acoust. Soc. Am. **123**(5), 3878 (2008)
11. Perrot, P., Aversano, G., Chollet, G.: Voice disguise and automatic detection: review and perspectives. Prog. Nonlinear Speech Process., 101–117 (2007)
12. Evans, N.W.D., Kinnunen, T., Yamagishi, J.: Spoofing and countermeasures for automatic speaker verification. In: Proceedings of the Interspeech, pp. 925–929 (2013)
13. Kinnunen, T., Wu, Z.Z., Lee, K.A., et al.: Vulnerability of speaker verification systems against voice conversion spoofing attacks: the case of telephone speech. In: Proceedings of the 2012 IEEE International Conference on Acoustics, Speech and Signal Processing (ICASSP), pp. 4401–4404. IEEE (2012)
14. Leon, P.D., Pucher, M., Yamagishi, J., et al.: Evaluation of speaker verification security and detection of HMM-based synthetic speech. IEEE Trans. Audio Speech Lang. Process. **20**(8), 2280–2290 (2012)
15. Black, A.W., Zen, H., Tokuda, K.: Statistical parametric speech synthesis. In: Proceedings of the 2007 IEEE International Conference on Acoustics, Speech and Signal Processing-ICASSP 2007, vol. 4, IV-1229–IV-1232. IEEE (2007)
16. Ma, Y., Ren, Z., Xu, S.: RW-Resnet: a novel speech anti-spoofing model using raw waveform. arXiv preprint arXiv:2108.05684 (2021)
17. Korshunov, P., Goncalves, A.R., Violato, R., et al.: On the use of convolutional neural networks for speech presentation attack detection. In: IEEE International Conference on Identity, pp. 1–8. IEEE (2018)
18. Dinkel, H., Chen, N., Qian, Y., et al.: End-to-end spoofing detection with raw waveform CLDNNS. In: Proceedings of the 2017 IEEE International Conference on Acoustics, Speech and Signal Processing (ICASSP), pp. 4860–4864. IEEE (2017)
19. Liu, P., Zhang, Z., Yang, Y.: End-to-end spoofing speech detection and knowledge distillation under noisy conditions. In: Proceedings of the 2021 International Joint Conference on Neural Networks (IJCNN), pp. 1–7. IEEE (2021)
20. Huang, L., Pun, C.M.: Audio replay spoof attack detection by joint segment-based linear filter bank feature extraction and attention-enhanced DenseNet-BiLSTM network. IEEE/ACM Trans. Audio Speech Lang. Process. **28**, 1813–1825 (2020)
21. Gong, Y., Yang, J., Poellabauer, C.: Detecting replay attacks using multi-channel audio: a neural network-based method. IEEE Sign. Process. Lett. **27**, 920–924 (2020)

22. Chen, B., Luo, W., Luo, D.: Identification of audio processing operations based on convolutional neural network. In: Proceedings of the 6th ACM Workshop on Information Hiding and Multimedia Security, pp. 73–77 (2018)

23. Renza, D., Lemus, C.: Authenticity verification of audio signals based on fragile watermarking for audio forensics. Expert Syst. Appl. **91**, 211–222 (2018)

24. Ghobadi, A., Boroujerdizadeh, A., Yaribakht, A.H., et al.: Blind audio watermarking for tamper detection based on LSB. In: Proceedings of the 2013 15th International Conference on Advanced Communications Technology (ICACT), pp. 1077–1082. IEEE (2013)

25. Sathya, A., Swetha, J., Das, K.A., et al.: Robust features for spoofing detection. In: Proceedings of the 2016 International Conference on Advances in Computing, Communications and Informatics (ICACCI), pp. 2410–2414. IEEE (2016)

26. Das, K.A., George, K.K., Kumar, C.S., et al.: Modified gammatone frequency cepstral coefficients to improve spoofing detection. In: Proceedings of the 2016 International Conference on Advances in Computing, Communications and Informatics (ICACCI), pp. 50–55. IEEE (2016)

27. Alzantot, M., Wang, Z., Srivastava, M.B.: Deep residual neural networks for audio spoofing detection. In: Proceedings of the Interspeech 2019, pp. 1078–1082 (2019)

28. Zhan, J., Pu, Z., Jiang, W., et al.: Detecting spoofed speeches via segment-based word CQCC and average ZCR for embedded systems. IEEE Trans. Comput. Aided Des. Integr. Circ. Syst. **41**(11), 3862–3873 (2022)

29. Tian, X., Xiao, X., Chng, E.S., et al.: Spoofing speech detection using temporal convolutional neural network. In: Proceedings of the 2016 Asia-Pacific Signal and Information Processing Association Annual Summit and Conference (APSIPA), pp. 1–6. IEEE (2016)

30. Ji, Z., Li, Z.Y., Li, P., et al.: Ensemble learning for countermeasure of audio replay spoofing attack in ASVspoof2017. In: Proceedings of the Interspeech, pp. 87–91 (2017)

31. Lavrentyeva, G., Novoselov, S., Malykh, E., et al.: Audio replay attack detection with deep learning frameworks. In: Interspeech, pp. 82–86 (2017)

32. Cui, S., Huang, B., Huang, J., et al.: Synthetic speech detection based on local autoregression and variance statistics. IEEE Sig. Process. Lett. **29**, 1462–1466 (2022)

33. Sun, X., Fu, J., Wei, B., et al.: A self-attentional ResNet-LightGBM model for IoT-enabled voice liveness detection. IEEE Internet Things J. **10**(9), 8257–8270 (2022)

34. Hua, G., Teoh, A., Zhang, H.: Towards end-to-end synthetic speech detection. IEEE Sig. Process. Lett. **28**, 1265–1269 (2021)

35. Li, X., Li, N., Weng, C., Liu, X., Su, D., Yu, D., Meng, H.: Replay and synthetic speech detection with Res2Net architecture. In: Proceedings of the IEEE International Conference on Acoustics, Speech and Signal Processing (ICASSP 2021) (2021)

36. Todisco, M., et al.: ASVspoof 2019: future horizons in spoofed and fake audio detection. In: Proceedings of the Interspeech, pp. 1008–1012 (2019)

37. Das, R.K., Yang, J., Li, H.: Long range acoustic features for spoofed speech detection. In: Proceedings of the Interspeech, pp. 1058–1062 (2019)

38. Lai, C.-I., Chen, N., Villalba, J., Dehak, N.: ASSERT: anti-spoofing with squeeze-excitation and residual networks. In: Proceedings of the Interspeech, vol. 2019, pp. 1013–1017 (2019)

39. Zeinali, H., Stafylakis, T., Athanasopoulou, G., Rohdin, J., Gkinis, I., Burget, L., Černocký, J.: Detecting spoofing attacks using VGG and SincNet: BUT-omilia submission to ASVspoof 2019 challenge. In: Proceedings of the Interspeech, pp. 1073–1077 (2019)

40. Lavrentyeva, G., Novoselov, S., Tseren, A., Volkova, M., Gorlanov, A., Kozlov, A.: STC antispoofing systems for the ASVspoof2019 challenge. In: Proceedings of the Interspeech, pp. 1033–1037 (2019)

# Speech Emotion Recognition Based on Recurrent Neural Networks with Conformer for Emotional Speech Synthesis

Xin Huang[1], Chenjing Sun[1], Jichen Yang[2(✉)], and Xianhua Hou[1]

[1] School of Electronics and Information Engineering, South China Normal University, Foshan 528225, China
[2] School of Cyber Security, Guangdong Polytechnic Normal University, Guangzhou 510665, China
nisonyoung@163.com

**Abstract.** Speech emotion recognition is the basis of emotional speech synthesis, a good speech emotion recognition system can learn more emotional expressions in speech and help in the synthesis of emotional speech. However, there are a number of issues that make the speech emotion recognition task difficult, including background noise and the distinct speech features of each speaker. The widely recognized speech emotion recognition system ACRNN extracts local features from speech signals using CNN, and its attention mechanism concentrates on the emotional content of the speech data. However, because only a single attention module is used, it is unable to simultaneously attend to the information from distinct representation subspaces at different locations, nor is it able to acquire long-term global information. The paper proposes CoRNN, which applies Conformer to replace CNN and attention module, with the purpose of overcoming the shortcomings of ACRNN. The experimental results on IEMOCAP dataset demonstrate that the unweighted average recall of the proposed CoRNN can achieve 65.53%, which improves 0.79% comparing with ACRNN.

**Keywords:** Speech emotion recognition · Emotional speech synthesis · Conformer

## 1 Introduction

The development of text-to-speech (TTS) technology makes the machine synthesized voice no longer cold and can better imitate human speech [1]. However, the current synthesized voice is still insufficient in emotional expressiveness, and it is necessary to further improve the system's emotional speech synthesis ability. Speech emotion recognition (SER) is the basis of emotional speech synthesis, and

J. Cai et al. (Eds.): SPNCE 2023, LNICST 525, pp. 268–277, 2025.
https://doi.org/10.1007/978-3-031-73699-5_19

can serve it, specifically in: the final synthesis stage of emotional speech synthesis system needs to provide the emotional embeddings of the desired emotion, and an excellent SER system can extract the emotional embeddings that contains more emotionally relevant information; for the voice input into the emotional speech synthesis system, the SER system can be used to first identify its emotional category, so as to eliminate the emotion-related information. Therefore, this paper focuses on the study of SER.

SER is widely used in network teaching, smart home, emotion conversion, expressive speech synthesis and other fields, which has important research value [2]. In recent years, people have conducted in-depth research on SER using acoustic features and a variety of machine learning (ML) and deep learning (DL) models. DL provides a variety of models for SER research to more accurately extract emotional states from speech. Deep neural network (DNN) models are often utilized to develop representations from low-level audio characteristics [3]. SER research usually uses convolutional neural networks (CNNs) and recurrent neural networks (RNNs) based on long short-term memory (LSTM) to extract local information in speech sequences. In CNN-based SER instances such as [4], CNN is often used to obtain time-frequency information derived from spectral features, while in LSTM-based instances such as [5], LSTM is used to focus on extracting sequence correlations of speech time series.

Convolutional Recurrent Neural Network (CRNN) was firstly proposed on raw audio samples for SER [6]. Then at the base of CRNN and attention mechanism, Chen et al. proposed a combination of attention model and convolutional recurrent neural network (ACRNN) for SER [7]. Because of its good performance, it has become a popular SER method to date.

The ACRNN mainly consists of three modules: CNN, Bidirectional Long Short-Term Memory (BiLSTM) and attention module, in which, CNN is used to extract local feature, BiLSTM plays the role of capturing contextual information and attention module is used to focus on emotion part. Though ACRNN is still extensively utilized in many domains, including expressive speech synthesis [8]. It has two drawbacks, one is that it is unable to extract long-term global information because it only makes use of CNN to capture local feature, the other is that only one single attention module in ACRNN is unable to attend to input from different representation subspaces at different positions simultaneously.

In order to settle down the two issues in ACRNN, in this paper, a method of CoRNN is proposed by using Conformer [9] to modify ACRNN. Further speaking, CNN and attention modules in ACRNN are swapped out for conformer. The reasons are as follows:

- Conformer has the ability to capture both global and local features simultaneously. The reason behind this is that Conformer is mainly composed of Transformer [10] and CNN, wherein Transformer can capture global information while CNN can be used to capture local feature.
- Conformer's multi-head attention module allows it to concurrently attend to data from different representation subspaces at different positions. Therefore, the model is more capable of sequence modeling for the relative dependency between features at different positions.

- Two half-step feed-forward layers are used in the Conformer, and the non-linear activation function is introduced, so the nonlinear fitting ability and performance ability of the network can be improved.
- Conformer can extract better representation for emotion recognition.
- Conformer is effective in dealing with long-distance dependencies, and can make up for the problem that LSTM cannot deal with long-term dependencies.

The remaining parts of the paper are as follows. Section 2 details the architecture of the BiLSTM and Conformer based CoRNN. Section 3 introduces the database and experimental setup. Section 4 reports the studies on IEMOCAP dataset. Finally, Sect. 5 concludes the paper.

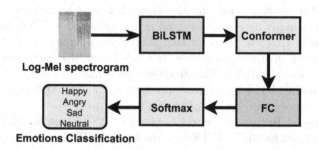

**Fig. 1.** Schematic diagram of CoRNN architecture for SER.

## 2   CoRNN

The structure of the CoRNN is shown in Fig. 1. From Fig. 1, it can be found that there are totally four modules in CoRNN, which are BiLSTM, Conformer, fully connected layer (FC) and softmax, in which the diagram of Conformer can be found in Fig. 2. The 3-D log-Mel spectrogram is fed into the BiLSTM network to capture the contextual features, and then the Conformer structure is connected to extract both local and global information of the sequence, and finally the classification is performed. Firstly, we introduce the role of each module briefly. BiLSTM is used to capture contextual information, Conformer is used to extract global and local features, FC plays the role of line transformation and Softmax is used to obtain the prediction probability of each emotion category of the input speech as the output. The emotion label corresponding to the dimension with the highest probability is the predicted emotion.

Next, the two principal modules in CoRNN, which are BiLSTM and Conformer, will be introduced in detail.

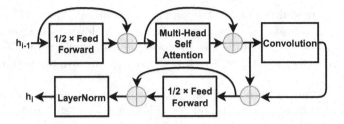

**Fig. 2.** The architecture of Conformer Block.

## 2.1 BiLSTM

RNNs introduce recurrent connections within layers, enabling parameters to be shared across time [11]. LSTM neural network is a variant of RNN. Relying on its unique mechanism, LSTM can process feature information with long interval distance, which is suitable for predicting temporal sequences. Therefore, it performs well in natural language processing and has been introduced into SER. In this paper, BiLSTM [12] is used. Compared with LSTM, BiLSTM combines the advantages of long short-term memory network and bidirectional recurrent neural network, which can better capture the temporal bidirectional context information of speech data, so it is more robust.

BiLSTM consists of two LSTM layers with opposite directions, which can simultaneously consider features from past and future timesteps, so it can capture the temporal bidirectional context information of speech data.

## 2.2 Conformer

When extracting the emotional representation of the speaker, the focus is on extracting the local and global features of the speech. Among them, global context modeling can increase the robustness of speaker feature extraction. CNN extracts features through local perception, so it can extract local features of speech well, but it is poor in capturing global features. While Transformer has good performance in capturing long-range global context dependencies, but has low local attention [13].

To extract emotional features more efficiently, we use the Conformer structure that can model both global and local features, as shown in Fig. 2. Transformer model is good at capturing global features but has low local attention, while CNN has a good ability to extract local features but is poor at capturing global features. Conformer is a combination of CNN and Transformer, which possesses the feature extraction capabilities of both, and thus can capture both local and global features of speech very well. The key components of the Conformer architecture include multi-head self-attention module (MHSA) and convolution module (Conv). The MHSA module can expand the ability of the model in sequence modeling of the relative dependency between features in different positions. Its relative position encoding module makes the model more robust to speech of different lengths [14].

The Conv module consists of Pointwise convolution layers, 1D Depthwise convolution layers, and also includes a BatchNorm layer to accelerate model convergence. The Conv module uses the local modeling ability of CNN to obtain the local features of sequences, which is the key to improve the performance of the model.

Different from the encoder of the Transformer model, the Conformer structure contains two feed-forward modules (FFN) with half-step residual connection, which are located before the MHSA module and after the Conv module. The addition of FFN introduces a nonlinear activation function that improves the nonlinear fitting ability of the network and improves the performance of the model. Such a structure can yield better results compared to a single FFN [15].

When the input feature $h_{i-1}$ is fed into the Conformer architecture, the output feature $h_i$ is generated as follows:

$$\widetilde{h}_i = h_{i-1} + \frac{1}{2}\text{FNN}(h_{i-1}) \tag{1}$$

$$h'_i = \widetilde{h}_i + \text{MHSA}(\widetilde{h}_i) \tag{2}$$

$$h''_i = h'_i + \text{Conv}(h'_i) \tag{3}$$

$$h_i = \text{LayerNorm}(h''_i + \frac{1}{2}\text{FNN}(h''_i)) \tag{4}$$

where $h_{i-1} \in R^{d \times T}$, $h_i \in R^{d \times T}$, $d$ is the dimension of the Conformer, and $T$ is the frame length.

## 3   Database and Experimental Setup

The suggested CoRNN is assessed using the Interactive Emotional Dyadic Motion Capture database (IEMOCAP) [16]. The following four categories of emotions-happy, neutral, angry and sad-are taken from the database's improvisation version, which has 2280 utterances [7]. In our assessment, 10-fold Cross Validation is employed.

In addition, the openEAR toolkit [17] is used to extract traditional speech emotion feature log-Mel spectrogram [11] in this work. Then its delta and delta-delta features are computed based on the log-Mel. The log-Mel, delta, and delta-delta features are synthesized into a 3-D log-Mel set as input to minimize the effect of speaker differences. To facilitate batch training, the 3-D log-Mel spectrogram of every utterance with 3 s length by truncating or padding before entering the CoRNN. For the padding process in this study, we employ the zero-padding method.

Our work uses the Python platform to deploy experiments, and the network uses the Adam optimizer to optimize the classification cross entropy. In the network parameters, the batchsize for single training of the CoRNN model is set to 40, the learning rate is set to $10^{-3}$, and the overall dropout of the model is set to 0.2. The last model selected is the one that has been trained across 250 epochs. Owing to the non-uniform label distribution, Unweighted Average Recall (UAR)) [18] is employed as a performance statistic for CoRNN, helping to prevent the model from being overfit to a particular category.

## 4    Experimental Results and Analysis

The experimental findings (UAR(%)) on IEMOCAP dataset using CoRNN are displayed in Table 1. It can be seen that using the CoRNN model proposed in this paper, the UAR can achieve a result of 65.53%, which is a good recognition effect.

**Table 1.** Experimental results on IEMOCAP dataset using CoRNN in terms of UAR(%)

| Models | UAR |
|--------|-------|
| CoRNN  | 65.53 |

### 4.1    Ablation Experiment of CoRNN

In order to better verify the effectiveness of the CoRNN, ablation experiments were carried out respectively:

- **CoRNN**: Extract the 3-D log-Mel feature of speech, and calculate its deltas, and delta-deltas to obtain a three-dimensional Mel spectrogram, which is input to the CoRNN for emotion classification.
- **w/o Conformer**: 3-D log-Mel spectrogram is only input into BiLSTM.
- **w/o BiLSTM**: 3-D log-Mel spectrogram is only input into Conformer.

Table 2 displays the outcomes of the experiment. The findings of the experiment show that the UAR value of the CoRNN model after deleting the Conformer network or BiLSTM network is smaller than the UAR value obtained by the original model, which means that the emotion recognition performance of the separate BiLSTM model and the separate Conformer model is not as good as the CoRNN model. An significant part of the CoRNN model recognition process involves the BiLSTM and Conformer networks.

**Table 2.** Ablation experiment results on IEMOCAP dataset using CoRNN in terms of UAR(%)

| Models | UAR |
|---|---|
| CoRNN | 65.53 |
| w/o Conformer | 63.68 |
| w/o BiLSTM | 59.76 |

## 4.2   Confusion Matrix Analysis

To compare and examine the experimental outcomes even more, confusion matrix is used here. Figure 3 shows the confusion matrix of the CoRNN.

By observing the confusion matrix of CoRNN's experimental results in the figure, it is discovered that the model significantly improves the ability to identify the emotions of anger and sad, but has a poor recognition effect on the emotions of happy and neutral, both of which are often recognized into each other. The reason may be that the small size of the happy category data, its feature acquisition is insufficient. The neutral category has not been able to capture its features well because of its own emotional factors are not prominent enough. These issues will be investigated in future work.

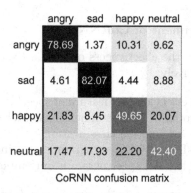

CoRNN confusion matrix

**Fig. 3.** Confusion matrix of CoRNN with the UAR of 65.53% on the IEMOCAP dataset

## 4.3   Comparison with the State-of-the-Art Systems

Here, we would like to compare the proposed CoRNN with other existing systems. To this end, Table 3 shows the comparison between CoRNN and other existing systems on the IEMOCAP dataset in terms of UAR. In which,

- **Raw Speech + CRNN** [19]: Taking raw speech as input, a parallel CNN is used to extract both long-term and short-term interactions from the raw

speech. The features that were captured are fed into a CNN and LSTM classification module. Convolutional layers pick up high-level information, while LSTM layers handle long-term temporal modeling.
- **3-D log-Mel features + ACRNN** [7]: The CRNN model is used to train high-level feature representations of speech segments, the attention model is employed to assess the value of a sequence of high-level representations to the resulting emotion representation, and the three-dimensional Mel spectrogram is obtained as the input.

**Table 3.** Comparison with the state-of-the-art systems on IEMOCAP dataset in terms of UAR(%)

| Systems | Features | Models | UAR |
|---|---|---|---|
| 1 | Raw Speech | CRNN | 60.23 |
| 2 | 3-D Log-Mel | ACRNN | 64.74 |
| Proposed | 3-D Log-Mel | CoRNN | 65.53 |

Our system is first contrasted with the CRNN system. Unlike the system in this paper, which uses hand-crafted acoustic features, the CRNN system uses CNN to extract features from raw speech, which are more general and contextual. However, the data size of the IEMOCAP dataset is too small to capture sufficiently accurate features. The experimental results show that the UAR value of the CoRNN system is increased by 5.3% compared with CRNN system. It reflects the effectiveness of the speech emotion recognition system proposed in this paper.

Second, our system is compared with the commonly used ACRNN systems, both of which take the 3-D log-Mel spectrum as input. Only CNN, BiLSTM and attention mechanism are used in the ACRNN system. The results show that the UAR of the CoRNN system is 0.79% higher than that of the ACRNN system, which indicates that the Conformer model has more advantages in the SER task than the ordinary attention model plus CNN.

To sum up, the proposed system based on CoRNN in this work outperforms other systems to a certain extent.

## 5   Conclusion

This paper modifies ACRNN to enhance SER's performance to better serve emotional speech synthesis. The CoRNN model is proposed that uses the Conformer module to replace the CNN and attention modules in the original model to improve the model's ability to extract global and local features. At the same time, the BiLSTM network is combined to achieve the goal of extracting more comprehensive emotional representation from various aspects. The effect of using

CoRNN for SER is better than that of using ACRNN, according to experimental results on the IEMOCAP dataset. In addition, the proposed system also outperforms some previous systems. Thus the proposed system can provide emotional embeddings containing more emotionally relevant information for emotional speech synthesis systems to improve the emotional expressiveness of synthesized speech.

**Acknowledgments.** The author gratefully acknowledges the support of NSFC (62001173, 62171188).

# References

1. Lei, Y., Yang, S., Xie, L.: Fine-grained emotion strength transfer, control and prediction for emotional speech synthesis. In: 2021 IEEE Spoken Language Technology Workshop (SLT), pp. 423–430 (2020)
2. Zhong, S., Yu, B., Zhang, H.: Exploration of an independent training framework for speech emotion recognition. IEEE Access **8**, 222533–222543 (2020)
3. Han, K., Yu, D., Tashev, I.: Speech emotion recognition using deep neural network and extreme learning machine. In: Interspeech 2014, pp. 223–227. Singapore, Malaysia (2014)
4. Zhang, S., Zhang, S.L., Huang, T., Gao, W.: Speech emotion recognition using deep convolutional neural network and discriminant temporal pyramid matching. IEEE Trans. Multimedia **20**(6), 1576–1590 (2018)
5. Xie, Y., Liang, R., Liang, Z., et al.: Speech emotion classification using attention-based LSTM. IEEE/ACM Trans. Audio Speech Lang. Process. **27**, 1675–1685 (2019)
6. Trigeorgis, G., Ringeval, F., Brueckner, R., et al.: Adieu features? End-to-end speech emotion recognition using a deep convolutional recurrent network, In: 2016 IEEE International Conference on Acoustics, Speech and Signal Processing (ICASSP), pp. 5200–5204 (2016)
7. Chen, M., He, X., Yang, J., Zhang, H.: 3-D Convolutional recurrent neural networks with attention model for speech emotion recognition. IEEE Signal Process. Lett. **25**(10), 1440–1444 (2018)
8. Liu, R., Sisman, B., Gao, G., Li, H.: Expressive TTS training with frame and style reconstruction loss. IEEE Trans. Audio Speech Lang. Process. **29**, 1806–1818 (2021)
9. Gulati, A., Qin, J., Chiu, C.C., et al.: Conformer: convolution-augmented transformer for speech recognition. In: Proceedings of Interspeech, pp. 5036–5040 (2020)
10. Vaswani, A., Shazeer, N., Parmar, N., et al.: Attention is all you need. In: Advances in Neural Information Processing Systems (NIPS 2017), pp. 5998–6008 (2017)
11. Latif, S., Rana, R., Khalifa, S., et al.: Survey of deep representation learning for speech emotion recognition. IEEE Trans. Affect. Comput. **14**(2), 1634–1654 (2021)
12. Graves, A., Schmidhuber, J.: Framewise phoneme classification with bidirectional LSTM and other neural network architectures. Neural Netw. **18**(5–6), 602–610 (2005)
13. Zhang, Y., et al.: MFA-conformer: multi-scale feature aggregation conformer for automatic speaker verification. In: Proceedings of Interspeech 2022, pp. 306–310 (2022)

14. Dai, Z., Yang, Z., Yang, Y., et al.: Transformer-XL: attentive language models beyond a fixed-length context. In: Proceedings of the 57th Annual Meeting of the Association for Computational Linguistics, pp. 2978–2988. Association for Computational Linguistics, Florence, Italy (2019)
15. Lu, Y., Li, Z., He, D., et al.: Understanding and improving transformer from a multi-particle dynamic system point of view, arXiv preprint arXiv:1906.02762 (2019)
16. Busso, C., Bulut, M., Lee, C.C., et al.: IEMOCAP: interactive emotional dyadic motion capture database. Lang. Resour. Eval. **42**, 335–359 (2008)
17. Eyben, F., Wöllmer, M., Schuller, B.: OpenEAR-introducing the Munich open-source emotion and affect recognition toolkit. In: 2009 3rd International Conference on Affective Computing and Intelligent Interaction and Workshops, pp. 1–6 (2009)
18. Schuller, B., Batliner, A., Steidl, S., Seppi, D.: Recognising realistic emotions and affect in speech: state of the art and lessons learnt from the first challenge. Speech Commun. **64**, 1062–1087 (2011)
19. Latif, S., Rana, R., Khalifa, S., et al.: Direct modelling of speech emotion from raw speech, arXiv preprint arXiv:1904.03833 (2019)

# Route Privacy-Preserving Authentication Scheme Based on PUF in VANETs

Hanwen Deng[1,2], Yining Liu[1,2(✉)], and Dong Wang[1,2]

[1] School of Computer Science and Information Security, Guilin University of Electronic Technology, Guilin 541004, China
lyn7311@sina.com
[2] School of Mathematics and Computing Science, Guilin University of Electronic Technology, Guilin 541004, China

**Abstract.** Due to the exposure of transmitted messages in public channels within Vehicular Ad-Hoc Network (VANET), many authentication schemes have been proposed to safeguard security and privacy. And in existing schemes, to expedite the authentication process for Vehicle-to-Infrastructure (V2I) communication, vehicles requesting authentication information from Certification Authority (CA) regarding the RSUs they are expected to encounter before the journey is recommended. However, the viability of the aforementioned schemes rely on two challenging prerequisites: complete trustworthiness of CA and the assurance that the Onboard Units (OBUs), which store secret keys permanently, remain impervious to physical attacks and cloning attempts. Hence in this paper, we propose a route privacy-preserving authentication scheme based on PUF in VANETs. Basing on Oblivious Transfer (OT) method, we let CA complete authentication keys distribution without knowing the route plan of a vehicle. We utilize Physically Unclonable Function (PUF) to minimize the exposure of private key. And as the output of a PUF is easily affected by objective factors, Fuzzy Extractor (FE) is used in our scheme to correct the challenge-response pair of it. In addition, the detailed security analysis proves that our scheme can meet the security requirements. Finally, the experimental analysis suggests that our scheme is lower than the other schemes in terms of time complexity.

**Keywords:** VANETs · Route Privacy · Oblivious Transfer · Physically Unclonable Function · Fuzzy Extractor

## 1 Introduction

In modern society, personal vehicles have become increasingly essential for not only convenience but also for easy mobility. Nonetheless, they give rise to issues such as traffic congestion and car accidents. To address these concerns, Vehicular Ad-Hoc Networks (VANETs) have been devised to provide safe and comfortable travel for passengers. They enable communication between different entities

J. Cai et al. (Eds.): SPNCE 2023, LNICST 525, pp. 278–296, 2025.
https://doi.org/10.1007/978-3-031-73699-5_20

using Wi-Fi technology and, as a result, have become a widely researched technology [2]. VANETs use Vehicle-to-Infrastructure (V2I) and Vehicle-to-Vehicle (V2V) communication, primarily relying on Dedicated Short Range Communication (DSRC) protocol [1]. The three entities taking part in VANETs are Certification Authorities (CAs), Road Side Units (RSUs), and vehicles.

As security is an issue that can not be ignored because transmitted messages are exposed to public channels, requirements such as authentication and integrity must be achieved [8]. Moreover, In most cases, present solutions provide unforgeability and non-repudiation of messages for ensuring message legitimacy [3]. However, traditional security requirements are insufficient for VANETs because of the features of exposed wireless communication, privacy preserving is critical in VANETs [9].

In order to preserve identity privacy, anonymous identity is proposed to hide the real identity of a vehicle. As some adversaries are able to link the content of message if the anonymous identity is fixed [5], many existing authentication schemes in VANETs suggest to generate different and temporary pseudonyms before every communication, which means that unlinkablility is achieved. Meanwhile, aiming at achieving traceability, Conditional Privacy-Preserving Authentication (CPPA) schemes have been proposed to curtail interference by malicious users by reveal their true identities [4].

However, as real time authentication between RSUs and high-speed vehicles is intolerable for the delay-sensitive applications in VANETs [7], route planning is introduced in VANETs to speed up V2I authentication process [6]. For privacy protection, sensitive information like vehicle's route must not be disclosed, even to entities. Due to both CA and RSUs are semi-trusted, additional measures are needed to preserve route privacy. Moreover, the effectiveness of the existing route privacy-preserving authentication schemes depends on two demanding prerequisites which are hard to guarantee: the absolute trustworthiness of CA and the guarantee that OBUs, responsible for permanently storing secret keys, remain impervious to physical attack and cloning attempts. Consequently, this paper proposes an authentication scheme in VANETs that is able to preserve route privacy and resist physical attacks.

## 1.1 Motivation and Contributions

In order to tackle the challenges associated with maintaining route privacy and countering physical attacks in VANETs, we propose a route privacy-preserving authentication scheme based on PUF in VANETs. Our scheme incorporates a k-out-of-n Oblivious Transfer method, allowing a vehicle to securely request authentication keys for RSUs it will encounter while keeping its route plan confidential from CA. Furthermore, we employ a combination of PUFs and fuzzy extraction techniques to effectively safeguard the private key from physical attack. Our key contributions are summarized below.

- We propose a route privacy-preserving authentication scheme based on PUF in designed to fulfill the security and privacy requirements of vehicles in

VANETs. In our scheme, the V2I authentication process is able to sped up with the guarantee that the private key will not be exposed by physical attacks and the achievement of route privacy when CA is not considered to be fully trusted.
- We conducted a detailed analysis of our scheme while ensuring that it meets the necessary security requirements. Our findings suggest that the proposed scheme effectively preserves the privacy of vehicles, even in complex and harsh conditions. Additionally, our scheme is characterized by low time complexity.

## 1.2   Outline of the Rest Paper

Related work is outlined in Sect. 2 In Sect. 3, we introduce the system model and threat model, meanwhile, a overview of Group Rings, Oblivious Transfer Protocol, Physical Unclonable Function and Fuzzy Extractor is provided. We introduce the proposed scheme detailedly in Sect. 4. Next, Sect. 5 evaluates the security of the route privacy-preserving authentication scheme based on PUF in VANETs while Sect. 6 offers a performance evaluation of it. At last, the conclusion of the paper is done by us.

## 2   Related Work

In this section, we provide an overview of different authentication schemes that address privacy and security concerns in VANETs. We examine each protocol individually, discussing their respective pros and cons.

Security is a crucial concern that cannot be overlooked since transmitted messages are vulnerable to public channels. Therefore, it is imperative to ensure that certain requirements, such as authentication and integrity, are met in order to safeguard the confidentiality and accuracy of the information being transmitted [3]. As Traditional security requirements are inadequate for VANETs due to the unique characteristics of exposed wireless communication, privacy preservation is widely research [9]. Aiming at preserving identity privacy, Mundhe et al. [11] utilize ring signature to generate identities to prevent property of vehicles from leakage. Ahamed et al. [12] proposed an efficient anonymous mutual and batch authentication scheme in VANETs, which is able to perform anonymous batch authentication. However, the problem is, the achievements of these existing schemes are not enough for the stability of the system. Because of the lack of the tracing and punishment mechanism, the adversary can disrupt the system without any price.

Therefore, in order to reveal the real identity of adversary, the conditional privacy-preserving authentication is widely researched in the last decades. Based on public key infrastructure (PKI), Khodaei et al. [18] check the certificate to verify the identity of a vehicle. However, as the use of digital certificates can result in increased transmission and storage overhead, CPPA schemes based on identity are proposed. Utilizing bilinear pairing, Zhang et al. [19] proposed to use multiple certificate authorities to achieve conditional privacy. Because there are some disadvantages in performance of bilinear pairing-based schemes which is unacceptable in delay-sensitive scenes, another cryptography tool Elliptic Curve Cryptosystem (ECC) is often used by authentication schemes in VANETs. Based on ECC, Lin et al. [13] proposed a scheme that organizes the vehicles into several groups managed by group leaders so as to reveal the real identities of malicious vehicles. Nevertheless, the high velocity of the vehicle during the journey renders it unsuitable for delay-sensitive applications [7], route planning is introduced in VANETs to speed up V2I authentication process [6]. As it is hard to guarantee the reliability of CA, Liang et al. [22] proposed a route planning authentication scheme aimed at safeguarding the privacy of vehicle routes while acquiring authentication keys from CA. Based on China's remaining theorem, in the route privacy scheme of Yan et al. [23], the malicious vehicles can be revoked efficiently.

While the aforementioned schemes appear to prioritize security and privacy, it is important to acknowledge that the security of OBUs is often perceived as excessively idealistic due to their inherent resource limitations. Given that OBUs frequently store private keys of associated entities, the system's security may be compromised by cloning or physical attacks [24]. In an environment lacking physical security, it is crucial to urgently develop a solution that not only has low cost implications but also effectively mitigates the risk of adversarial compromise of remote unmonitored devices. Baseing on unavoidable variations in the manufacturing process, the Physical Unclonable Function (PUF) is specifically designed to offer a hardware-unique mapping [25]. Renault et al. [26] utilized PUF to spread secret keys by RSUs. According to their scheme, vehicles have the capability to receive emergency tokens from RSUs, and only authorized vehicles possess the decryption capability. Likewise, based on PUF, Umar et al. [28] proposed a identity-based anonymous authentication scheme in VANETs. They employed fundamental cryptographic operations to reduce costs, while also incorporating PUF as a countermeasure against physical attacks. However the schemes mentioned above ignored the fact that chip aging, environmental variations such as temperature, and other factors can introduce noise, which can result in bit flipping and potentially impact the response of PUF. Additional methods should be figured to solve the problem.

In conclusion, the practicality of numerous schemes falls short, prompting our objective to propose an authentication scheme for VANETs that not only safeguards the privacy of vehicle routes but also effectively thwarts physical attacks on the system. Furthermore, we analyze the differences between the related schemes, which are shown in Table 1.

## 3    Preliminaries

In this section, the System Model, Threat Model, Group Rings, Oblivious Transfer Protocol, Physical Unclonable Function, Fuzzy Extractor and Design Goals of the proposed scheme are described respectively.

Table 1. Existing Schemes: A Comparative Summary

| Scheme | Year | Methods | Strenghts | Limitations |
|---|---|---|---|---|
| [11] | 2018 | Ring signature | Providing signature unforgeability | Lack of providing traceability and protection for physical attack |
| [12] | 2018 | Bilinear pairing | Providing mutual authentication and data integrity | Lack of providing traceability and unlinkability. High computational overheads |
| [18] | 2021 | PKI | Providing reduction on certificate revocation lists distribution overhead | High storage overheads. Lack of providing protection for physical attack |
| [19] | 2017 | Bilinear pairing | Providing simultaneous verification of many messages | Lack of unlinkability. High computational overheads |
| [26] | 2021 | PUF | Providing protection against physical attack | Lack of providing methods to correct the noisy response of PUF. Storing response of PUF in RSUs which is unsafe |
| [28] | 2021 | ECC and PUF | Providing low-cost authentication and rotection against physical attack | Lack of providing methods to correct the noisy response of PUF |
| [23] | 2022 | ECC and Chinese remainder theorem | Providing route privacy and malicious vehicles revocation | Lack of providing protection for physical attack |

## 3.1 System Model

Figure 1 illustrates the system model of out route privacy-preserving authentication scheme based on PUF in VANTEs. There are three entities in the model: Certification Authority (CA), Road Side Unit (RSU), and vehicle.

– **CA:** CA plays a crucial role in the proposed scheme by utilizing its exceptional computing and storage capabilities to perform two primary tasks: storing information related to RSUs and vehicles, and facilitating the authentication process between them. Although CA is expected to follow established protocols, it cannot be entirely relied upon. This is due to the fact that CA has an inherent interest in obtaining sensitive privacy information about vehicles, including real-time location and routes.

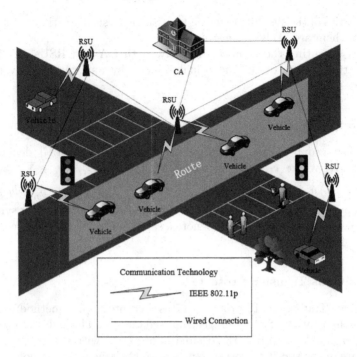

**Fig. 1.** System model.

- **RSU:** RSUs are strategically placed along the roadside and serve as intermediaries between CA and vehicles. Their primary function is to provide driving convenience to vehicles within their coverage area, including information on road conditions. Furthermore, RSUs also facilitate communication between vehicles that are situated within their range.
- **Vehicles:** Each vehicle is equipped with an OBU. OBU is in charge of communicating with other entities: CA, RSUs and OBUs.

## 3.2   Threat Model

In the proposed scheme, the Initial phase and registration phase are performed in a secure channel while the security of the communications between vehicles and the other entities (CA, RSUs, vehicles) could not be guaranteed. What calls for special attention is that although both CA and RSUs should adhere to defined protocols strictly, they are curious about the sensitive privacy of vehicles such as routes and speed. Additionally, the time of all entities is kept in sync and the identities of all RSUs are public. The assumptions of the adversary model are described as follows:

- It is assumed that an attacker has the ability to intercept, modify, delete, and replay any information transmitted over the public channel. This includes all forms of communication that are not securely encrypted or protected.

- The entities of the system are facing the risk of physical attacks, secret parameters of them are likely to be stolen.
- Besides executing the protocol honestly, both CA and RSUs are likely to obtain the privacy of the individual vehicles by analyzing legally received messages.

### 3.3  Group Rings

For a Given group $G$ and a commutative ring $R$. The $R[G]$ denote a set of $\sum_{g_i \in G} r_i g_i$, where $r_i \in R$. In which we have $\sum_{g_i \in G} a_i g_i + \sum_{g_i \in G} b_i g_i = \sum_{g_i \in G} (a_i + b_i) g_i$ and $\sum_{g_i \in G} a_i g_i \cdot \sum_{g_i \in G} b_i g_i = \sum_{g_i \in G} \left( \sum_{g_i g_k = g_i} a_j b_k \right) g_i$ [17]. In this paper, we denote $Z_q[S_m]$ for $R = Z_q$ and $G$ is the $m$-degree symmetric group. What's more, $M_l(Z_q[S_m])$ denote a set of $l * l$ matrices that is considered as a semi-group over $Z_q[S_m]$.

### 3.4  Oblivious Transfer Protocol

An Oblivious Transfer (OT) protocol [17] is a cryptographic method utilized to safeguard the privacy of users in electronic commerce. Through the use of OT, the receiver is able to obtain the desired information without the sender being made aware of the specific selection. In $k$-out-$n$ OT scheme, we denote Alice has $n$ messages and Bob wants to get $k$ of them. Specifically, Bob can only get what he has chosen, meanwhile, Alice knows nothing about Bob's choice [10]. Figure 2 shows the process of the mentioned $k$-out-$n$ OT scheme.

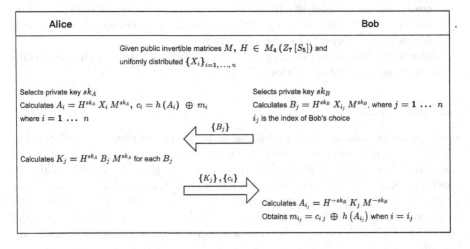

**Fig. 2.** $k$-out-$n$ OT scheme.

### 3.5 Physical Unclonable Function

A Physical Unclonable Function (PUF) is a device that transforms an input bit-string, also known as a challenge, into an output bit, which is referred to as a response. This transformation is achieved by utilizing a specialized microelectronic circuit within the PUF that is highly responsive to variations in signal propagation delay. Variations in manufacturing processes result in slight delays among the fabricated circuits. These delays, combined with the intentional design of the delay-sensitive PUF circuit, impact the response to identical challenge bits across different instances of circuit fabrication. As the delay cannot be controlled, the PUF becomes unclonable, providing a means for unique authentication in devices that incorporate such embedded PUFs [20]. Let $Cha$ and $RE$ denote challenge and the response respectively, in this paper, a PUF function can be described as $RE = PUF(Cha)$.

### 3.6 Fuzzy Extractor

It's worth noting that chip aging, environmental variations such as temperature and some other factors can introduce noise, leading to bit flipping and potentially affecting the PUF response. Consequently, the demand for helper data algorithms becomes imperative to address errors in PUF responses and ensure the independence and uniform distribution of response bits. These algorithms play a crucial role in fulfilling the requirements of PUF-based authentication and key generation processes [21]. In this paper, we introduce Fuzzy Extractor(FE) to generate the reproduction parameter to correct the noisy response. The two algorithms in FE are denoted as $Rep()$ and $Gen()$ respectively. Specifically, let $RE$ denote the input parameter, $(SK, RP) = Gen(RE)$, where $SK$ is secret key and $RP$ is reproduction parameter to be saved. The recovery process is $SK^* = Rep(RE^*, RP)$ where there is a certain error between $RE$ and $RE^*$.

### 3.7 Design Goals

- **Route Privacy:** Under the assumption that CA is partially untrusted, we are supposed to ensure that the routes of vehicles remain undisclosed to any entity.
- **Mutual identity authentication:** In order to ensure the validity of the messages transmitted in the public channel, We need to guarantee that only the senders of the messages could prove that who they are claimed to be.
- **Identity Traceability:** Once a malicious vehicle is detected, its real identity could be revealed by the RSU cluster even though all the vehicles use pseudonyms through the communications.
- **Identity Unlinkability:** This implies that neither attackers nor any other entities can deduce the identity of a specific vehicle by linking two authentication messages transmitted by that vehicle.
- **Physical Attack Resistance:** It means that even if the OBUs of vehicles are under physical attack, for instance, being captured by adversaries, the secret key cannot be obtained by them.

– **Replay Attack Resistance:** This implies that the replayed messages are unable to pass the verification process of any entity within the system.

## 4 The Proposed Scheme

In this section, we introduce our route privacy-preserving authentication scheme. Meanwhile, we list the main notations in proposed scheme as Table 2.

**Table 2.** Main Notations

| Notations | Descriptions |
| --- | --- |
| $h_0, h_1$ | Secure hash functions |
| $M, H$ | Invertible matrices |
| $E_{sym}$ | Symmetry encryption algorithm |
| $RSU_i$ | The $i$-th RSU |
| $v_j$ | The $j$-th vehicle |
| $sk_{CA}, sk_{v_j}$ | Private key of each entity |
| $K_i$ | Authentication key of $RSU_i$ |
| $K_R$ | Symmetric key of all RSUs |
| $RID_j$ | Real identity of $v_j$ |
| $AID_j$ | Associated identity of $v_j$ |
| $PID_j$ | Pseudonym of $v_j$ |
| $PUF$ | Physical unclonable function |
| $Gen, Rep$ | Generation and reproduction functions of fuzzy extractor |

### 4.1 Initial Phase

In this phase, CA is supposed to set necessary parameters of system with the coordination of RSUs.

1. CA chooses a random number $sk_{CA} \in Z_q^*$ as private key, it then selects a secure parameter $\lambda$ and generates two collision-resistance hash functions $h_0 : \{0,1\}^* \to Z_q^*$ and $h_1 : M_4 (Z_7 [S_5]) \to \{0,1\}^\lambda$.
2. To meet the requirements of the system, CA selects a symmetric encryption algorithm denoted as $E_{sym}$. This algorithm is utilized to encrypt the plaintext message $m$ by performing the operation $c = E_{sym}(k, m)$, where $c$ represents the resulting cipher and $k$ is the secret key. Subsequently, the received cipher $c$ is decrypted by executing the operation $m = D_{sym}(k, c)$ to obtain the original plaintext message.
3. We assmue that there are $n$ RSUs in the jurisdiction of CA which indicated as $\{RSU_i\}_{i=1,2,\cdots,n}$. CA assigns $n$ authentication keys $\{K_i\}_{i=1,2,\cdots,n}$ for them and select one symmetric key $K_R$.

4. CA randomly chooses invertible matrices $M, H \in M_4 (Z_7 [S_5])$ and uniformly distributed $\{X_i\}_{i=1,\dots,n}$. Then, CA calculates $A_i = H^{sk_{CA}} X_i M^{sk_{CA}}$ and the ciphers $c_i = h_1 (A_i) \oplus K_i$ for $i = 1, \dots, n$.
5. CA securely retains the values $sk_{CA}$ and $\{c_i\} i = 1, 2, \cdots, n$. It transmits the symmetric key $K_R$ to all RSUs through a secure channel. Additionally, CA publicly broadcasts the following elements: $\left\{ h_0, h_1, E_{sym}, M, H, \{X\}_{i=1,\dots,n} \right\}$.

## 4.2 Registration Phase

Every vehicle needs to register into the system through the registration Phase. Figure 3 reflects the registration process.

1. Let us assume that there will be a maximum of $m$ vehicles. When a vehicle, denoted as $v_j$ ($j = 1, 2, \cdots, m$), signs up, it generates a challenge $Cha_j$ and computes response $R_j$ using PUF as $R_j = PUF(Cha_j)$. Subsequently, in order to obtain the reproduction parameter $RP_j$, $v_j$ calculates $(sk_{v_j}, RP_j) = Gen(R_j)$. It is worth mentioning that $sk_{v_j}$ will not be stored. Finally, it sends its real identity $RID_j \in Z_q^*$ to CA.
2. Upon receiving the $RID_j$ from $v_j$, CA chooses a random number $r_j$ for $v_j$ and generates its corresponding associated identity as $AID_j = RID_j \oplus h_0(sk_{CA}||r_j)$. It is important to note that CA has the capability to periodically update the value of $AID_j$. Then, the pseudonym of $v_j$ is generated by calculating $PID_j = E_{sym}(K_R, AID_j)$. Subsequently, CA transmits the associated identity and pseudonym $\{AID_j, PID_j\}$ to the respective vehicle.

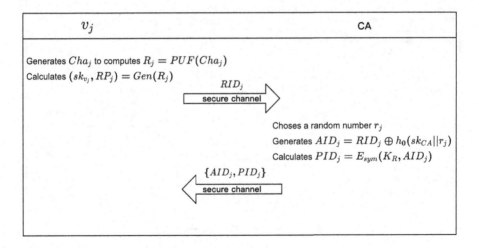

**Fig. 3.** Registration phase.

### 4.3   Route Planning Phase

In this phase, we introduce the route planning phase before a journey of $v_j$. Figure 4 reflects the route planning process

1. The vehicle $v_j$ chooses an appropriate shortest path algorithm such as SPFA algorithm. Suppose that the result of the shortest path algorithm suggests that $v_j$ would pass $Path_j = \{RSU_1, RSU_2, \cdots, RSU_a, \cdots, RSU_w\}$ ($w <= n$). Then it obtains $R_j^* = PUF(Cha_j)$ and generates it secret key by calculating $sk_{v_j} = Rep(R_j^*, RP_j)$.

2. According to the $Path_j$, the vehicle $v_j$ keeps its choice $ch$ ($ch = 1, \cdots, w$), and calculates $B_{ch} = H^{sk_{v_j}} X_{j_i} M^{sk_{v_j}}$ for $1 \leq j_i \leq n$. In addition, $v_j$ generates the timestamp $t_0$ and constructs $\iota_{j,1} = h_0(AID_j\|t_0)$, $\iota_{j,2} = h_1(B_{ch})$ and sends $\{\iota_{j,1}, \iota_{j,2}, t_0, \{B_{ch}\}, AID_j\}$ to CA.

3. On receiving message from $v_j$, CA checks the legality of $AID_j$ and verifies $\iota_{j,1}$, $\iota_{j,2}$ and $t_0$. If the checking process succeeds, CA computes $R_{ch} = H^{sk_{CA}} B_{ch} M^{sk_{CA}}$ for $ch = 1, 2, \cdots, w$, generates the timestamp $t_1$ to constructs $\mu_1 = \{h_0(t_1\|c_i)\}_{i \in \{1,2,...,n\}}$, $\mu_2 = \{h_1(R_{ch})\}_{ch \in \{1,2,...,w\}}$ and sends them back to $v_j$ with all ciphers $\{c_i\}_{i \in \{1,2,...,n\}}$.

4. In order to get the authentication keys of wanted RSUs in $Path_j$, $v_j$ first verifies $\mu_1$, $\mu_2$ and $t_1$. If the verification succeeds, it computes $A_{j_i} = H^{-sk_{v_j}} R_{ch} M^{-sk_{v_j}}$. Finally, $v_j$ could obtain $K_{ch} = c_{j_i} \oplus h_1(A_{j_i})$ while CA could not know which $c_i$ the $v_j$ has chosen.

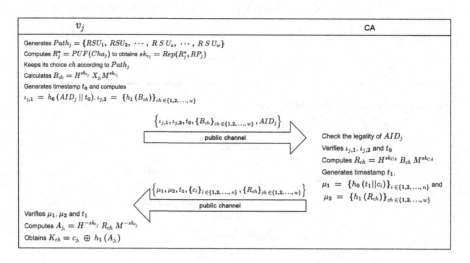

**Fig. 4.** Route Planning phase.

### 4.4   Mutual Authentication Phase

As both of the vehicles and RSUs are probably attacked, before they share information with each other, they have to do the mutual authentication. Figure 5 reflects the mutual authentication process.

1. When the vehicle $v_j$ enters the coverage of $RSU_i$, both of them need to prove their validation. The vehicle $v_j$ selects a random number $r_{j_i} \in Z_q^*$. Then, $v_j$ generates the timestamp $t_2$ and message $m_0$, to calculates $sm_{j_i} = E_{sym}(K_i, AID_j \|t_2\| m_0 \|PID_j\| r_{j_i})$, $\phi_j = h_0(PID_j \|AID_j\| sm_{j_i} \|t_2)$, where $j_i \in \{1, \ldots, n\}$. Finally, $\{sm_{j_i}, \phi_j, t_2, PID_j, AID_j\}$ is sent to $RSU_i$.
2. After $RSU_i$ receives, it first calculates $content_{j_i} = D_{sym}(K_i, sm_{j_i})$ to decrypt the cipher. The checking process is to judge whether $\phi_j$ is valid using hash function $h_0$. If it passes, then it calculates $AID_j^* = D_{sym}(K_R, PID_j)$, only if the equation $AID_j^* = AID_j$ holds, it means that the authentication of $v_j$ is complete, otherwise, $RSU_i$ rejects the request. Next, $RSU_i$ generates the timestamp $t_3$ and message $m_1$, calculates $sm_{i_j} = E_{sym}(K_i, h_0(r_{j_i} + 1) \|t_3\| m_1)$ and $\sigma_i = h_0(i \|t_3\| m_1 \|sm_{i_j})$. It sends $\{sm_{i_j}, \sigma_i, t_3, i\}$ back to $v_j$ at last.
3. On receiving the response, $v_j$ calculates $content_{i_j} = D_{sym}(K_i, sm_{i_j})$. It then verifies the validation of $\sigma_i$ from $content_{i_j}$, if it passes, the communication between $v_j$ and $RSU_i$ is finally established.

## 5   Security Analysis

In this section, the security analysis is provided to demonstrate that the proposed scheme has meets all of out design goals.

**Theorem 1.** *The proposed scheme can achieve route privacy.*

*Proof.* During the route planning phase, vehicle $v_j$ obtains authentication keys through Oblivious Transfer (OT). The only relevant parameter for $v_j$ in CA's possession is $B_{ch} = H^{sk_{v_j}} X_{j_i} M^{sk_{v_j}}$. If CA intends to determine the route, it must deduce $X_{j_i}$ by factoring $B_{ch}$ into $H^{sk_{v_j}}$, $X_{j_i}$, and $M^{sk_{v_j}}$, then identify the value of $j_i$ by comparing $X_{j_i}$ with other matrices. However, this task cannot be accomplished due to the protection provided by $H^{sk_{v_j}}$ and $M^{sk_{v_j}}$, as it is based on the Group Factorization Problem [29].

**Theorem 2.** *The proposed scheme can achieve mutual identity authentication.*

*Proof.* In the proposed scheme, since RSUs are semi-trusted, RSUs and vehicles have to complete identity authentication with each other before establishing communication channel.

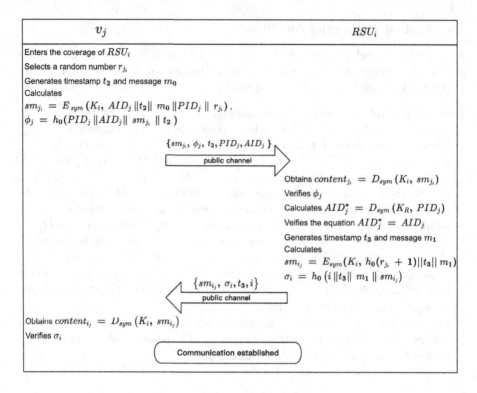

**Fig. 5.** Mutual authentication phase.

- On the one hand, the vehicle $v_j$ obtains the authentication key $K_i$ of $RSU_i$ in the route planning phase. If the adversary wants to disguise as a legal vehicle, it needs to obtain the matrix $X_{j_i}$ to get $K_i$ to encrypt message using $E_{\text{sym}}$. However, it is tough for it as the proof of **Theorem 1** mentioned above. If the adversary wants to tamper the message of $v_j$, $RSU_i$ can penetrate the attack by the hash function $h_0$ and reject it.
- On the other hand, $RSU_i$ has access to the random number $r_{j_i}$ generated by $v_j$. In order to establish its legitimacy, $RSU_i$ is required to respond with $h_0(r_{j_i}+1)$. Importantly, only the authorized RSU possesses the authentication key necessary to decrypt the cipher transmitted by $v_j$.

**Theorem 3.** *The proposed scheme can achieve identity traceability.*

*Proof.* In our proposed scheme, when a malicious vehicle $v_j$ is detected, CA is able to reveal its real identity because $AID_j = RID_j \oplus h_0(sk_{CA}||r_j)$ and CA is responsible to store $sk_{CA}$ and $r_j$. Moreover, in order to guarantee that the associate identity can be traced, $RSU_i$ is supposed to verifies the availability of the pseudonyms by calculating $AID_j^* = D_{sym}(K_R, PID_j)$, only if the equation $AID_j^* = AID_j$ holds, it means that the authentication of $v_j$ is complete. In the event that a malicious vehicle $v_j$ is detected, CA has the capability to disclose its real identity. This is possible because $AID_j = RID_j \oplus h_0(sk_{CA}||r_j)$, and CA is responsible for securely storing both $sk_{CA}$ and $r_j$. Furthermore, to ensure traceability of the pseudonyms sent by $v_j$, $RSU_i$ is required to verify the validity of it by computing $AID_j^* = D_{sym}(K_R, PID_j)$. Only when the equation $AID_j^* = AID_j$ holds true, it signifies that the authentication of $v_j$ is successful.

**Theorem 4.** *The proposed scheme can achieve unlinkability.*

*Proof.* Due to the periodic updating of vehicle pseudonyms, it becomes impossible for an adversary to establish a connection between multiple messages originating from the same vehicle.

**Theorem 5.** *The proposed scheme can resist physical attack and cloning.*

*Proof.* The private key $sk_{v_j}$ of vehicle $v_j$ is not directly stored in OBU. To derive its private key, $v_j$ is required to compute the noisy results as $skn_j = PUF(Cha_j)$. Subsequently, it calculates $sk_{v_j}$ using the reproduction parameter $RP_j$ as $sk_{v_j} = Rep(skn_j, RP_j)$. As a result, even if OBU becomes a target of physical attacks or cloning attempts, adversaries are unable to obtain $sk_{v_j}$ and exert influence on other entities.

**Theorem 6.** *The proposed scheme can resist replay attack.*

*Proof.* Each time an entity intends to transmit messages via the public channel, timestamps and random numbers are integrated into the public messages. Consequently, adversaries are unable to successfully pass the verification process due to the inclusion of freshness indicators.

## 6   Performance Evaluation

This section presents a comprehensive analysis of the computational and communication workload associated with the proposed scheme, along with a comparative assessment against several recent schemes. To assess the computation overhead, we implemented the proposed scheme using Java 15 on a desktop computer featuring an Apple M1 Pro processor with a clock frequency of 3.20 GHz, running on macOS 13 operating system. The average operation time of the simulation, calculated over 1000 iterations, is displayed in Table 3. It is important to note that the computational burden of certain operations, such as XOR, has been disregarded due to their relatively minor impact on efficiency when compared to other operations.

### 6.1   Computational Overhead

In the proposed scheme, as the registration phase is an one-time process, we ignore the computation burden of it in this subsection. In route planning phase, as we assume that the total number of RSUs is $n$ and the path of the vehicles would include $w$ RSUs. To begin with, in order to obtain its secret key, the

**Table 3.** Execution

| Notation | Description | Execution time (ms) |
|---|---|---|
| $T_h$ | Hash function execution | 0.001 |
| $T_a^{ecc}$ | Point addition execution on ECC | 0.016 |
| $T_m^{ecc}$ | Scalar multiplication execution on ECC | 0.669 |
| $T_i^{mtx}$ | Matrix inverse execution | 0.002 |
| $T_m^{mtx}$ | Matrix multiplication execution | 0.003 |
| $T_e$ | Encrytion of AES | 0.037 |
| $T_d$ | Decryption of AES | 0.016 |
| $T_{PUF}$ | PUF simulation | 0.113 |
| $T_{fe}$ | Fuzzy extractor execution | 0.417 |

vehicle is supposed to perform PUF and FE once, then it needs to execute matrix multiplication $2\log sk_{v_j} + 2w$ times, hash function $w + 1$ times to prepare for the request. On receiving the response from CA, the vehicle $v_j$ is supposed to perform 2 matrix inverse, $2w$ matrix multiplications and $w + n$ hash evaluations. Therefore, $(2\log sk_{v_j} + 4w)T_m^{mtx} + (n + 2w + 1)T_h + 2T_i^{mtx} + T_{PUF} + T_{fe} = 0.006\log sk_{v_j} + 0.014w + 0.001n + 0.58ms$ is cost by $v_j$. As for CA, it needs to perform hash function $2w + n + 1$ times and matrix multiplication $2w$ times. The total cost of CA is $0.008w + 0.001n + 0.001ms$. Figure 6 reflects the relationship between the system computation burden, the number of RSUs in the route of vehicle and the total computation burden in this phase.

**Table 4.** Comparison of computation overheads in authentication phase

| Scheme | Computation overheads |
|---|---|
| [10] | $8T_h + 11T_m^{ecc} + 4T_a^{ecc}$ |
| [14] | $11T_h + 4T_m^{ecc}$ |
| [15] | $2T_h + 5T_m^{ecc}$ |
| [16] | $10T_h + 10T_m^{ecc} + 3T_a^{ecc}$ |
| Our scheme | $5T_h + 2T_e + 3T_d$ |

In the mutual authentication phase, the vehicle $v_j$ ought to Before sending message, the vehicle $v_j$ ought to perform AES encryption and hash function once respectively. On receiving the response from $RSU_i$, in order to verify the validation of $RSU_i$, it has to perform AES decryption once and hash function once finally. Thus, the computation burden of $v_j$ in mutual authentication phase is $2T_h + T_e + T_d = 0.054ms$. As mentioned above, in order to check the validation of $v_j$, $RSU_i$ has to obtain $PID_j$ and then deduce $AID_j$. Double AES decryption and a hash operation would be done. Then $RSU_i$ needs to execute AES

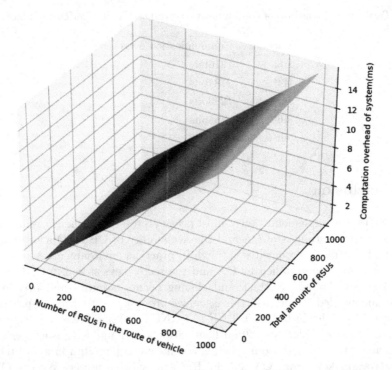

**Fig. 6.** Relationship between system computation overheads, number of RSUs in the route of vehicle and total computation overheads.

decryption once and hash function twice respectively to response. The total cost of $RSU_i$ is $3T_h + T_e + 2T_d = 0.072ms$. In Table 4, we list the comparison of computation burden between other related schemes as they could be implemented in the same way.

## 6.2  Communication Overhead

In this subsection, our focus is solely on analyzing the communication cost associated with the mutual authentication process, as the route planning phase occurs only occasionally. To estimate the communication overhead, we make reasonable assumptions regarding the bit-lengths of the output of hash function (SHA-128) and symmetric encryption (AES-128) are both 128bits. The length of an ECC point, a timestamp are 160bits and 32bits respectively. We calculate and compare the communication overhead of the protocols in Table 5.

Hence, our scheme not only offers enhanced security compared to other relevant schemes but also maintains a lower overhead, making it more suitable for the requirements of VANETs.

**Table 5.** Comparison of communication overhead in authentication phase

| Scheme | Communication overhead |
|---|---|
| [10] | 1216bits |
| [14] | 2784bits |
| [15] | 1280bits |
| [16] | 864bits |
| Our scheme | 832bits |

## 7 Conclusion

In VANETs, the implementation of most privacy-preserving schemes relies on the complete trustworthiness of CA and the availability of OBUs. Obviously, guaranteeing these two prerequisites is tough in practical environment. As the route of a vehicle may be obtained by CA and the secret keys stored in OBUs might be leaked when physical attack and cloning occurs, security and privacy can not be safeguarded. To address this issue, we propose a route privacy-preserving authentication scheme based on PUF in VANETs. While preserving route privacy, our scheme accelerates V2I authentication speed and defends against physical attacks. To implement our scheme, a vehicle can plan its route and request authentication keys from CA for the RSUs it will encounter. We use OT to ensure that CA has no knowledge of which authentication keys the vehicle has chosen. Furthermore, a vehicle's secret key must be generated by PUF using its challenge. And as s the output of a PUF is easily affected by objective factors, fuzzy extractor is used in our scheme to correct the noise. Finally, our scheme has a lower computation burden compared to other relevant schemes.

## References

1. Cui, J., Wei, L., Zhang, J., et al.: An efficient message-authentication scheme based on edge computing for vehicular ad hoc networks. IEEE Trans. Intell. Transp. Syst. **20**(5), 1621–1632 (2018)
2. Khan, A.A., Abolhasan, M., Ni, W., et al.: A hybrid-fuzzy logic guided genetic algorithm (H-FLGA) approach for resource optimization in 5G VANETs. IEEE Trans. Veh. Technol. **68**(7), 6964–6974 (2019)
3. Wei, L., Cui, J., Xu, Y., et al.: Secure and lightweight conditional privacy-preserving authentication for securing traffic emergency messages in VANETs. IEEE Trans. Inf. Forensics Secur. **16**, 1681–1695 (2020)
4. Wang, Y., Liu, Y., Tian, Y.: ISC-CPPA: improverd-security certificateless conditional privacy-preserving authentication scheme with revocation. IEEE Trans. Veh. Technol. **71**(11), 12304–12314 (2022)
5. Saini, K., Namdev, K., Rai, K.: TMAPS: a trust-based mutual authentication and privacy in VANET. In: 2022 3rd International Conference for Emerging Technology (INCET), pp. 1–7. IEEE (2022)

6. Ahmad, A., Din, S., Paul, A., et al.: Real-time route planning and data dissemination for urban scenarios using the internet of things. IEEE Wirel. Commun. **26**(6), 50–55 (2019)
7. Zhang, H., Yu, J., Obaidat, M.S., et al.: Secure edge-aided computations for social internet-of-things systems. IEEE Trans. Comput. Soc. Syst. **9**(1), 76–87 (2020)
8. Song, J., Liu, Y., Shao, J., et al.: A dynamic membership data aggregation (DMDA) protocol for smart grid. IEEE Syst. J. **14**(1), 900–908 (2019)
9. Lin, C., He, D., Huang, X., et al.: BCPPA: a blockchain-based conditional privacy-preserving authentication protocol for vehicular ad hoc networks. IEEE Trans. Intell. Transp. Syst. **22**(12), 7408–7420 (2020)
10. Zhang, X., Zhong, H., Cui, J., et al.: LBVP: a lightweight batch verification protocol for fog-based vehicular networks using self-certified public key cryptography. IEEE Trans. Veh. Technol. **71**(5), 5519–5533 (2022)
11. Mundhe, P., Yadav, V.K., Verma, S., et al.: Efficient lattice-based ring signature for message authentication in VANETs. IEEE Syst. J. **14**(4), 5463–5474 (2020)
12. Ahamed, A.B.S., Kanagaraj, N., Azees, M.: EMBA: an efficient anonymous mutual and batch authentication schemes for vanets. In: 2018 Second International Conference on Inventive Communication and Computational Technologies (ICICCT), pp. 1320–1326. IEEE (2018)
13. Lin, X., Sun, X., Ho, P.H., et al.: GSIS: a secure and privacy-preserving protocol for vehicular communications. IEEE Trans. Veh. Technol. **56**(6), 3442–3456 (2007)
14. Wei, L., Cui, J., Zhong, H., et al.: Proven secure tree-based authenticated key agreement for securing V2V and V2I communications in VANETs. IEEE Trans. Mob. Comput. **21**(9), 3280–3297 (2021)
15. Kumar, V., Ahmad, M., Mishra, D., et al.: RSEAP: RFID based secure and efficient authentication protocol for vehicular cloud computing. Veh. Commun. **22**, 100213 (2020)
16. Wang, J., Zhu, Y.: Secure two-factor lightweight authentication protocol using self-certified public key cryptography for multi-server 5G networks. J. Netw. Comput. Appl. **161**, 102660 (2020)
17. Wang, X., Kuang, X., Li, J., et al.: Oblivious transfer for privacy-preserving in VANET's feature matching. IEEE Trans. Intell. Transp. Syst. **22**(7), 4359–4366 (2020)
18. Khodaei, M., Papadimitratos, P.: Efficient, scalable, and resilient vehicle-centric certificate revocation list distribution in VANETs. In: Proceedings of the 11th ACM Conference on Security & Privacy in Wireless and Mobile Networks, pp. 172–183 (2018)
19. Zhang, L., Wu, Q., Domingo-Ferrer, J., et al.: Distributed aggregate privacy-preserving authentication in VANETs. IEEE Trans. Intell. Transp. Syst. **18**(3), 516–526 (2016)
20. Millwood, O., Miskelly, J., Yang, B., et al.: PUF-phenotype: a robust and noise-resilient approach to aid group-based authentication with DRAM-PUFs using machine learning. IEEE Trans. Inf. Forensics Secur. **18**, 2451–2465 (2023)
21. Badshah, A., Waqas, M., Muhammad, F., et al.: AAKE-BIVT: anonymous authenticated key exchange scheme for blockchain-enabled internet of vehicles in smart transportation. IEEE Trans. Intell. Transp. Syst. **24**(2), 1739–1755 (2022)
22. Liang, Y., Liu, Y., Gupta, B.B.: PPRP: preserving-privacy route planning scheme in VANETs. ACM Trans. Internet Technol. **22**(4), 1–18 (2022)
23. Yan, Z., Zhang, J.: Path privacy-preserving scheme based on oblivious transfer protocol. In: 2022 10th International Conference on Intelligent Computing and Wireless Optical Communications (ICWOC), pp. 6–10. IEEE (2022)

24. Alfadhli, S.A., Lu, S., Chen, K., et al.: MFSPV: a multi-factor secured and lightweight privacy-preserving authentication scheme for VANETs. IEEE Access **8**, 142858–142874 (2020)
25. Wallrabenstein, J.R.: Practical and secure IoT device authentication using physical unclonable functions. In: 2016 IEEE 4th International Conference on Future Internet of Things and Cloud (FiCloud), pp. 99–106. IEEE (2016)
26. Renault, É., Mühlethaler, P., Boumerdassi, S.: Communication security in vanets based on the physical unclonable function. In: ICC 2021-IEEE International Conference on Communications, pp. 1–6. IEEE (2021)
27. Umar, M., Islam, S.K.H., Mahmood, K., et al.: Provable secure identity-based anonymous and privacy-preserving inter-vehicular authentication protocol for VANETS using PUF. IEEE Trans. Veh. Technol. **70**(11), 12158–12167 (2021)
28. Habeeb, M., Kahrobaei, D., Koupparis, C., Shpilrain, V.: Public key exchange using semidirect product of (semi)groups. In: Jacobson, M., Locasto, M., Mohassel, P., Safavi-Naini, R. (eds.) ACNS 2013. LNCS, vol. 7954, pp. 475–486. Springer, Heidelberg (2013). https://doi.org/10.1007/978-3-642-38980-1_30
29. Habeeb, M.E., Kahrobaei, D., Koupparis, C., et al.: Public exchange using semidirect product of (semi)groups. In: Applied Cryptography and Network Security (2013)

# Stable NICE Model-Based Picture Generation for Generative Steganography

Xutong Cui[1], Zhili Zhou[2]($\boxtimes$), Jianhua Yang[3], Chengsheng Yuan[1], and Weixuan Tang[2]

[1] Engineering Research Center of Digital Forensics, Ministry of Education, Nanjing University of Information Science and Technology, Nanjing 210044, China
yuancs@nuist.edu.cn

[2] Institute of Artificial Intelligence, Guangzhou University, Guangdong 510006, China
zhou_zhili@163.com, twei@gzhu.edu.cn

[3] School of Cyber Security, Guangdong Polytechnic Normal University, Guangdong 510006, China
yangjh86@gpnu.edu.cn

**Abstract.** Steganography is one of most important techniques for covert communication. In recent years, generative steganography, which transforms a secret information into a generated picture, is a prospective steganography-resistant technique. Nevertheless, it is difficult to achieve a good trade-off between information hiding ability and extraction accuracy because of the low efficiency and irreversibility of the secret-to-picture conversion. In order to solve this problem, this paper proposes a secret message-driven picture generation solution for generative steganography. The presented SM-IG scheme is founded on the design of a stable version of the Nearly Independent Component Estimation (Stable NICE) model, allowing for a stable bijection mapping between a potential space with simple distributions and an picture space with complex distributions. During the secret to picture conversion, a latent vector is constructed, driven by a given secret message, which is then mapped to the generated picture via the Stable NICE modelAs a result, the secret information is eventually converted into the generated picture. Due to the good efficiency and reversibility of the SM-IG scheme, this steganography method has high hiding capability and accurate message extraction accuracy. The experiments prove that the proposed SM-IG can simultaneously realise good-level hiding capacity (as much as 4 bpp) and precise extraction accuracy (close to 100% accuracy) without compromising the required resistance to detection and imperceptibility.

**Keywords:** Steganography · Generative steganography · Information hiding · Digital forensics

© ICST Institute for Computer Sciences, Social Informatics and Telecommunications Engineering 2025
Published by Springer Nature Switzerland AG 2025. All Rights Reserved
J. Cai et al. (Eds.): SPNCE 2023, LNICST 525, pp. 297–314, 2025.
https://doi.org/10.1007/978-3-031-73699-5_21

# 1 Introduction

Picture steganography is a technique for hiding secret messages in cover pictures, allowing secret communication without suspicion [1–3]. The advantage of steganography is that it hides the happening of secret communication and thus ensures the safety of secret message transmission [1–3].

Generally, the traditional steganography methods take an existing picture as a cover and secret message is embedded in it by modifying the cover picture. However, they will inevitably cause the cover picture to become distorted, especially with high concealed payloads. In this case, a well-designed implicit analyzer is able to detect the existence of hidden information [4]. Some researchers have proposed "generative steganography" to resist the detection of steganalyzers [5–7]. However, these methods can only convert short secret messages into low-dimensional inputs to the generative model, and can only construct one-way mappings between the input message and the picture content, making the secret to picture conversion process low efficiency and non-reversible. As a result, very limited hiding power or the inability to accurately extract secret messages from the generated picture limits the applicability of these methods to practical steganography tasks.

Based on the above analyses, in order to realize large-volume hiding and precise extraction of secret messages, how to design efficient reversible conversion between secret information and pictures is crucial for generating steganography. To this end, we design a flow-based generative model, *i.e..*, Stable version of Near Independent Component Estimation (Stable NICE) model, to enable a stable bijective mapping between high-dimensional potential vectors and pictures. Based on the designed Stable NICE model, we propose the SM-IG scheme to achieve an efficient and reversible conversion between the secret information and produced pictures for messages hiding and extraction.

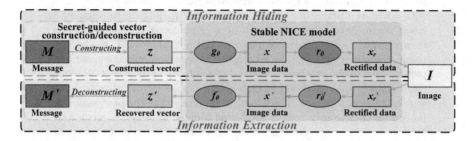

**Fig. 1.** The framework of SM-IG scheme for generative steganography based on the Stable NICE model.

Figure 1 illustrates the structure of the SM-IG steganography generation scheme on the basis of the stable NICE model. The proposed steganographic approach has the following advantages over existing generative steganographic approaches.

(1) The proposed SM-IG scheme demonstrates high efficiency and reversibility, resulting in a maximum high hiding capacity (up to 4 $bpp$) and almost 100% accuracy in the extraction of secret messages.
(2) The pictures produced can remain high quality as the hidden payload grows.
(3) Existing steganographers are still unlikely to defeat the proposed steganography method because the steganography method generates a new picture as a steganographic picture instead of modifying the existing picture for information hiding.

## 2   Related Work

Generative steganography, different from conventional steganography, allows you to hide secret messages without having to change the cover picture, providing a promising performance of anti-detectability. Existing methods for generative steganography can be broadly classified into two categories: methods based on texture synthesis and methods based on GANs.

Xu et al. [8] converted secret messages directly into complex texture pictures for steganography. Li et al. [9] converted the secret information to a fingerprint picture by mapping it to fingerprint phase. However, the meaningless of texture pictures could arouse the suspicion of attackers.

Luckily, the modern generative deep learning models, i.e., Generative Adversarial Networks (GANs) [10], are capable of producing new significant pictures which look very real, i.e., "realistic-looking pictures". Consequently, a number of generative steganographic approaches converted the secret messages into the realistic-looking pictures based on GANs. Cao et al. [11] converted a given secret message to attribute labels of the anime characters and generated anime characters with GAN [12] constrained by the labels. Then, Illustration2Vec [13] is used to extract the labels of anime characters and then convert them to secret messages by long short-term memory network (LSTM).Qin et al. [14] established a mapping dictionary between object labels and binary message sequences after detection by using Faster RCNN [15], and then employed the GANs to generate stego-picture with corresponding labels. However, the hiding capacity of these generative steganography methods is very limited, since very limited amount of information can be carried by simple labels and semantic information.

To enhance hiding capacity, some picture generative steganographic approaches constructed a mapping between secret message and a noise signal, and then fed the noise signal to GANs for stego-picture generation. Hu et al. [7,16] fed the noise signal encoded by the secret message to Deep Convolutional GAN (DCGAN) [17], since the DCGAN has the ability of generating high-quality stego-pictures that looks realistic. To improve the quality of the generated picture, Li et al. [18] adopted Wasserstein GAN Gradient Penalty (WGAN-GP) [19] instead of DCGAN for steganography. Arifianto et al. [20] converted the secret message to a word vector by employing a word2vec model [21]. The word vector is fed to the GANs to generate the stego-picture. However, GANs only establish a unidirectional mapping relationship from low-dimensional input information to high-dimensional pictures. Thus, the above GANs-based steganography methods may fail to precisely recover secret messages from these produced pictures, particularly when the payload is high.

In conclusion, it is difficult for the current generative steganographic methods to realise a feasible balance between hiding power and secret message extraction accuracy, which restricts the task of steganography in practice.

To achieve accurate extraction and high-capacity hiding of secret information simultaneously, in this paper, we attempt to design the Stable NICE model to enable a stable bijective-mapping between high-dimensional latent vectors and pictures. Then, based on the designed Stable NICE model, we propose the SM-IG scheme to realize an efficient and reversible transformation between the secret message and generated picture for information hiding and extraction. Consequently, while maintaining the anti-detectability and imperceptibility desirable for generative steganography, the suggested method achieves high-level information hiding capacity and precise message extraction simultaneously.

## 3   Designed Stable Nice Model

In this paper, the SM-IG scheme is proposed for picture generative steganography, which is implemented by a flow-based model. Thus, to implement the scheme, we first design a proper flow model, *i.e.*, Stable NICE model, to realize a stable bijective-mapping between latent space and picture space.

NICE model enables a bijective-mapping between picture space and latent space. However, as the bijective-mapping is not stable enough, directly applying the original NICE model for the SM-IG scheme will affect the information extraction significantly. Further details are below.

As Fig. 1 illustrates, in the secret message to picture conversion process of SM-IG scheme, driven by a provided secret message, a latent vector $z$ is constructed and then mapped to an picture data $x$ for picture generation. The generated picture is then reverse mapped to the latent vector to extract information. If the original NICE model is employed to map the constructed latent vector $z$ to the picture data $x$, it is found that $x$ contains some exceptional elements, which are out of the value range [0,1]. That is mainly caused by the finite size of training dataset and the errors of bijective-mapping between continuous latent space and discrete picture space. To generate the picture from $x$, the original NICE model directly removes these exceptional elements in $x$. The information loss of $x$ makes the recovered latent vector $z'$ quite different from the original one $z$, as shown in Fig. 2(a). That will affect the extraction of secret message significantly. Therefore, it is not a good choice to directly apply the original NICE model to implement the SM-IG scheme for generative steganography.

To address this issue, it is straightforward to normalize all the values of picture data $x$ to the range of [0,1] for picture generation. However, if some exceptional elements of $x$ have very large or small values, the normalization causes a lot of elements of $x$ to be changed significantly, which will decrease the quality of generated picture, as shown in Fig. 2. To accurately extract secret message

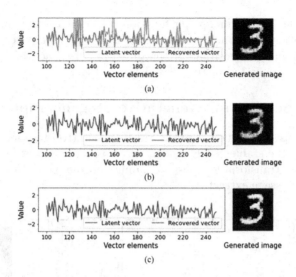

**Fig. 2.** Different recovered latent vectors and generated pictures, which are obtained by (a) NICE model with removal of exceptional elements of picture data, (b) NICE model with picture data normalization, and (c) NICE model with picture data rectification (Stable NICE model), respectively.

without affecting the qualities of generated pictures, we design a stable version of NICE model, called as Stable NICE model, by adding a pair of rectification functions into the original NICE model, as shown in Fig. 1. The rectification functions are described as follows.

Instead of simply normalizing the original picture data $x$, an invertible rectification function $r_\alpha$ is learned to rectify $x$ before picture generation, and its inverse function is used to recover the original picture data $x$ from the generated picture. The rectification function and its inverse function are defined by

$$x_r = r_\Theta(x) = [\tanh(\alpha_1 x + \alpha_2) + 1]/2 \tag{1}$$

$$x = r_\Theta^{-1}(x_r) = \frac{1}{2\alpha_1} \log_2 \left( \frac{x_r}{1 - x_r} \right) - \frac{\alpha_2}{\alpha_1} \tag{2}$$

The function $r_\Theta(\cdot)$ensures that the exceptional elements of $x$ are rectified to the range of [0,1] while most of other elements are adjusted slightly so as to generate the high-quality picture; Its inverse function $r_\Theta^{-1}(\cdot)$ allows accurate recovery of original picture data and latent vector for information extraction.

To learn the function parameters, we consider two objectives: (1) Minimizing the difference between the recovered latent vector $z'$ and the original one $z$, and (2) Minimizing the difference between the picture $I$ generated by rectifying the data $x$ and the picture $I_0$ generated by directly removing the exceptional elements of $x$. Thus, the function parameters are learned by Genetic algorithm using the following equation. More details of learning process are given in Sect. 5.

$$\min_{\alpha \in A}(\|z' - z\| + \|I - I_0\|) \tag{3}$$

Owing to the bijective-mapping functions of original NICE model and the added rectification functions, the Stable NICE model can ensure good stability of bijective-mapping between latent space and picture space while maintaining high qualities of generated pictures, as shown in Fig. 2(c).

## 4     SM-IG Scheme for Generative Steganography

Figure 1 illustrates the structure of the SM-IG generative steganography scheme on the basis of the stable NICE model, which is composed of two phases: the secret to picture transform for message hiding and the secret to picture inverse transform for message extraction.

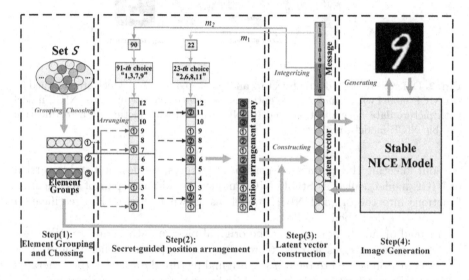

**Fig. 3.** The illustration of S2I transformation for information hiding.

### 4.1     S2I Transformation for Information Hiding

As shown in Fig. 3, the task of secret messages to pictures convert is to hide messages. First, we group a set of randomly sampled elements and choose a part of proper elements from each group. Then, a high-dimensional latent vector $z$ is constructed by arranging the selected elements at the corresponding relative locations, driven by the given information. Finally, the built vector $z$ is mapped to a generated picture $I$ via the Stable NICE model. Consequently, long secret messages can be naturally hidden in the generated picture $I$.

Thus, the processing of the S2I transform consists of four steps: element grouping and selection, secret-guided location arrangement of elements, latent vector construction, and picture generation, as shown in Fig. 3. The specific steps are as follows.

**Step (1): Element grouping and choosing.** In NICE model, It is common to randomly sample a suite of $N_T$ elements from the standard Gaussian distribution to build a $N_T$-dimensional potential vector for picture generation, as each component of latent space follows the standard Guassian distribution. Consequently, the values of randomly sampled elements follow an approximate Guassian distribution.

To hide a given secret message $M$, if we encode the message straight away as the elements for latent vector construction, the distribution of these elements is likely to be very different from the distribution of randomly sampled elements, *i.e.*, approximate Guassian distribution, which will pose threats to security of hidden message. To avoid this issue, do not directly encode secret messages as elements, we encode it as the corresponding location arrangement for the $N_T$ randomly sampled elements to construct the latent vector $z$. More details are given as follows.

For a standard Guassian distribution, we first split the range of [-2,2] into $K$ parts and make the probability values of each part to be equal, because the $N_T$ elements sampled from the standard Gaussian distribution are mostly fall into the range. According to the $K$ range parts, the $N_T$ sampled elements are split into $K$ groups, denoted as $\{G_i | 1 \leq i \leq K\}$.

As shown in Fig. 2(c), using the stable NICE model for information extraction, while it is possible to recover the constructed potential vectors, they remain somewhat dissimilar to the recovered potential vectors. This is mainly because certain components of the created concealed vectors that are near group boundaries are displaced towards adjoining groups. This displacement is caused by the bijective mapping error between the concealed continuous space and the discrete pictures space. That will affect the accuracy of information extraction. Thus, select the $n$ elements closest to the centre of each group to get $N$ elements to construct latent vector, which are unlikely to be transferred to adjacent groups. Consequently, $N = K \times n$ and $N \leq N_T$. It is notable that $K$ and $n$ are shared between communication participants in advance to hide and extract information.

**Step (2): Secret-guided location arrangement of elements.** A set of corresponding locations, controlled by a given secret message $M$, is assigned to each group $G_i$ of $n$ elements. Select $n$ locations in the location set *pos*, which registers the $[N - (i - 1)n]$ locations remaining after ordering the elements, where $(i-1)n$ denotes the number of locations taken by the elements of $1 - th$ to $(i - 1) - th$ groups. The count of options to select $n$ locations from *pos* can be calculated by $\omega_i = C(N - (i-1)n, n)$, where $C(x, y)$ denotes the count of options to select $y$ locations from $x$ locations. Therefore, $\lfloor \log_2 \omega_i \rfloor$-bit secret information can be encoded as the location order of elements of $G_i$.

The pseudo-code of Algorithm 1 details the secret bootstrap location arrangement for each group of elements. Also shown in Fig. 3 is an instance of a secret guide location arrangement. Assuming that $N = 12$ elements are selected from $K = 3$ groups $\{G_i | 1 \leq i \leq 3\}$, with each group containing $n = 4$ elements. Since there are 12 elements to arrange, the original set of locations for the arrange-

---

**Algorithm 1.** Secret-guided location arrangement of elements

---

**Input:** Secret bitstream: $M ='$ $01011010010110'$, Number of groups: $K$, Number of chosen elements in each group: $n$, Number of chosen elements in total: $N$;

**Output:** Array of location arrangement: $Ind=(Ind[1],Ind[2],\ldots,Ind[N]$;

1: $r \leftarrow M$;                          ▷ Record number of remaining locations
2: $pos \leftarrow (1,2,3,\ldots,N)$;          ▷ Record remaining locations
3: **for** $i = 1$ to $K-1$ **do**
4:     $\omega_i = C(r,n)$;    ▷ Compute number of choices of selecting $n$ locations from $r$ locations
5:     $m \leftarrow \text{Read}(M, \lfloor\log_2\omega_i\rfloor)$;   ▷ Read the next $\lfloor\log_2\omega_i\rfloor$ bits from $M$ as a positive decimal integer $m$
6:     $sel \leftarrow \text{Select}(m, pos, n)$;        ▷ Select $n$ locations from $pos$ guided by $m$
7:     **for** $p$ in $sel$ **do**
8:         $Ind[p] \leftarrow i$;                     ▷ Set $Ind[p]$ as the group No., i.e., $i$
9:     **end for**
10:    $r \leftarrow r - n$;
11:    $pos \leftarrow \text{PosDelete}(pos, sel)$;                  ▷ Remove $sel$ from $pos$
12: **end for**
13: **return** $Ind$

---

ment of these elements is represented as $pos = (1,2,3,\ldots,12)$. The elements of each group are placed into the set of locations chosen from $pos$, which is driven by a provided secret bit-stream $M ='$ $01011010010110'$. Additional details are provided below.

The locations of the 4 elements in group $G_1$ should be chosen from the 12 locations in $pos$, so the amount of selections is $C(12,4) = 495$. Since 495 options can be represented as $\lfloor\log_2 495\rfloor = 8$ bits of secret information, we take the first 8 bits from the secret bit-stream, i.e., $'01011010'$, as the decimal integer $m = 90$. Next, the $(m+1) = 91 - th$ location, i.e. the locations "1,3,7,9", is chosen in dictionary sequence to arrange elements in $G_1$. Therefore, we determine the location of elements in first group to be $Ind[1]$, $Ind[3]$, $Ind[7]$, $Ind[9]$, i.e., $Ind[1]=Ind[3]=Ind[7]=Ind[9]=1$. That implies the locations "1,3,7,9" will be employed to align the elements of $G_1$.

Likewise, arranging the $n = 4$ elements of $G_2$, 4 locations must be selected from the residual 8 locations in $pos$, so there are $C(8,4) = 70$ to choose from. $\lfloor\log_2 70\rfloor = 6$ bits of secret message can be concealed in 70 selections. Therefore, Then read the next 6 bits from the secret bit stream, i.e., $'010110'$, as the decimal integer $m = 22$. Next, the $(m+1) = 23 - th$ location choice i.e., the locations "2,6,8,11", is chosen in dictionary sequence to order the four elements of $G_2$. Therefore, we determine the location of elements in $G_2$ i.e., $Ind[2]=Ind[6]=Ind[8]=Ind[11]=2$. That implies the locations "2,6,8,11" will be employed to align the elements of $G_2$.

Driven on provided secret information $M$, the location Alignment array $Ind = (1,2,1,3,3,2,1,2,1,3,2,3)$ can be obtained finally. Hence, the secret message $M$ is coded to be an arrangement of the locations of these elements. The below steps can be used to structure potential vectors, which is indicated by this array $Ind$.

**Step (3): Latent vector construction.** Arranging the array$Ind$ based on the locations it gets, the four elements in $G_1$ are placed in the "1-$th$, 3-$th$, 7-$th$, and 9-$th$" locations, the four elements in $G_2$ in the "2-$th$, 6-$th$, 8-$th$, and 11-$th$" locations, and the elements of groups $G_3$ are placed in the est of the locations in a random sequence. Get a $N$-dimensional vector by joining these aligned elements. As with a sum of $N_T$ sampling elements, another $N_T - N$ elements are straight joined at the last of the vector to get the eventual $N_T$-dimensional latent vector $z$.

**Step (4): picture generation.** Randomly scramble elements of $z$ using a private $Key$ that is shared among the communicating participants, after constructing the $N_T$-dimensional latent vector z. Then the perturbation vector is projected onto the produced high-quality picture by the Stable NICE model. Eventually, the produced picture is employed as steganographic pictures for secret correspondence.

Under the recommended SM-IG programme, since the space of locational arrangements of $N$ chosen elements is large enough for structuring high-dimensional potential vectors, the secret information in the structured vectors is efficiently encoded. In addition, the stable bijective-mapping between the structured vector and the produced picture can be achieved by the Stable NICE model. Therefore, the proposed SM-IG scheme has good efficiency and reversibility, which enables steganography with huge hiding volume and accurate secret message recovery.

Furthermore, by using the Stable NICE model, the constructed vector can be projected to a high-quality picture, and the message concealment can be achieved by producing fresh pictures instead of changing already existing ones. As a result, the proposed steganography method is ideally resistant to detection and unnoticeable, as demonstrated by the experiments in Sect. 5.

### 4.2   Reverse S2I Transformation for Information Extraction

Since message recovery is the reverse procedure of information concealment, the secret information can be obtained from the produced picture by implementing the reverse S2I transformation. The process of information extraction contains two major steps: latent vector extraction and secret message recovery.

**Step (1): Latent vector recovery.** At the receiver side, the Stable NICE model inversely maps the received picture into a latent vector. Then, the recovered latent vector $z$ can be obtained by the location sequence of the latent vector elements, which is recovered by the shared $Key$.

**Step (2): Secret message extraction.** Recover the potential vector with $K$ and $n$ known to both communicating parties and denote it as $z'$, and regroup the first $N = Kn$ elements of $z'$ using the method used in the information hiding phase. Get the location of elements of each group $G_i$, and according to get the location to determine its corresponding $No.$ in the location list, where the location list has $C(N-(i-1)n, n)$ possible options. Following step (2) of the information hiding phase, we can determine that the choice No. is $(m_i + 1)$ and the corresponding $m_i$ is the decimal integer of relevant secret bit. Therefore, the corresponding selection number No. can be determined based on the location of $n$ elements in each group $G_i$ to get $m_i$, then $m_i$ transformed to the relevant secret bit. Once all the bits are got, they are concatenated to extract the ultimate secret information $M'$.

## 4.3   Hiding Capacity Analysis

The hiding capacity of SM-IG scheme is analyzed in this subsection. As mentioned in Sect. 4.1, for $i$-$th$ group, $\lfloor \log_2 \omega_i \rfloor$-bit secret message can be embedded in the order of locations of its elements, where $\omega_i = C(N - (i-1)n, n)$. Therefore, the sum of bits that can be encoded as the location order for all groups is computed by

$$BN_{S2I} = \sum_{i=1}^{K-1} \lfloor \log_2 \omega_i \rfloor \tag{4}$$

It fulfils the formula.

$$\left( \sum_{i=1}^{K-1} \log_2 \omega_i \right) - K + 1 < \sum_{i=1}^{K-1} \lfloor \log_2 \omega_i \rfloor \leq \sum_{i=1}^{K-1} \log_2 \omega_i \tag{5}$$

where,

$$\sum_{i=1}^{K-1} \log_2 \omega_i = \log_2 \prod_{i=1}^{K-1} C(N - (i-1)n, n) \tag{6}$$

In accordance with the Stirling approximation, the below results can be obtained.

$$\sum_{i=1}^{K-1} \log_2 \omega_i \approx \log_2 \left( \left( \frac{1}{\sqrt{2\pi}} \right)^{K-1} \frac{(Kn)^{Kn+\frac{1}{2}}}{n^{K(n+\frac{1}{2})}} \right)$$
$$= -(K-1)\log_2 \sqrt{2\pi} + \left( Kn + \frac{1}{2} \right) \log_2 K - \frac{K-1}{2} \log_2 n \tag{7}$$

Suppose that all the $N_T$ sampled elements are selected and divided into $N_T$ groups, $i.e.$, $N = N_T$ and $K = N_T$, with each group containing only $n = 1$ element for message hiding. The scale of the training pictures employed in the experiments are $28 \times 28 = 784$, and the latent vector $N_T$ is constructed with the same dimension as the scale of these pictures, hence $N_T = 784$. Based on Eqs.

(5) and (7), the greatest $BN_{S2I}$ is estimated to be approximately in the region of (5721,6504], and thus the largest number of bits hidden in per picture pixel ($bpp$) can theoretically be about $6504/784 \approx 8.3$, which is a very high level.

According to Eq. (6), larger $K$ and $n$ can result in better message hiding power but less accurate of message extraction. This will be analyzed in Sect. 5.2

## 5    Experiments

Within this section, firstly, we describe the experimental setup including training datasets, model training details, experimental environment, and assessment standards. Secondly, the influence of the parameters of the SM-IG scheme is analysed and discussed. That is, the effect of the number of element groups $K$ and the number of elements $n$ selected in each group. Thirdly, the validity of Stable NICE model is verified for the proposed method. Lastly, the performances of suggested SM-IG is evaluated and compared with the prior art in terms of resistance to detection and imperceptibility.

### 5.1    Experiment Settings

As the Stable NICE model consists of original NICE model and the rectification functions, we first train the original NICE model and then train the rectification functions.

**Training Datasets:** In [22], it is proven that the original NICE model trained on picture datasets can effectively generate high quality pictures. Therefore, in our experiments, we used two picture datasets, *i.e.*, MNIST dataset [23] and EMNIST dataset [24], to separately train the NICE model. The MNIST database is the dataset of 70K pictures, while the EMNIST database contains 145.6K pictures. The sizes of all the pictures in the two datasets are $28 \times 28$.

**Model Training Details:** By maximising the objective function defined in Eq. (6), the NICE model is trained. The learning rate of the training process is $10^{-3}$. After 1500 training epochs on the two datasets, two trained NICE models are obtained, respectively. After obtaining the trained NICE models, we learn the parameters of the rectification functions defined in Eq. (7) and (8). To this end, we construct a set of 1000 latent vectors $Z$ in the manner prescribed in Sect. 4.1 and then input the set into the NICE model trained on the MNIST database with or without the rectification function $r_\alpha$ to generate the two picture sets $I$ and $I_0$, respectively. Then, the picture set $I$ is reversely mapped by the trained NICE model to obtain the set of recovered latent vectors $Z'$. Then, by minimizing the objective function defined in Eq. (9) with Genetic algorithm, we can determine the parameters, *i.e.*, $\alpha_1 = 3.0349$ and $\alpha_2 = -1.1655$.

**Evaluation Criteria:** In the experiments, we use the following evaluation criteria to assess the hiding power, extraction accuracy, detection resistance and imperceptibility of different steganography methods.

*Hiding Capacity:* The number of bits per pixel (*bpp*) is used to assess the information hiding ability of most picture steganography methods. It represents the number of secret bits hidden in per pixel. Also, we assess the hiding capacity $IH_C$ by *bpp*.

*Extraction Accuracy:* The length of the initial secret bit stream may differ from the length of the recovered secret bit stream because of the hiding manner of suggested steganographic methods. Thus, we assess the precision of message extraction by calculating the Edit Distance (ED) between the original secret bit stream $M$ and the extracted secret bit stream $M'$. The accuracy rate is computed by

$$IE_A = 1 - \frac{ED(M, M')}{\max[Len(M), Len(M')]} \tag{8}$$

where, $Len(M)$ and $Len(M')$ are used to computing the lengths of bitstream $M$ and $M'$, respectively.

*Anti-detectability:* The following detection error rates were used to assess the performance of anti-detection against the steganalyser.

$$P_E = \min_{P_{FA}} \frac{1}{2}(P_{FA} + P_{MD}) \tag{9}$$

where $P_{FA}$ is the false-alarm (FA) probability of steganalyzer and $P_{MD}$ is the missed-detection (MD) probability of steganalyzer. A larger $P_E$ implies that the steganography method has a higher resistance to detection against the steganography analyse [25].

## 5.2   Parameter Impacts

In the presented SM-IG scheme, there are two key parameters in order to construct the latent vectors: $K$ and $n$, are the amount of groups of elements and the number of elements selected from each group, respectively. We evaluate the effect of the parameters on the performance of the suggested scheme in terms of hiding capacity and extraction accuracy. In this experiment, we adopt the trained Stable NICE model, which consists of the original NICE model trained on the MNIST dataset and the rectification functions trained on the set of 1000 constructed latent vector as described in previous subsection.

Figure 4 illustrates the effect of parameters on the proposed SM-IG. As shown in this diagram, the larger K and n are, obviously, the higher the hiding power. Since bigger $K$ and $n$ provide a bigger space for arranging the locations of the elements to structure the potential vectors, which allows to hide more secret bits in the produced pictures by the structured potential vector. Nevertheless, as $K$ and $n$ increase, the precision of message recovery decreases for the following

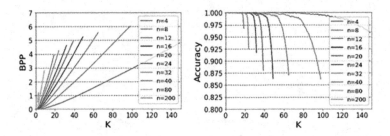

**Fig. 4.** The impacts of parameters $K$ and $n$ in the aspects of hiding capacity and extraction accuracy for SM-IG scheme.

reasons. Increases in $K$ and $n$ leads to more elements close to the group boundary, which makes the group $Nos.$ of these elements fragile. Thus, it is quite different for the group $Nos.$ of elements in the recovered latent vector and those in the raw latent vector, which significantly impacts the precise of message recovery.

According to Fig. 4, under the condition of perfect accuracy rate of information extraction, i.e., $IE_A = 1.0$, the hiding capacity of SM-IG can reach up to 4.3 $bpp$. As shown in Fig. 4, to reach the desired level of hiding capacity $IH_C$, there are several combinations of $(K, n)$ to choose from. For instance, when SM-IG require the hiding capacity of $IH_C = 4$ $bpp$, the set of $(K, n)$ are (23,32), (29,24), (33,20), (40,16), (50,12), (70,8) and (128,4). Moreover, with some hiding power, smaller $K$ usually leads to higher extraction accuracy. Thus, the smallest $K$ in the parameter combination, $i.e.$, (23,32), can be selected to obtain the desired hiding capacity $IH_C = 4$ $bpp$. In this way, it is possible to establish parameter combinations $(K, n)$ for SM-IG that achieve a desired level of hiding power. These combinations can then be utilised in subsequent experiments.

### 5.3   Validity of Stable NICE Model

After setting the parameters in the above manner, we observe the validity of the designed Stable NICE model in this subsection. To this end, we test the accuracies of information extraction of SM-IG scheme with different levels of hiding payloads when using original NICE model or Stable NICE model. We denote the corresponding methods as NICE+SM-IG, S-NICE+SM-IG.

Figure 5 shows the accuracies of information extraction of the two methods with different levels of hiding payloads. From this figure, the accuracy of the method decreases as the hidden payload increases. It is clear that the accuracies of S-NICE+SM-IG is much higher than that of NICE +SM-IG. That indicates Stable NICE model can improve the information extraction accuracy significantly for SM-IG.

### 5.4   Performance Evaluation and Comparison

In this subsection, we evaluate and compare the performance of different steganographic methods in terms of accuracy, resistance to detection and impercepti-

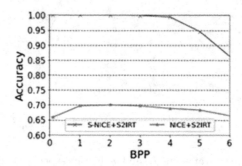

**Fig. 5.** Information extraction accuracy of SM-IG scheme when using original NICE model or Stable NICE model.

bility of information extraction under different hidden payloads. These methods include the following.

S-UNIWORD [26]: This well-known traditional steganography method is implemented based on a heuristically defined distortion function.

UT-6HPF-GAN [27]: It is a conventional steganographic approach and employs the distortion function learnt by the GAN.

SWE [16]]: The generative steganographic approach is named as steganography without embedding (SWE), where the secret information is encoded by fed into the DCGAN for stego-pictures generation.

S-NICE+SM-IG: In this approach, the proposed SM-IG scheme is implemented based on Stable NICE model for generative steganography.

In S-NICE+SM-IG, the stable NICE model trained on MNIST and that trained on EMNIST are employed to produce stego-pictures.

**Information Extraction Accuracy:** The message extraction precision (values of $IE_A$) of SWE, S-NICE+SM-IG with increasing hidden payload is shown in Table 1.

**Table 1.** The message extraction precision of stego-pictures of those methods with different hiding payloads.

| Methods | Hiding payloads (*bpp*) | | | | |
|---|---|---|---|---|---|
| | 0.1 | 0.5 | 1.0 | 2.0 | 4.0 |
| SWE | 0.9983 | 0.8323 | 0.7096 | 0.6981 | 0.6844 |
| S-NICE+SM-IG | **1.0000** | **1.0000** | **1.0000** | **1.0000** | **0.9943** |

Obviously, the proposed steganographic methods, *i.e.*, S-NICE+SM-IG, is much more accurate than other generative steganography methods*i.e.*, SWE, in terms of message extraction precision and under various hidden payloads. Also, when the hiding payload were between 0.1 *bpp* and 4 *bpp*, the extraction accuracy rate remained at a very high-level ($IE_A \approx 1.0$). That is mainly because the approach has good efficiency and reversibility in secret-to-picture transformation process.

Therefore, the suggested generative steganography method can realize both hiding capacity (up to 4 *bpp*) and precise extraction of secret information (almost 100% accuracy rate).

**Anti-detectability:** In terms of estimating and comparing the anti-detection properties of different steganographic methods, the well-known steganalyzers, *i.e.*, SRM [15] and XuNet [3], used to check the existence of hidden messages in a steganographic picture. Among them, SRM is a steganalyser founded on a set of high-dimensional manual steganalysis features, and XuNet is a steganalyser founded on an improved CNN steganalysis structure. By using the two steganalyzers, the detection error rate $P_E$ is calculated in the same way as described in Sect. 5.1 to assess the anti-detectability performance of various steganographic methods.

**Table 2.** The values of $P_E$ of four steganographic methods with different hiding payloads.

|  | Methods | Hiding payloads(*bpp*) | | | | |
|---|---|---|---|---|---|---|
|  |  | 0.1 | 0.5 | 1.0 | 2.0 | 4.0 |
| SRM | S-UNIWORD | 0.4229 | 0.1824 | 0.0493 | - | - |
|  | UT-6HPF-GAN | 0.4414 | 0.2489 | 0.0615 | - | - |
|  | SWE | 0.4987 | - | - | - | - |
|  | S-NICE+SM-IG | **0.5007** | **0.5011** | **0.4998** | **0.5002** | **0.5001** |
| XuNet | S-UNIWORD | 0.4461 | 0.1925 | 0.0712 | - | - |
|  | UT-6HPF-GAN | 0.4690 | 0.2971 | 0.0787 | - | - |
|  | SWE | 0.4991 | - | - | - | - |
|  | S-NICE+SM-IG | **0.5001** | **0.4997** | **0.4986** | **0.5008** | **0.5002** |

Table 2 shows the anti-detection behaviour of these methods for various hidden payloads (values of $P_E$) . From this table, we can draw a couple of observations.

For the low hiding payloads (0.1–0.5 *bpp*), we can observe that the generative steganographic approaches, *i.e.*, S-NICE+SM-IG and SWE, Outperforms traditional steganography methods by a wide margin, *i.e.*, S-UNIWORD and UT-6HPF-GAN. This is because these steganography generating methods do not need to modify the carrier picture and directly generate a new picture as a steganographic picture, and it is difficult for steganographers to discover the existence of hidden information.

For the high hiding payloads (larger than 0.5 $bpp$), it is obvious that the anti-detectability performances of S-NICE+SM-IG and SWE remain at high levels ($P_E$ is about 0.5); On the contrary, the properties of the other methods inclusive of S-UNIWORD and UT-6HPF-GAN, is obviously degraded. In S-UNIWORD and UT-6HPF-GAN, the more secret information that is hidden in the cover picture, the more misrepresentation occurs, since secret information is hidden by altering the existing cover picture. As a result, steganographic analysers are more likely to easily detect these steganographic methods, especially at high hidden payloads. Note that for UT-6HPF-GAN and S-UNIWORD, the values of $P_E$ will be null if the payload is greater than 1 $bpp$, as they are unable to get the hiding capacity greater than 1 $bpp$. Also, as shown in Table 1, when the hiding payload is larger than 0.1, the SWE is unable to extract the hidden information while the hidden load is greater than 0.1, and the corresponding $P_E$ value of the SWE is null for following reasons. In SWE, the secret information is coded as a low-dimensional noise signal of DCGAN for generating a steganographic picture, and the information extractor is trained to extract the secret information from the steganographic picture. These make SWE difficult to achieve high hiding capacity with accurate information extraction. Thus, the high hiding power of SWE, S-UNIWORD and UT-6HPF-GAN comes at the cost of security performance or message extraction precision.

As a summary, the proposed steganographic approach, $i.e.$, S-NICE+SM-IG, can achieve desirable anti-detectability performances against the steganalyzers even at a very high hiding payload (4 $bpp$).

# 6    Conclusion

This work provides a new idea of generative steganography. A secret message-driven picture generation scheme (SM-IG) based on the designed Stable NICE model has been proposed for generative steganography. The proposed steganographic approach can obtain promising hiding capacity (over 4 $bpp$) while preserving the desired resistance to detection and unnoticeability, and dramatically outperforms state-of-the-art steganographic methods.

To conduct covert communication, many practical steganography tasks require hiding large amounts of message in an picture while preserving high extraction precision and desired resistance to detection and imperceptibility. These tasks can be well implemented by the proposed steganographic approach. Consequently, the proposed approach has important practical significance in the field of information hiding. As the NICE model is good at generating pictures, in the proposed steganographic approach, the secret messages are converted to the generated pictures. Going forward, we plan to extend the presented method by exploring additional flow models to generate other common types of pictures, for instance, face photos and landscape pictures for steganography.

**Acknowledgements.** This work is supported in part by the National Natural Science Foundation of China under Grant 62372125, Grant 61972205, Grant 62102462, in part by the Guangdong Basic and Applied Basic Research Foundation under Grant no.2022A1515010108, in part by the Guangdong Natural Science Funds for Distinguished Young Scholar under Grant 2023B1515020041, and in part by the Collaborative Innovation Center of Atmospheric Environment and Equipment Technology (CICAEET) fund, China.

# References

1. Filler, T., Judas, J., Fridrich, J.: Minimizing additive distortion in steganography using syndrome-trellis codes. IEEE Trans. Inf. Forensics Secur. **6**(3), 920–935 (2011)
2. Zhou, Z., Mu, Y., Wu, Q.: Coverless picture steganography using partial-duplicate picture retrieval. Soft. Comput. **23**(13), 4927–4938 (2019)
3. Wan, S., Gu, R., Umer, T., Salah, K., Xu, X.: Toward offloading internet of vehicles applications in 5G networks. IEEE Trans. Intell. Transp. Syst. **22**(7), 4151–4159 (2020)
4. Xu, J., et al.: Hidden message in a deformation-based texture. Vis. Comput. **31**(12), 1653–1669 (2015)
5. Saito, M., Matsui, Y.: Illustration2vec: a semantic vector representation of illustrations. In: SIGGRAPH Asia 2015 Technical Briefs, pp. 1–4 (2015)
6. Li, J., et al.: A generative steganography method based on WGAN-GP. In: Sun, X., Wang, J., Bertino, E. (eds.) ICAIS 2020. CCIS, vol. 1252, pp. 386–397. Springer, Singapore (2020). https://doi.org/10.1007/978-981-15-8083-3_34
7. Holub, V., Fridrich, J., Denemark, T.: Universal distortion function for steganography in an arbitrary domain. EURASIP J. Inf. Secur. **2014**(1), 1–13 (2014). https://doi.org/10.1186/1687-417X-2014-1
8. Wu, K.C., Wang, C.M.: Steganography using reversible texture synthesis. IEEE Trans. Picture Process. **24**(1), 130–139 (2014)
9. Li, S., Zhang, X.: Toward construction-based data hiding: from secrets to fingerprint pictures. IEEE Trans. Picture Process. **28**(3), 1482–1497 (2018)
10. Girshick, R.: Fast R-CNN. In: Proceedings of the IEEE International Conference on Computer Vision, pp. 1440–1448 (2015)
11. Cao, Y., Zhou, Z., Wu, Q.M.J., Yuan, C., Sun, X.: Coverless information hiding based on the generation of anime characters. EURASIP J. Image Video Process. **2020**(1), 1–15 (2020). https://doi.org/10.1186/s13640-020-00524-4
12. Jiang, W., Hu, D., Yu, C., Li, M., Zhao, Z.Q.: A new steganography without embedding based on adversarial training. In: Proceedings of the ACM Turing Celebration Conference-China, pp. 219–223 (2020)
13. Radford, A., Metz, L., Chintala, S.: Unsupervised representation learning with deep convolutional generative adversarial networks. arXiv preprint arXiv:1511.06434 (2015)
14. Li, S., Zhang, X.: Toward construction-based data hiding: from secrets to fingerprint pictures. IEEE Transactions on picture Processing **28**(3), 1482–1497 (2018)
15. Fridrich, J., Kodovsky, J.: Rich models for steganalysis of digital pictures. IEEE Trans. Inf. Forensics Secur. **7**(3), 868–882 (2012)
16. Hu, D., Wang, L., Jiang, W., Zheng, S., Li, B.: A novel picture steganography method via deep convolutional generative adversarial networks. IEEE Access **6**, 38303–38314 (2018)

17. Peng, J., Sun, P., Zhang, L., Kuber, K., McLernon, D.: Timing synchronization for OFDMA femtocells in the presence of co-channel interference. In: 2012 8th International Wireless Communications and Mobile Computing Conference (IWCMC), pp. 1215–1220. IEEE (2012)

18. LeCun, Y.: The MNIST database of handwritten digits (1998). http://yann.lecun.com/exdb/mnist/

19. Xu, J., et al.: Hidden message in a deformation-based texture. Visual Comput. **31**(12), 1653–1669 (2015)

20. Arifianto, A., et al.: EDGAN: disguising text as picture using generative adversarial network. In: 2020 8th International Conference on Information and Communication Technology (ICoICT), pp. 1–6. IEEE (2020)

21. Jin, Y., Zhang, J., Li, M., Tian, Y., Zhu, H., Fang, Z.: Towards the automatic anime characters creation with generative adversarial networks. arXiv preprint arXiv:1708.05509 (2017)

22. Dinh, L., Krueger, D., Bengio, Y.: Nice: non-linear independent components estimation. arXiv preprint arXiv:1410.8516 (2014)

23. Le, Q., Mikolov, T.: Distributed representations of sentences and documents. In: International Conference on Machine Learning, pp. 1188–1196. PMLR (2014)

24. Cohen, G., Afshar, S., Tapson, J., Van Schaik, A.: Emnist: extending MNIST to handwritten letters. In: 2017 International Joint Conference on Neural Networks (IJCNN), pp. 2921–2926. IEEE (2017)

25. Luo, Y., Qin, J., Xiang, X., Tan, Y.: Coverless picture steganography based on multi-object recognition. IEEE Trans. Circuits Syst. Video Technol. **31**(7), 2779–2791 (2020)

26. Goodfellow, I., et al.: Generative adversarial nets. In: Advances in Neural Information Processing Systems, vol. 27 (2014)

27. Xu, G., Wu, H.Z., Shi, Y.Q.: Structural design of convolutional neural networks for steganalysis. IEEE Signal Process. Lett. **23**(5), 708–712 (2016)

# Computer-Generated Image Forensics Based on Vision Transformer with Forensic Feature Pre-processing Module

Yifang Chen, Guanchen Wen, Yong Wang, Jianhua Yang[✉], and Yu Zhang

Guangdong Polytechnic Normal University, GuangZhou 510665, GuangDong, China
yangjh86@gpnu.edu.cn

**Abstract.** The correct distinction between highly realistic computer-generated (CG) images and photographic (PG) images has become an important area of research. In recent years, most of the CG image forensics methods are proposed based on deep learning, but the detection performances of these methods still need to be improved, especially in terms of robustness and generalization. To tackle these issues, we leverage the *Vision Transformer* (ViT) model, which excels in capturing the global features of images, and design a Forensic Feature Pre-processing (FFP) module to further improve the detection performance. Experiments are conducted on a large-scale CG image benchmark (LSCGB), which is a challenging dataset for CG image detection. The proposed approach can achieve high detection accuracy. Extensive experiments on different public datasets and common post-processing operations demonstrate our approach can achieve significantly better generalization and robustness than the state-of-the-art approaches.

**Keywords:** Computer-generated images · Vision Transformer · Robustness · Generalization

## 1 Introduction

Nowadays, computer-generated (CG) images, which are often generated by using computer graphics techniques (e.g., 3D rendering techniques [1,2]) or advanced deep learning algorithms such as autoencoders (AE) [3,4] and Generative Adversarial Networks (GANs) [5,6], are difficult to recognize with the naked eye and may present potential risks to social stability if used maliciously. Therefore, it is of primary importance to develop reliable methods to distinguish CG images from photographic (PG) images, which are captured by digital cameras and accurately and objectively record real-world scenes.

In recent years, deep neural networks, such as Convolutional Neural Networks (CNNs), have been successfully used for CG image forensics due to their powerful

J. Cai et al. (Eds.): SPNCE 2023, LNICST 525, pp. 315–325, 2025.
https://doi.org/10.1007/978-3-031-73699-5_22

learning ability [7–9]. Bai et al. [10] contributed a Large-Scale CG images Benchmark (LSCGB). They further proposed a texture-aware network to serve as a strong baseline for the new benchmark based on the observation that the texture feature is an effective representation to distinguish CG and PG images. Yao et al. [11] proposed a CG image detection method by applying transfer learning and convolutional attention to consider both the shallow content features and the deep semantic features of the image, thereby improving the accuracy of identifying CG images. Gangan et al. [12] proposed a Multi-Colorspace fused EfficientNet [13] model by parallelly fusing three EfficientNet networks. Each of the three networks operates in a different colorspace, i.e., RGB, HSV, and LCH to provide high classification accuracies for the task of detecting CG images. Meena et al. [14] found that the high-frequency noise features of CG images are significantly different from those of PG images, so they can be utilized as complementary discriminate features to improve detection performance. Therefore, they proposed a two-stream network to respectively extract RGB color features and high-frequency noise features obtained from Spatial Rich Model (SRM) [15] filters.

Despite CNNs having been proven effective tools for CG image forensics, they tend to learn local visual discriminative features (e.g., color, texture, and edges) of the images and fail to capture global correlation among different image regions due to the limitation of receptive fields. Since all the regions of a CG image are synthesized, a wide range of artifacts that span the entire image can be created in the computer-generated process. Therefore, these global features are also crucial in CG image forensics for providing essential information regarding the artifacts of generation. Vision Transformer (ViT) [16] have recently emerged as a competitive alternative to CNNs and increasingly be applied to the image forensics tasks, such as the detection of splicing [17], deepfakes [18], and recaptured screen images [19], etc. Compared with CNNs, the cascaded self-attention modules in ViT can help it to capture long-range feature dependencies and reflect complex spatial transformations to capture the global features.

In this work, we apply ViT specifically to CG image forensics and design it to further improve its detection performance. Instead of inputting image patches in conventional ViT, we propose a Forensic Feature Pre-processing (FFP) module to first convert the input images to feature maps which is beneficial to CG image forensics. The FFP module mainly comprises a convolutional block and a SRM filter block, which extract distinct spatial features and noise domain features from the input images, respectively. In the convolutional block, the input images are successively passed to a convolutional layer, a batch normalization layer, and a maximum pooling layer. In the SRM filter block, the input images are split into three color channels, i.e., $R$, $G$, and $B$, and then processed by three different SRM filters, respectively. The SRM filters can learn noise-based distinct features which have been proven to be effective for CG image detection in [14]. In Fig. 1, we show the features obtained from the images taken from LSCGB [10] by the three SRM filters. It can be seen that the SRM filters tend to suppress image content and focus on the local noise features of the images.

Our main contributions are as follows: (1) We specifically adapt ViT for CG image forensics. The images are first converted into discriminative features and then inputted into the ViT, rather than inputting image patches in conventional ViT. (2) A Forensic Feature Pre-processing (FFP) module is propped to highlight the discriminative information between CG and PG images. (3) Experimental results demonstrate that the proposed method achieves strong robustness against post-processing operations and generalization on different CG image datasets.

**Fig. 1.** The top-to-bottom images are respectively the original images taken from LSCGB [10] and the images of their RGB channels after passing through SRM filters.

## 2 Proposed Method

### 2.1 Overall Network Architecture

The architecture of the proposed ViT is shown in Fig. 2. Firstly, the input images go through the FFP module to be converted into feature map patches. These patches are then flattened and mapped to a sequence of token embeddings. These token embeddings are then combined with an additional class token, and the resulting embeddings are fed into a series of stacked transformer encoder blocks. Finally, the resulting output is input to the classifier for classification. In this work, the ViT-B/16 model [16] serves as the baseline model.

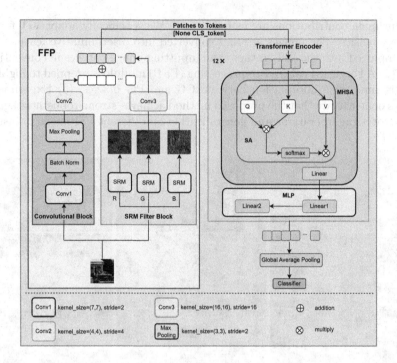

**Fig. 2.** The network architecture of the proposed method.

In order to further improve the detection performance of ViT, we made some improvements to it. Firstly, conventional ViT directly labeled patches with the fixed size from the original input image. This simple recognition makes it difficult for the model to extract local features of some basic structures in the image [20,21]. However, local features also contribute to CG image forensics. In order to take full advantage of local features and global features, we leverage the advantage of CNNs in extracting local features from images by using a convolutional block to extract local features. Secondly, local noise is one of the key features that can be used to differentiate CG images from PG images [14]. Therefore, we introduce a SRM filter block to extract the noise features which provide complementary clues for CG image detection.

Additionally, CNNs frequently use global average pooling layers before the final classifier to integrate visual features from different spatial locations to guarantee translation invariance (i.e. the network's predicted class for the object in the image isn't changed with the translation of their position), which is an important property of CNN. However, ViT differs from CNN in that it uses an additional class (CLS) token for performing classification, rather than relying on translation invariance. Based on the above mentioned, we use global average pooling to gain the classification features instead of the CLS token.

## 2.2 Forensic Feature Pre-processing Module

In order to fully mine the discriminative properties between CG and PG images, we designed the Forensic Feature Pre-processing (FFP) module. As shown in Fig. 2, the FFP module comprises a convolutional block for extracting local feature maps, a SRM filter block for extracting noise-based feature maps, and two convolutional layers for converting these feature maps into patches.

In the convolutional block, we leverage the advantage of convolution operations to extract local features, because ViT is not as proficient as CNNs in capturing local features such as texture and edges in shallow layers [21]. These local features also contribute to CG image forensics. The convolutional block consists of a convolutional layer, a batch normalization layer, and a maximum pooling layer. For the input image $x \in R^{H \times W \times 3}$, the output of the convolutional block can be denoted as:

$$x_l = MaxPool\left(BN\left(Conv1\left(x\right)\right)\right) \tag{1}$$

where $x_l \in R^{I \times J \times C}$, $(H,W)$ is the size of the input image, $(I,J)$ is the size of the output of the convolutional block, and $C$ is the number of channels.

The SRM filter block is applied to extract noise-based discriminate features. As shown in Fig. 2, an input image is split into three color channels, i.e., R, G, and B. For $k_{th}$ color channel $x^k$ of size $H \times W$, one SRM filter $F^k$ is used to extract the local noise feature $x_h^k$

$$x_h^k = F^k\left(x^k\right) \tag{2}$$

where $k = 1, 2, 3$ is the number of color channels. Figure 3 shows the weights of three SRM filters used in the SRM filter block. For each color channel, the size of local noise feature maps $x_h^k$ can be calculated as follows:

$$\left\lfloor \frac{H + 2p - k}{s} + 1 \right\rfloor \cdot \left\lfloor \frac{W + 2p - k}{s} + 1 \right\rfloor \tag{3}$$

where $p$ represents padding, $s$ represents stride, $(k, k)$ represents the filter size and $\lfloor \cdot \rfloor$ represents the floor function. In this work, to maintain consistency between the image through the SRM filter and the original image, we set $(k, k)$ as $(5,5)$, $s$ as 1, and $p$ as 2. The noise-based discriminate features are extracted from each color channel and the final output is $x_h$.

$$\frac{1}{4}\begin{bmatrix} 0 & 0 & 0 & 0 & 0 \\ 0 & -1 & 2 & -1 & 0 \\ 0 & 2 & 4 & 2 & 0 \\ 0 & -1 & 2 & -1 & 0 \\ 0 & 0 & 0 & 0 & 0 \end{bmatrix} \quad \frac{1}{12}\begin{bmatrix} -1 & 2 & -2 & 2 & -1 \\ 2 & -6 & 8 & -6 & 2 \\ -2 & 8 & -12 & 8 & -2 \\ 2 & -6 & 8 & -6 & 2 \\ -1 & 2 & -2 & 2 & -1 \end{bmatrix} \quad \frac{1}{2}\begin{bmatrix} 0 & 0 & 0 & 0 & 0 \\ 0 & 0 & 0 & 0 & 0 \\ 0 & 1 & -2 & 1 & 0 \\ 0 & 0 & 0 & 0 & 0 \\ 0 & 0 & 0 & 0 & 0 \end{bmatrix}$$

Fig. 3. The weights of three SRM filters $F^1$, $F^2$ and $F^3$.

Both the output of convolutional block $x_l$ and the output of SRM filter block $x_h$ are split into patches of size $(P, P)$ and added together to the new patches $x_p \in R^{\frac{H}{P} \times \frac{W}{P} \times (P^2 \times 3)}$. It can be noted as:

$$x_p = Conv2\,(x_l) + Conv3\,(x_h) \tag{4}$$

Then the feature map patches $x_p$ are flattened and mapped to a series of token embeddings $x_t \in R^{N \times D}$, where $N = HW/P^2$ and $D = P^2 \times 3$ are the number and the size of token embeddings, respectively.

## 2.3   Transformer Encoder

The transformer encoder consists of twelve stacked ViT blocks, where each block comprises two sub-layers: Multi-Head Self-Attention (MHSA) and Multi-Layer Perceptron (MLP). Layer normalization (LN) [22] is applied prior to each sub-layer, with a residual connection surrounding them.

In the MHSA layer, token embeddings are linearly transformed into $qkv$ (i.e., queries $Q \in R^{N \times D}$, keys $K \in R^{N \times D}$, and values $V \in R^{N \times D}$) spaces, which are split and fed to self-attention (SA) modules for twelve executions in parallel. The resulting outputs are concatenated and projected. The SA module can be noted as:

$$Attention(Q, K, V) = softmax \left( \frac{QK^T}{\sqrt{D}} \right) V \tag{5}$$

In the MLP layer, the element-wise operations are performed, which are applied individually to each token. It comprises two linear transformations, separated by a non-linear activation GELU [23]. It can be noted as:

$$MLP(x) = Linear2\,(GELU\,(Linear1\,(x))) \tag{6}$$

For the MHSA, by calculating the dot product, the similarity between different tokens can be calculated to obtain long-range and global attention. And the corresponding values of V are linearly aggregated. For the MLP, each token is performed dimension alteration and non-linear transformation, thereby enhancing the representation ability of the token.

## 3   Experiments

### 3.1   Experiment Setup

The benchmark database used in this study is the LSCGB proposed by Bai et al. [10], which is the state-of-the-art database for CG image forensics. The LSCGB contains 71,168 CG images and 71,168 PG images. All images are randomly divided into training set, testing set, and validation set according to the same ratio in [10] to 7:1:2. The input images are conducted the same processing in [10]. The experiments are carried out using PyTorch library on a single NVIDIA GTX3090. The total number of training epochs is set to 50. The Adam [24] is used as the optimizer, and the batch size is set to 32. For CNN-based methods and our ViT-based method, the learning rate is initialized to 0.0001 and 0.005 respectively, and scheduled to decrease by 10% every five epochs.

## 3.2 Evaluation of Robustness

In this section, we evaluate the robustness of our proposed method against various post-processing operations. We consider four common post-processing operations with different parameters: JPEG compression (quality factor (QF) $\in$ $\{90, 80, 70\}$), image scaling (up by 20% or down by 20%), image blur (median blur and mean blur, kernel size $\in \{3 \times 3\}$), and Gaussian noise addition (zero mean and $\sigma \in \{1, 1.5\}$).

We compare our method with the state-of-the-art methods mentioned above and ViT. The testing results are reported in Table 1. It can be observed that the basic ViT can achieve satisfying performance and our proposed method further improves the performance. Our method achieves an accuracy of 95.55% on the original testing dataset, which is approximately 5% higher than other methods. Under various post-processing operations, our method has an average accuracy close to 90%, which outperforms others in the comparison by more than 10%. Specifically, compared to the accuracy on the original dataset, our method shows an average accuracy decrease of 5.27%, 1.48%, 7.37%, and 1.50% under four types of post-processing operations respectively. In comparison, the best-performing CNN-based method among others, as demonstrated by Bai et al. [10], suffers a larger decrease in average accuracy of 11.93%, 3.03%, 21.95%, and 8.14% under the same conditions.

As shown in Fig. 4, the detection of CG images becomes increasingly challenging as the intensity of the post-processing operation increases. The performance of other state-of-the-art methods declines sharply, particularly for images that have undergone median filtering. In contrast, our method maintains a high level of detection accuracy in all scenarios. These results demonstrate the superior robustness of our method against post-processing operations compared with other CNN-based methods.

**Table 1.** The detection accuracy under post-processing operations

| Methods → Operations ↓ | Bai [10] | Yao [11] | Gangan [12] | Meena [14] | ViT [16] | Ours |
|---|---|---|---|---|---|---|
| Origin. | 91.73 | 91.26 | 90.56 | 90.82 | 94.88 | **95.55** |
| JPEG QF = 90 | 84.28 | 83.17 | 82.24 | 82.69 | 90.76 | **91.43** |
| JPEG QF = 80 | 78.89 | 78.29 | 76.68 | 76.84 | 88.31 | **90.29** |
| JPEG QF = 70 | 76.24 | 75.91 | 73.45 | 74.57 | 86.45 | **89.13** |
| Scaling Up 20% | 89.36 | 87.78 | 86.94 | 87.34 | 93.98 | **94.31** |
| Scaling Down 20% | 88.04 | 88.16 | 85.32 | 86.42 | 93.45 | **93.84** |
| Median 3×3 | 71.74 | 70.88 | 69.93 | 70.45 | 88.13 | **88.61** |
| Mean 3×3 | 67.83 | 66.39 | 64.74 | 65.83 | 87.59 | **87.75** |
| Noise $\sigma = 1$ | 84.55 | 82.73 | 81.17 | 81.92 | 93.78 | **94.36** |
| Noise $\sigma = 1.5$ | 82.64 | 81.71 | 80.08 | 81.37 | 93.43 | **93.75** |

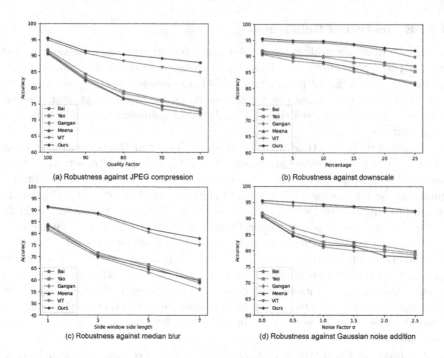

**Fig. 4.** The robustness against post-processing operations.

### 3.3 Evaluation of Generalization Ability

Cross-domain generalization poses a challenging problem for image forensics methods based on deep learning. Therefore, we demonstrate the performance of our method and other state-of-the-art methods in cross-domain scenarios in this section. We also adapt LSCGB dataset [10] as the benchmark training dataset and evaluate the detection performance on four separate datasets used for cross-domain testing: the Columbia dataset [25], consisting of 2400 images; the dataset proposed by Tokuda et al. [26], consisting of 4850 CG images and 4850 PG images; the dataset proposed by Rahmouni et al. [27], consisting of 3600 images; and the dataset proposed by He et al. [28], consisting of 6800 CG images and 6800 PG images.

As shown in Table 2, our model shows an improvement in accuracy compared to ViT across these four datasets. Moreover, compared to the approach proposed by Bai et al. [10], which performs the best among all CNN-based detection methods, our method respectively achieves 5.99%, 2.35%, 12.76%, and 6.53% improvements in cross-domain accuracy on the four datasets. These results highlight that our method also outperforms other CNN-based methods in cross-domain generalization.

**Table 2.** The detection accuracy on cross-domain datasets

| Methods⟶ Datasets ↓ | Bai [10] | Yao [11] | Gangan [12] | Meena [14] | ViT | Ours |
|---|---|---|---|---|---|---|
| Origin. | 91.73 | 91.26 | 90.56 | 90.82 | 94.88 | **95.55** |
| Columbia [25] | 78.59 | 70.14 | 73.49 | 72.46 | 84.51 | **84.58** |
| Tokuda [26] | 91.70 | 90.91 | 87.45 | 85.28 | 93.95 | **94.05** |
| Rahmouni [27] | 76.83 | 75.39 | 69.42 | 73.14 | 87.75 | **89.59** |
| He [28] | 84.18 | 82.35 | 77.41 | 83.81 | 90.46 | **90.71** |

**Table 3.** Ablation experiments on the proposed method

| Methods⟶ Scenarios ↓ | ViT (Baseline) | w/o SRM Filter Block | w/o Conv. Block | Ours |
|---|---|---|---|---|
| Origin. | 94.88 | 95.42 | 95.21 | **95.55** |
| JPEG QF = 90 | 90.76 | 91.20 | 90.94 | **91.43** |
| JPEG QF = 80 | 88.31 | 89.56 | 88.86 | **90.29** |
| JPEG QF = 70 | 86.45 | 88.74 | 88.17 | **89.13** |
| Rahmouni [27] | 87.75 | 89.06 | 88.35 | **89.59** |

### 3.4  Ablation Study

In this section, we assess the convolutional block (Conv. Block) and the SRM filter block in terms of robustness against post-processing operations. We test their performances on the original dataset, the dataset edited by JPEG compression (quality factor (QF) $\in \{90, 80, 70\}$) and the dataset proposed by Rahmouni et al. [27].

As shown in Table 3, on the original dataset, the accuracy without the SRM filter block is 95.42%, and without the convolution block is 95.21%. Without the SRM filter block, the average accuracy declines by 0.45% under JPEG compression compared to our proposed method. Similarly, without the convolutional block, the average accuracy witnessed a decrease of 0.96% under the same conditions. On the dataset proposed by Rahmouni et al. [27], without the SRM filter block and the convolutional block, the accuracy decreases by 0.53% and 1.24%, respectively. The performance degradation confirms that utilizing the SRM filter block or the convolutional block effectively improves the performance of the model.

## 4  Conclusion

In this work, we propose a novel ViT with Forensic Feature Pre-processing (FFP) module for CG image forensics tasks. The advantage of ViT in capturing global features contributes to distinguishing CG images from PG images, and the FFP module which exploits the discriminative information further improves the detection performance. Extensive experiments have shown that our method outperforms state-of-the-art methods, especially in terms of cross-domain generalization and robustness against post-processing operations. In further work, the proposed framework will also be extended and modified to tackle more image forensic applications, such as image tampering detection.

**Acknowledgment.** This work was supported in part by the National Natural Science Foundation of China (Nos. 62102100, 62102462), the Guangzhou Technology Plan Project (No. 202201011258), the Natural Science Foundation of Guang dong (Nos. 2022A1515 010108, 2023A1515011084), and the Talent fund of Guangdong Polytechnic Normal University (Nos. 2021SDKYA127, 2022SDKYA027, 99166990223).

# References

1. Shum, H., Kang, S.B.: Review of image-based rendering techniques. In: Proceedings of SPIE, vol. 4067, pp. 2–13 (2000)
2. Goswami, P.: A survey of modeling, rendering and animation of clouds in computer graphics. Vis. Comput. **37**(7), 1931–1948 (2021)
3. Kingma, D.P., Welling, M.: Auto-encoding variational bayes. arXiv preprint arXiv:1312.6114 (2013)
4. Huang, H., li, Z., He, R., Sun, Z., Tan, T.: IntroVAE: introspective variational autoencoders for photographic image synthesis. In: Proceedings of 32nd International Conference on Neural Information Processing Systems, vol. 31, pp. 52–63 (2018)
5. Creswell, A., White, T., Dumoulin, V., Arulkumaran, K., Sengupta, B., Bharath, A.A.: Generative adversarial networks: an overview. IEEE Signal Process. Mag. **35**(1), 53–65 (2018)
6. Goodfellow, I., et al.: Generative adversarial networks. Commun. ACM **63**(11), 139–144 (2020)
7. Nguyen, H.H., Tieu, T.N.D., Nguyen-Son, H.Q., Nozick, V., Yamagishi, J., Echizen, I.: Modular convolutional neural network for discriminating between computer-generated images and photographic images. In: Proceedings of the 13th International Conference on Availability, Reliability and Security, pp. 1–10 (2018)
8. Huang, R., Fang, F., Nguyen, H.H., Yamagishi, J., Echizen, I.: A method for identifying origin of digital images using a convolutional neural network. In: Proceedings of Asia-Pacific Signal Information Processing Association Annual Summit and Conference (APSIPA ASC), pp. 1293–1299 (2020)
9. Zhang, R.S., Quan, W.Z., Fan, L.B., Hu, L.M., Yan, D.M.: Distinguishing computer-generated images from natural images using channel and pixel correlation. J. Comput. Sci. Technol. **35**, 592–602 (2020)
10. Bai, W., et al.: Robust texture-aware computer-generated image forensic: benchmark and algorithm. IEEE Trans. Image Process. **30**, 8439–8453 (2021)
11. Yao, Y., Zhang, Z., Ni, X., Shen, Z., Chen, L., Xu, D.: CGNet: detecting computergenerated images based on transfer learning with attention module. Signal Process. Image Commun. **105**, 116692 (2022)
12. Gangan, M.P., Anoop, K., Lajish, V.: Distinguishing natural and computer generated images using Multi-Colorspace fused EfficientNet. J. Inf. Secur. Appl. **68**, 103261 (2022)

13. Tan, M., Le, Q.: EfficientNet: rethinking model scaling for convolutional neural networks. In: Proceedings of International Conference on Machine Learning, pp. 6105–6114 (2019)
14. Meena, K.B., Tyagi, V.: Distinguishing computer-generated images from photographic images using two-stream convolutional neural network. Appl. Soft Comput. **100**, 107025 (2021)
15. Fridrich, J., Kodovsky, J.: Rich models for steganalysis of digital images. IEEE Trans. Inf. Forensics Secur. **7**(3), 868–882 (2012)
16. Dosovitskiy, A., et al.: An image is worth $16 \times 16$ words: transformers for image recognition at scale. In: Proceedings of International Conference on Learning Representations (2020)
17. Sun, Y., Ni, R., Zhao, Y.: ET: edge-enhanced transformer for image splicing detection. IEEE Signal Process. Lett. **29**, 1232–1236 (2022)
18. Heo, Y.J., Yeo, W.H., Kim, B.G.: Deepfake detection algorithm based on improved vision transformer. Appl. Intell. **53**(7), 7512–7527 (2023)
19. Li, G., Yao, H., Le, Y., Qin, C.: Recaptured screen image identification based on vision transformer. J. Vis. Commun. Image Represent. **90**, 103692 (2023)
20. Yuan, K., Guo, S., Liu, Z., Zhou, A., Yu, F., Wu, W.: Incorporating convolution designs into visual transformers. In: Proceedings of the IEEE/CVF International Conference on Computer Vision, pp. 579–588 (2021)
21. Mao, X., et al.: Towards robust vision transformer. In: Proceedings of IEEE/CVF Conference on Computer Vision and Pattern Recognition, pp. 12042–12051 (2022)
22. Ba, J.L., Kiros, J.R., Hinton, G.E.: Layer normalization. arXiv preprint arXiv:1607.06450 (2016)
23. Hendrycks, D., Gimpel, K.: Gaussian error linear units (GELUs). arXiv preprint arXiv:1606.08415 (2016)
24. Kingma, D.P., Ba, J.: Adam: a method for stochastic optimization. arXiv preprint arXiv:1412.6980 (2014)
25. Ng, T.T., Chang, S.F., Hsu, J., Pepeljugoski, M.: Columbia photographic images and photorealistic computer graphics dataset. Columbia University, ADVENT Technical Report, pp. 205–2004 (2005)
26. Tokuda, E., Pedrini, H., Rocha, A.: Computer generated images vs. digital photographs: a synergetic feature and classifier combination approach. J. Vis. Commun. Image Represent. **24**(8), 1276–1292 (2013)
27. Rahmouni, N., Nozick, V., Yamagishi, J., Echizen, I.: Distinguishing computer graphics from natural images using convolution neural networks. In: 2017 IEEE Workshop on Information Forensics and Security (WIFS), pp. 1–6. IEEE (2017)
28. He, P., Jiang, X., Sun, T., Li, H.: Computer graphics identification combining convolutional and recurrent neural networks. IEEE Signal Process. Lett. **25**(9), 1369–1373 (2018)

# VoIP Steganalysis Using Shallow Multiscale Convolution and Transformer

Jinghui Peng[1]($\boxtimes$), Yi Liao[1], and Shanyu Tang[2]

[1] School of Cyber Security, Guangdong Polytechnic Normal University, Guangzhou 510665, Guangdong Province, China
jinghuipeng@gpnu.edu.cn
[2] Cybersecurity and Criminology Centre, University of West London, St. Mary's Road, W5 5RF London, UK

**Abstract.** Steganography is an effective method for transmitting secret information, but it can also be used for illegal activities such as terrorism, organized crime and data theft, etc. To solve the problem of steganography being used for malicious purposes, steganalysis technology has been developed. Steganalysis aims to detect whether the data has been steganography and identify whether it contains secret information, which is a kind of reverse process of steganography. VoIP data stream usually has high redundancy, which makes it an ideal carrier for steganography. In this paper, a Steganalysis Transformer (SAT) VoIP voice steganalysis method based on Transformer neural network is proposed with VoIP voice as the research object. The method first encodes the relative position of the features extracted from VoIP voice signals, combines the multi-scale convolution method to improve the local feature extraction to obtain more detailed feature information, transforms the high-dimensional sparse matrix into the low-dimensional dense features by mapping, and then realizes the steganalysis analysis through the feature extraction by the improved Transformer; the proposed SAT method is able to obtain the global features from the shallow layer and learn the high quality intermediate features. Experiments show that the SAT method proposed in this paper has superior performance, and the accuracy of VoIP steganalysis reaches 96.41%.

**Keywords:** Steganography · Steganalysis · Neural Network · Attention Mechanism · Transformer

## 1 Introduction

The way to protect the privacy and security of data is generally through the use of cryptographic techniques, by encrypting the content of the communication so that only the person who has the key can decrypt and view the communication. Cryptographic techniques have been widely used to encrypt plaintext data, transmit the ciphertext over the Internet, and decrypt the ciphertext at the receiving end to extract the plaintext [1]. However, since the ciphertext does not make much sense when interpreted, a hacker or intruder can easily detect that the information sent over the channel was encrypted

J. Cai et al. (Eds.): SPNCE 2023, LNICST 525, pp. 326–351, 2025.
https://doi.org/10.1007/978-3-031-73699-5_23

rather than plaintext, which naturally increases the curiosity of malicious hackers or intruders to cryptanalyze the ciphertext for attacks and makes them more likely to be targeted. Information hiding technology is to secretly embed the hidden information to be transmitted into the normal information by some specific methods, so that the secret information can be transmitted by the transmission of normal information at the same time without being detected, and it is an important research direction in the field of information security [2].

Steganography is a branch of information hiding technology, which aims to carry out secret communication without causing suspicion or detection by a third party, so as to ensure the security and privacy of communication [3]. Steganography can hide secret information in another information medium, which is generally called carrier, and the carrier can be images, voices, texts, videos, etc. There are two basic research methods for VoIP voice steganography: the steganography with the payload as the carrier in the voice stream of VoIP real-time transmission, and the steganography based on the network protocol. The payload-based VoIP voice steganography method exploits the redundancy of the voice stream itself and embeds secret information in the redundant bits of the carrier voice stream, which has better concealment and larger hidden capacity [4]. The payload-based VoIP voice steganography usually uses two basic steganographic algorithms, Least Significant Bit (LSB) steganography and Quantized Index Modulation (QIM) steganography. Steganography is difficult to detect and manipulate, and its correct use can ensure information security, but unfortunately, at present, steganography is mostly used in illegal activities, mainly involving terrorism, organized crime and data theft. For example, when spreading malicious software, hackers hide malicious software in ordinary files to steal users' personal information, control computers, and so on. The risk and impact of malicious use of steganography must be paid attention to, and there are huge security risks.

In order to solve the security risks caused by the malicious use of steganography, prevent the malicious use of steganography and protect information security, the most effective method is steganalysis, which can effectively detect steganography. It appears at the same time as steganography, which is antagonistic to each other. It was first used to evaluate the strength of steganography. The purpose of steganalysis is to analyze whether the carrier is steganographic, which belongs to the problem of pattern recognition or machine learning classification [5]. When the steganography algorithm embeds the secret data, the original data must be modified, and some statistical characteristics of the original data must also be modified. Therefore, we can distinguish whether it is steganographic by learning and analyzing the difference between the characteristics of the original data and the modified data. Steganalysis has a common pattern. Firstly, it extracts some feature information from the carrier of sample data, and then analyzes and classifies this feature information to detect whether the carrier is steganographic [6]. In addition, steganalysis has a very wide range of applications, such as network security, intelligence monitoring, legal forensics, etc. In the field of network security, steganalysis can be used to detect and prevent network attacks, prevent the spread of malicious software and data leakage; it is used to decrypt the secret information of terrorists and provide support for the fight against terrorism; it is used to crack the information of criminals and provide evidence for case investigation and evidence collection. Steganalysis is of great significance in protecting network and data security, promoting the development of steganography, and contributing to social security and stability.

## 2 Relate Work

The research stage of steganalysis can be roughly divided into two stages: In the first stage, Rich Model (RM) [7] is usually used to manually extract the features of the best results; in the early stage, statistical strategies are usually used to manually classify the extracted statistical features; After machine learning is mature, binary classifiers are used for classification (the common ones are ensemble classifier (EC) [8], support vector machine (SVM) [9] and perceptron; In the second stage, with the rapid development of deep learning [10], steganalysis also began to apply the method of deep learning, which can automatically extract relevant features and learn to detect steganography. At present, the steganalysis method of deep learning has shown strong performance in accuracy, robustness and detection efficiency, and gradually replace the traditional method, which is the mainstream research trend.

According to the format, audio steganalysis can be divided into steganalysis technology for compressed format (such as MP3 and AAC) and steganalysis technology for uncompressed format (such as WAV). According to the correlation characteristics of split vector quantization (VQ) codewords with linear predictive coding filter coefficients changed after QIM steganography, a model called quantized codeword correlation network (QCCN) is constructed, which is based on the split VQ codewords from adjacent audio frames. A high-performance detector is constructed by using support vector machine (SVM) classifier. It can effectively detect steganography used in G.723.1 and G.729 low bit rate audio codec.

In terms of compressed audio, Jin et al. [11] proposed a steganalysis technique to detect mp3stego steganography in 2016. Mp3stego changes the quantized modified discrete cosine transform coefficient (QMDCT) during the compression process, which affects the correlation between adjacent QMDCT's of the audio coverage. Therefore, Markov features can be extracted from the carrier audio and steganography audio to describe the correlation between QMDCT, and then these features are crossed through the preprocessing steps to select the best features to train the support vector machine classifier. The experimental results show that this method has high detection accuracy in the case of low embedding rate. In 2020, Wang et al. [12] proposed another steganalysis technique for MP3, which extracts the steganalysis features of MP3 by calculating the QMDCT coefficient matrix of MP3, and uses rich high-pass filtering technique to improve the sensitivity of the technique to noise signals. The author found that each replacement of a QMDCT coefficient changes a Huffman codeword. For this reason, they proposed a correlation measurement module, which is used to measure the correlation between point and $2 \times 2$ and $4 \times 4$ detect any possible changes in the QMDCT coefficient matrix on blocks. To reduce the dimension of the features and to select the optimal feature, an empirical threshold is applied. For the classification task, the ensemble classifier is trained.

Li [13] proposed a steganalysis method in low bit rate coded voice stream to detect the steganography of VoIP in compressed domain. According to the correlation characteristics of split vector quantization (VQ) codewords with linear predictive coding filter coefficients changed after QIM steganography, a model called quantized codeword correlation network (QCCN) is constructed based on the split VQ codewords of adjacent audio frames. A high-performance detector is constructed by using Support Vector Machine (SVM) classifier. It can effectively detect steganography used in G.723.1 and G.729 low bit rate audio codec.

For uncompressed format, it includes two methods: cooperative method and non-cooperative method. In the first method, the technique is based on the comparison between the estimated carrier signal and the steganography signal. There are many methods for estimating the carrier signal, including denoising, carrier linear basis, re-embedding and so on. However, it is also possible to estimate the steganalysis signal used for calibration, which was discovered by Ghasemzadeh et al. [14]. The authors proposed a general steganalysis technology based on calibration, which is a reliable audio steganalysis system based on Mel Frequency Cepstral Coefficient (R-MFCC), generating a model with the largest deviation from the HAS model and using genetic algorithm to optimize the dimension of features. In their technology, signals and random messages are embedded using re-embedding method. The energy feature is extracted, in which each signal and the re-embedding signal are divided into many blocks, and the energy of each block is calculated. Then, the energy of each block corresponding to the signal and its re-embedding is subtracted. Finally, the statistical properties of the energy features, including mean, skewness, standard deviation and kurtosis, are selected to train the SVM classifier. Their techniques have been evaluated with a variety of steganography techniques. The experimental results show that this method has a good detection effect in the case of pertinence and universality.

The non-cooperative method extracts feature directly from the audio signal based on the embedded feature domain. Han et al. [14] proposed a linear prediction method that extracts linear prediction LP features from segmented audio files. According to the experiment, the author found that LP parameters can significantly discriminate carrier and hidden information. Therefore, LP coefficients, LP residuals, LP spectra and LP Cepstral coefficients are extracted from time domain and frequency domain. The SVM classifier is trained based on the features extracted from the cover signal and the steganography signal. Extensive experiments have been conducted on different embedding rates and different steganography techniques have been tested. The results show that compared with the popular steganalysis technology at that time, the proposed technology is effective.

Traditional audio steganalysis schemes usually analyze the relevant feature information extracted manually or use traditional machine learning methods. The accuracy of the analysis results of traditional methods can usually be guaranteed at a high level. However, compared with deep learning, traditional audio steganalysis methods also have some problems. First, the algorithm is not universal enough to obtain features that are effective for most audio steganalysis algorithms; in terms of efficiency, it is far inferior to the currently mature deep learning method, and it cannot process data with large feature dimensions. Due to the concept of depth feature, neural networks have become a trend in deep learning and classification tasks in recent years. Both efficiency and accuracy reflect the power of deep learning. Neural networks also have better robustness and effectiveness. Steganalysis based on deep learning is also increasingly applied and needs more research.

Under the influence of this environment, most of the steganalysis methods in recent years are deep learning. The experimental results also show that steganalysis based on deep learning method is the appropriate research direction. In 2015, steganalysis began to enter the field of deep learning, which is different from the traditional machine learning methods. Qian [15] first added the method of deep learning to the research of steganalysis. They proposed that the task of steganalysis can be regarded as a formulaic binary classification problem to distinguish cover objects and steganalysis objects, and constructed the detection model of steganalysis through two steps of feature extraction and classification. Regarding the development of convolutional neural networks for classification tasks, since the proposal of AlexNet, more and deeper neural networks have been proposed, such as VGG and GoogleNet, and RESNET has solved the problem of gradient disappearance caused by too deep network depth. In 2018, Mehdi Boroumand [16] and others built a steganalysis model based on the deep residual network inspired by the deep residual network. The experimental results show that it has been relatively improved in the area of JPEG images. On this basis, researchers have tried various improved and optimized neural network models for steganalysis, which have achieved good results.

Convolutional neural network in audio steganalysis, Chen [17] first proposed a audio steganalysis model (ChenNet) based on convolutional neural network (CNN) to detect LSB (least significant bit matching) steganalysis in time domain. Then, Lin [18] improved the convolutional neural network model and used the truncated linear unit and residual module, which were effective in image steganalysis, to optimize it. Experiments proved the effectiveness of the model optimization. For the steganalysis of MP3, Ren [19] proposed a universal audio steganalysis method of MP3 and AAC (Advanced Audio Coding) based on the deep residual network (RESNET) and used the audio spectrum as the network input. Taking the spectrogram as the input feature can effectively detect voice steganography based on ACC and MP3. At the same time, taking the spectrograms of different sizes as multi-scale input, a group of high-pass filters are designed to distinguish the spectral energy differences between time and frequency caused by different steganography methods. The classification results are obtained by using the deep residual network training, this scheme has relatively better performance than the scheme using quantized modified discrete cosine transform MDCT coefficient and Mel spectrum as feature input. Zhang [20] also proposed a audio steganalysis method based on time domain, improved the convolutional neural network and used the deep residual method to build the model.

Inspired by the inception module, Li [21] and others used different convolution kernels in their model to increase the width of CNN architecture, and then connected them and tried to use different activation modules dam to form a new CNN architecture for image steganalysis. The experimental results are better than the existing models. The multi-scale network structure is used for multi-scale feature fusion. Different sizes of convolution kernels are used to obtain different outputs, and then the depth superposition becomes a new output feature. In CNN, the receptive field of the high-level network is different from that of the low-level network. The network extracts target features by layer-by-layer abstraction method. Different scale features have different effects on the results of the classification task. The model can be optimized by multiscale convolution kernel. The multi-scale model is derived from the proposed architecture of a deep convolutional neural network code named Inception [22].

Using the deep learning method to study VoIP steganalysis, Lin et al. [23] proposed an effective online steganalysis method to detect QIM steganalysis. This method is based on the code word correlation model of recurrent neural network (RNN), which can separate the relevant features into carrier audio and steganalysis audio, and then effectively detect QIM steganalysis. This method is the first deep learning network applied to the steganalysis task of network flow. In 2019, Yang [24] proposed a correct method that can combine the advantages of CNN and LSTM architecture, which uses bidirectional long-term and short-term memory recurrent neural network (BI-LSTM) to capture long-term context information in the carrier, and then uses CNN to capture local and global features and time carrier features to detect QIM-based steganalysis.

In the same year, Yang [25] analyzed the correlation of carriers and proposed a novel and very fast steganalysis method for VoIP streams. The vector quantization codewords are mapped into the semantic space, and only a hidden layer is used to extract the correlation between codewords. This method can quickly and accurately detect possible steganalysis in VoIP streams. In 2020, Yang et al. [26] designed a lightweight neural network called fast correlation extraction model (FCEM), which extracts features from VoIP frames only based on an attention variant called multi-head attention, and is significantly superior to the relatively complex recurrent neural network (RNN) and convolutional neural network (CNN) in terms of accuracy and time efficiency. In 2020, hu [27] designed a hierarchical representation network to solve the steganalysis problem of QIM steganography in low bit rate audio signals, and applied the three-level attention mechanism to different convolution blocks, so that it can pay different attention to contents of different importance in audio frames.

In 2022, Yang [28] developed a multi-channel convolutional sliding window (CSW) to analyze the correlation between a given frame and adjacent frames in VoIP signals, using two different channels to extract high-level features and low-level features, respectively, and analyzed the classification after linear layer fusion. This method has good performance in the steganography scheme with low embedding rate, and has greatly improved the detection efficiency of the model. It almost realizes the real-time detection in the process of VoIP communication. The above methods have limitations on the generality of many audio steganalysis methods. This method is mainly used to detect the steganography of QIM, and the effect of other steganography needs to be further studied.

Li [29] proposes a general frame-level steganalysis method for low bit-rate compressed audio. It uses the dual-domain representation method in time domain and compression domain to extract rich features from audio frames, and introduces an adaptive local correlation enhancement module to effectively model local features, which compensates for the shortcomings of the traditional transformer-based model. In 2022, Tian [30] proposed that in VoIP steganalysis, integer and fractional pitch delays are used as inputs, and a subframe splicing module is designed to organically integrate the integer and fractional pitch delays of subframes for real-time detection. A spatial fusion module based on pre-activated residual convolution is designed to extract pitch spatial features and gradually increase its dimension to find more subtle steganographic distortion to improve the detection effect, in which the group extrusion weighted block is introduced to reduce the information loss in the process of increasing the feature dimension. A time fusion module is designed that uses stacked LSTM to extract pitch time features, and a gated feedforward network is introduced to learn the interaction between different feature maps while suppressing useless features for detection.

At present, in the field of steganalysis, the methods based on deep learning have gradually replaced the traditional methods. Researchers have focused on deep learning. At present, the steganalysis methods based on deep learning have been continuously improved in accuracy and other aspects, and have caught up with and surpassed the traditional methods. At the same time, they are absolutely ahead in efficiency. But at present, audio steganalysis based on deep learning is still in its infancy, and there is a lot of research space. Many problems, such as the accuracy of low embedding rate, need to be further improved.

According to the current research on audio steganalysis, although the traditional audio steganalysis methods can usually achieve detection, the efficiency is far less than that of audio steganalysis based on deep learning. In this paper, the work of VoIP steganalysis mainly focuses on the neural network based on multi-scale and attention mechanism, and improves the accuracy and efficiency of the model by optimizing and adjusting the depth model and algorithm. The main contents of this paper are as follows: A voice steganalysis method of VoIP based on transformer is proposed. In order to solve the problem of high resource consumption in the optimization depth network, combining the respective advantages of transformer and CNN, the model uses the relative position coding method to obtain the location information missing in the model, multi-scale convolution operation is introduced to obtain the local feature information, which is complementary to transformer, and the SAT neural network model is constructed for VoIP steganalysis. The multi-head self-attention mechanism improves the processing ability of long sequence audio data, enhances the generalization ability of the model, and realizes the high efficiency and high accuracy of VoIP steganalysis.

## 3  Proposed Model for VoIP Steganalysis

Transformer is a self-attentive neural network model originally used in natural language processing. It can effectively process long sequence data. Compared with CNN and RNN, the computational complexity of each layer is lower, but the local information acquisition ability is not as good as CNN and RNN [31]. In order to give full play to the respective advantages of CNN and transformer, form a benign complement, and reduce the computational resources and training time of the model under the premise of ensuring the detection accuracy. Our proposes a steganalysis transformer (SAT) method based on transformer neural network to analyze VOIP voice data, so as to recognize the steganalysis information embedded in VoIP voice signal. The technologies including relative position coding [32], multi-scale feature fusion method, mapping method, self-attention mechanism, residual connection and normalization are adopted. The relative position coding is used to obtain the accurate position information in the self-attention calculation process, the multi-scale feature fusion method is used to improve the local feature extraction to obtain the detailed information, and the mapping method is used to adjust the sample shape. The self-attention mechanism reduces the dependence on external information, it can better capture the internal correlation of features and solve the problem of long dependence. The residual connection can prevent the gradient from disappearing, and the normalization can improve the generalization ability and effect of the model. Through the experimental verification of the model, it is proved that the SAT method can train faster and effectively detect the hidden information in VoIP audio signal.

We propose a VoIP steganalysis method based on satellite neural network, design a low-cost neural network model, and ensure the accuracy of hidden information detection at the same time. We use multi-scale feature fusion method and multi-head self-attention mechanism to improve the performance. The voice steganalysis method of VoIP based on SAT is proposed. By combining transformer and CNN for modeling, the advantages of both can be complemented, the generalization ability of the model can be improved, and the modeling ability of spatial and temporal features of the model can be enhanced. At the same time, the acquisition of global and local features is taken into account. The parallel computation of transformer greatly reduces the computational cost, and the strong feature extraction ability of CNN ensures the recognition accuracy of the model.

As shown in the Fig. 1, in our method to detect whether the VoIP voice carries secret information, we first preprocess the original VoIP voice data to extract the linear prediction parameters and adaptive codebook parameters in the voice signal, and then divide the two sets of features into training set and test set. The training set is used for training the SAT neural network model, and the test set is used for experimental testing. In the model training, the audio data samples are coded by relative position, and then the features are fused after multi-scale convolution, and then the fused features are mapped. The improved transformer module is used to compute self-attention, and multiple are superimposed to form multi-head self-attention. Combined with residual and normalization operations, the multi-layer perceptron classifier is used for classification, The steganalysis of VoIP audio is completed by distinguishing carrier samples from carrier samples. After the error of the model converges, the SAT model is stored and tested online with the test set, and the output results are used to determine whether the audio signal carries secret information.

## 3.1 Pre-processing VoIP Data

Before entering neural network model training, the data must be pre-processed. This process can control the data quality, standardize the data and optimize the algorithm. In the process of VoIP covert communication, it is necessary to sample the original VoIP voice signal and convert the analog voice signal to digital signal before it can be transmitted by the network. Usually, the WAV format is used as a lossless voice file format to store high quality voice data and protect the steganography information from damage. Next, the wav format must be converted into a pure PCM voice file. The PCM voice file does not contain any other metadata. After that, the pure voice data

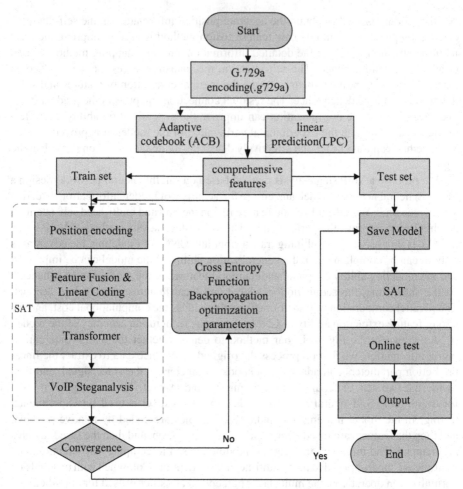

**Fig. 1.** Flow chart of SAT steganalysis algorithm

needs to be encoded into the PCM format. The encoders commonly used in VoIP voice communication include G.729, G.723.1, AMR, G.729A, etc.

According to the principle of VoIP communication, analog voice signals are converted into digital voice signals and compressed to reduce the bandwidth and delay of data transmission. Then, after negotiation, the compressed digital voice signal is divided into multiple packets for packet transmission, and header information is added to each packet. Unused fields of the protocol header are usually used to hide information; after receiving the digital voice signal data packet, the receiver reconstructs the header information to obtain a complete digital voice signal. Finally, the digital voice signal is restored to an analog voice signal and played back to complete the VoIP voice communication. Steganography is usually embedded in the compression coding process, so we extract the corresponding feature parameters in the compression coding for steganalysis.

The audio sample we use uses the coding format of G.729A. G.729A can provide high quality, high bit rate audio communication, and can compress the 16kHz, 16-bit precision PCM audio signal to a bit rate of 8kbps, ensuring high audio quality and low delay. Generally, the steganography of VoIP payload is concentrated in this compression process, so the corresponding decoder is used to obtain the corresponding features. The steganography method used in VoIP payload usually affects LPC parameters and ACB parameters, so extracting these two audio parameters as the input of neural network can effectively detect VoIP steganography.

We divided the G.729A compressed audio samples with sampling time of 1s into 100time frames, and extracted 7 LPC parameters and ACB parameters from each time frame. In order to meet the operation requirements of the subsequent neural network models, the combined features added one dimension. Finally, the data set is divided, the training set is used for model training, and the test set is used for evaluation test. Then, the position coding information is added, and the relative position coding is used to add the dominant position information to the sample.

### 3.2  Modeling and Training

Build a SAT model for training, and save the model after convergence for subsequent testing. The constructed model mainly consists of four main parts: location coding, feature fusion, linear coding and transformer. Location coding solves the missing location information in the computation of the attention mechanism. Feature fusion obtains local and global information. Linear coding is realized by mapping. The features within the method are used by transformer to compute self-attention and solve the problem of long-distance feature detection of time series.

### 3.3  Online Test

After the model is saved, the model structure and the saved optimal parameters are reproduced. The test set is put into the model for evaluation and testing, and the predicted label is obtained. The results are obtained after comparing with the real label, and whether the secret information is carried in the output carrier is obtained.

The overall structure of the SAT model is shown in Fig. 2. There are four parts in total. Figure 2(a) is the overall structure of the model, including data preprocessing part, position coding part, multi-scale feature fusion part, and improved transformer part. Figure 2(b) is an enhanced transform module, where norm represents the normalization operation. Here, layer normalization is used to reduce the gradient disappearance problem. X is an abstract multi-head self-attention module. MLP is a multilayer perceptron composed of a full connection layer, which also combines the operation of residual connection. Figure 2(c) is a multi-scale feature fusion module, which includes convolution operations and pooling of different scales. Figure 2(d) is the multi-head self-attention calculation module, which is the core of the transformer. The samples after linear coding calculate self-attention, and the superimposed h heads are fused to form multi-head self-attention.

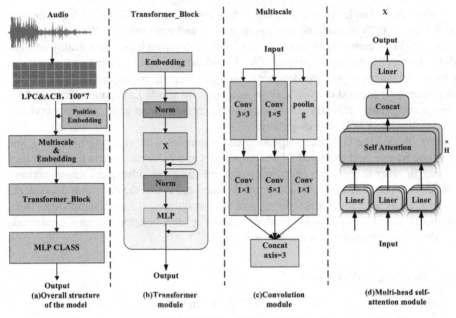

**Fig. 2.** SAT model structure

## 3.4 Relative Position Encoding

Position encoding describes the location and relationship of entities in the sequence and gives a unique representation to each element in the sequence. The self-attention used in the transformer neural network is a global operation that is insensitive to location information. Changing the location coding between two elements will not affect the result, and it does not have the ability to learn the word order of RNN. Therefore, it is necessary to add position encoding information. The traditional CNN model, due to its local processing mechanism, that is, it only works on several neighbors of the target element, so it will be limited in dealing with the problem of long sequence, but the relative position between elements can be noticed. Some previous work has also shown that CNN can learn some position information through padding, but how to express the position explicitly is still a problem. So, although there are some CNN operations in the model, this chapter marks the position information by adding position encoding to the encoding process.

The commonly used position encoding methods are absolute position encoding and relative position encoding. Absolute position coding generally uses learnable absolute position encoding, that is, the representation of each position is added directly to the representation of the token as a learnable vector. There are also problems with this method: (1) The position encoding itself needs to be learned by a large amount of data. If the length of the training set exceeds the maximum length, the model cannot learn the position information; (2) the relative relationship between position vectors is not exploited. Relative position encoding requires only a limited number of position codes that can express the relative position of any length, so it can process any length of data.

Relative position coding refers to the direct consideration of the relative position between two tokens when calculating the attention score. The output calculation elements $z_i$ are the weighted sum of the input elements of the linear transformation, and the relative position information is taken into account, which can be expressed as Formula 1.

$$z_i = \sum_{j=1}^{n} \alpha_{ij}(x_j W^V + a_{ij}^V) \tag{1}$$

Calculate the weight coefficient using the Softmax activation function:

$$\alpha_{ij} = \frac{\exp e_{ij}}{\sum_{k=1}^{n} \exp e_{ik}} \tag{2}$$

Compare the compatibility functions of two input elements to calculate $e_{ij}$, and add the relative position calculation:

$$e_{ij} = \frac{(x_i W^Q)(x_j W^K + a_{ij}^K)^T}{\sqrt{d_z}} \tag{3}$$

### 3.5 Feature Fusion and Linear Encoding

CNN can capture local dependencies well, and transformer can obtain global dependencies by using multi-head self-attention mechanism. The two methods complement each other. At the same time, to further verify the effectiveness of the multiscale method proposed in the previous chapter, the multiscale feature fusion method proposed in the previous chapter is added to the SAT model to introduce the convolution operation.

The various operations of VIT [33] and Swin Transformer [34] in patch embedding are all for the purpose of adjusting the size of the input. A large input size is too expensive for the transformer to process, so the same processing method as for text is adopted for the image to ensure that the transformer can process it, so we can also process the audio samples accordingly. Patch embedding in vit is used to convert two-dimensional images into a series of one-dimensional patch embeddings. The input size is (H × W × C), According to Patch Size to get the size of P × P, The number of image blocks of is N = H × W/ P2. Where n can be understood as the sequence length, and the dimension Dim (size P2 × C) of each element in each sequence, It is called patch embedding.

The linear encoding in our model is realized by the mapping layer, and the size of the audio sample after preprocessing and extracting the feature parameters is 100 × 7. Since the audio samples are divided according to the time frame during feature extraction, we take the length of the time frame 100 as the sequence length, and the 7-dimensional features are mapped to the corresponding sample dimension. The final dimension is to maintain the same size of the original input data and the element relationship of the original sequence.

## 3.6   Transformer Module

Our model improves the transformer module, maintains the overall structure of the model, abstracts the core part, and reduces the residual operation, making it more suitable for VoIP voice steganalysis. At the same time, it does not overlap the module many times to reduce the complexity of the model. The performance advantage of the transformer is mainly due to its structure. When we abstract the multi-head self-attention of the encoder part, we get the module Meta-former [35], and use the multi-head self-attention method in the abstract block. Self-attention can reduce the dependence on external information and pay more attention to the internal correlation of data, so as to solve the problem of long dependence. Using multi head self-attention can make the model focus on multiple key information in the whole situation, so as to solve the problem of self-attention over focus on itself. Therefore, the transformer architecture is maintained in the model construction to verify the effectiveness of the attention mechanism in VoIP voice steganalysis.

$$X = InputEmbedding(x) \tag{4}$$

where, $x$ is the input of the sample, and X is the input of the transformer after the embedding.

The two residual connections can be expressed as:

$$X = Attention(LN(x)) + x \tag{5}$$

where, $x$ is input, Attention is multi-head self-attention, LN is layer normalization, and batch normalization can also be attempted.

$$X = \sigma(LN(x)W_1)W_2 + x \tag{6}$$

where it is mainly composed of a two-layer MLP with nonlinear activation, $x$ is the output of the first remaining connection, and the activation function here is ReLU (or GELU). The two-layer MLP with nonlinear activation has two full connection layers. After passing through a full connection layer, it is activated by the ReLU function and then connected to a full connection layer to get the output.

The structure of the MLP is shown in Fig. 3. There are two complete connection layers and a ReLU activation function.

Self-attention in Transformer is the core of it. Self-attention can be thought of as learning a relationship, the relationship between the current element and other elements in a sequence, and the dependency can be computed directly regardless of the distance. The attention function can be described as mapping a query and a set of key-value pairs to the output, which can be obtained by calculating the weighted sum of the values.

Attention function in the model through the matrix way to achieve parallel computing. First calculate the point multiplication result of query and all keys, and then multiply by the scaling factor 1/k d to prevent the product result from being too large. Send the above calculation results to the Softmax function to obtain the weight corresponding to the value. According to this weight, you can configure the value vector to get the final output. The process of calculating the output of attention relationship can be simply expressed as the function attention (Q, K, V), and the calculation formula is:

$$Attention(Q, K, V) = Softmax\left(\frac{QK^T}{\sqrt{d_k}}\right)V \tag{7}$$

MLP

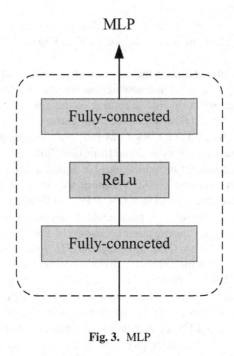

**Fig. 3.** MLP

The multi-head attention module is shown in Fig. 2(d). Multi-head self-attention uses multiple queries to compute and select multiple information from the input information in parallel. Each attention focuses on different parts of the input information, initializes multiple groups of different (Q, K, V) matrices by different coding forms to compute multiple attention, and then connects them. Its calculation formula is expressed as:

$$MultiHead(Q, K, V) = Conact(head_1, \ldots, head_n)W^o head_1$$
$$= Attention(QW_i^Q, KW_i^K, VW_i^V) \tag{8}$$

Finally, MLP is also used to achieve classification, and sigmoid function is used to output the samples that distinguish steganography from non-steganography. Or add a classification label in the embedding to output the same classification effect.

## 4   Results and Discussion

### 4.1   Data Set

The dataset we use is from VStego800k, which is a large dataset for voice steganalysis over VoIP, and is a mixture of different steganography algorithms, embedding rate, and quality factors. The duration of all samples in the data set is uniformly shortened to 1 s, and the collected audio signals are mixed with male and female speakers, Chinese and English. This dataset contains 814592 streaming audio clips, which are divided into 50000 samples as the test set and the remaining samples as the training set. VStego800k uses two typical streaming audio steganography algorithms for each steganographic sample, and randomly selects the embedding rate of 10% -40% to embed secret information.

The audio sample data set used in the experiment is a total of 310000 Chinese audio samples, including steganographic and non-steganographic samples, with a ratio of 1:1. In this chapter, the data set is divided according to the ratio of 8:2, and gets 248000 samples as the training set and 62000 samples as the test set. The sample steganography method is randomly selected from CNV-QIM [36] pitch steganography method [37], and the embedding rate is randomly selected from 10%, 20%, 30%, and 40%.

Each segment of the sample is divided into 100 time frames. In each frame, a total of 7 data including LPC features and ACB features are extracted. Finally, the shape of the feature sample in the input model is $100 \times 7$. For the feature parameter selection, it is based on the steganography of LPC parameters. It can be observed that the relevant special effects of split vector quantization codeword of linear predictive coding filter coefficients have changed after QIM steganography. In audio coding, the LPC coefficients of each frame are extracted and converted into line spectral frequency (LSF) coefficients. Then the LSF coefficients are coded using the VQ format. Low bit rate audio coders typically use split VQ. For example, in the G.729 or G.723.1 standards, the quantized LSF coefficients are described by the quantized codeword set $C = \{C1, C2, C3\}$, where C1, C2, and C3 are codewords selected from codebooks C1, C2, and C3, respectively. The QIM steganography scheme hides the secret information in the VQ process. This method is easy to implement and has low computational complexity. Therefore, this method is suitable for establishing covert channel in VoIP. Compared with MFCC Mel Cepstral Coefficient or LPL Linear Perceptual Prediction, which are commonly used by mainstream audio recognition systems in the past, LPC used in this chapter is based on the characteristics of human voice mechanism, which mainly distinguishes different vocals and vowels by the formant distribution position. Formants are areas where the energy of sound is relatively centralized in the spectrum. The frequency and bandwidth of formant can be well calculated by using LPC parameters to characterize the sound. The steganography method in the example is based on the fact that the LPC parameters will also change to a certain extent after steganography, so the extracted LPC features can be used as learning parameters.

ACB parameter is a parameter extracted from pitch feature. Pitch parameter is an important feature parameter in audio signal processing, which is used to describe the pitch periodicity of audio signal. Pitch period refers to the time of sound wave vibration repetition in each cycle of audio signal, and it is one of the most periodic parts of a audio signal. Pitch extraction algorithm is usually used to extract pitch period from audio signal and represent it as pitch parameter. Pitch frequency refers to the number of repeated pitch cycles per second in the audio signal, which is also the reciprocal of the pitch cycle. It can reflect the speaker's voice pitch, tone change and other information. Pitch intensity refers to the energy of the pitch part in the audio signal. It can reflect the speaker's emotional state, speaking posture and other information. Pitch phase refers to the difference between the start position and end position of the pitch part in a audio signal. It can reflect the speaker's speaking speed, voice mode, and other information.

Pitch-based steganography uses the pitch periodicity of audio signals to hide information. The embedding process of hidden information: convert the information to be hidden into binary code, and select different embedding schemes according to the parity of pitch periods. For example, when the pitch period is even, "0" and "1" can be represented by positive and negative cadence, while when the pitch period is odd, "0" and "1" can be represented by high and low rise and fall. In the process of pitch steganography, small amplitude change determines the value of pitch period, so the extracted pitch feature information can effectively enable the model to learn and classify. LPC parameters and ACB parameters can be steganography using either LSB or QIM. Therefore, selecting these two feature parameters can perform most of the VoIP voice steganalysis to improve the universality of the model.

## 4.2 Evaluation Index

The common evaluation indicators of steganalysis include accuracy, detection time, false detection rate and missing detection rate. Detection accuracy is the most important. The model training time is also a reference index. The detection time can reflect the detection efficiency of the model, but it is affected by the computer configuration. Steganalysis is a binary classification task in deep learning, so we can refer to the evaluation index of binary classification. There are two kinds of steganalysis samples, including cover and stego. Set stego as positive sample P = Positive and cover as negative sample N = Negative. There are:

$$acc = \frac{X_{tp} + X_{tn}}{X_{tp} + X_{tn} + X_{fp} + X_{fn}} \qquad (9)$$

where: $acc$ is the accuracy, $X_{tp}$ is the number of samples correctly classified as steganographic, $X_{tn}$ is the number of samples correctly classified as non-steganographic, $X_{fp}$ is the number of non-steganographic samples incorrectly classified as steganographic, $X_{fn}$ classifies the number of steganographic samples as non-steganographic samples for errors [38]. At the same time, the following indicators can reflect the performance of the model:

The detection sample duration is used as an evaluation index to assess the performance of steganography detection.

$$\overline{T} = \frac{T_{test}}{T_{Sam}} \qquad (10)$$

where: $\overline{T}$ is the average detection duration, $T_{test}$ is the total duration, $T_{Sam}$ is the total length of the sample.

## 4.3 Experimental Environment

The model designed in this paper is written in Python language based on Tensorflow2.4 deep learning framework, and runs on win10 system with Intel ® Core™ I7-12700kf, GPU adopts NVIDIA GeForce RTX4090. The main parameters of the training process are set as follows: the learning rate is 0.001 by default, the batch size is set to 64, and the optimizer uses Adam.

**4.4  Experimental Results**

Table 2 shows the experimental results of VoIP steganalysis based on the SAT model. It can be seen that the final accuracy of the experimental results is at a high level. In the total of 62000 test samples, 1637 cover samples were detected as stego samples, and only 785 stego samples were misjudged as cover samples, that is, stego samples were not correctly detected. The test recall rate reached 97.46%, the accuracy rate of the test results reached 96.41%, and the comprehensive evaluation index F1 score was 96.45%, which can prove the effectiveness of the proposed method for VoIP steganalysis. Figures 4 and 5 shows the confusion matrix drawn based on the experimental results. From the confusion matrix, we can intuitively see that the performance of the VoIP steganalysis model is good in detecting stego-like positive samples, and can detect positive samples with secret information (Table 1).

**Table 1.** Sample processing method

| Encoder | Steganographic algorithms | Parameters | Sample length | Embedding rates |
|---------|---------------------------|------------|---------------|-----------------|
| **G.729A** | CNV-QIM | LPC | 1s | 0–40% |
| **G.729A** | PMS | ACB | 1s | 0–40% |

**Table 2.** Experimental result

| TP | TN | FP | FN | FPR | FNR | Precision | Recall | F1 | ACC |
|----|----|----|----|-----|-----|-----------|--------|----|----|
| 30251 | 29523 | 1570 | 656 | 5.04% | 2.12% | 95.06% | 97.78% | 96.45% | 96.41% |

Figure 4 describes the process that the accuracy of the model of the training set and the test set continues to improve with the number of iterations, where the number of iterations is set to 20, and the number of iterations refers to the process of updating the weight parameters each time during the training process. Typically, we need to train the model repeatedly until the performance of the model tends to be stable. In Figs. 4, 5 and 6, the number of iterations is set to 20, and the model has improved significantly within this number of iterations. However, it should be noted that too few iterations can lead to under-fitting of the model, while too many iterations can lead to over-fitting. ACC reflects the model's accuracy of detection; ACC refers to the model's accuracy of detection, that is, the proportion of predicted results that agree with the actual results. The higher the ACC, the higher the accuracy of the model. Therefore, we hope to evaluate the performance of the model and adjust and optimize it by monitoring the ACC on the training set and the test set. From the training process diagram of the experiment, it can be seen that the accuracy of the training set increases and converges with the number of iterations, and the test validation set gradually increases with the number of iterations and finally tends to be stable. The accuracy of the training set with 20 iterations is 99.4%, and the accuracy of the test set is 96.41%.

Figure 5 describes the change in the loss function, which is an indicator to measure the difference between the predicted value and the actual value of the model. The loss value is the value calculated by the model according to the loss function in the training process. The loss value essentially reflects the performance of the model in the training process. The larger it is, the closer the predicted result of the model is to the real value, i.e., the better the performance of the model. The training loss gradually decreased and converged, and the loss value of the test set also tended to be stable after falling to a certain level. The loss value has two main functions: on the one hand, it is used to evaluate the performance of the model. During the training process, the super-parameters of the model can be adjusted according to the change of the loss value to achieve better performance; on the other hand, it is used to optimize the model. During back propagation, we need to use the loss value to update the model parameters by gradient descent to continuously optimize the model.

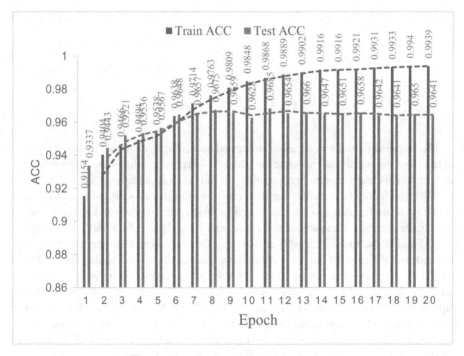

**Fig. 4.** Visualization of the training process

## 4.5 Comparative Analysis

In order to evaluate the performance of the proposed model, we compare the performance of the algorithm from many aspects, including comparing the different structures of the model and the existing VoIP steganalysis methods.

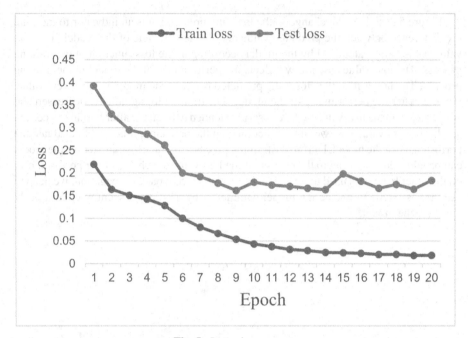

**Fig. 5.** Loss change curve

The model structure was adjusted and tested accordingly, as shown in Table 3. When we removed the multi-scale module and the self-attention module from the model, the model could not learn the effective parameters, and the final detection accuracy was only 50.21%, which could not detect the secret information in the VoIP voice signal. After removing the multi-scale module, multi head self-attention module and position coding module, the accuracy of the whole model decreased by 2.28%, 2.31% and 1.18%, respectively. Finally, the multi-head self-attention in the transformer structure is abstractly replaced, and the channel attention mechanism used in the table is replaced. It is found that the decrease in detection accuracy is not very large, which is 0.9% lower than the full model in this chapter. The results show that the attention mechanism can effectively improve the voice steganalysis performance of VoIP, and the structure of the transformer can give full play to its advantages of global modeling. Therefore, it is proved that multi-scale feature fusion method and attention mechanism are effective methods to improve the accuracy of voice steganalysis in VoIP.

In order to verify the VoIP voice detection performance of the proposed method, the detection performance of the proposed method is compared with several existing methods in mixed random samples. The mixed samples are randomly selected by steganography method, and the embedding rate is 0.1bps-0.4bps. As shown in Table 4, the comparison methods are SS-QCCN [39], CCN [40], RSM [23], FSM [25], and SFFN [27], and all the methods are tested on the mixed sample test set VStego800K. It can be seen from the table that some existing VoIP steganalysis methods do not perform well in the mixed samples with low embedding rate and short sampling time, and the detection accuracy is less than 90%, while the SAT method proposed in this paper has an accuracy, precision, recall

**Table 3.** Comparing different model structures

| Model structure | Accuracy | Effect |
|---|---|---|
| Remove multi-scale and self-attention modules | 50.21% | Decrease 46.20% |
| Remove multi-scale modules | 94.13% | Decrease 2.28% |
| Remove multiple self-attention modules | 94.10% | Decrease 2.31% |
| Remove position encoding modules | 95.23% | Decrease 1.18% |
| Replace self-attention modules | 95.51% | Decrease 0.9% |
| Proposed full model | 96.41% | - |

and F1 score of more than 95%. CCN and SS-QCCN are traditional machine learning methods based on manual features and classifiers. It can be clearly seen that the proposed method is superior to the traditional machine learning method in the case of complex test samples. RSM-SM, FSM and SFFN are some existing VoIP steganalysis methods based on deep learning. From the perspective of detection accuracy, this method is superior to these methods. Compared with the FSM with the best results among the existing methods, the accuracy of the methods in this chapter has been improved by 7.16%. The above experimental results show that the proposed algorithm has good performance in VoIP steganalysis, and can effectively detect the steganography in VoIP audio signals.

**Table 4.** Compare existing methods

| Steganalysis method | ACC | Precision | Recall | F1 Score |
|---|---|---|---|---|
| PROPOSED | 0.9641 | 0.9506 | 0.9778 | 0.9645 |
| SS-QCCN | 0.6117 | 0.6595 | 0.4617 | 0.5432 |
| CCN | 0.5542 | 0.5544 | 0.5517 | 0.5531 |
| RSM-SM | 0.5174 | 0.5103 | 0.8605 | 0.6407 |
| FSM | 0.8925 | 0.8885 | 0.8115 | 0.8100 |
| SFFN | 0.7048 | 0.7206 | 0.6689 | 0.6938 |

To verify the efficiency of the model proposed in this paper, we compared the training time and detection time of the model. The training time and detection time of the model are greatly affected by the hardware equipment. The total number of samples in one round of training is 24000, and the average detection time is the average detection time of each sample in the test. As shown in Table 5, the method proposed in this paper compared with the method of multi-scale and attention mechanism has been shortened to one third under both indicators. Under the condition of detecting the VoIP voice samples with a length of 1s, the detection time has been reduced by 0.68ms, but the detection accuracy has been slightly reduced by 0.94%. The experimental results show that the method proposed in this paper has been greatly improved in terms of efficiency. Under the premise of ensuring the detection accuracy, it reduces the computational resources and training time of the model, and improves the efficiency of detecting VoIP voice steganography. The average time required by several different methods to detect the steganography information in the audio signal with the sampling time of 1 s is compared. Sat method and MAS method are the average detection time tested in the experimental environment. The detection sampling time of 1 s is 0.32 ms and 1 ms, respectively. Other method data are from FCEM [26]. The detection time of RSM-SM [23] and RCNN [24] methods takes longer than other methods, 4.165 ms and 3.754 ms respectively, HRN [39] method takes 0.512 ms, and FCEM method takes only 0.281 ms to complete the detection.

**Table 5.** Comparison of 1-s sample detection time

| Steganalysis method | Average detection time | Average training time per step |
|---|---|---|
| PROPOSED | 0.32 ms | 21 ms |
| MAS | 1 ms | 64 ms |
| RSM-SM | 4.165 ms | - |
| RCNN | 3.754 ms | - |
| HRN | 0.512 ms | - |
| FCEM | 0.281 ms | - |

Compare the FCEM method based on multi-head self-attention with the method based on CNN [41]. FCEM is a neural network constructed by using only multi-head self-attention, which realizes fast detection of VoIP steganography. Compared with the traditional audio steganalysis method, the CNN method has higher detection accuracy, stronger robustness and higher computational efficiency.

The FCEM model and the CNN model are reproduced and tested in the same environment. Figures 6 and 7 compare the accuracy, false positive rate and false negative rate of these methods, respectively. Sat is the method of this paper, in which the accuracy of this method is improved by 2.21%, the false positive rate is reduced by 1.4%, and the false negative rate is reduced by 3.13% compared with the FCEM method using only multi-head self-attention; compared with CNN, the accuracy of this method is increased by 4.61%, the false positive rate is reduced by 4.93%, and the false negative rate is reduced by 2.78%.

The experimental results in Figs. 6 and 7 show that the SAT method used in this paper can better detect the steganographic information in the mixed samples, and can achieve effective VoIP steganalysis. Compared with the FCEM model, it shows that the convolution operation introduced by the multi-scale module used in this chapter can compensate for the problem of local information certainty in the transformer, and the combination of the two is benign and complementary. Compared with the CNN model, the attention mechanism can obtain more global features, which proves that the SAT neural network proposed in this paper is an effective voice steganalysis method for VoIP.

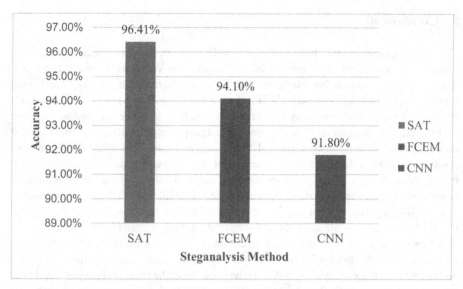

**Fig. 6.** Comparison of Accuracy with CNN and FCEM

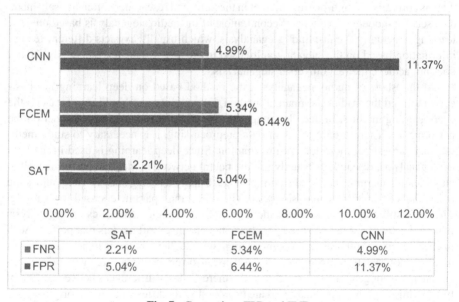

|        | SAT    | FCEM   | CNN     |
|--------|--------|--------|---------|
| ■FNR   | 2.21%  | 5.34%  | 4.99%   |
| ■FPR   | 5.04%  | 6.44%  | 11.37%  |

**Fig. 7.** Comparison FPR and FNR

## 5 Conclusion

The wide application and characteristics of VoIP network streaming media make it an excellent carrier for covert communication. Research on VoIP-based voice steganography and steganalysis has become a research hotspot. The malicious use of covert communication technology will make VoIP information security more serious. At present, the VoIP steganalysis technology is generally not mature, so it needs to further improve the theoretical system and technical framework. This paper proposes a SAT model based on transformer neural network for VoIP voice steganalysis. This method uses relative position coding to effectively obtain the relationship between sequence elements; combining the multiscale of the previous method, the convolution operation is introduced to enhance the capture of local information, and the dimension of the feature map is reduced by mapping; optimizing the transformer architecture, solving the problem of learning distance dependence with self-attention, and improving the processing ability of long audio sequences to achieve higher detection efficiency and accuracy. Experimental results show that the SAT model can detect steganography with low embedding rate, and the detection accuracy is 96.41%. At the same time, the detection time is also better than most existing methods, which can effectively detect malicious steganography. At the same time, the research also has some limitations. For the field of audio steganalysis, there is currently no high-quality data set in the field, and researchers often use self-made data sets for model experiments. Second, most of the audio steganalysis based on deep learning is actually "semi-blind" steganalysis, which usually extracts different feature information based on the steganography used in the data set for learning analysis, and does not achieve the real universal steganalysis.

At this stage of audio steganalysis, the method based on deep learning has basically replaced the traditional manual method. Future research should also focus on the deep learning method. In deep learning, the size of the data has a great impact on the performance. Therefore, in terms of data preprocessing, it is necessary to study methods that can extract more feature information. Since deep learning is used in the field of steganalysis, researchers usually use the neural network model that performs well in classification learning tasks at the current stage to apply it to steganalysis tasks, and some researchers optimize steganalysis by studying the feature parameters used for learning. There are still many things to consider according to the characteristics of steganalysis in neural networks. Many deep steganalysis models only graft models that perform well in classification. At the same time, there are many excellent methods in neural networks that have not been tested. Steganalysis tasks are also very different from general classification tasks. For general classification tasks, there are large differences between different types, while the steganalysis samples are usually slightly different from the original samples by a small amount of modification, which is a place that needs special attention. At the same time, considering the timeliness of real-time streaming media, we need to balance the accuracy of the model and the detection efficiency of the model. For the transformer-based method, this method has been proved to have excellent performance in various fields, but there is not much research in the field of steganalysis at present, so we need to verify the effectiveness of this method from more angles. In future research on steganalysis, it should be noted that unlike other deep learning classification tasks, steganalysis itself pays more attention to details, and its characteristics should be taken into account in the research.

**Acknowledgments.** This work was supported in part by the Education Department of Guang-dong Province under Grant 2021KTSCX063, Special topic of basic and applied basic research in Guangzhou under Grant SL2023A04J01043, Guangdong Regional Joint Fund under Grant 2022A1515110693and GPNU Science Foundation under Grant 2021SDKYA 025.

# References

1. Priscilla, C.V., Hemamalini, V.: Steganalysis techniques: a systematic review. J. Surv. Fisher. Sci. **10**(2S), 244–263 (2023)
2. Dalal, M., Juneja, M.: Steganography and Steganalysis (in digital forensics): a cybersecurity guide. Multimedia Tools Appl. **80**(4), 5723–5771 (2020)
3. Peng, J., Jiang, Y., Tang, S., et al.: Security of streaming media communications with logistic map and self-adaptive detection-based steganography. IEEE Trans. Depend. Sec. Comput. **18**(4), 1962–1973 (2019)
4. Yi, X., Yang, K., Zhao, X., et al.: AHCM: adaptive Huffman code mapping for audio steganography based on psychoacoustic model. IEEE Trans. Inf. Forensics Secur. **14**(8), 2217–2231 (2019)
5. Peng, J., Tang, S.: Covert communication over VoIP streaming media with dynamic key distribution and authentication. IEEE Trans. Industr. Electron. **68**(4), 3619–3628 (2020)
6. Chaharlang, J., Mosleh, M., Rasouli-Heikalabad, S.: A novel quantum steganography-Steganalysis system for audio signals. Multimedia Tools Appl. **79**(25–26), 17551–17577 (2020)
7. Fridrich, J., Kodovsky, J.: Rich models for steganalysis of digital images. IEEE Trans. Inf. Forensics Secur. **7**(3), 868–882 (2012)
8. Kodovsky, J., Fridrich, J., Holub, V.: Ensemble classifiers for steganalysis of digital media. IEEE Trans. Inf. Forensics Secur. **7**(2), 432–444 (2011)
9. Cortes, C., Vapnik, V.: Support-vector networks. Mach. Learn. **20**, 273–297 (1995)
10. Lecun, Y., Bengio, Y., Hinton, G.: Deep learning. Nature **521**(7553), 436–444 (2015)
11. Jin, C., Wang, R., Yan, D.: Steganalysis of MP3Stego with low embedding-rate using Markov feature. Multimedia Tools Appl. **76**(5), 6143–6158 (2017)
12. Wang, Y., Yi, X., Zhao, X.: MP3 steganalysis based on joint point-wise and block-wise correlations. Inf. Sci. **512**, 1118–1133 (2020)
13. Li, S., Jia, Y., Kuo, C.C.J.: Steganalysis of QIM steganography in low-bit-rate speech signals. IEEE/ACM Trans. Audio Speech Lang. Process. **25**(5), 1011–1022 (2017)
14. Ghasemzadeh, H., Tajik Khass, M., Khalil Arjmandi, M.: Audio steganalysis based on reversed psychoacoustic model of human hearing. Dig. Sig. Process. **51**, 133–141 (2016)
15. Qian, Y., Dong, J., Wang, W., et al.: Deep learning for steganalysis via convolutional neural networks. In: Media Watermarking, Security, and Forensics 2015. SPIE, vol. 9409, pp. 171–180 (2015)
16. Boroumand, M., Chen, M., Fridrich, J.: Deep residual network for steganalysis of digital images. IEEE Trans. Inf. Forensics Secur. **14**(5), 1181–1193 (2018)
17. Chen, B., Luo, W., Li, H.: Audio steganalysis with convolutional neural network. In: Proceedings of the 5th ACM Workshop on Information Hiding and Multimedia Security, pp. 85–90 (2017)

18. Lin, Y., Wang, R., Yan, D., et al.: Audio steganalysis with improved convolutional neural network. In: Proceedings of the ACM Workshop on Information Hiding and Multimedia Security, pp. 210–215 (2019)
19. Ren, Y., Liu, D., Xiong, Q., et al.: Spec-resnet: a general audio steganalysis scheme based on deep residual network of spectrogram. arXiv preprint arXiv:190106838 (2019)
20. Zhang, Z., Yi, X., Zhao, X.: Improving audio steganalysis using deep residual networks. In: Wang, H., Zhao, X., Shi, Y., Kim, H., Piva, A. (eds.) Digital Forensics and Watermarking. IWDW 2019. Lecture Notes in Computer Science(), vol. 12022. Springer, Cham (2020). https://doi.org/10.1007/978-3-030-43575-2_5
21. Li, B., Wei, W., Ferreira, A., et al.: ReST-Net: diverse activation modules and parallel subnets-based CNN for spatial image steganalysis. IEEE Signal Process. Lett. **25**(5), 650–654 (2018)
22. Szegedy, C., Vanhoucke, V., Ioffe, S., et al.: Rethinking the inception architecture for computer vision. In: Proceedings of the IEEE Conference on Computer Vision and Pattern Recognition, pp. 2818–2826 (2016)
23. Lin, Z., Huang, Y., Wang, J.: RNN-SM: fast steganalysis of VoIP streams using recurrent neural network. IEEE Trans. Inf. Forensics Secur. **13**(7), 1854–1868 (2018)
24. Yang, H., Yang, Z., Huang, Y.: Steganalysis of VoIP streams with CNN-LSTM network. In: Proceedings of the ACM Workshop on Information Hiding and Multimedia Security, pp. 204–209 (2019)
25. Yang, H., Yang, Z., Bao, Y., et al.: Fast steganalysis method for VoIP streams. IEEE Signal Process. Lett. **27**, 286–290 (2019)
26. Yang, H., Yang. Z., Bao, Y., et al.: Fcem: a novel fast correlation extract model for real time steganalysis of VOIP stream via multi-head attention. In: ICASSP 2020–2020 IEEE International Conference on Acoustics, Speech and Signal Processing (ICASSP), pp. 2822–2826. IEEE (2020)
27. Hu, Y., Huang, Y., Yang, Z., et al.: Detection of heterogeneous parallel steganography for low bit-rate VoIP speech streams. Neurocomputing **419**, 70–79 (2021)
28. Yang, Z., Yang, H., Chang, C.-C., et al.: Real-time steganalysis for streaming media based on multi-channel convolutional sliding windows. Knowl.-Based Syst. **237**, 107561 (2022)
29. Li, S., Wang, J., Liu, P.: General frame-wise steganalysis of compressed speech based on dual-domain representation and intra-frame correlation leaching. IEEE/ACM Trans. Audio Speech Lang. Process. **30**, 2025–2035 (2022)
30. Tian, H., Qiu, Y., Mazurczyk, W., et al.: STFF-SM: steganalysis model based on spatial and temporal feature fusion for speech streams. IEEE/ACM Trans. Audio Speech Lang. Process. **31**, 277–289 (2022)
31. Han, K., Xiao, A., Wu, E., et al.: Transformer in transformer. Adv. Neural. Inf. Process. Syst. **34**, 15908–15919 (2021)
32. Shaw, P., Uszkoreit, J., Vaswani, A.: Self-attention with relative position representations. arXiv preprint arXiv:1803.02155 (2018)
33. Dosovitskiy, A., Beyer, L., Kolesnikov, A., et al.: An image is worth 16x16 words: transformers for image recognition at scale. arXiv preprint arXiv:2010.11929 (2020)
34. Liu, Z., Lin, Y., Cao, Y., et al.: Swin transformer: hierarchical vision transformer using shifted windows. In: Proceedings of the IEEE/CVF International Conference on Computer Vision, pp. 10012–10022 (2021)
35. Yu, W., Luo, M., Zhou, P., et al.: Metaformer is actually what you need for vision. In: Proceedings of the IEEE/CVF Conference on Computer Vision and Pattern Recognition, pp. 10819–10829 (2022)
36. Xiao, B., Huang, Y., Tang, S.: An approach to information hiding in low bit-rate speech stream. In: IEEE GLOBECOM 2008–2008 IEEE Global Telecommunications Conference, pp. 1–5. IEEE (2008)

37. Huang, Y., Liu, C., Tang, S., et al.: Steganography integration into a low-bit rate speech codec. IEEE Trans. Inf. Forensics Secur. **7**(6), 1865–1875 (2012)
38. Gupta, A., Chhikara, R., Sharma, P.: A review on deep learning solutions for steganalysis. Int. J. Comput. Dig. Syst. (2023)
39. Yang, H., Yang, Z., Bao, Y., Huang, Y.: Hierarchical representation network for steganalysis of QIM steganography in low-bit-rate speech signals. In: Zhou, J., Luo, X., Shen, Q., Xu, Z. (eds.) Information and Communications Security. ICICS 2019. Lecture Notes in Computer Science(), vol. 11999. Springer, Cham (2020). https://doi.org/10.1007/978-3-030-41579-2_45
40. Li, S.-B., Jia, Y.-Z., Fu, J.Y., et al.: Detection of pitch modulation information hiding based on codebook correlation network. Chin. J. Comput. **37**(10), 2107–2116 (2014)
41. Wang, Y., Yi, X., Zhao, X., et al.: RHFCN: fully CNN-based steganalysis of MP3 with rich high-pass filtering. In: ICASSP 2019–2019 IEEE International Conference on Acoustics, Speech and Signal Processing (ICASSP), pp. 2627–2631. IEEE (2019)

# Author Index

Printed in the United States
by Baker & Taylor Publisher Services